CONCORDIA UNIVERSIT

QA11.M215

PERSPECTIVES ON SECONDARY MATHEMATI

C0-AYE-796

3 4211 000086879

WITHDRAWN

PERSPECTIVES ON SECONDARY MATHEMATICS EDUCATION

PERSPECTIVES ON SECONDARY MATHEMATICS EDUCATION

Edited by

JERRY A. Mc INTOSH
Indiana University

KLINCK MEMORIAL LIBRARY
Concordia Teachers College
River Forest, Illinois 60305

Prentice-Hall, Inc., Englewood Cliffs, New Jersey

Copyright © 1971 by Prentice-Hall, Inc.
Englewood Cliffs, New Jersey

All rights reserved. No part of this book may
be reproduced in any form or by any means
without permission in writing from the publisher.

13–660795–0

Library of Congress Catalog Card Number: 70–115133

Current printing (last digit):

10 9 8 7 6 5 4 3 2 1

PRENTICE-HALL INTERNATIONAL, INC., *London*
PRENTICE-HALL OF AUSTRALIA PTY. LTD., *Sydney*
PRENTICE-HALL OF CANADA LTD., *Toronto*
PRENTICE-HALL OF INDIA PRIVATE LIMITED, *New Delhi*
PRENTICE-HALL OF JAPAN, INC., *Tokyo*

Printed in the United States of America

95809

Contents

1

Evolution of
Mathematics Education, 1

2

Methods, 61

3
Curriculum, 141

4

Research, 209

Preface

There is much evidence to support the position that "modern mathematics" was becoming quite popular prior to the launching of Sputnik during the fall of 1957. Still, there are those who deny this and can justify their position with considerable documentation. However, the clarification of the two diametrically opposed positions is tedious and the resolving of the issue is purely academic.

Of consequential significance is the verification of the revolution of school mathematics in this country today. This revolution has had a profound effect not only upon students but upon parents and the general citizenry as well, who have been dramatically concerned. Although this revolution in mathematics education— beginning in the late 1950's and early 1960's—is quite evident, even more astonishing is the impact of the continuing production of revolutionary materials and formulations of new interpretations of modern mathematics. Indeed, these changes are staggering, and no end is in sight, as evidenced by current publications such as "The Continuing Revolution in Mathematics" which is sponsored by the National Council of Teachers of Mathematics.

This continuing revolution in school mathematics is associated with many forms and kinds of mathematics content, including booklets designed for the instruction of specific technical units, computer-assisted instruction, games, films, film strips, and film loops. Although these different *forms* of instructional material clearly illustrate the large variety available today as compared with the 1950's, these changes are no less revolutionary than the changes in *content*. For example, it is almost commonplace in forward-looking schools for much of the mathematics content currently being taught to have been included in the college mathematics curriculum of students who were preparing to become secondary mathematics teachers during the pre-Sputnik era.

Although the revolution in school mathematics has caused mathematics educators to re-examine their philosophies, it has raised more questions than it has provided answers. And although this is discouraging, we must recognize that it is only through continual questioning that significant advancement can be achieved. This continuing concern in mathematics education is evidenced by the increasing demand for the services of professional mathematics educators.

The present book of readings is designed primarily for the future teacher of secondary school mathematics, and hopefully will be of assistance to the experienced teacher who wishes to become more familiar with contemporary thought in mathematics education. Clearly, this book would be inadequate as a complete reference source for an undergraduate methods course, but it can profitably be utilized as one of several reference sources.

Although methodology is not treated in depth in these readings, several documented references to pedagogy have been included, in addition to the description of situations which have inherent implications for methodology. The purpose of the introductory material to each section is to provide the reader with several possible interpretations as he proceeds. He will undoubtedly find that some elements of his philosophy will be reinforced, whereas others will be altered to varying degrees. Most important, it is hoped that the reader will form a unique and increasingly consistent philosophy of the teaching of secondary school mathematics.

JERRY A. MCINTOSH

1

Evolution of

Mathematics Education

Clearly, the recent evolution of mathematics education is composed of many factors, the most identifiable of which is Sputnik. Numerous less publicized factors have contributed significantly to the evolution. Two of the more important factors in this category include the mathematical competence which our technological society is demanding of its citizenry and the general trend toward an increasing level of abstraction and sophistication in the contemporary secondary school curriculum.

Each individual views the evolution of mathematics education in a unique way in light of his past experiences and the subsequent interpretation of these experiences. The degree of compatibility and internal consistency of information and decision making which emerges is directly proportional to the quality of one's philosophy. With this rather coarse description of a philosophical base, the editor hopes to provide the reader with authoritative information for formulating a position about the evolution in school mathematics.

Some of the selections provide direct interpretations of the evolution as described from different vantage points, interpretations which may vary only slightly in some articles but vary a great deal or even be diametrically opposed in others. On the basis of these interpretations, the reader can evaluate his own judgment relative to the evolution in mathematics education.

The Ancients Versus the Moderns: A New Battle of the Books

MORRIS KLINE

INTRODUCTION

... The major part of my talk is a critique of the movement to teach modern mathematics in the high schools. My understanding of what this movement amounts to has been derived from talks I have heard, from conversations with numerous advocates of the movement, from printed materials, and from articles appearing in *The Mathematics Teacher* and other journals. In particular, there is a rather definitive article written by Dean A. E. Meder in *The Mathematics Teacher* for October 1957. This article appeared to be so important in presenting the views of the Commission on Mathematics that tens of thousands of preprints were run off and distributed around the country. But just a month ago, Dean Meder and I debated with each other at Ohio State University, and Dean Meder presented previews of the Commission's forthcoming recommendations that were more moderate than those advocated in the published article. I am not at all satisfied with the more moderate views either, and I shall try to show why a

Reprinted from *The Mathematics Teacher*, LI (October, 1958), 418–27, by permission of the author and the National Council of Teachers of Mathematics. Copyright © 1958 by the National Council of Teachers of Mathematics. This material was originally presented at the Thirty-sixth Annual Meeting of the National Council of Teachers of Mathematics at Cleveland, Ohio on April 11, 1958. Morris Kline is Professor of Mathematics and Chairman of Undergraduate Mathematics, Washington Square Campus, New York University.

little latter. However, the moderation may indicate that perhaps insofar as the Commission is concerned, modern mathematics is dying. But I recall that it took thirty stabs to kill Caesar. Moreover, if this hydra called modern mathematics has lost one of its heads, there are others to be chopped off. I shall proceed therefore to do the dirty work.

CRITICISM THAT TRADITIONAL MATHEMATICS IS OUTMODED

My first objection is perhaps more of a quarrel about words rather than about substance, about arguments presented by the modernists rather than about the subject matter they are proposing. Nevertheless I believe that the point I shall make warrants some attention. The argument most often offered by the modernists is that the mathematics we have been teaching is outmoded because it is several hundred years old. This argument impresses people because we are prone in our modern civilization to believe that what is new is automatically better than what is old. To people who believe that a 1958 automobile is already out of date by the fall of 1958 it seems immediately clear that 300-year-old mathematics must be hopelessly antiquated. Leaving aside the question of whether a 1958 automobile is really better than its predecessors, let me point out that if there is one subject in which up-to-dateness is totally irrelevant, it is mathematics. Mathematics has been built solidly, at least since

Greek times, and generally the later developments have depended logically upon the earlier ones. Mathematics is, in other words, a cumulative development. Hence the older portions do not become antiquated or useless. In a subject such as physics, a new theory will often entirely replace an old one. For example, we no longer speak of a phlogiston theory of combustion. But this is not true of mathematics. The geometry of Euclid and the trigonometry of Hipparchus and Ptolemy, although 2,000 years old, are still not replaced by a new geometry and trigonometry that show the old subjects to be incorrect or useless.

Moreover, the modernists themselves do not wish to throw out all of the older mathematics. They would teach some Euclid and some trigonometry. They certainly wish to teach the calculus and coordinate geometry that are 300 years old. If the argument that what is old is definitely bad is a sound one, then certainly all of the old mathematics should be thrown out.

Now I know that the modernists don't mean to argue that what is old is necessarily bad. Hence all that I ask is that the modernists stop emphasizing the word "modern" with all its connotations. That word serves only as propaganda or as an appeal to an argument by analogy, and every mathematician knows that an argument by analogy is not reliable.

The modernists also give the impression that the topics they recommend are the main ones now claiming the attention of mathematicians. But many more mathematicians are still advancing such subjects as ordinary and partial differential equations, integral equations, numerical analysis, algebraic geometry, integral transform theory, approximation procedures, and other branches of analysis. These modern mathematical interests and activities somehow have escaped mention.

VALUE OF MODERN MATHEMATICS FOR MATHEMATICS PROPER

Let us put aside, however, any contentions about a weak or misdirected argument and examine on its own merits the contents which the modernists advocate. The modernists would replace material currently taught by such topics as symbolic logic, Boolean algebra, set theory, some topics of abstract algebra such as groups and fields, topology, postulational systems, and statistics. I have no objection to the introduction of statistics, but I should like to examine the value of the other subjects from the standpoint of their central position in the body of mathematics and from the standpoint of application.

As for importance in the body of mathematics, I believe it is fair to say that one could not pick more peripheral material. Let me consider a few of these subjects, for example, symbolic logic. No mathematician except a specialist in problems of mathematical logic uses symbolic logic. First of all, every mathematician thinks intuitively and then presents his arguments in a deductive form, using words, familiar mathematical symbols, and common logic. This is true of 99.9 per cent of all the mathematics that has been created. Specialists in foundation problems, who have to worry about the ambiguities and imprecision of ordinary language, do resort to symbolic logic. But even these people know what they want to say intuitively and *then* express their thoughts in special symbols. Let us be clear that the symbolic logic does not control or direct the thinking; it is merely the compact written expression of the real thinking. One must know what he wants to say before he puts it in symbolic form and, indeed, make sure that the symbols express what is intended rather than that the symbols tell him what he means to say. Hence not only is symbolic logic *not* used by almost all mathematicians, but those who do use it do their effective thinking first in more common language. Moreover, if the investigations in symbolic logic have taught us anything, it is that this medium cannot encompass any significant portion of mathematics.

Let us consider next the centrality of topology in mathematics. Topology is a new and as yet relatively untried branch of mathematics. It makes no contribution to the essential subject matter of algebra, trigonometry, coordinate geometry, calculus, and differential equations. As to its role in geometry, Euclidean geometry, non-Euclidean geometry, projective geometry, and differential geometry are far more basic. Let me also add a caution here. Such topics as the Königsberg bridge problem, the four-color problem, and the Möbius band are not topology. They are incidental details, curiosities, and amusements of the caliber of magic squares. The real matter of topology has not even been mentioned by the modernists; hence they should not deceive themselves and others that they are teaching topology.

Boolean algebra plays no role at all in mathematics. Set theory, which is closely related, is used only in topology and in the foundations of the theory of real functions and of the theory of probability. Set theory, then, plays a limited role in mathematics.

Insofar as elementary mathematics is concerned the concepts of abstract algebra are of use only in unifying some fundamental branches. After one knows the various types of real numbers, complex numbers, vectors, matrices, and transformations, it is nice to learn that these many mathematical entities have a few properties in common. But if one does not know, and know thoroughly, these basic subjects, then the group concept, for example, has nothing to offer. It appears to be an empty subject, an arbitrary creation of mathematical phantasy.

VALUE OF MODERN MATHEMATICS FOR APPLICATIONS

And now let me consider the second value claimed for these modern topics, namely, their use today in applications. My evaluation is that they are practically useless. Some examples have been offered to show how Boolean algebra and symbolic logic can be used to form committees. But these committees will do less good than some of our Congressional committees. Of course such applications are totally artificial. The claim is made that Boolean algebra is used to design switching circuits. This claim is technically correct, but it justifies teaching Boolean algebra to high school students about as much as the argument that the Presidency of the United States is important because it publicizes the game of golf. The claim is made that the newer mathematics is wanted by the social scientists. Here we must face some hard facts. Except through statistics, the social sciences have made no real applications of mathematics and, in fact, are still getting nowhere fast. The social sciences are hardly sciences, let alone mathematical sciences. If fifty or 100 years from now the social sciences make some significant use of mathematics, any kind of mathematics, we'll teach it. But even then there will be some question as to whether it should be taught on the high school level.

It seems curious to me that when the modernists talk about applications they make no mention of the application of mathematics to mechanics, sound, light, radio, electricity, atomic and nuclear theory, hydrodynamics, aerodynamics, geophysics, magnetohydrodynamics, elasticity, plasticity, chemistry, chemical physics, physical biology, and the various branches of engineering. If there are ten people in this world designing switching circuits, there are 100,000 scientists in these other fields. And what mathematics is used in these fields I have mentioned? Because I work in a large institute devoted to applied mathematics, I believe I can tell you. The subjects are algebra, geometry, trigonometry, coordinate geometry, the calculus, ordinary and partial differential equations, series, the calculus of variations, differential geometry, integral equations, theory of operators, and many other branches of analysis.

THE EFFICIENCY OF THE ABSTRACT APPROACH TO TRADITIONAL MATHEMATICS

The modernists often claim that they wish to teach much of the standard material but that they will do so more efficiently through a unified point of view made possible by the modern concepts. The prime example they offer is the concept of a field, and the presumed advantage of teaching fields first is that the rational, real, and complex numbers form a field. Setting aside for the moment the difficulties young people may have in learning the concept of a field, let us see what is gained. When one has a field, one has a system of elements that combine under two operations. These operations satisfy five properties: closure, the associative and commutative laws, and the exist-

ence of an identity and of an inverse. In addition, there is the distributive law connecting the two operations. Suppose a student knew all these properties. Would he be able to add 2 and 2? Would he be able to add fractions, irrationals, complex numbers? No. And the reason is that just because the field properties are those which are *common* to all these systems of numbers, they automatically wipe out any distinguishing features. The field concept wipes out just those important processes which are needed to operate with these basic number systems. I conclude that a person with an excellent knowledge of fields could not even make change in a grocery store. To put it otherwise, fields do not explain the types of numbers and operations with them. In fact, it is just the reverse. A good understanding of the various number systems explains the concept of a field. Hence insofar as efficiency is concerned, the time that is wasted is the time spent teaching the abstract concept.

The same kind of argument applies to a subject such as topology. Even if we really taught topology and not the curiosities commonly described as topology, the students could not with this knowledge find the area of a triangle, because by very definition topology is not concerned with particular metirc geometries We would still have to teach the specialized geometry.

Let us remember that the more general the mathematical concept, the emptier it is.

TEACHING THE ABSTRACT BEFORE THE CONCRETE

The modernists make other claims for their material. They say that their material is a new point of view as much as new content. This is true, but what is the point of view? In the first place, *their* modern mathematics is highly abstract. Groups, rings, and fields, as I have already indicated, are abstractions from various more concrete algebras. Topology is a generalization of Euclidean, non-Euclidean, and projective geometry. Postulational systems are an abstraction from the deductive structure of the various branches of mathematics. Even the simple concepts have become abstract. The old-fashioned x which used to stand for an unknown number is now the place holder for the pronumeral of the name of a number, or is it the pronumeral of the place holder of the number of names? Of numbers themselves we can no longer speak. We have only names for numbers. The numbers themselves are in heaven.

How can we expect students to learn the abstract before the concrete? I thought that the educators were the ones who always stressed that the concrete must come first. Certainly if one judges by the time it took great mathematicians to learn the concrete cases, one can hardly believe that the abstract ideas can be taught to young people. It took mathematicians a few thousand years to understand the irrational number, and yet we presumably can teach Dedekind cuts to high school people. It took mathematicians 300 years to understand complex numbers, but we can teach at once that a complex number is an ordered pair of real numbers. It took about 1,000 years to understand negative numbers, but now we have only to say that a negative number is an ordered pair of natural numbers and, presto, the idea is learned. From Galileo to Dirichlet, mathematicians struggled to understand the concept of a function, but now domain, range, and ordered pairs such that no two second members may be different for the same first member do the trick. From the ancient Egyptians and Babylonians to Vieta and Descartes, no mathematician realized that letters could be used to stand for a class of numbers, but now we are told that the simple notion of set

yields the concept immediately. The point of an investigation such as topology came to mathematicians after they had analyzed Euclidean and the other geometries I have mentioned, but somehow these other geometries are apparently not needed to see the point of topology.

Were these great mathematicians really not so great, or are there not intrinsic diffculties in all these concepts that cannot be hurdled by jumping into abstractions?

CRITICISM OF THE MODERNIST RIGOR

The second major change in viewpoint which the modernists advocate is more rigor. We can no longer present Euclidean geometry à la Euclid but must present it à la Hilbert. Dedekind cuts and Peano's axioms are the new order of the day in teaching numbers. And symbolic logic must rectify the weaknesses of Aristotelian logic.

The desire to incorporate more rigor is ill-advised for many reasons. First of all, the capicty to appreciate rigor must be developed. The capacity to appreciate rigor is a function of the age of the student and not of the age of mathematics. Those who do not believe that mathematical maturity is needed to appreciate rigor should be guided in this matter, too, by the history of mathematics. For 2,000 years after it was created, the best minds in Western civilization accepted Euclidean geometry as the prime example of rigor. Will young people, then, appreciate the deficiencies in Euclidean geometry? For 2,000 years the mathematicians worked with whole numbers, fractions, and irrational numbers on an intuitive basis. Despite the fact that many of them were troubled by the difficulties in the concept of the irrational number, they did not succeed in eliminating those difficulties until the sophisticated concept of Dedekind cuts or Cantor sequences was created. If it took mathematicians so long to arrive at the logical concept of the irrational number, can we believe that young people will appreciate it at once? The introduction of symbolic logic, insofar as it is an effort to provide rigor, is likewise countered by the historical fact that Aristotelian logic not only sufficed for 2,000 years but, as I pointed out in another connection, still is the logic used by practically all mathematicians.

As a matter of fact, much of this rigor does little good. Let us consider the real number system. As I just remarked, mathematicians used the various types of real numbers for thousands of years and knew all along exactly what properties these numbers must have. But, having become somewhat rigor-conscious and conscience-stricken in recent times, they decided that they must supply a logical basis for the number system. And so they started with Peano's axioms, and by introducing couples of natural numbers, couples of signed numbers, Dedekind cuts, and the like, they managed to build up a logical basis for what they had known and used all along. Having done so, they forget all about this artificial, formal, and meaningless structure and continue to use numbers on the intuitive level just as they had done prior to the logical construction. All that the rigor accomplished was that the mathematicians salved their consciences.

The presentation of mathematics in rigorous form is ill-advised on other counts. Mathematics must be understood intuitively in physical or geometrical terms. This is the primary pedagogical objective. When this is achieved, it is proper to formulate the concepts and reasoning in as rigorous a form as young people can take. But let us always remember that the rigorous presentation is secondary in importance. As Roger Bacon said, "Argument concludes a question; but it does not make us feel certain, or acquiesce in the contemplation of truth, except the truth also be found to be so by experience." Let me cite some other wise advice in this connection. Three hundred years ago Galileo said, "Logic, it appears to me, teaches us how to test the conclusiveness of any argument or demonstration already discovered and completed; but I do not believe that it teaches us to discover correct arguments and demonstrations." And Pascal said somewhat impertinently, "Reason is the slow and tortuous method by which those who do not know the truth discover it." The proper finesse rather than logic is what is needed to do the correct thing. Of recent vintage is the observation by Herman Weyl, "Logic is the hygiene which mathematics practices to keep its ideas healthy and strong." If I may exaggerate slightly, I would put it that rigor is the gilt on the lily of real mathematics.

There is another point about the introduction of rigor which, I believe, has been lost sight of. In presenting rigorous developments of the number system and of geometry we first have to make the students aware of the difficulties and then meet them. The reason for this in the case of numbers is that the students have long understood numbers intuitively through their elementary school training. In the case of geometry, students use figures which automatically take care of the very points, such as order, which the rigorous presentation covers. Hence we have to spend a great deal of time in making a student aware of what he has accepted on an intuitive or visual basis and then prove these facts. The student is unimpressed. He knew all this before. In fact, he fails to grasp just what we are after. Are we trying to prove the obvious? Surely, he thinks, we can't be that foolish.

I might say parenthetically that the entire emphasis on rigor today is most anomalous. There never was a time when the question of what is rigorous mathematics was less clear. I cannot enter here upon the history of rigor or on the difficulties in building mathematics rigorously, but I will point out that there are serious and unresolved controversies concerning what is rigorous mathematics. We do know that many mathematicians are sufficiently skeptical of whether we shall ever settle this question to make sarcastic remarks such as "logic is the art of going wrong with confidence"; "the virtue of a logical proof is not that it compels belief but that it suggests doubts"; "a mathematical proof tells us where to concentrate our doubts." Not only have the standards of rigor varied from one age to another, but today rigor in mathematical logic is one thing; rigor in foundations is another; rigor in analysis is still another; and rigor in applied mathematics is entirely different. The whole attempt to inject rigor in mathematics has amounted to picking up jewels only to discover serpents underneath.

THE ISOLATION FROM REALITY

The modernist program is deficient in another respect. It ignores completely the primary reason for the existence of mathematics and the chief motivation for the study of mathematics, namely, the investigation of nature. Mathematics is significant and vital because it is the chief instrument for the study of the physical world. On the other hand, the pure mathematics which the modernists wish to present is pointless mathematics, a manipulation of meaningless symbols which can appeal only to an esoteric group.

Let me consider an example of how far the modernists depart from reality. The real number system and Euclidean geometry are in themselves abstractions from reality, but at least students can

see their relationship to the physical world or it can readily be made evident. In undertaking to teach deductive structure, the modernists propose to use abstract and artificial postulational systems. The significant systems, such as Euclidean geometry and the real number system, are too complex. It is true that these physically significant deductive systems are complex, but even if students do manage to get some glimpse of deduction from artificial systems, what will they conclude? After studying meaningless axioms and meaningless theorems, their natural conclusion will be that the whole business is meaningless.

The traditional curriculum is already meaningless, and by heading for abstract mathematics the modernists are moving farther away from reality. To teach pure mathematics apart from physical problems is to lose the gold and keep the iron in the ore of real mathematics. The meaning of mathematics, if I may be somewhat paradoxical, is not in mathematics.

OMISSION OF THE LIFE AND SPIRIT OF MATHEMATICS

Another objection to the modernists' program that is directed toward their aim to be rigorous and abstract is that it fails to present the life and spirit of mathematics. Mathematics is a creative or inventive process, deriving ideas and suggestions from real problems, idealizing and formulating the relevant concepts, posing questions, intuitively deriving a possible conclusion, and then, and only then, proving the hunch or intuitive argument deductively. Intuition and construction are the driving forces of mathematics.

All of these values are ignored in a presentation of finished, abstract, rigorous mathematics. This version is in fact an emasculation of mathematics. It perhaps shows us how questions are answered, but not why they are put or how the answers are conceived. Arithmetic, algebra, geometry, trigonometry, and the calculus did not come about by manipulating meaningless symbols or by playing games according to rules. To have students like and understand mathematics we must help them create it for themselves. As their experiences increase and as they encounter the need for stricter formulation and checks on intuition, their appreciation of the need for proof, rigor, and finished presentations will grow.

THE NEW POSITION OF THE COMMISSION ON MATHEMATICS

I mentioned at the beginning of this talk that a month ago Dean Meder presented the forthcoming recommendations of the Commission on Mathematics and that these were not as extreme as the views I have been attacking. But I also said that these views were equally unsatisfactory. As I understand his remarks, it appears that the first year of high school algebra will hardly be changed. The word "set" is to be introduced, but that is all. If this is all, then I do not see that anything is really being recommended insofar as this year's work is concerned. The word "set" means no more than "class" or "collection." It is a word that any teacher might think of using without expecting to be honored for thinking of it. The word is not a magic formula that will suddenly illuminate mathematics or make the subject attractive.

Insofar as the second year's work is concerned, the major change seems to be to cut down on Euclidean geometry and to substitute coordinate geometry for the discarded material. To my mind, this change is not significant. In the first place, if we are talking about the college preparatory group and if the first two years are intended as preparation for

later work, then the amount of Euclidean geometry that would be taught is not enough. The argument that coordinate geometry will be used to prove further results of Euclidean geometry is not strong. Proofs by coordinate geometry may be more systematic but are much clumsier. Moreover, students will be frightened by the amount of algebra they have to use. Algebra is the bane of students.

The recommendations for the third and fourth years were in part agreeable. There are parts of trigonometry, such as logarithmic solution of triangles, that can be discarded, and the introduction of statistics is, I believe, warranted.

But the major criticism I would make of even this more moderate program is that if it backs away from modern mathematics it only backs into a minor reshuffling of the traditional curriculum. In view of the fact that we have failed miserably to put mathematics across with the traditional curriculum, it seems to me that the Commission's recommendations are not going to improve the teaching of mathematics.

PRINCIPLES OF A NEW APPROACH TO THE CURRICULUM

Genuine improvement of the curriculum does call for drastic revision, though not of course by resorting to modern mathematics and not by merely reshuffling the traditional mathematics. Just what should we be doing? Let me begin by stating that we have not thus far correctly analyzed the weakness in the present curriculum. The trouble is not that we are teaching outmoded mathematics, except for one or two topics. Rather, the trouble lies in the way in which we approach the material we teach. I shall try to indicate the principles which would guide a revision of our present approach.

Have you ever taken into account

how intrinsically more difficult it is to arouse interest in mathematics than in history or literature? Mathematics of any kind is abstract, and the role that it plays in human thought is not a priori clear, whereas every student knows what history is about, why he is expected to study history, and what he might gain from it.

My first principle, then, is that we must begin our teaching of mathematics by seeking to arouse interest in the subject. If this is agreed upon, then we should select material which will serve the purpose of arousing interest. But what interest can young people find in simplifying fractions, in factoring, in exponents, in the quadratic formula, and in all the other dirty, intrinsically meaningless, boring processes that we teach in first-year algebra? The fact is that we have been guided in our choice of material not by the effort to arouse interest but to teach the mathematics that will be needed in the subsequent study of the subject. Our concern, in other words, has been with preparation for the future. But with such an introduction to mathematics, few students want a future in the subject.

Some people may object that we cannot afford to waste years in arousing interest. Let us suppose, to take the worst possibility, that nothing we teach in the first two years will advance the student technically, Have we then lost two years? Not at all. Since we wish to interest more students in mathematics and we now discourage and lose most of the students who take the subject, the "preparation" we now give them for advanced work is wasted and in addition we have built up a dislike that hurts us. Actually we would not lose any time. Since students work hard at what they like, those who go on will readily make up for lost time because they have become interested. Moreover, we would be teaching some technique while solv-

ing interesting problems. Further, if we succeed in giving students some insight into the purposes and ways of mathematics and into the uses of technique, the students will really learn what they are taught, and we shall not have to repeat the meaningless techniques in intermediate algebra and college algebra courses.

My second principle is that regardless of how we arouse interest in mathematics, even if it be through games, we must supply motivation and purpose to the mathematics we teach. This means that we must motivate each topic with a genuine problem and show that the mathematics does something to solve that problem. But let us be clear on this point. For young people, at least, the motivation for a mathematical idea or method is *not* a more advanced mathematical idea or method. The motivation for learning about functions is not to learn how to differentiate or integrate functions. In view of the actual motivation for the creation of mathematics, the motivation we can use is the solution of simple, genuine, and basic physical problems. Of course the social sciences, art, and music also provide good problems. The motivation must not be confused with the mathematics that will be used to solve the problem, but the motivation should be there.

Third, since even the great mathematicians think intuitively, we must all be sure that the intuitive meaning of each mathematical idea or procedure is made intuitively clear to the students. This intuitive side of mathematics is in fact the essence of the subject. Mathematics is primarily a series of great intuitions. The way to make the meaning of an idea clear is to present it in the intuitive setting that led to its creation or in terms of some simple modern equivalent. Physical or geometrical illustrations or interpretations will often supply this meaning. Thus $s = 16t^2$

is not just a quadratic function. It is a law of falling bodies, and s and t have definite and clear physical meanings. The fact that $s = 16t^2$ and not $16t$ also has an important physical significance and makes the quadratic feature impressive. Numerical examples, and especially examples wherein the process or theorem fails, help to make meanings clear.

Of course something must be done to teach the concept of proof and the language of mathematics, even though symbolism and sparse presentation of proofs often conceal the ideas. Proof should be emphasized mainly in establishing what is not obvious and even runs counter to untrained intuition. Insofar as rigor is concerned, E. H. Moore's precept is applicable, "Sufficient into the day is the rigor thereof." And by the day I mean the student's age. Fortunately, young people (and even older ones) will accept as rigorous and acquire a feeling for proof from proofs that are really not rigorous. Is this deception? I call it pedagogy. At any rate, it is no more deception than we practice on ourselves. As our own capacity to appreciate more rigorous proofs increases, we are able to see flaws in the cruder proofs taught to us and to master sounder proofs. But again let me warn you that there are no final rigorous proofs. Not all the symbolism of modern symbolic logic, Boolean algebra, set theory, postulational methods, and topology can make mathematics rigorous, and these ideas certainly do not make mathematics more understandable or acceptable to young people.

Fourth, knowledge is a whole, and mathematics is a part of that whole. Mathematics in every age has been part of the broad cultural movement of the age. We must relate the mathematics to history, science, philosophy, social science, art, music, literature, logic, as well as to any other development which the topic in hand permits. We should try as far as possible to organize our material so that the development of the mathematics proper is related to the development of our civilization and culture. At the very least, each *major* topic should be imbedded in the cultural context which gave rise to it and should be capped by a discussion of what the creation has done to influence the development of our civilization.

I shall not attempt in this brief talk to give a detailed outline of courses. I will say that my conception of the first two years of high school mathematics would entail a radical revision of the present curriculum. I have worked on material for high school and college courses, and I am convinced that we can make mathematics attractive and meaningful. In fact, the present high position of mathematics in our culture means that the subject does have extraordinary interest, purpose, meaning, and significance. We cannot doubt, then, that it is possible to make the subject live.

The Ancients Versus the Moderns:
A Reply

ALBERT E. MEDER, JR.

... Professor Kline refers to an article of mine in *The Mathematics Teacher* of October 1957 as one from which he derived, in part at least, his understanding of the nature of the movement to teach modern mathematics in the high school. However, there is not one word in this article in advocacy of the views opposed by Professor Kline in his paper. My article was not a presentation of the nature of the movement to teach modern mathematics in the high school or an argument in its behalf; it was rather an attempt to explain the nature of modern mathematics. It stated in so many words that "many teachers have been presenting traditional content from a point of view accurately described as modern"; emphasized that "the same fact can often be discussed from the traditional point of view of algebra as a form of manipulative skill, or from the modern point of view of algebra as a study of mathematical structure." It pointed out that new subject matter had developed from the axiomatic point of view, described what some of the new subject matter was, and made the following statements concerning the teaching of secondary school mathematics:

Reprinted from *The Mathematics Teacher*, LI (October, 1958), 428–33, by permission of the author and the National Council of Teacher of Mathematics. Copyright © 1958 by the National Council of Teachers of Mathematics. Albert E. Meder, Jr., is Professor of Mathematics, and Vice Provost and Dean of the University, Rutgers University, New Brunswick, N.J.

We are asking that teachers familiarize themselves with certain basic concepts—new in form but familiar in part in substance—and creatively utilize these simplifying and unifying concepts in their teaching once again to make the study and learning of mathematics a stimulating, interesting, and vitalized intellectual adventure.

I am confident that Professor Kline does not mean to attack that kind of teaching.

There are essentially two aspects of Professor Kline's paper that I find objectionable: First, the vague generalizations, entirely undocumented, concerning the views held by the "modernists," and second, the inference drawn from what has not been said by the "modernists." No one could object, though he might disagree, if Professor Kline quoted specific statements made by those whose views he is attacking, gave their source, and explained why he thought they were erroneous. But he does not do this. He neither documents his generalizations nor does he even define his terms. Moreover, he draws inference from the fact that certain statements have not been made. This is indefensible.

I shall now list some of Professor Kline's undocumented generalizations and comment upon them;

1. "The argument most often offered by the modernists is that the mathematics we have been teaching is outmoded because it is several hundred years old." I submit that this statement is not documented because it cannot be documented; nobody would be fool-

ish enough to make such a statement.

I have myself often stated that the mathematics we teach is seventeenth-century mathematics. But this statement has never, to the best of my knowledge and belief, been coupled with the statement that *therefore* it is outmoded. Parts of what we teach certainly are outmoded, not because they are old but because they are antiquated. Professor Kline is quite correct in saying that in mathematics, knowledge does not become useless because it is old. Nevertheless, it can become antiquated in the sense that it is no longer the most appropriate material for inclusion in a secondary school curriculum.

Professor Kline says: "If the argument that what is old is definitely bad is a sound one, then certainly all of the old mathematics should be thrown out." Agreed. Since, however, it is obvious that all of the old mathematics should not be thrown out, it follows that the hypothesis that what is old is definitely bad is false.

Professor Kline ends his discussion on this point by asking that the "modernists" stop emphasizing the word "modern." He thinks this word has a propaganda aspect that he regards as bad. For myself, I would be perfectly willing to eschew the word. I suspect, however, that Professor Kline would not like our ideas any better if we described them by some phrase other than "modern mathematics."

2. "The modernists would replace material currently taught by such topics as symbolic logic, Boolean algebra, set theory, some topics of abstract algebra such as groups and fields, topology, postulational systems, and statistics."

Professor Kline does not like the word "modern" because it is "propaganda"; I do not like his word "replace" because it is not quantified. How much material currently taught is to be replaced by the topics listed? All? A great deal? A little? It makes a great difference. This generalization is so broad as to be almost meaningless.

The fact is that it is proposed by the Commission on Mathematics to include in the secondary school program, in place of some small part of material currently taught, some small part of set theory and abstract algebra. I know of no proposal to include symbolic logic, Boolean algebra, or topology. It is proposed to include statistics, but since Professor Kline agrees that this is unobjectionable, I shall not discuss this proposal.

It may be that someone somewhere wants to do some of these things that the Commission does not propose. That is precisely the point; statements should be documented.

3. The next generalization has to do with the importance in the body of mathematics of such topics as symbolic logic, topology, Boolean algebra, and abstract algebra. Professor Kline thinks none of these is of any real significance. He is entitled to his opinion. My contention is that his opinion is irrelevant. Since it is not proposed to teach these topics as central in the development of mathematics, it is irrelevant whether Professor Kline thinks they are central or whether he thinks they are not. Actually, I think that he has less interest in some rather fascinating parts of mathematics than he ought to have. I probably have less interest in some parts of mathematics that he thinks exciting than he would think I ought to have. The fact is that no human being can possibley learn all mathematics, however much all of us would like to do so, and therefore a selection has to be made. But it is surely a rash generalization for any one of us to say that the mathematics in which we happen to be interested is more important than the mathematics in which someone else happens to be interested.

I would like to make one other remark on this point. Our opinion of the importance or difficulty of any branch of mathematics is likely to be related to the order and the time in which we ourselves learned it. Generally speaking, subjects learned in the graduate school or from our own reading are apt to seem more remote to us than the subjects we were taught in secondary school or college. But if one learned in school or college the subjects we learned later and vice versa (assuming the possibility of doing this, to some extent), then it is altogether likely that the relative difficulty and importance of the topics would also seem quite different to such an unconventional learner. All of us need to beware of this pitfall.

While I am most certainly not advocating teaching topology and symbolic logic in junior high school, I do say that if this were done, the student who had been so taught would almost certainly have a different psychological attitude toward these subjects than do Professor Kline and I.

Finally, Professor Kline by his own admission is not a specialist in symbolic logic, topology, Boolean algebra, or abstract algebra; why not let someone who is a specialist speak concerning the importance of these subjects?

4. The next vague generalization is that these modern topics are practically useless in their applications. I am glad that Professor Kline said, "My evaluation here is that they are practically useless." Many others would completely disagree with him.

5. The next vague generalization made by Professor Kline is that the abstract approach to traditional mathematics is relatively inefficient. He argues that because a person understood the concept of a field he would not know how to add 2 and 2. He states further, "A person with an excellent knowledge of fields could not even make change in a grocery store." Well, who ever said that he could? The purpose of teaching the concept of a field is not to enable a person to make change in a grocery store. Here we have two laudable objectives, although Professor Kline apparently thinks only one of them is laudable. The first objective is to teach arithmetic. We believe in this. The second objective is to teach the structure of algebra. We believe in this, too, even though Professor Kline doesn't.

6. The next vague generalization is summed up in the question: "How can we expect students to learn the abstract before the concrete?" The answer is we can't and we don't. On this point I completely agree with Professor Kline: It is essential to teach intuitive, concrete notions before abstractions can be taught.

Moreover, on June 8, 1957, Professor Carl B. Allendoerfer, a member of the Commission on Mathematics, addressed a letter to Professor Kline that included the following statements:

Abstract concepts. No one in his right mind would teach these before the concrete material. Certainly abstraction is hard, but it is still necessary. I favor introducing it earlier than is done at present, but not before the students are ready for it, Many of the laws of algebra (the axioms of a field) are easier to understand and much more useful than the arbitrary "rules" which now appear in elementary algebra books. There is no reason why they should not be taught and used—but only after the proper intuitive foundation has been laid. . . .

Finally, let is never be said that anyone on the CEEB Commission favors teaching mathematics in reverse by doing abstractions first and then coming to the concrete illustrations. We do, however, favor the gradual introduction of the abstract at a rate considerably faster than is done at present. We are sure that this is both possible and desirable.

Despite this statement by a member of the Commission, Professor Kline still insists that the "modernists" advocate teaching "the abstract before the concrete."

7. "The second major change in viewpoint which the modernists advocate is more rigor."

This generalization is not documented because it cannot be documented. No such position has been advocated.

On this point also Professor Allendoerfer stated the position of the Commission in his letter to Professor Kline almost a year before Professor Kline delivered the address on which I am commenting. He said:

Rigor. Of course the level of rigor must suit the age and maturity of the student. But this does not mean to dispense with it entirely. I think that you have missed the point on the teaching of logic. Actually it is not lost on young people. My experience has been that they lap it up. The sole object of teaching it is to help the students understand the structure of the deductive process—not to make logicians out of them. Too many students have been through geometry and only memorized the theorems. I favor a brief session on logic to let the students see what they are trying to do. The logic, however, should be brief and should not interfere with the mathematics as such.

It would take far more space than I have a right to expect to discuss Section VII of Professor Kline's paper in detail. I will therefore merely make two remarks: First, much of what he says, properly understood, is of course correct; second, it does not give, in my opinion, a true picture of the relative importance of intuition and rigor in mathematics. But this is a matter of opinion, and a discussion of it would not be germane to this debate.

8. "The modernist program . . . ignores completely the primary reason for the existence of mathematics and the chief motivation for the study of mathematics, namely, the investigation of nature." The "primary reason for the existence of mathematics" is a matter of

opinion (though I think Professor Kline is probably right about it), but surely the "chief motivation" for the study of mathematics may differ for different individuals and be differently considered by different philosophers.

Moreover, the primary reason for the existence of mathematics may not be either the primary reason for the inclusion of the subject in the school curriculum or the primary criterion for the selection of curricular content. And it is certainly an unwarranted assumption that the chief motivation for the study of mathematics is identical for all individuals. I am sure that the desire to investigate nature is the chief motivation for some students; I am equally sure it is not the chief motivation for all. This certainly was not what led me to major in mathematics, for example.

9. Finally, there is a vague generalization to the effect that the proposed program "fails to present the life and spirit of mathematics." Then follows one of the really good paragraphs in Professor Kline's paper.

All I can say is that of course we desire to have mathematics so taught. The quotation from my own article in *The Mathematics Teacher* of last October given at the beginning of this article is sufficient comment on this unjustified generalization.

Let us turn now to Professor Kline's "arguments from silence":

1. "The modernists also give the impression that the topics they recommend are the main ones now claiming the attention of mathematicians."

Why should anyone think that topics recommended for inclusion in the secondary school curriculum are the main topics claiming the attention of mathematicians? I submit that, on the contrary, one would be justified in forming the impression that topics recommended for inclusion in the secondary school course would most likely not be topics of principal interest to research mathematicians. It is not likely that school boys and research mathematicians would have the same principal interests, nor that topics most suitable for instruction would be also those most suitable for research.

But the truth of the matter is that it may well be considered irrelevant, in a discussion of the secondary school curriculum, to comment on the activities of research mathematicians. Because irrelevant remarks are not made, it does not follow that they were not made because they were considered unimportant.

2. "It seems curious to me that when the modernists talk about applications, they make no mention of the application of mathematics to mechanics, sound, light, radio, electricity, atomic and nuclear theory, hydrodynamics, aerodynamics, geophysics, magnetohydrodynamics, elasticity, plasticity, chemistry, chemical physics, physical biology, and the various branches of engineering."

There is nothing curious about this situation. If one is discussing the applications of "modern" mathematics, it is not to be expected that he will talk about the applications of classical mathematics. It is unfair to chide him because he does not discuss a topic different from the one he set out to discuss.

But there is a still better explanation: Rightly or wrongly, it is assumed to be common knowledge that classical mathematics has important applications to science and engineering.

Moreover, it is false to say that these applications are never mentioned. I quote from an article in the *College Board Review*, Winter 1958, an official publication of the agency that appointed the Commission on Mathematics:

In order to formulate a curriculum oriented to the needs of the second half of the twentieth century, the Commission had to ask what these needs were. It takes no narrow view here; it is interested in the needs of mathematics itself, of course, but it is also interested in the needs of the users of mathematics, and in the applications of mathematics. . . .

Thus, when the Commission speaks of the "needs" of the second half of the twentieth century, it means the needs of mathematics, *of physical science*, of social science, of technology, *of engineering*, of business, of industry [italics added].

I must now comment very briefly on that section of Professor Kline's paper entitled "The New Position of the Commission on Mathematics." First, I want to introduce a demurrer to the use of the word "new." The Commission on Mathematics does not have an old position or a new position. The position of the Commission on Mathematics has not changed. Professor Kline's understanding of it has changed, principally because he started talking about the point of view of the Commission without finding out what it was.

However, Professor Kline's statement of what he calls the new position of the Commission on Mathematics is just as distorted as his presentation of what he would have called the old position of the Commission on Mathematics. He says, "It appears that the first year of high school algebra will hardly be changed. The word 'set' is to be introduced, but that is all." This is not an accurate statement. I do, however, agree with Professor Kline that the word "set" is not a magic formula which will suddenly illuminate mathematics or make it attractive.

Again, to describe the "major change" of the geometry program as "to cut down on Euclidean geometry and to substitute coordinate geometry for the discarded material" is also a distortion. Professor Kline says this change is not significant; I disagree. However, that is not what the change is. The change is an attempt to teach the true nature of deductive reasoning, and also to teach a great deal more geometry more creatively than is now traditionally accomplished, as well as to make use of the fact that in the twentieth century geometry can be taught in a less cumbersome manner than in the time of the Greeks, principally because we have developed an adequate algebra.

Apparently Professor Kline does not like algebra because it is "the bane of students." I doubt that it is, but in any event this does not seem to be an adequate reason for not introducing algebraic or coordinate geometry into the high school program.

It is utterly amazing to me how Professor Kline can so freely criticize something of which he does not have full knowledge. He makes a few generalized, partly accurate, partly inaccurate statements concerning the "new position" of the Commission on Mathematics, and then criticizes it on the grounds that "if it backs away from modern mathematics it only backs into a minor reshuffling of the traditional curriculum."

Those of the readers of *The Mathematics Teacher* who have had the opportunity of seeing the Third Draft of the Report of the Commission on Mathematics know that the recommendations of the Commission on Mathematics are far from being a minor reshuffling of the traditional curriculum. To be sure, we do "back away" from modern mathematics in the sense that we do not "replace" the traditional material by "symbolic logic, Boolean algebra, topology, etc.," which is what Professor Kline thought we were going to do. The truth is, however, that we never had any intention of doing what he thought we were going to do; neither are we going to propose what he now thinks we are. My advice is that Professor Kline wait until he reads the Report of the Commission before he criticizes the Commission's position.

In conclusion, I will comment on Professor Kline's "Principles of a New Approach to the Curriculum." Unfortunately these principles are also vague generalizations: We must teach mathematics by seeking to arouse interest in the subject; we must supply motivation and purpose to the mathematics we teach; we must be sure that the intuitive meaning of each mathematical idea or procedure is made intuitively clear to the students: knowledge is a whole and mathematics is a part of that whole.

Well, of course I agree with all of these generalizations. But I must say that I do not agree with the presuppositions underlying these platitudes.

First, Professor Kline assumes that "it is intrinsically more difficult to arouse interest in mathematics than in history or literature." I just don't believe it. I taught mathematics for twenty-two years before becoming a full-time administrative officer, my experience is that this assumption is not true. Certainly it is correct to say that mathematics of any kind is abstract, and the role that it plays in human thought is not a priori clear. But it is not correct to say that "every student knows what history is about, why he is expected to study history, and what he might gain from it."

Second, with respect to motivation and purpose, Professor Kline believes that such motivation is to be found in the solution of simple, genuine, and basic physical problems, and he will also admit problems from the social sciences, art, and music. It is not clear whether this is the only possible motivation, or the best possible motivation. I do not agree with either assumption, however.

Finally, Professor Kline ends on the same note of vague generalization with which he started. He says that he has a conception of the first two years of high school mathematics that would entail a radical revision of the present curriculum, but he does not tell us what it is. I submit that if he has such a revision, he is under an intellectual obligation to reveal it.

Having finished Professor Kline's paper and these comments upon it, I am left with one unanswered question. I am wondering whether in point of fact, Professor Kline really likes mathematics. I do not deny that he is a mathematician, and one of considerable competence. I do not deny that he is a teacher of mathematics, and from the views he expresses concerning mathematical pedagogy, I am inclined to believe that he is a good teacher of mathematics. But I think that he is at heart a physicist, or perhaps a "natural philosopher," not a mathematician, and that the reason he does not like the proposals for orienting the secondary

school college preparatory mathematics curriculum to the diverse needs of the twentieth century by making use of some of the concepts developed in mathematics during the last 100 years or so is not that this is bad mathematics, but that it minimizes the importance of physics.

The assumption can, of course, be wrong. But it is an assumption that explains Professor Kline's apparent antipathy to all parts of mathematics not directly related to physical applications, his desire to teach mathematics by means of physical problems, his feeling that mathematics is intrinsically less interesting than other subjects, and his evident distaste for abstraction and rigor.

The Second Revolution in Mathematics

CARL B. ALLENDOERFER

"The first step in the learning of any mathematical subject is the development of intuition."

INTRODUCTION

This meeting is being held almost exactly seven years after the first revolution in mathematics was stimulated by the successful firing of the first earth satellite, Sputnik I, by the Russians. Although this revolution had been brewing ever since World War II and before, the

Reprinted from *The Mathematics Teacher*, LVIII (December, 1965), 690–95, by permission of the author and the National Council of Teachers of Mathematics. Copyright © 1965 by the National Council of Teachers of Mathematics. This material was originally presented as an address delivered before the NCTM at Atlanta, Georgia, November 20, 1964. Carl B. Allendoerfer is Professor of Mathematics, University of Washington, Seattle.

launching of Sputnik I can be taken as the date on which the revolution entered its active phase and after which real progress began to be made. It is, therefore, appropriate at this meeting to review what has happened in these seven years, to take stock of the present state of the revolution, and to discuss the proper direction for the second revolution which is about to follow upon the heels of the first

HISTORY OF THE FIRST REVOLUTION

I shall begin by describing the history of the first revolution as I have seen it develop. This is a personal account which is not built on any serious historical research, and so it may omit the contributions of many people. In essence, however, I believe it to be accurate.

It is of importance to observe at the outset that this revolution began in the colleges, for this orientation has had a great influence on how the revolution has proceeded. A small number of mathematicians returned to their colleges from World War II and began to reassume their teaching duties. During the war we had been aware of exciting developments in mathematics such as game theory, linear programing, new methods in statistics, and the applications of these to operations analysis. When we returned to the classroom, we found the old curriculum dull and sterile and having far too little contact with the living mathematics which we knew. In the large universities the GI bulge made curricular reform impossible, but at the smaller colleges new materials were produced at a surprising rate. We had no NSF, no summer writing groups, and virtually no secretarial help. Frequently I typed my own mimeographed material a day or two ahead of the class, and on one occasion sorted out the sheets with the aid of the president of the college, who had come to my office on a matter of college business. Various preliminary versions of new materials were prepared in this fashion, and word began leaking out to the schools that something was happening in some of the colleges.

Through my colleague and coauthor, Cletus Oakley, this situation came to the attention of the Committee on Examinations of the College Entrance Examination Board, which began to wonder whether changes in the schools were necessary in view of what was happening in the colleges. It has been the long-term policy of the College Board to base its examinations on what was actually being taught and not to sponsor curriculum reform by changing its examinations. On this occasion the Board was so impressed with the need that it violated this policy and decided to help change the school mathematical curriculum. The Board then appointed the Commission on Mathematics under the chairmanship of Professor A. W. Tucker of Princeton University. This Commission contained university and college mathematicians as well as leaders in school mathematics. This appointment was a momentous event, for it was the first time in a generation (at least) that school and college teachers of mathematics had sat down together to discuss their joint problems in an atmosphere which was suitable for a free exchange of ideas.

The Commission consulted with other groups which were springing up, such as that at the University of Illinois, and took a good hard look at school mathematics for the college-capable student. We found many places where improvements were long overdue, wrote these up in detail, and issued our report. This was available in preliminary form when Sputnik I went off, and it laid the groundwork for the major events that came later.

If it had not been for Sputnik I, this report might have suffered the fate of many educational documents and been filed in the archives, with little effort being made to implement it. As things turned out, the public demanded action, federal funds suddenly became available, the mathematical community organized SMSG, and the fat was in the fire. The first versions of the SMSG materials were available in the autumn of 1959 and were generally released in revised form for use in 1960. So now we have had five years of experience with them and can begin to form judgments of their effectiveness.

Although SMSG never said so explicitly, the history so far makes it clear that the SMSG materials were generally aimed at college-capable students. It was recognized that there were other students in the schools, and some people expressed pious hopes that with some simplification the SMSG materials could be made useful for them as well. I have seen no sign, however, that this was ever pressed very hard.

Since its initial set of publications, SMSG has gone on to publish many other helpful materials and has extended its writing to the elementary school. Its influence has been very great, and I support it wholeheartedly. It is remarkable that that so much was accomplished in so short a time. But there is even more that needs to be done.

PRESENT STATE OF THE REVOLUTION

In my opinion, the revolution has now moved out of its most dynamic stage of development into the stage of refinement and consolidation. The SMSG books are available in their revised forms, and so are the Illinois materials. Commercial writers have had a chance to catch the flavor of the movement, and a sprinkling of good, modern commercial textbooks have been published. What is the present impact of all this effort?

When we come to a meeting such as this, we get the impression that the battle is won and that most schools are "wall to wall" with SMSG, Illinois, Ball State, or some other modern program. When we talk to mathematicians at Ivy League Universities, we learn that "nearly" every entering student has studied calculus in high school, and that calculus is disappearing as a university-level freshman course. The physicists are delighted and are stiffening the mathematical requirements for their beginning courses. The revolution has long since been won, and the next steps are being pushed with vigor.

I submit to you that we should be very suspicious of this type of euphoria,

and that the revolution is far from being won. I do not know of any general national survey of what has happened in the schools, but I should like to refer to a limited survey conducted by the College Board and published in 1963.[1] The data are for 1962. Admittedly this is out of date, but this seems to be the usual state of educational statistics. The Board surveyed 181 schools that normally send a reasonable number of candidates to the College Board Mathematics Achievement Tests. These are generally the more ambitious schools, so this is certainly a biased sample of high schools in the country as a whole. This is a group which I would expect to be "wall to wall" with modern programs but not so.

28 per cent did not teach the structure of the number system.
34 per cent did not teach set theory.
56 per cent did not teach logic.
30 per cent did not teach probability.
30 per cent gave no attention to calculus.

Although 86 per cent reported the use of SMSG materials, the large majority of them did so at one grade level only, most frequently the ninth.

If these premier schools are so far from "wall to wall," what about the rest of the country? My own observations lead me to conclude that the good city and suburban schools are using modern materials for their top students but that very little has happened in their standard courses offered for the less gifted. It is still not uncommon for me to find teachers in rural or small-town schools to whom SMSG and modern mathematics are little more than an unpleasant rumor. I conclude that the revolution is very far from being won and that we shall be making a tragic mistake

[1] The preparation in mathematics of candidates who take the intermediate or advanced mathematics tests, by Donald J. Malcom. Educational Testing Service. Princeton, N.J., 1963.

if we assume that the glowing reports from sophisticated centers in the country are truly representative.

Let us review how the revolution took place. It was guided by college people and was largely aimed at the college-capable students. The construction of the curriculum and the preparation of the text materials were not based upon any theory of learning or educational research; they represent solely what the writers thought to be best in the light of their knowledge of mathematics and their experience in the classroom.

In spite of all the thunder and lightning, I believe that we have not made any really fundamental change in school mathematics. We have taken a structure, which was well built to start with, have shifted its partitions, redecorated its rooms, put in new and faster elevators, dressed up the lobby, and cleaned the grime off the exterior. Certainly it is more livable than it used to be, but it is still intended for the use of the upper classes. We have not gone to the back streets and done anything with the (educational) slums, and we have hardly thought about new types of structures which are properly suited to the modern age. It is high time that we moved into these new areas of activity.

THE CAMBRIDGE REPORT

So now we come to the second revolution in mathematics. The first salvo of this revolution was the Cambridge Report *Goals for School Mathematics* (Houghton Mifflin, 1963). This ambitious document was prepared by a group of mathematicians and other scientists selected from the most prestigious institutions in the country. They call for a complete reconstruction of the mathematics curriculum, beginning in the elementary school and proceeding upward through the high school to the colleges. An important

feature of their plan is that two years of calculus be taught in the high school together with substantial courses in linear algebra and probability. This is to be accomplished by improving the mathematical program in the elementary school to the point where it includes much of the present first two years of the high school. The report is full of caveats to the effect that this plan is a goal to be achieved in a decade or two and that it cannot be implemented until there has been a major overhaul in the training of mathematics teachers in both the elementary schools and the high schools. I shall not dwell on the details of this report, for I urge every mathematics teacher to read it for himself.

Although there is much to commend in this report and although it is well hedged with caveats (which I have taken to heart), it is my position that this report goes in the wrong direction if it is intended as the outline for the second revolution in mathematics.

In the first place, I detect that the authors have succumbed to the euphoria about which I spoke earlier. They are used to students from the limited number of schools which have succeeded in implementing the first revolution in mathematics, and they seem to suppose that their experience is typical of the rest of the country. If their assumption is correct, their report is actually rather modest. During the past thirty years we have moved instruction in calculus for these honor students from the sophomore year of college to the senior year of high school. By tightening up just a little bit more, we can surely gain another year and teach two years of calculus in the high school. There are, indeed, school systems which can implement this report in the next few years if they put their minds to it. My first objection, however, is that this is a program for the superelite and that it is misleading to suppose that it can be adopted widely throughout the nation in any foreseeable period.

My second objection is that the report is very vague when it describes exactly what is to happen in the elementary school. A few of the writers of the report taught for several weeks in elementary schools and discovered what they could get away with. This is a far cry from what can be done on a regular basis by even the most highly qualified elementary teachers. I have asked several of these writers about their reactions to current psychological research on how young children learn mathematics, and found that they treat it with scorn. Whether this view is shared by all members of the Cambridge Group may be open to question, but at least the report shows no knowledge of the work of these psychologists. Until much more research of this kind has been done and its results incorporated into the curriculum, the program for the elementary school which is outlined in this report can be offered only to the most gifted young children.

My third objection is that the report completely ignores the very substantial problem of what mathematics should be taught to the lower seven-eights of the ability group, and in particular to the lower third. The first revolution has not had any impact upon this lower third, and here the mathematics community is in serious trouble. These are the children who in the past would grow up to take unskilled jobs, but these jobs are disappearing. These children include the culturally deprived and those who are likely to be the poor of the next generation. Our mathematical curriculum cannot ignore these people, and, in spite of some attention to them by the NCTM and SMSG, their problems have not been seriously faced. If the Cambridge Report is to be taken as the blueprint for curriculum reform in the next decades, these children will continue to be neglected, and this is something that we just cannot let happen.

OUTLINE OF THE SECOND REVOLUTION

What, then, have I to offer in the place of this report? In contrast to the first revolution, which began from the top down, I favor a revolution that rises from the bottom up. Surely it must know where it is going, but the research and development must begin in the elementary school and proceed upward to the colleges. Until we know what can be done in the elementary school, there is little point in even talking about the future program for the high schools.

How then do we begin? First I recommend that we do pay attention to the growing body of knowledge on how young children learn mathematics. Relatively few people in the world are working on this aspect of the problem, and they are far from arriving at definitive answers. Still, there is much that we can learn from their present tentative conclusions. In particular I draw your attention to the work of Professor Suppes, who is one of the few people in this country who have made contributions along these lines.

In order to be more specific, let me discuss what seems to me to be the greatest block to the learning of mathematics in the early grades. I have arrived at this by talking with several people who know much more about young children than I do, and my conclusions are still very tentative. I am referring to the matter of *intuition*. The first step in the learning of any mathematical subject is the development of intuition. This must come before rules are stated or formal operations are introduced. The trouble is that we know all too little about how to foster the growth of mathematical intuition. It is here that children differ very widely in their rate of growth. The most "brilliant" see things in a flash; with the slower ones, we give up and have them memorize. When these slower students have memorized a number of bits of mathematics without intuition or understanding, they begin to get confused and their "computer jams." They may be able to add and multiply, but they do not know *when* to add and when to multiply. Before long they are mathematical failures, and no amount of remedial work seems to help very much. It is to such people that we try to teach "senior arithmetic" or even what one of my friends calls "prenatal mathematics," a popular course in many junior colleges. Most of this effort is wasted; for by the time these students have reached high school or college, they have such a block against mathematics that few teachers have the skill to reach their minds.

So first we must learn how to develop intuition in all our young children. Since the rate at which this can be done will vary greatly with the child, students will proceed with their mathematics at markedly differing speeds. Perhaps we must abandon textbooks, with their prescribed grade levels, and work from sets of task cards or short pamphlets which the teacher can present to each student when he is ready.

The task of working all this out is an enormous one. More mathematicians and psychologists need to be recruited to undertake the basic research. New types of teaching materials need to be prepared to take this research into account, and elementary teachers need to be trained to use these materials. This is clearly a very long-range program, which will be even more expensive than all the work of the first revolution. It is time that the problem be recognized and that a start be made.

The impact of such a program on the high schools would be truly revolu-tionary. It is not easy to see what form mathematical education in the high schools would take, and so I do not propose to make the mistake of my Cambridge friends in outlining a high school program before I know what kind of foundations it will have in the elementary school.

INTERIM STEPS

Since the construction of a really sound elementary curriculum is a long time off, and since the problems of the lower- and upper-ability groups are currently with us, we must proceed to try to solve these with the tools and information we have at hand. For the upper group, the problems are not too difficult. We can speed up the acceleration and follow many of the ideas of the Cambridge Report—and the sooner the better.

The problem of the lower-ability group is much more difficult. I have identified the elementary school as the place where the damage is done, and it is here that we must begin. There is already enough psychological knowledge to make our first tentative applications of it to the curriculum. These, however, cannot be handled by the usual, general-purpose elementary teacher. Our first step, then, should be the general adoption of the scheme of having arithmetic in the grades taught by arithmetic specialists. This is frequently advocated, but few school systems have done anything about it!

I saw such a scheme in operation in the summer of 1963 when I visited Hobart, Tasmania. I was a guest at an Infant's School, which incorporated the first three grades. The school was in a working-class neighborhood, and some of the children were delightful little thugs, already on the road to being delinquent. There were six teachers for the five rooms in this school, and they traded teaching duties around. The senior teacher was the arithmetic specialist. I watched her all morning and was much impressed by the arithmetic understanding and skills that her pupils were absorbing. We can do the same if we only have the will to do it.

A second interim step is to put much more emphasis on remedial work in arithmetic in the high schools for those who need it. Funds for such work should be available in connection with President Johnson's poverty program. I know that isolated groups are, indeed, working on this; but I do not believe that sufficient manpower and effort are being directed into this kind of work. The problem here is even more difficult than that of the elementary school; for first we must overcome the mathematical blocks that exist in these young people, and then we must teach them from scratch, using materials and techniques that appeal to their more mature psychology. School mathematicians alone cannot do this job; we must recruit college mathematicians, psy-

chologists, even sociologists, and make a largescale effort.

CONCLUSION

So we have much to do, and there will never be a dull moment for those of us who are conscientious about mathematical education. Among our jobs are:

1. Implementation of the first revolution in all the grades of all our schools.
2. Construction, with the help of psychologists, neurosurgeons, and others, of a drastically different elementary curriculum in mathematics adjusted to the learning patterns of young children. When this has been completed, we can turn to a new curriculum for the high schools.
3. Interim steps, including acceptance and implementation of the general principle that arithmetic should be taught by specialists in the elementary schools and an all-out team effort to solve the problem of remedial instruction in arithmetic in the high schools and colleges.

A Second Look at Modern Mathematics
SISTER MARY PETRONIA

Since "modern mathematics" has been with us now for about ten years, perhaps it would be profitable to take another look at it and its implications. So that there may be no misunderstanding, it seems imperative to me that

Reprinted from *The Catholic Educator*, XXXVII, Nos. 3 and 4 (November and December, 1966), 63–66, 27–30 (also published by Scott, Foresman and Company in 1967), by permission of the author and the publisher. Sister Mary Petronia is Associate Professor of Mathematics and Chairman of the Mathematics Department, Mount Mary College, Milwaukee, Wisconsin.

I say what I mean by "modern mathematics," because many persons talk about it, and yet, if they were questioned as to what they mean, they would not be able to explain. To my way of thinking it would be better to speak of a modern program of mathematics, as changes in both method and content are involved. Some new topics—not new in the field of mathematics, but new in the sense that they are introduced earlier in the curriculum—have been added, it is true, but there is also a decided difference in purpose, approach, and attitude. The modern program of mathematics regards mathematics as a system of thinking rather than a set of arbitrary rules, as a system better learned by understanding the structure and principles of mathematics than by memorization of facts.

Essentially, then, it implies a reorganization of traditional subject matter with the addition of explaining where rules come from and where they lead, some new content, and a decidedly new teaching approach, all within the framework of the unifying concepts that form the basis of the structure of mathematics as a whole. The main objective and primary concern of a modern program is to have the student understand why he does what he does. Its approach is one of investigation, experimentation, and discovery. It aims to make mathematics intellectually exciting and challenging. "Modern mathematics" started as a sincere effort on the part of our best educators to improve the quality of the teaching of mathematics, and it has grown into a force that is spreading over the entire country. It really has made mathematics come "alive."

I would also like to make it clear that I do have faith in a modern program of mathematics and feel it holds much promise. I sincerely believe that *if* "modern mathematics" is taught properly, it is decidedly better than the way most of us learned it. In addition, it should produce more critical readers and much better thinkers.

In the light of what I have just written, I would like to make some comments on several of the modern trends in mathematics today.

SETS

The topic of sets has been very prominent in conversation and literature today so much so that to some persons it *is* "modern mathematics." This, of course,

is a mistake. I do not intend to discuss sets, set relationships, nor set operations as such, but rather to discuss, to some extent, the use of sets in an elementary school mathematics program. I am not entirely convinced that set notation and set symbolism should be used in the lower grades. I feel that it has no genuine significance there and that there are exercises that would be more profitable to small children than to have them struggling to make braces and other set symbols, which have little or no meaning for them. Yet, I think the language of sets is both convenient and profitable and should be used at the very beginning. It can and should serve as a unifying factor in a mathematics program. In setting up any mathematical system, one begins with a set of elements. In fact, all mathematics begins with a study of collections of objects, and "set" is one of the simplest words one can use for such a collection. It is essential for children to have some means of identifying the elements that belong to a particular set, a means of telling whether or not an element belongs to a set. Children can then match the elements of one set with those of another set to find out whether there are just enough, more than enough, or not enough. This gives rise to equivalent and non-equivalent sets, terms which small children need not use. It is sufficient if they can do the matching and explain what is happening.

This comparison of sets gives rise to the idea of number. Sets, whose elements match exactly, have the same number, and we give this number a name. If a first set has more (or less) elements than a second set, we say the number of the first set is greater (or less) than the number of the second set. We can order sets according to their manyness and then arrange the number names of these sets in the same order as the order of the sets. Finally, then, we obtain a set of number names, in order, which can be used in place of the ordered sets. This in turn enables us to count, that is to find the number of a set of objects or to find the position of a particular object in an ordered set, giving rise to the cardinal and ordinal use of number. However, counting would certainly be limited if we failed to extend our system for naming numbers. So we develop a system of numeration, a system for naming numbers by means of grouping by tens, and the use of the principles of place value and addition. It is this decimal system of numeration which is the basis for all the algorisms used in computation in arithmetic. There are systems of numeration constructed with bases other than ten. These are commonly referred to today as "number bases." Though they may not be too useful, they furnish interesting and enriching experiences for children.

We can extend these ideas to the concepts of addition and multiplication. We can think about the joining of sets; for example, a set of three objects is joined by a set of four objects to form a set of seven objects. The mathematical analogue of this physical situation is $3 + 4 = 7$, read "3 plus 4 equals 7." We must be careful to distinguish; we join sets but we add numbers. Viewed in this way, addition is the process of finding the cardinal number of a set which is the union of two disjoint sets, sets having no elements in common. We can think of joining 3 disjoint sets, each of which contains 4 objects, forming a set of 12 objects. The mathematical analogue of this would be: $3 \times 4 = 12$. Consequently, we can think of multiplication as the process of finding the cardinal number of the union of a number of disjoint sets each of which contains the same number of elements. More attention will be given the other processes later in this article.

It might be wise at this point to comment briefly on the introduction and reading of signs. This is something I feel strongly about, and it is part of good mathematics to give signs their proper names. Signs of operations like $+$, $-$, $\times$, $\div$ should be introduced very carefully, and once so introduced, teachers should insist that children read them correctly. $3 + 4 = 7$ should be read "3 plus 4 equals 7" right from the start and $7 - 5 = 2$ should be read "7 minus 5 equals 2." Signs of relation like $=$ (equals), $>$ (greater than), $<$ (less than) should not be introduced too early, lest the children merely manipulate signs without regard for the meaning the sign is to convey. It would seem to me that, in general, the teacher at any level would be the best one to judge whether or not his class is ready as far as the use of the symbol is concerned.

There is the danger that teachers might teach an isolated unit on sets, just for the sake of sets or in order to say that they are teaching "modern mathematics." This would be a mistake, and a serious one. For in this way the students would not see how the concept of sets fits into the whole picture of mathematics and how it is, perhaps, the most significant concept which runs like a thread through all mathematics. The more we know about and use mathematics, the better we can understand why mathematicians say that the concept of set is a unifying, clarifying, and simplifying factor for all of mathematics.

PRECISION OF LANGUAGE

In thinking about precision of language, doubtless the distinction between number and numeral would head the list. A number is a property of a set, that property that tells how many elements there are in the set. A numeral is a name for a number or a symbol used to represent a number. Essentially, to distinguish between a number and a numeral is to distinguish between a thing and the name of a thing. If the things considered are physical entities, then we seem to have little difficulty in making the distinction. For example, no one would confuse the four-legged animal we call a cat with the word "c–a–t" written on a chalkboard, nor the girl Mary with the name "Mary." But if things are abstract entities such as we deal with in mathematics, it becomes considerably more difficult to make the distinction between the name of the thing and its referent, the thing itself. Since numbers are abstractions and cannot be perceived by any of the five senses, they are often confused with their names. I do think a teacher ought to be very careful to use correct terms, since this helps children to learn better and to think better. However, he should not do this to the extent that it would make him strained in his classroom or hesitant about which word to use. It is important that a student understand the distinction between number and numeral, so that he may realize the difference between actually operating with numbers and merely manipulating symbols representing those numbers.

This is only one item in regard to precision of language. There are many others, such as distinguishing between a line and the picture of a line, a point and the dot used to represent the point. Not only should the language of mathematics be precise, it should also be used correctly. I have known of college professors who utterly confused elementary school teachers by speaking about equal sets and equivalent sets as though the terms could be used interchangeably.

The idea that a number may have different names is easy for children to grasp. Finding different names for numbers opens a vast and exciting field for children to explore. Actually much of mathematics is finding different names for numbers and then being creative enough to choose that name which is most convenient for a particular situation. Some programs, in naming numbers, speak of standard names and operational names. This is very convenient. For example, the standard name for the number fifteen would be 15, whereas examples of operational names would include $7 + 8$, $20 - 5$, 3×5, and others. Requiring children to give names for a number using variations of symbols and signs provides opportunities for interesting practice, ingenuity, and good learning. To illustrate, children might be asked to give names for the number 15, using two symbols and one sign as $6 + 9$, or three symbols and two signs like $13 + 7 - 5$ or $2 \times 7 + 1$. Teachers often fail to extend this idea beyond whole numbers, and in doing so, lose a valuable opportunity to have children learn and see relationships. For, rational numbers and other kinds of numbers too have many names. Names for seven-eights might include $\frac{1}{2} + \frac{3}{8}$, $7 - 6\frac{1}{8}$, and $\frac{5}{6} + \frac{3}{8} - \frac{1}{3}$.

There is another aspect of number naming which is very useful and should be encouraged, 7,000 could be renamed as 7 thousands, 700 tens, or 70 hundreds. This reminds me of an incident I had the joy of experiencing in a fourth-grade classroom. A boy had this subtraction to perform:

$$\begin{array}{r} 7,000 \\ -\ 2,756 \\ \hline \end{array}$$

His reasoning went like this. I cannot take 6 ones from 0 ones, so I will take a ten. I have 700 tens. If I take one ten and change it to ones, I will then have 699 tens and 10 ones. Now I am all set to subtract. You will have to agree with me that this boy's method was extremely efficient. His performance gave evidence of understanding. In particular, he knew that 7,000 had many names, and he chose to use the one that best suited his purpose—namely, 699

95809

tens, ten ones. It would indeed be remarkable if we as teachers could have all those we teach understand situations like this and consequently perform as efficiently as this boy. These are some ideas that every teacher could and should be using in his classroom.

PROPERTIES OF OPERATIONS ON NUMBERS

Some teachers seem to think that in "modern mathematics" children need no longer learn automatic response to the basic facts in the four processes. What a mistake! We still want children to know their basic facts! Otherwise they have not the necessary foundation on which to build. However, in a modern program of mathematics the way in which children learn these facts ought to be different. Teachers should have children understand the meaning of the facts, furnish a host of experiences in which the facts are developed, and then provide meaningful and interesting practice to help the children know their facts correctly and speedily. There are some mathematics teachers today who say that drill is not needed. Perhaps they would rather substitute "sustained attack." I grant that if children learned with more understanding, less time would have to be devoted to drill. Yet, it is my opinion that even the most talented children need a certain amount of drill—not pure drill of course and not drill before understanding, but interesting means of giving children the necessary repetition for retention.

Even at the first-grade level, through many and varied experiences with sets of objects and the action of joining sets, children can learn that $3 + 4 = 4 + 3$, a particular example of the commutative principle with respect to addition. They may even understand this idea before they learn that $3 + 4 = 7$ and $4 + 3 = 7$. Likewise, later in a similar manner, they can discover that $3 \times$ $4 = 4 \times 3$, an example of the commutative principle with respect to multiplication. In like manner children could be lead to discover the associative principles of addition and multiplication. Should small children, because they have gained understanding of these principles, be expected to rattle off these big words—commutative, associative, and the like? It always amuses me when teachers tell me how their little second-graders can say these big words but it does not really impress me.

Do not misunderstand! I do want children to learn as much mathematics as they can and good mathematics! I would much prefer that they have complete understanding of the principle and can show me why they know that it does not make any difference in what order numbers are added rather than lack this knowledge and be able to refer to the principle by name. It seems to me that very often teachers fail to have students extend these principles to situations including numbers other than whole numbers, sometimes not even beyond the basic facts. This is not good mathematics! These principles should be extended to other situations where they apply—for example, children should see that $\frac{2}{3} + \frac{1}{2} = \frac{1}{2} + \frac{2}{3}$, $7.5 \times 8.3 = 8.3 \times 7.5$, $25 \times 728 = 728 \times 25$, and the like. Eventually from the study of many particular cases, students will discover the commutative principles of addition and multiplication: for every replacement of a and b, $a + b = b + a$ for the operation of addition and $ab = ba$ for the operation of multiplication. Teachers should proceed with the associative principle in the same manner.

The distributive principle seems to give teachers more difficulty, perhaps because it includes both addition and multiplication. Yet, by the use of pictures, the idea of sets, and renaming numbers, the principle can be demonstrated simple and clearly. Let us illustrate. We might start with 3×7. Then rename 7 as $2 + 5$, so we have $3 \times (2 + 5)$, which means 3 sets with $2 + 5$ elements in each set and could be pictured like this:

```
   x x    x x x x x ⎞
   x x    x x x x x ⎬ 3 sets
   x x    x x x x x ⎠
    2  +     5
```

But then taking another look at the picture, without adding or removing any elements, we also see that we have 3 sets with 2 elements in each set and 3 sets with 5 elements in each set, which translated into mathematical language would be: $(3 \times 2) + (3 \times 5)$. Consequently, abstracting from the physical situation, $3 \times (2 + 5)$ must name the same number as $(3 \times 2) + (3 \times 5)$. Eventually, by the process of induction, children could derive the distributive principle: for every replacement of a, b, and c, $a \times (b + c) = (a \times b) + (a \times c)$.

This principle provides numerous worthwhile applications. It should of course be extended beyond the whole numbers. I think children who really understand this principle should be strongly urged to perform certain multiplications mentally through its use. For example, 8×17 could be thought of as $8 \times (10 + 7)$; then $8 \times 10 = 80$ and $8 \times 7 = 56$, and $80 + 56$ can be renamed as 136. Also, renaming $5\frac{1}{4}$ as $5 + \frac{1}{4}$, $12 \times 5\frac{1}{4}$ can be renamed as 63.

Just a few words about what I like to call V.I.N.'s. Initials are used for so many things in our day and age. We can find application for them in mathematics too. What are V.I.N.'s? They are "*V*ery *I*mportant *N*umbers." They are none other than zero and one, the identity elements for addition and multiplication, respectively. We know that adding zero to any given number or multiplying any given number by one does not have the given number lose its identity. This makes zero and one really unique. Further, if children are lead to discover and understand the role of zero and one in the different operations, then they have already learned much arithmetic. Many of the errors made in mathematics are due to a lack of understanding of how these very important numbers behave.

INVERSE OPERATIONS

This title indicates another trend of "modern mathematics," the attempt to show that the different operations in mathematics are related and how they are related. Subtraction is the inverse of addition, the "undoing" of addition, if you will. In the physical world we put two sets together, say sets A and B, to obtain a third set, set C. In this case we have joined sets. The mathematical analogue of this is addition. Now we can also remove the set A from the set C, leaving the set B remaining. In this case we have separated sets. The mathematical analogue of this is subtraction. It is from this idea that we formulate the definition of what it means to subtract one number from another. To subtract a number a from a number c means to find a number b such that $b + a = c$. This definition is basic and important. I am not suggesting that small children be able to recite this definition, but I would want them to be applying it endlessly. I would especially recommend emphasizing this definition in two ways. First, when teachers ask for another name for, say, $7 - 2$, children should be taught to realize that they are looking for a number n, that when 2 is added to it, the result will be 7. What number does n represent? Secondly, teachers should repeatedly question children by asking: "How do you know that $7 - 2 = 5$?" To children who understand substraction the answer should be evident. $7 - 2 = 5$ because $5 + 2 = 7$. Let us not stop here. We must make extensions and show that this definition of subtraction holds throughout mathematics. That is what makes it so significant. We must keep children mindful of what number they are looking for when they subtract and how to prove they are right, once they have obtained the number.

Similarly, division is the inverse of the operation of multiplication. To divide a number a by a number b means to find a number c such that $c \times b = a$. Many elementary teachers find it difficult to see or to explain why division by zero is impossible. In the light of the definition above, this becomes easy to see and not in the least mysterious. To illustrate, suppose I want to divide 5 by 0. To translate this to terms of multiplication it means I am looking for that number n, which when multiplied by 0, will yield 5. Now what number n times 0 is equal to 5? Any number times 0 is equal to 0. Therefore, there is no number n, such that $n \times 0 = 5$. So it is impossible to divide 5 by 0.

If teachers consistently kept students mindful of subtraction and division as inverse operations of addition and multiplication, children would see more sense in mathematics and find it easier to understand. Likewise, at higher levels, students would have less difficulty in learning how to perform these operations on integers and other types of numbers.

PROBLEM SOLVING

The concept of an equation (more precisely, condition) as the expression of the structure of a problem situation is being used more and more. Traditionally the critical phase of problem solving has been the choice of the operation to be used, and to make that choice, children very often have been taught to depend upon clue words or phrases. The modern tendency is to make the translation of the problem situation into an equation the critical phase. Without a doubt the modern approach is better. Repeatedly we hear it said that children cannot solve problems because they cannot read them. What we really mean is that the children cannot interpret the problem situation. The STA (Seeing Through Arithmetic) approach to problem solving, in my opinion, is excellent. In fact, I think it is the only program which really has a *method* of problem solving, and this method is developed consistently and logically throughout this program. Regardless of program, the method could be used to advantage. It regards *action* as the key word to problem solving. In problem situations we may have the joining of sets, the separating of sets, or the comparison of sets. Children are taught which signs convey which actions. Essentially the method itself consists of four steps: having children visualize the action taking place in the problem or having children get a mental picture of what is going on in the problem, translating that action into the symbols of mathematical language or writing the condition that fits the structure of the problem, determining the means of finding the missing numeral in the condition, and lastly, relating the result obtained to the physical situation from which it came. This method is excellent because it forces children to think. The child's writing of the condition as a record of his thought gives evidence that this thinking has taken place, because unless a child understands the nature of the problem, he cannot write the condition. The condition is simply an arithmetic sentence that tells the story of the problem in shortened form and gives the teacher a clear idea of how the child has interpreted the problem situation. Relating the result to the physical situation from which it came provides an opportunity for the child to check on the reasonableness of his answer.

Let us consider just one simple problem to illustrate: "Debbie has some dolls. Lou gave her two more dolls. Now Debbie has 5 dolls. How many dolls did Debbie have at first?" In this problem we know that Debbie had some dolls but we do not know how many, so we will let n stand for that number. Then Lou gave her 2 more dolls, and so we can imagine this set of dolls joining the set that Debbie already had. The sign that indicates this action is the plus sign. After the two sets were joined, Debbie had 5 dolls. So we may write $n + 2 = 5$.

It may be well for us to observe that the ability to express mathematical ideas by using signs and symbols is a necessary prerequisite to the ability of writing the condition to fit the structure of a problem. This shows again how extremely important it is that signs and symbols be carefully introduced, be given their proper meaning, and that the meaning be properly understood by children.

In solving the above problem traditionally, we probably would have thought about it as a subtraction problem. But if a child writes $5 - 2 = n$, he has not translated the situation correctly. What he has done is express the necessary computational procedure to obtain a replacement for n.

It is important to notice that there are two ideas involved in this method—the situation and the computation. These two, for a particular problem, may or may not be the same. In the problem given above, they are not the same. The situation is an additive one, since in the physical world, one set is joining another. The computation required to find the correct replacement for n is subtraction.

MATHEMATICAL SENTENCES

In programs where children are expected to translate problem situations into mathematical sentences, children are faced with the need of solving conditions such as $n + 5 = 11$, $4n = 28$, $n - 5 = 8$, and the like. The question might be raised as to whether or not teachers should expect children to solve them according to a set of rules, as they do later in algebra. This is definitely not the case! What we want children to do at the beginning is to work with objects or pictures of objects in determining solutions for these conditions in the hope that children may begin to make generalizations on their own. At this stage conditions should be solved on an intuitive and informal basis and not by the axiomatic methods used in algebra at the secondary level.

It may seem to some teachers that requiring children to write equations to fit the structure of problem situations is again making children perform according to pattern and thus conclude that this method is no better than the traditional. This is far from the truth! It is important for teachers to realize that there are some problems for which more than one mathematical sentence can be written. Teachers should respect the creativity of the children and accept the sentence as correct if the children can justify the sentence they write.

In writing about problem solving, I would like to point out that it is very good to give children conditions and have them make up problems of their own to correspond with the given conditions. This gives them the opportunity to be creative and to develop their ability for problem solving. It is likely, too, that teachers may learn more about their students by observing the types of problems they construct.

USE OF RATIOS

Ratios are extremely useful in problem solving. Not all texts and programs treat ratio in the same way. I prefer to use it as it is used in the STA (Seeing Through

Arithmetic) Program, in which a ratio is considered to be a name for a pair of numerals written one over the other to express a relation in situations involving rate or comparison. If we consider it in this sense, then we must distinguish between the ratio $\frac{2}{5}$, which could be read *2 for 5*, if it represents a rate and might mean that 2 of something was selling for 5 cents or *2 is to 5*, if it represents a comparison and might mean that something was shared in the ratio of 2 to 5, and the fractional numeral $\frac{2}{5}$, which would be read two-fifths and means two of the five equal parts into which some whole was divided.

Very many problems in mathematics involve the idea of rate or comparison and can be solved very simply by setting up and solving conditions involving ratios. Children must first be introduced to the basic ideas of rate and comparison and see how they can use ratios to express these basic ideas. By supplying experiences, we can have children discover that different ratios may express the same rate. For example, suppose we say that we can buy 6 objects for 15¢. We might ask the children to separate both the set of objects and the set of cents into subsets, so that they would have the same number of subsets of objects and cents. The set of objects, then, would be divided into 3 subsets with 2 objects in each subset; the set of cents into 3 subsets with 5 cents in each subset. Then children could be led to see that each subset of objects could be matched with each subset of cents. Consequently, they would realize that it must be true that they could buy 2 objects for 5 cents and conclude that *2 for 5¢* must express the same rate as *6 for 15¢*. So $\frac{2}{5}$ and $\frac{6}{15}$ must be equivalent ratios, ratios expressing the same rate. Through further guidance and study children could learn how to compute to replace a ratio with an equivalent ratio, and that by multiplying or dividing both terms of a ratio by the same number they

can obtain another ratio that expresses the same rate or comparison.

Suppose we consider a simple application. Assume oranges are selling for 2 for 15¢. How many oranges can we buy for 60¢? Traditionally this would be a multiple-step problem. Ratio simplifies the whole procedure. The rate at which oranges are selling is 2 for 15¢, written as the ratio $\frac{2}{15}$. We want to know how many oranges we can buy for 60¢. We do not know the number we can buy as yet, so we will let n stand for that number and write the ratio as $n/60$. Now we have two ratios, each of which expresses the same rate. In other words, we have two equivalent ratios, and so we may write: $2/15 = n/60$. Now all we have to do is to find the correct replacement for n. This we can do by asking ourselves what 15 would have to be multiplied by to obtain 60, namely 4. Then that is the number we must multiply 2 by to find the number n stands for. So we find that we can buy 8 oranges for 60¢.

Naturally, children would later have to learn a method by which they could find the missing numeral in conditions involving situations in which the terms of one ratio were not whole-number multiples of the corresponding terms of the other ratio. This can readily be done by introducing the cross-products method.

The use of ratio in the solution of per cent problems completely does away with the memorization of formulas involving rate, percentage and base. How can ratio be used in the solution of per cent problems? First, students must be taught to understand that per cent is a means of expressing a comparison with 100, that is, a ratio in which the second term is always 100. Likewise, they learn that whenever they meet a comparison situation in which a ratio can be set up with a second term of 100, they can express that comparison as a per cent. Consequently, in the ratio method all problems involving per cent are set up in the same way, simply as an equality of two ratios, in which one numeral is missing and the second term of one of the ratios is 100. Comparing this with the traditional method of solving per cent problems, in which three cases are studied, each case requiring its own individual method of solution, it can readily be seen that the ratio method provides a method that cannot be surpassed in simplicity and clarity. In case some of my readers are not familiar with this method, let us consider this problem, ordinarily classified as the third type: 25% of those enrolled at a certain college are freshmen. If there are 200 freshmen at that college, what is the total enrollment at that college?

If students have been taught to think about a per cent as a ratio in which the second term is 100, they will readily translate the 25% to 25/100. Since in this ratio the first term represents the number of freshmen, the first term in the second ratio will have to do the same. Consequently, it will be $200/n$, where n represents the total number of students. Setting the two ratios equal, we have $25/100 = 200/n$. We can easily see that the correct replacement for n is 800. So there are 800 students enrolled at that college.

Most children find the process of changing from one measure to another measure difficult. This procedure can be greatly simplified through the use of ratio. This is true whether the measures be linear, square, or cubic, or whether the measures be in different systems. Care must be taken, of course, to have the two ratios represent the same comparison. All children need to do is to express the basic relation between the two measures as a ratio, then equate it to another ratio expressing the same relation—one of whose terms will be represented by the given measure and the other by a placeholder. For example,

suppose we had to change 81 cubic feet to cubic yards. The basic ratio is 27/1, since there are 27 cubic feet in 1 cubic yard. The second ratio is $81/n$. Then $27/1 = 81/n$, and n stands for the number 3.

The concept of ratio is a beautiful and powerful one. It is a relation, and as such, it provides a good basis for the study of relations in more advanced mathematics, and also for functions, which are special kinds of relations. It has innumerable applications in elementary mathematics and serves as a useful tool in the sciences.

DISCOVERY

Though the use of guided discovery is thought of as one of the modern trends, it is not really new. Good teachers have been using it for a long time. The discovery method, properly used, should produce children who are alert, curious, creative, interested. It is a technique that leads students to discover principles and make generalizations. It stimulates thought, develops the minds of those we teach, and makes them ever more prepared to use the knowledge they already have and apply it to new situations. It makes students willing to make intelligent guesses about various situations and then to test whether or not their guesses prove to be right. There is no neat package to hand teachers to give them this technique. Yet it can be acquired. Teachers must try not to tell the children all the answers but to ask them the "critical questions" —the questions that will urge the children to go from step to step until they have made a "discovery." This implies that teachers must permit children the freedom to make mistakes and to ask questions. It also implies maximum discovery on the part of children and minimum exposition on the part of teachers. This method of "creative" teaching is the very opposite of "this is the way you do it" type. At every stage of development we should give children opportunities to be creative and to discover, because once they have made a discovery, the concept or principle discovered will be well fixed in their minds and there is surely more reason to hope it will be better retained. Even if not all the children in a class have made the discovery, certainly presentation after a careful build-up is far superior to just presentation by rule. Repeated use of guided discovery helps children to increase their mathematical ability—especially in being ingenious in finding methods of solutions when they are confronted with difficult or unfamiliar problems. When I speak of discovery in this sense, I do not mean that a child must discover something that has not been known before. I simply mean that to the child it must be a discovery—an insight, a seeing and an understanding of something he has not seen nor understood before. Such a discovery on the part of a child gives him much satisfaction and a joy "no one can take from him." It urges him on to further discoveries.

Let me cite a few examples of this type of discovery. A certain teacher had the habit of presenting her students with an example the students had not encountered before. She would ask them to think about ways of finding the answer. On this particular occasion the example given was: $8\frac{1}{5} - 3\frac{4}{5}$. One boy figured it out this way: "1 from 4 is 3, 3 from 5 is 2, $\frac{2}{5}$. 3 from 7 is 4. The answer is 4 and $\frac{2}{5}$." The teacher had the feeling that this could not be right. So she tells how she went home and tried a number of examples of the same type, using the boy's method. To her surprise each time she tried, she found the correct result, and so she realized the method must be sound. Next day she asked the boy to explain his reasoning. His explanation went like this: "I took 1 from the 4, because that told me how many fifths I was short in order to make the subtraction, so that I had to take that many fifths from the five-fifths, which I obtained from the 1, which I took from the 8."

I observed another incident in a fourth grade, in which the multiplication tables were being studied, that I would like to share with you. It both amused and thrilled me. The fact under consideration was 4×9. These four things were on the board:

$4 \times 9 = \square$ Four 9's are

x x x x x x x x x
x x x x x x x x x
x x x x x x x x x
x x x x x x x x x

$9 \times 4 = \square$

The child at the board was having difficulty and was about to resort to counting. Another child promptly volunteered that he knew it was 36. When questioned as to how he knew so quickly, he responded: "I knew that if I put one more x in each row, then there would be ten x's in each row, and 4 tens would be 40. Then if I took away those 4 that I put there, there would be 36 left." Good thinking? Another boy in the back of the room did not understand the child's explanation and asked about it. The teacher had the first boy go to the board and show what he meant. He did it just like a little professor. After this explanation, understanding came to the boy in the back of the room, and he chanted, "Oh, now I see. I could have thought of that myself."

To be a "creative" teacher, one who can get his students to perform at their maximum potential and find joy in that performance, is not an easy task but is a rewarding one.

SUMMARY

I have discussed many of the modern trends in mathematics today. All are good, if used properly. "Modern mathematics," as I said before, aims to have children understand why they do what they do. What could not be good about that? Teachers, let us be diligent and use every effort to have those we teach understand the why of mathematics so that they may learn to appreciate and enjoy it.

In the teaching of mathematics, especially at the lower levels, I think there is the danger of becoming too abstract too soon—not giving children enough use of physical materials in an arithmetic class, making the transition from the concrete to the abstract before children are really ready for it. Children need a great diversity of types of experiences. Of course teachers must be careful not to let the pendulum swing too far in either direction, the concrete or the abstract. In the first case children will become too dependent on physical things or pictures or tools and will never acquire the habit of thinking abstractly. In the second case they may be able to manipulate symbols and signs efficiently but never really understand what it is all about.

It has often been said, and it is true, that teachers are apt to teach the way they have been taught rather than the way they have been taught to teach. Teachers, let us not be in this category! Rather, let us constantly have a research attitude, continuously examining our methods of teaching with a view to improving them. A good mathematics program depends not so much on the text as on the teacher and his methods of teaching. The teacher is really the key.

In our teaching let us endeavor to give those we teach a better understanding of the basic concepts and structure of mathematics and thus provide for them a richer and firmer foundation for more advanced mathematics. Mathematics possesses power and beauty. We as teachers should aim to have children realize this. I think that every elementary teacher should be so convinced of the continuity in the mathematics program as a whole, that he would deliberately and emphatically use ideas that have been presented before as a basis for teaching new concepts; and looking ahead, would stress the ideas that are significant and make generous use of relationships between concepts and processes. Doubtless the more mathematical background a teacher has, the more readily he can do this.

To make a mathematics program really effective, our teachers must be adequately prepared by persons who really know mathematics. There must be unity on the part of the teaching staff, all working for the same good cause. Each teacher should know, at least to some extent, the school mathematics program as a whole, that he may teach what he has to teach as part of that whole. Further, he should be particularly familiar with the material that precedes what he is to teach and that which follows, so that he may build well on what the children have previously learned and may stress what is significant so that the teacher who follows him may have solid ground on which to build.

The Revolution at Sputnik-Plus-Ten
FRANCIS J. MUELLER

...[T]he title of [this reading]... may suggest a speech on foreign affairs. But to members of the National Council of Teachers of Mathematics, there is little question as to what *the* revolution refers to: It is our revolution in mathematics education.

The reference to Sputnik in the title is essentially relevant, though indirectly so. As a point of historical fact, our revolution in mathematics education had begun well before Sputnik took flight in 1957. For example, the Commission on Mathematics had been appointed by the College Entrance Examination Board two years before, in 1955, though its report was not published until after Sputnik had made history. By 1957 the University of Illinois was well along with its pioneering work. Those who attended the annual conventions of the Council in the early 1950's could not help but be aware of impending changes. Moreover, it can be shown that many of the features that were to emerge after 1957 in the new secondary school mathematics curricula—where the revolution tended to concentrate in the beginning—had

Reprinted from *The Mathematics Teacher*, LX (November, 1967), 696–706, by permission of the author and the National Council of Teachers of Mathematics. Copyright © 1967 by the National Council of Teachers of Mathematics. This material was originally presented at the opening general session of the Forty-fifth Annual Meeting of the National Council of Teachers of Mathematics in Las Vegas, Nevada, April 18, 1967. Francis J. Mueller is Academic Dean, College of Arts and Sciences, United States International University, California Western Campus, San Diego.

already found their way into revised elementary school mathematics programs as much as a decade before, under the heading "meaningful arithmetic."

What can be attributed to Sputnik, however, is this: As never before, Sputnik focused public attention upon the problems of education in a highly dramatic way. As never before, educators found a willing ear. Curriculum planners who had previously recognized the serious need to update the science and mathematics offerings in the schools and who had already formed ideas on what to do about it, were suddenly listened to and granted support.

The cry, "We dare not fall behind the Russians," sometimes darkly hinted, sometimes blatantly affirmed, became something of a touchstone that unleashed torrents of money for the purpose of bringing about reforms in science and mathematics instruction. In all, it was a classic instance of a right response for a wrong reason. But, let me hasten to add, in the realm of practical politics that is a rather trivial distinction. Frankly, without this unexpected, though admittedly questionable, incentive, many of the curriculum visionaries (both pre- and post-1957) would probably still be weak voices crying in the wilderness. Certainly we would not be as far along as we are today.

So, in a sense, the flight of Sputnik marked the beginning of our public life in mathematics education. Indirectly, Sputnik gave us an almost instant thrust from the shade of previous anonymity and public unconcern into the sudden glare of widespread attention and scrutiny. This year, 1967, marks the tenth anniversary of that event, a particularly appropriate time for taking stock. Although taking stock usually involves a combination of appraising glances backward and hopeful looks forward, it is not my plan . . . to dwell much upon the past. I feel as did Charles Kettering, the famous inventor and industrialist, when he said, "I am far more interested and concerned about the future, because that is where I am going to be spending the rest of my life." (It is interesting to note that he was heard to make that remark when he was about 78 years old!)

But before I dismiss the past, I should like to draw attention to what seems to me to be a rather significant item, one that has substantial relevance for the future, and one that tends to be overlooked. It is this: Those of us who have been active in mathematics education for somewhat more than ten years, who have lived and worked through that turbulent period, tend to assume that most of our colleagues in mathematics education are also personally acquainted with its chain of events. We unconsciously tend to feel that the majority of those who share our particular professional concerns share also a common heritage; that they, too—for the most part—have been witnesses to the full march of progress in mathematics education that we have seen.

Increasingly, and very likely at a more rapid pace than many of us may realize, such a contention is losing validity. In a very recent national survey made by the Research Division of the National Education Association it was found that the median number of years of teaching experience for teachers in schools across the nation was but eight years. For men it was much less— six and a half years; for women it was ten years. These statistics relate to schoolteachers generally. For mathematics teachers they are probably high, particularly when you consider the relatively more attractive competing opportunities for employment open to people with mathematical competence.

Even so, this means that more than half of the mathematics teachers in this country today have no *professional* recollection of the "old" days, those days before 1957. In fact, very little more than a third of today's classroom teachers (37 per cent) can point to as many as fifteen years of teaching experience.

To students of revolutions, this is not a surprising development. More than anything else, it accounts for the tendency of movements to change direction along the way, as new people are recruited or otherwise come aboard and as long-term objectives are reevaluated.

There is a subtle but very important effect involved here, one that the older revolutionaries should note well. They should recognize that current victories and accomplishments are not nearly so impressive to the newcomers as they are to those who have been involved for some time. Ideas and objectives that seemed radical a decade ago, but which time and great effort have made workable, are achievements that rightfully evoke feelings of pride among the early revolutionaries. But to the later revolutionaries, such things are relatively commonplace. To the newcomer, the situation has been more or less that way during most of this time on the scene.

In this, we have a fact that the leadership of any movement can ignore only at the peril of its cause. That the leadership of a movement tends to be heavily vested in its senior members is a natural development, but it is somewhat less than natural for those senior members to be completely objective about the differing viewpoints and values expressed by the junior members.

We must not forget that revolutions are essentially transformations, movements away from things as they were toward new ground, new objectives. Certainly those of us who can personally compare the present with the past of ten or fifteen years ago realize that a transformation of great magnitude has taken place in the field of mathematics education over the intervening years.

But yesterday's baselines are no longer of major importance. Where we are today becomes the important and relevant bench mark. From it a new order of priorities develops. New goals evolve; new objectives are sighted. These become the fuel for the continuation of our revolution in the years immediately ahead.

Along the way new names will become prominent in the affairs of mathematics education. New prophets will arise among us, and some of the earlier prophets will fade. I can say this partly because it is an inevitable consequence of progress and human attrition; and partly because I foresee a significant and imminent shift in emphasis in our field, from current areas of prime concern to other areas of concern.

I wish I could say that I foresee this shift taking place peacefully, fraternally, dispassionately. But I am afraid that I cannot. In fact, I see the next ten years as being every bit as turbulent and controversial—perhaps even traumatic —as the past ten years. It is just that the turmoil is likely to be felt more in different quarters. Indeed, it may well turn out that some of the principal givers of turmoil over the past decade will be the main getters of it in the next.

METHODOLOGY

What, then are some of these new prime areas of concern that will engage us in the years immediately ahead?

Two categories of problems seem readily apparent. To say that they are not especially popular among us today would probably qualify as the understatement of the evening. But I am convinced that they will be popular soon because their need for treatment is already at the urgent level and simply cannot be avoided much longer.

The first of these two categories bears a rather tarnished word for a label. It is not quite a dirty word, except perhaps in a few quarters. The word I refer to is *methodology*.

Let me begin my commentary with an excerpt or two from an article written by Professor B. F. Skinner, the eminent and articulate behaviorist scholar of Harvard University. Among other things it will tend to show that we in mathematics education are not alone in our relative unconcern for pedagogy— whatever comfort that may be. In the October 16, 1965, issue of *The Saturday Review*, under the title "Why Teachers Fail," Skinner wrote this:

The most widely publicized efforts to improve education show an extraordinary neglect of method. Learning and teaching are not analyzed, and almost no effort is made to improve teaching as such. The aid which education is to receive usually means money, and the proposals for spending it follow a few, familiar lines. We should build more and better schools. We should recruit more and better teachers. We should search for better students and make sure that all competent students can go to school and college. We should multiply teacher-student contacts with films and television. We should design new curricula. All of this can be done without looking at teaching itself. We need not ask how those better teachers are to teach those better students in those better schools, what kinds of contact are to be multiplied through mass media, or how new curricula are to be made effective.

Perhaps we should not expect questions of this sort to be asked in what is essentially a consumer's revolt.... Today the disaffected are the parents, employers, and others who are unhappy about the [results] of education. . . . It is perhaps natural that consumers should turn to the conspicuous shortcomings of plant, personnel and equipment, rather than to method.

Skinner then goes on to point out that teachers at the college level typically receive no help or instruction in teaching, while those who are to teach at the elementary and secondary levels do get some instruction, principally advice and counsel from experienced teachers. But, as Skinner states, even this meager effort for prospective elementary and secondary teachers is under attack, to which he makes this telling comment:

It is argued that a good teacher is simply one who knows his subject matter and is interested in it. Any special knowledge of pedagogy as a basic science of teaching is felt to be unnecessary.

The attitude is regrettable. No enterprise can improve itself to the fullest extent without examining its basic processes. A really effective educational system cannot be set up until we understand the process of human learning and teaching. Human behavior is far too complex to be left to casual experience, or even to organized experience in the restricted environment of the classroom. Teachers need help. In particular they need the kind of help offered by a scientific analysis of behavior.

This indictment, which Skinner levels at education generally, fits us in mathematics education all too well, I am afraid. To me, his comments are cogent and timely and represent the wave of the future.

Skinner's use of the word "consumer" suggests an analogy that seems appropriate to our situation in mathematics education. Through it, perhaps I can bring into better focus some of our problems of the future, as I see them.

Mathematics education in this country in the 1950's might be compared to an old reliable company, a business establishment that had served the public well for generations, but one in which growing obsolescence was becoming painfully evident. To continue to serve the public, which desperately needed its product, modernization was called for. To accomplish this modernization, a new management team was brought into the company. In effect, the new management team has been the collective leadership that has done most to stimulate progress in mathematics education over the past decade.

Realistically, the place to start a rejuvenation program is with the product. Although the product is not sufficient to keep a firm in business, it is a necessary condition. The product of mathematics education is subject matter, the content of the courses; and it is this feature upon which mathematics education has largely concentrated its attention over the past ten years.

The results that have been wrought in that time have been remarkable, to say the least. New items and complete product lines have been developed; some old lines have been discarded and others extensively renovated. In all, the total product mix today represents an impressive array of mathematics of better quality, mathematics of potentially greater power and utility, and mathematics that bears a far more authentic resemblance to that which is in the mainstream of contemporary mathematical thought.

While the products and the mixes are not ideal, and further improvement is warranted and can be expected, that phase of our enterprise now seems much less urgent, less demanding of our greatest energy and resources. Currently, other needs, some of them longstanding, now seem relatively more important. In other words, the time is here, or at least very near at hand, for us in mathematics education to shift the focus of our attention from the product to the consumer—our students and the public at large.

Now I don't mean to suggest that the consumer has been completely ignored over the past ten years. He hasn't. But attention given to him has been marginal at best and certainly meager in terms of results. Nor is this to find fault with the direction in which we have been going. For without good mathematics to teach, the rest becomes a relatively empty exercise. Consequently, first priority rightfully went to product development.

Moreover, in launching a campaign it is prudent to concentrate one's forces initially in areas where the chances of success are best. Not only was cleaning up the content comparatively much easier than appreciably stepping up the consumer's comprehension and retention of the subject, but assistance was readily available across the campus in mathematics departments to help accomplish the content cleanup. On the other hand, nowhere at the time could comparable assistance be found to cope with the much more difficult consumer-type problems. The state of the psychologists' art had simply not progressed that far.

Whereas these are good and defensible reasons for our past preoccupation with product development, there existed still another general reason, which now seems to be of lesser validity, but which continues to prevail among us. It is based upon a deceptively naive assumption, namely, that if the mathematics fare is improved, student comprehension and retention and many other consumer problems will more or less take care of themselves automatically.

Many perceptive classroom teachers have questioned such a contention right along, but it has not been popular to give expression to such views—at least not publicly, though teachers certainly have among themselves. But now they are beginning to see support in a growing consensus, and some objective evidence is beginning to surface. The latest and among the most significant can be found in the report of the recent study made by the International Project for the Evaluation of Educational Achievement. In the study, 133,000 students in twelve highly industrialized countries were tested on how well they learned mathematics. As you may know, the American students fared very poorly, near or at the bottom of the list in some of the most important categories.

I have not had a chance as yet to read the full report—it was published just a few weeks ago—but advance summaries of it were published widely in many newspapers and news magazines. The *New York Times* account stated that the researchers in the study saw nothing in the data to suggest that differences in student performance could be attributed to differences in the mathematical offerings in the various countries. In other words, the contents of the programs were comparable. Nor did the researchers feel that any country had an edge over other countries in relative amounts of native mathematical talent. However, these researchers did feel that student interest in the subject and personal incentive were relevant factors in how the various nations scored. And I need not remind you that "interest" and "incentive" are more properly matters of methodology than of content.

But, unfortunately, methodology is a term that evokes a distasteful image, both inside and outside the academic community. In part, that poor image is justified; but in much larger part, it is not. Perhaps we in education should take our cue from the funeral directors who cloak the blunter realities of death in syrupy euphemisms. Perhaps we should coin a new word, a more palatable word, for methodology.

That is an alternative, but to me a less-than-honest one. For it would seem to confirm *all* of the demeaning attacks upon this absolutely essential part of every teacher's stock-in-trade. It would seem to confirm many of the pompous, self-righteous pronouncements that we have heard so often among us that set content in contradistinction to method. No matter what a person's persuasion, if he teaches, he can no more divorce himself from some sort of methodology than he can separate his smile or frown from his face.

It has been my observation that a great many of those teachers who most violently disclaim the relevance of methodology themselves practice a rather singular form of methodology. It might be described as *assign-and-test*, a methodology in which the teacher does precious little teaching, but nevertheless holds the student responsible for learning.

That sort of rugged-individualistic approach to instruction may be effective with a few students, perhaps those who are going to learn anyway, regardless of the capability of the teacher; but it certainly is not a way to optimize instruction for the great majority of students. Can you imagine how a commercial company would prosper with such a sink-or-swim approach to sales? I can think of only one set of circumstances in which a firm with that type of sales philosophy could survive. That would be a situation in which the company had an absolute monopoly on a much-needed product. Under such conditions, perhaps it could remain in business. And when you think of it, this is probably not too farfetched an analogy to the way in which the enterprise of formal education is and has been conducted.

At this point, let me stress that what you are hearing me say tonight should not be interpreted as the belated wailings of some kind of unreconstructed educator. On the contrary, practically all of my past professional involvements in mathematics education have been related to the product, or content. In this respect, at least, I have been in the mainstream. But what prompts my plea tonight for greater attention to matters of pedagogy is what seems to me to be a fact: That the improved brand of mathematical content we now have available is a necessary but, in itself, not a sufficient means to achieve the mathematical literacy that our society requires now and in the future. Attention to *how* we teach mathematics— plainly stated, methodology—now constitutes for us, I believe, an imperative of the greatest magnitude.

In support of my position, let me direct your attention to a significant development that is taking place, one of which I suspect not many people in education are as yet fully aware. This is a buildup that, once its impressive forces are sufficiently marshaled, will culminate in the greatest competitive offensive upon the *means of learning* that history has ever seen. The invention of the printing press will pale in comparison.

Why is it, do you suppose, that giant electronic firms like IBM and General Electric and vast media corporations such as Time and CBS are buying up and merging with textbook publishers, both large and small? To diversify? To enhance their annual reports with additional profit-making divisions?

Possibly, but certainly much more than that.

Up to now, these publishing firms have controlled the most important of methodological devices—the textbook. As a consequence, publishing companies are today the greatest private, or privileged, repositories of current academic content to be found anywhere. In order to launch the offensive I speak of, it is a matter of essential logistics to have immediately available, and under exclusive control, such stores of academic content. The main objective these corporate giants have set for themselves, however, is not to expand their particular cache of content, nor to push it into deeper reaches; their main objective is to outdo their competitors in ability to incorporate this academic knowledge into the minds and actions of learners. In short, their mission is one of teaching.

Clearly . . . this is a matter of critical importance. Not only should we be aware of its development and strive to keep abreast of it, but, indeed, I feel that we should be eager and active contributors to it. To do that effectively, to make a significant contribution, will call for a considerable change from what our prevailing attitude and central interests have been. Specifically, there must be a change from heavy emphasis upon product to perhaps even heavier emphasis upon the problems of the consumer.

It can be done, this redirection, and it must be done. But, again, it is not likely to be done without much grinding of gears and perhaps even the snapping of a few. On the other hand, the potential rewards are considerable. For one, by virtue of its contribution, the Council could enter upon an era of even greater prestige and worth than is its good fortune to enjoy at the moment. Up to now, the "teachers" part of the title of our organization has been suppressed, and the "mathematics" part accented. Events of the next ten years, I suspect, will restore a rightful balance to that term which best describes our professional effort: *teachers of mathematics.*

TOOL SUBJECT

Let me now move on to a second area of concern, a second category of problems that also pleads for representation among our new priorities. This category is not completely unrelated to methodology, yet I think it is sufficiently different to warrant a place of its own among

the new goals of our continuing revolution. Fortunately, we can do something about this class of problems almost immediately; but unfortunately, not easily, because it, too, requires a change of mind-set among us, a mind-set that is perhaps even more rigid than the one currently held toward methodology.

The category I now refer to may also be labeled by a single word. In this case it is a word that many would classify as one of those dirty, four-letter Anglo-Saxon expressions. I refer to the word *tool*, particularly as it is used in that so-called disgusting phrase, "mathematics as a tool subject."

In the not-too-distant past, it was perfectly respectable to refer to mathematics as a tool. Of course, it could be expressed more elegantly, say, "mathematics, handmaiden to the sciences." And from the beginning down to the nineteenth century, the status of a servant was practically the only one mathematics knew. Then, in the nineteenth century, mathematics attained independence. It achieved a completeness and internal consistency that it had not known before. Mathematics continued to be useful to other disciplines, but now it was dependent upon none of them, as it had been dependent in the past. With its new-found freedom, mathematics established its own goals to pursue. Its mentors of the past—engineering, physical science, and commerce—now became no more than its peers, often less in the eyes of members of the mathematical community.

This attitude of aloofness still prevails, and few among us have not been guilty to some extent of reveling in it. Consider the usual expressions of mathematicians and most of today's mathematics educators, as they try to capture the essence of mathematics for the reader or the listener. Much will be heard about the integrity of mathematics, its beauty, its structure, and all of the other features that relate to mathematics as an end in itself. But rarely, if at all, will you find utility getting anywhere near equally prominent billing.

Yet only a small minority of the population of this country sees mathematics primarily as an end in itself. And, almost exclusively, that minority is made up of mathematicians and mathematics educators. The rest of the population has a completely different image. They see mathematics only as a very useful means to other ends, a powerful and incisive tool of wide applicability.

I don't think that I stretch matters unduly when I say that there exists today something akin to the two worlds described by C. P. Snow. In this case, those of the "tool world" are almost totally oblivious of the things that motivate, inspire, and stimulate the true mathematician. On the other hand —and probably this is less forgivable— it seems that most of the people of the mathematician's world are almost totally oblivious of the desires and motivations of those who seek mathematical knowledge as a device, a lever.

This is not to say that the drummer to which we in the mathematical community march is, or has been, a false drummer. On the contrary, marching to that drummer's beat, mathematics has become the most prolific and powerful of the basic disciplines. Yet we must not fail to recognize that there are other drummers and other marchers, going in other directions. There are legions of people who want and need mathematics, but only as a modest part of their basic marching equipment. And it is our job as mathematics educators, the prime distributors of the wares fashioned by the guild of mathematicians, to be alert to these needs and desires—and to provide.

What we have here is not a new problem, but its importance is growing at a geometric rate. As the useful potential of mathematics expands (and it is expanding enormously), it becomes increasingly incumbent upon us in mathematics education to organize new mixes of subject matter; to tailor the emphasis carefully; to find better and more effective ways of imparting the subject to those who, for their own purposes, rightfully see in mathematics simply a subservient means to more important ends.

Many of the school mathematics curricula that have been developed in the past decade, as well as the prevailing spirit in which these curricula have been wrapped, have been for the mathematical scholar. Utilitarian aspects have been almost totally ignored. The standard rebuttal is usually this: The viewpoint of the mathematics scholar and that of the users of mathematics should be compatible and essentially uniform.

But this I question.

Let me cite a personal experience of several years ago, an experience that pointed up the kind of double standard that exists among us. I was attending a meeting of the mathematics department of a university. Two items appeared on the agenda. The first had to do with a communication from the dean of business. In the diplomatic language of a petitioner, he was complaining about a statistics course that was staffed by the mathematics department but taken principally by business students. The failure rate in the course was high, the dean noted, and the emphasis upon theorems and proof seemed inappropriate for those students whose main purpose for taking the course was to gain a functional grasp of the subject so they could better cope with their business courses.

I need not describe to you the reactions within the mathematics department to that sort of nonsense. In polite though perhaps in not quite so diplomatic terminology, a reply was drafted to the dean of business. It pointed out that statistics is a branch of mathematics and that the treatment the course was getting—and would continue to get—was appropriately mathematical.

The next item on the agenda was the complaint of candidates for advanced degrees in mathematics about the kind of instruction they were receiving in the language department. Students who had not learned French or German as undergraduates had to take beginning courses in those subjects to prepare for the foreign language reading requirement for their advanced degrees. In these beginning language courses, there seemed to be extensive concentration upon primitive roots and word forms from which the modern version of the language evolved, much discussion of historical and cultural events that have influenced the course of the language, and so on. All of this seemed to run counter to their objective of gaining a quick facility for reading the language, the students complained.

So another letter was drafted. In it the members of the mathematics department stated, with suitable diplomacy, that this sort of emphasis and depth of background was perhaps appropriate for students majoring in the language, but all these mathematics students wanted was a limited, functional literacy in the subject so they could read mathematics written in that language; that was all.

The interesting thing was that not one of us, including myself at the time of the meeting, recognized the inconsistency of the two actions taken. Both seemed eminently reasonable by our usual professional criteria.

In some colleges and universities, the intransigence of mathematics departments in their relations with other departments that it is their duty to serve can only be described as monumental. Talk to deans and professors and students, particularly in some of our engineering schools, if you want specific evidence. And, sadly, I am beginning to

hear rumbles of this sort of thing at the junior college and community college levels. At the secondary level too, I am afraid, some of this kind of double standard exists.

To borrow a term from the professional communicators, we in education as it is conceived in the United States serve many publics. For the public that has both the capability and the interest to pursue mathematics with vigor, we are now doing a reasonably good job— certainly a better job than was done in the past. Granted there is still room for improvement in this quarter, but it is far less than that which exists between the current and the ideal in our service to our other publics.

Most immediately, there are our brethren in science. One of the better presentations of their dilemma appeared in *The Mathematics Teacher* in October 1966 under the title, "Mathematics and the Teaching of Science." In that article, author John J. Bowen stated in calm and measured tones what many of his fellow science educators express more vehemently. His concluding statement is especially pertinent here:

Not all students are captivated by the internal consistency of mathematics, and, for every one who makes it a career, there will be dozens to whom it is only an elegant tool.

Part of our disdain for applied mathematics is exhibited in attitudes toward the less able student. Those who do not do well in the usual mathematics courses are shunted into courses labeled "shop," "essential," or "consumer" mathematics. We proclaim a value system which says that applied mathematics is for dullards and assume that the better students will learn the applications by some mysterious osmosis. Speaking from twenty years of teaching science, I believe that this assumption is of doubtful validity. The better students, who took the regular courses in algebra, geometry, trigonometry, and even through the calculus, have difficulties in [the applications of mathematics to] science.

Howard F. Fehr makes a similar point, this time in the context of elementary school mathematics. In his article "Sense and Nonsense in a Modern School Mathematics Program," published in the February 1966 issue of *The Arithmetic Teacher*, he wrote:

The rise of modern science, and the concomitant creation of a technological society, compels us to give increasing weight to utilitarian demands for the more intense teaching of mathematics. In spite of the forces that are pointing mathematics in the direction of technology and science, the large experimental programs have so far almost completely ignored applications and the relation of the subject to science instruction. We should now recognize that if mathematics had not been useful, it would long ago have disappeared from our school curriculum as required study.

We would all do well, I think, to paste that last sentence on our desk tops for daily observation.

There is another factor of consequence in this "utility" area: the resurgence of vocational education. This stepchild in the family of professional education is gaining new stature, partly as a result of the various Great Society programs and partly by the very serious and growing shortage of skilled technicians, a shortage that could very well turn our coming technological millennium into a quagmire of broken-down, inoperative wonder-machines.

The mathematics needed by students in these programs is a good many cuts higher than that mastered by the typical academic dropout. But the mathematics they require is of a vastly different sort from what is usually proposed for the liberal arts student. Here and there in vocational education, new courses in mathematics are being prepared and tried. From what I can gather, they represent a forthright attempt to provide a mix and a relevance to better suit the technical student. And while my evidence is far from complete, I have a haunting impression that this kind of experimentation is taking place largely outside of what may be considered the mainstream of mathematics and mathematics education.

If this is so, it is an exceedingly unfortunate development—but not one without precedent. In line with my earlier comment, more than one school of engineering, as well as other major divisions of some universities, has found it expedient to offer its own mathematics courses because suitable courses were not available in the university's mathematics department. To let such a stalemate develop at the school-mathematics level would be tragic. But the signs are ominous.

I am convinced that teachers of students whose mathematical needs are different from our own would prefer to have our cooperation; but failing that, I am also convinced, they will strike out on their own. Although they would be the very first to admit that the product they are able to fabricate on their own will be inferior to what it might have been with our help, in their eyes that inferior product is to be preferred to what we may insist they take.

NONBEHAVIORAL OBJECTIVES?

Finally, and briefly, a comment or two about another development that is forming, one that is likely to exert significant influence upon many of the things that I have been talking about this evening. Last month I had an opportunity to hear Professor Henry Walbesser, of the University of Maryland, speak to a meetings of mathematics teachers under the interesting title "Help Stamp Out Nonbehavioral Objectives."

You didn't have to listen very long to realize how vulnerable we are in mathematics education. We, the missionaries and distributors of a product that knows no peer in precision and succinctness, do indeed state our objectives—our goals—in the vaguest sort of rhetoric, couched in soaring platitudes, rich in fervor and zeal, but utterly devoid of any measurable criteria.

Inspiring as this sort of thing has been to us in the past—particularly to those of us who already have the religion—the days of nonbehavioral objectives are probably numbered. Hastening their demise, among other forces, will be the growth of one of the most revolutionary developments to come in the next decade: computer-assisted instruction. Enormously patient and powerful as these electronic wizards are reputed to be, they could never begin to cope with the foggy objectives that supposedly guide us today in mathematics education.

Inevitably, we are going to be forced to decide just what it is the student is expected to learn under our instruction, and not only that, how we can tell whether or not he has learned it. More than anything else, I suspect, that kind of demand will bring to education a measure of realism not often matched since the day when the earliest caveman took his son aside and taught him some of the rudiments of survival.

Can it be done, this sort of specificity? In our time? In our circumstances? And particularly, in our subject? I honestly think that it can, though it will be an arduous and exasperating task. And along the way we'll probably have to withstand a lot of pedantic flak that will be thrown up to obscure matters, particularly in that idle debate of training versus education. But we'll simply have to learn to live with it, as with ants at a picnic, for the sake of the greater good.

IN CONCLUSION

These, then, are a few of the more prominent features of the shape of things to come, as they appear to me: events and pressures that will influence the course of education generally, and that of mathematics education particularly. They are, at the same time, potential annoyances and sources of great hope.

If what I have said . . . has any validity at all, no one could possibly . . . [think] that our revolution in mathematics education is in its dotage, or is anywhere near to being over. On the contrary, I believe that it can be accurately stated that our revolution has about completed an energetic and productive youth, and is now moving into an even more energetic and more productive middle age.

Now, I'll admit, to the young, those under thirty, middle age is Dullsville. But they are wrong, absolutely wrong—or so I have been told by my older friends who have achieved middle age. They adamantly affirm what they read in a *Time* article of about a year ago on the "command generation," the generation now at middle age around the world. The successful middle-ager was characterized in the article as a person with little taste for mock heroics and even less taste for overstatement. His eyes are relatively clear, it was stated, if at times somewhat troubled. His productive record is vast, and his potential is still enormous. While at times he may seem hesitant and confused, he has pride in his competence, his intelligence, his tenacity, and his staunch confidence in the future.

This, I submit, not only characterizes the successful middle-ager, but also describes very well the present condition of *the* revolution, at Sputnik-plus-ten.

A Report of the Cambridge Conference on School Mathematics

MARSHALL H. STONE

With the support of the National Science Foundation, Educational Services Incorporated held a small conference of 25 mathematicians and scientists at Cambridge, Massachusetts, between June 18 and July 12, 1963. The report of this conference has since become known as "The Cambridge Report." Its stated purpose was to present "tentative views upon the shape and content of a pre-college mathematics curriculum that might be brought into being over the next few decades. The Report is imbued with no such humble spirit as this modest declaration of aims would quite naturally lead one to expect. The unusual amount of publicity and fanfare with which the Report was launched reflected a zealous missionary spirit far from being tentative or tempered by any self-doubts. As Dr. Francis Keppel, United States Commissioner of Education, writes in his foreword,

The present report is a bold step. . . . It is characterized by a complete impatience with the present capacities of the educa-

Reprinted from *The Mathematics Teacher*, LVIII (April, 1965), 353–60, by permission of the author and the National Council of Teachers of Mathematics. Copyright © 1965 by the National Council of Teachers of Mathematics. This material is a book review of *Goals for School Mathematics: The Report of the Cambridge Conference on School Mathematics* (Boston: Houghton Mifflin Company, 1963). Marshall H. Stone is Andrew Macleish Distinguished Service Professor of Mathematics, and Chairman of the Mathematics Department, University of Chicago.

tional system. It is not only that most teachers will be completely incapable of teaching most of the mathematics set forth in the curricula proposed here; most teachers would be hard put to comprehend it. No brief period of retraining will suffice. Even the first-grade curriculum embodies notions with which the average teacher is totally unfamiliar.

None the less, these are the curricula toward which the school should be aiming. . . .

Can the goals set forth in this report be trusted? Can we be confident that the curricula set forth here will indeed be the optimum curricula for 1990? It should not disturb us to realize that any such confidence would be completely unwarranted. . . .

After reading the Cambridge Report with persistence and close attention, I realize that we cannot even be confident that the curricula set forth in it would be the "optimum curricula" for 1965, as measured in terms of the present needs and potentialities. And I confess that this does disturb me profoundly. It disturbs me all the more when I remind myself that the participants in the Cambridge Conference included not only some of the leading mathematicians, statisticians, and applied mathematicians of the United States, but also some of the most influential figures in the current reform movement—for instance, the Director of SMSG and the Chairman of CUPM. The reason for this reaction is my conviction that the goals proposed by the Cambridge Report fall short of those already formulated and already on the way to realization in Europe. It is imperative for the future of our country that our youth receive the best possible education in all fields, mathematics included, unless we are content to see others outstrip us in the various ways which count in our times—that is to say, intellectually, economically, and politically. I am reluctant to believe that the Cambridge Report represents the best thinking of which we in the United States are collectively capable in the field of mathematical education. Yet I am in no doubt whatsoever that the Report by implication rejects many of the bolder, more imaginative, and more profound modifications of the school mathematics curriculum that are beginning to win acceptance in Europe, both in the west and in the east.

Thus, as I see it, the merit of the Cambridge Report is not to be found in its substance—in that respect it is, quite bluntly, extremely disappointing—but rather in its willingness to challenge the extent of our current achievements in the field of mathematical education and to demand a thorough and uncompromising revision of the entire school mathematics curriculum from Grade K through Grade 12. The very cautious proposals of the Commission on Mathematics were enough to set off an effective movement in a direction that had already been pioneered to some extent by UICSM. This movement has resulted in substantial improvements in texts, teaching methods, and curricula for grades K–12 without venturing upon any fundamental or truly radical reforms in content or organization. Now there are signs that both SMSG and UICSM, the two most influential agents of reform in the United States, are losing momentum in the sense that neither is giving a place of importance to bold experiments with mathematical subject matter or its efficient organization into a curriculum radically different from the traditional one. This is most unfortunate, because we need to make a real break with tradition at this time, and we have already amassed enough evidence through imaginative experiments undertaken here and abroad to show that the reform demanded by current trends in mathematics and its widening fields of application is pedagogically feasible. The Cambridge Report should now give a new impetus to the American work of revision and reform, just when there is a psychological need for it. The discussions and experiments provoked by the report should lead to some decisive progress in our struggle to establish goals and standards for school mathematics at the high level demanded by our times and those which lie ahead of us.

I have just declared my opinion that the Cambridge Report is extremely disappointing. One's first impression that the Report is daring, comprehensive, and progressive in outlook does not stand up under examination. Instead, one sees that it is really superficial, confused, and shot through with wishful thinking of a shallow kind. It is superficial in its treatment of the content and organization of the mathematics curriculum; confused in the presence of the very deep reasons for a new, modern approach to algebra and geometry at the school level; and willful in its refusal to face up to the pedagogical difficulties involved in the sweeping changes it proposes.

The excuses one might try to make in explanation of these faults are pitifully weak. They could have been avoided, in large part, if the Cambridge Conference had been somewhat differently constituted and if the participants had all prepared themselves for their work by first learning what others here and abroad have been writing and doing about the problems of mathematical instruction during the past decade. At the Conference there were not enough teachers of mathematics experienced in dealing with boys and girls in everyday school situations, and there were not enough mathematicians distinguished by their thorough knowledge of what is really going on today in pure mathematics. The absence of school mathematics teachers resulted from a deliberate decision, as the Report explicitly states on page 3. Perhaps the preponderance of applied mathematicians and non-mathematicians was also intentional, though nothing is said about that. No doubt some of the participants were (or should have been) familiar with the main currents of contemporary thinking about mathematical education as represented in the reports of numerous conferences and study groups organized here and abroad during the last ten years; but it seems unlikely that the majority had even a bowing acquaintance with this rich material. Certainly the Report itself studiously avoids making any but the most fleeting references to what others have said, written, or done.[1] This solipsistic behavior is carried to the point of refusing to employ such a useful standard term as "structure," which constantly recurs in similar discussions elsewhere. Indeed, the concept itself is ignored, and with it the possibility of making such a beautiful and penetrating analysis of the organization of the mathematics curriculum as can be found in Professor

Choquet's recent article "L'Analyse et Bourbaki."[2]

If the aim is to create an impression that the Report is novel and highly original, only the naive reader will be deceived. The truth is that most of the individual ideas and proposals advanced in the Cambridge Report are neither novel nor original. Indeed, a surprisingly large portion of them have already been tried out—and with encouraging results —in certain American, European, or Asian schools. And in one country, Denmark, a program essentially as advanced as that proposed by the Cambridge Report (though not nearly so crowded) has already been officially adopted! By remaining silent about all these matters, the authors of the Report have deprived themselves of a fine opportunity to cite a lot of convincing evidence in support of their views and have made it difficult to emphasize and elaborate what is really new in their proposals.

The grand goal proposed by the Cambridge Report is to compress the mathematical program so that what is now taught over twelve years of school plus three of college can be completed by the end of high school; that is, in twelve years. How do the authors plan to achieve this goal? The means proposed are essentially those which have been put forward by everyone else who has seen the need for this kind of compression: the introduction of a great deal more mathematics into the elementary school program; better use of the opportunities for moving ahead in Grades 7 and 8; a more or less drastic reevaluation of topics to be included in the curriculum; a more tightly and skillfully organized presentation of the essential elements of school mathematics; and, finally, more stimulating

---

[1] I have searched carefully and have turned up only the following citations: UISCM, SMSG, and CUPM are mentioned on p. 2; the "R. Davis and P. Suppes projects" are cited parenthetically on p. 15; an article of Freudenthal, with mention of pedagogical approaches to geometry, is referred to on p. 38; an article of McShane is cited on 0. 65 as a guide to introducing the notion of limit; on p. 79 it is stated, without bibliographical references, that "Recently, in England and Germany, experimental courses (in geometry) have been developed in which the reflections have been used as the basic apparatus."

[2] L'Enseignement Mathématique, VIII (1962), 109–35.

and efficacious pedagogical methods aimed at developing important insights into the structure of mathematics as well as basic manipulative skills.

Two big questions are at once raised by the recommendations of the Report: (1) Should the curriculum it proposes be adopted, at least in principle? (2) Will the means envisaged open up a practicable way for attaining the stated goal? It seems to me that neither question is squarely faced or adequately answered by the Report. This is a great pity because, in my opinion, a really strong case can be made out for affirmative answers to both questions. The Cambridge Conference, for the reasons already mentioned, did not succeed in presenting this strong case.

Let us now take a look at what is certainly the key to realizing any goal so ambitious as that proposed by this Report, namely, the development of a rich mathematics program for the elementary school. It is quite clear, I think, that in order to move three years of college mathematics down in the high school it would be necessary to move a lot of mathematics down from the high school into the junior high school, and a good deal from the junior high school down into the elementary school. Although it may be true that there is a great deal of evidence, much of it recent, to persuade us of the bright child's capacity for learning a quite astonishing amount of mathematics at the elementary school level, we also have the strongest grounds for believing that the child's development proceeds at an irregular pace, responds sensitively to motivating influences of various kinds, and follows a time-pattern characterized by quite definite stages.

Where cautious optimism would therefore have been appropriate, the Cambridge Report indulges in extensive wishful thinking, exemplified by its sweeping and almost contemptuous dismissal (see pages 3–4) of Piaget's work as justifying "no conclusion relevant to our task." While this is not the place to analyze or appraise Piaget's voluminous and strikingly ingenious contributions to psychology, it must be pointed out that he not only built up a huge body of acute observations on the course of the child's mental and intellectual development but also evolved a subtle theory to explain them. It would be surprising indeed if Piaget had said the last word in so difficult a field of investigation, but this is no reason for imagining that a few key experiments will serve to demolish his work *in toto* or to prove that the patterns of development are so flexible as to present no important obstacles to the desires of curriculum reformers. Whatever light new advances in psychology may presently shed on these obstacles, we are not likely to enjoy in the immediate future enough firmly established scientific knowledge as a basis for teaching elementary school mathematics that we can throw all caution to the winds and ignore the practical lessons of accumulated experience.

Even though some of the participants in the Cambridge Conference certainly had either direct experience or special knowledge of the problems of teaching at the elementary level, the Report itself gives the impression of being overoptimistic and almost completely detached from reality in its discussion of elementary school mathematics. This impression is sharpened because the Report is quite vague as to how the rather extensive material proposed for grades K–6 (especially Grades 3–6) is to be organized and fitted into the classroom time available or likely to be available in a balanced program of elementary education. It seems to me that it would have been extremely useful to start from one of the existing new treatments of elementary school mathematics as a first approximation (for example, the SMSG program) and to describe the modifications needed to convert it into a program along the lines which appear to have been envisaged by the Conference. It would then have been easier to see whether enough time could be found to cover what the Report would consider as an adequate foundation for the detailed curricula that it would like to start off in Grade 7.

Of course, as the Report quite rightly insists, teaching methods play a very great role at the elementary level and determine to some extent the answer to the question of just how much mathematics can be taught in Grades K–6. The Report therefore devotes considerable space to a discussion of teaching methods. It urges emphasis on the discovery of patterns rather than on drill in manipulation and special techniques. It seems to me that more attention should have been paid here to the element of play in the child's first explorations of mathematics. Perhaps the authors felt that this was implicit in their remarks on the discovery method. However, there is good reason to be quite explicit and emphatic in proclaiming that the early years of school mathematics must be as close to pure fun as the teacher can make them. The verbalization and the drill can come later, when the child feels the need for them, as he will surely do if the teacher creates the right conditions in the classroom. The Report attaches great importance to interrelating and interweaving the different mathematical topics to be taken up throughout the school period and envisages the progressive broadening and deepening of the child's mathematical knowledge and insights by what is called "the spiral approach." It can hardly be said that there is anything very novel in these pedagogical ideas, though in some respects the Cambridge Conference may have tended to push them further than

other proposers have done. One cannot quarrel with the expression of these recommendations, but one may be pardoned for doubting that they are quite the magic solvent for the learners' difficulties that the Report appears to suggest.

Apart from a general enrichment of the elementary school mathematics curriculum by the inclusion of more arithmetic, algebra, and geometry, on the level of what the Report calls "premathematics," two specific recommendations of the Report are to be noted.

First, it is urged that the function concept be stressed in connection with set theory. Others have already made the same point, noting that the function concept is central to all mathematics, whether one refers to a function as an operation (in algebra and analysis) or as a mapping or transformation (in geometry); and that the concept can be introduced at a very early stage and developed gradually. Agreement on this suggestion should not be hard to reach, even though the function-concept used to be considered hard to teach to college freshmen!

Second, the summaries of the Report broadcast by ESI have stressed the Report's recommendation that from the very beginning the child should learn about the real number system, instead of being led by sharply distinguished stages through the natural numbers, fractions, and negative numbers to the rational number system and thereafter to the irrationals and the real number system. The Report is not explicit as to what this recommendation is intended to mean. If it means that contact between arithmetic and geometry should be maintained from the outset and used to introduce negative numbers and fractions very soon after some small natural numbers have become familiar to the student, one can only say that the proposal is quite reasonable and has already been carried out in a good many places. On the other hand, if it means that the irrational numbers are somehow to be injected in a necessarily vague and unprecise way into the child's consciousness of things mathematical, to play a role something like that assigned to the "either" in late nineteenth-century physics, then the proposal strikes me as extremely dubious. The real numbers are operationally too abstract (for instance, there is no explicit rule for determining *in every case* the nth digit of the sum of two decimal numbers) and sophisticated to have any place in the earliest grades; and if they are presented as "space-fillers" called on to occupy the interstices between the rational numbers they may prove to be more mystifying than helpful.

Kronecker said that God made the natural numbers and man made all the rest. Perhaps one should concede for the present purposes that nature produces the rational numbers but beyond that it is hard to go, particularly at the present moment when our physical notions of spacetime may be destined to suffer some very radical alterations. My own opinion is that the real numbers should not even be mentioned until the stage has been thoroughly set by the study of various finite and denumerably infinite number systems arising in arithmetic, algebra, and geometry. If such a preparation can be carried out in Grades K–6 or K–7 (and I see no reason why it cannot) then an adequate treatment of the real number system can be spread over Grades 7–8 or 8–9 in such a way that the grand goal of the Cambridge Report can still be attained. It seems to me that the time which would have to be devoted to handling the real number system successfully in the earlier grades would much better be used for introducing the function-concept and some important basic notions from modern abstract algebra.

By this time it should be apparent that in discussing the elementary school mathematics program the Cambridge Report makes some very big tacit assumptions which need to be brought out into the open and examined. The chief ones are to the effect that all children *can* and *should* be taught all the mathematics needed as a foundation for the curricula proposed in detail for Grades 7–12—curricula which will carry the student in six years to a point now reached only after nine.

It seems most unlikely that the majority of our elementary school children can master so much mathematics as this appears to imply. Even if one admits that all children should be exposed to the central ideas to be treated in the proposed elementary program, it seems entirely unreasonable to require more than a certain fraction (a third? a quarter?) of them to learn all the mathematics involved here. The Report speaks vaguely of providing for students to terminate their school mathematics studies (p. 42) somewhere along the line, presumably at the secondary level somewhere beyond Grades 8 or 9; but the Cambridge conferees surely would not have proposed that there should be separate and distinct programs for different groups of elementary school pupils (even though they quite clearly have made recommendations for the secondary shcool program which would compel branching and the setting up of separate streams).

This lack of realism and sense of proportion cannot be defended on the ground that the purpose of the conference was to define purely idealistic goals, possibly forever unattainable. The goals have meaning and viability only insofar as they are related to the needs and capacities of individual human beings and to the structure and functioning of the society in which those individuals participate. Mathematics itself may be abstract, but the teaching of mathematics is not. It is a terrible weakness of the Cambridge Report, therefore, that it does not ask, "What mathematics should we teach for *whom?*" So far as the secondary school curriculum is concerned, it was quite easy to say that the Cambridge Conference and its Report would deal exclusively with mathematics for the college-capable student, just as the whole reform movement has been doing for a decade. But this declaration will not do at all for the elementary school program, and it leaves a yawning void in the secondary program, so far as all students who are not college-bound are concerned. Certainly there are sound democratic ways of handling a common elementary school program that will allow for differences of ability and motivation, giving the slow learners the chance to move at their own pace through the essentials of arithmetic and geometry, and encouraging the quick to go fast and far in their exploration of elementary mathematics. No proposal for elementary school mathematics can be regarded as entirely satisfactory if it does not discuss those ways.

In the discussion of secondary school mathematics the Cambridge Report becomes much more explicit and detailed. Here two curricula for Grades 7–12 are offered. They are first presented in outline (as syllabi) and then discussed in considerable detail. The chief difference between them is in the treatment of algebra and of fundamental algebraic concepts. The first curriculum lays much more stress on basic ideas and techniques of abstract algebra and their relation to arithmetic and geometry. This curricular proposal was prepared by a committee of the Conference but provoked "widespread disagreement" in the group as a whole and led to the formation of a second committee to draw up an alternative proposal and "to bring out some of the area of disagreement" (p. 48).

The Report admits that the two curricula are "based upon different philosophies"—different for example, with respect to the role of modern abstract algebra—but (see p. 4) blandly tries to minimize the really fundamental nature of the disagreement. There is very good ground for believing that the two philosophies of which the Report speaks, without any attempt to define them, are irreconcilable—and not just within the little group which gathered in Cambridge but in the mathematical and scientific community as a whole. It is quite evident that the Cambridge group split decisively and could not work out a compromise. I consider this as very strong evidence of what I referred to previously as confusion "in the presence of the very deep reasons for a new, modern approach to algebra and geometry in school mathematics." I believe that to use the term "confusion" in referring to this situation is charitable. Since the Report does not define or discuss the real issues and obviously does its best to cover up the points at stake (look, for instance, at the completely inadequate attention paid to the group concept—the index at the end of the Report will be of assistance), a much harsher term could have been applied!

If I had been a member of the committee which submitted the first curriculum proposal, my philosophical convictions and my contentious nature would have led me to insist that the lines be drawn and the pros and cons set forth in the Report itself. Philosophy is not divorced from decision or action; and in the present case decisive action could have profound consequences for the future of mathematics and science in our country. For the Report to evade a major issue such as this does not contribute positively to the formulation of goals for school mathematics, but sows the seeds for eventual confusion in a much wider circle than just the Cambridge group.

In general, the first curriculum presented in the Report contains a good deal more mathematics and gives greater emphasis to general concepts than the second. However, the latter would go considerably further in analysis, taking up a greater number of the topics usually discussed in a college advanced calculus course. Naturally the achievement of the grand goals envisaged by the Cambridge Conference demands that such college subjects as analytic geometry, calculus, probability, linear algebra, and even differential equations find their places in both these curricula. Except for probability, which is initiated in Grades 7–8, these subjects are treated mainly in Grades 10–12. Both curricula devote the last two high school years to the calculus, including some of its applications and some differential equations. The second curriculum (pp. 45–46) would even start the calculus in Grade 9 and carry it there as far as the mean-value theorem and the fundamental theorem of the calculus! This naturally leaves more room later on for topics from advanced calculus.

The detailed descriptions given in the Report of these segments of college mathematics could have been lifted with little change from almost any good college announcement. Thus, in essence, the Cambridge Report just shifts downward by three years the existing college material which it proposes to incorporate in the secondary school curriculum without raising any question as to whether the prevailing college curriculum is also in need of some revision and improvement! This forces the present school mathematics downward by a like amount, producing marked congestion in Grades 7–8 in addition to that previously noted in Grades 3–6. It is my impression that the Conference simply did not have the time to think through the attendant curricular difficulties in a realistic way, and sought comfort in a certain amount of wishful

thinking and hand-waving, as well as in the thought that it was really only necessary to challenge others to do the hard work—of course, following the guidelines in the Report itself.

If there is any way to attain the ambitious goals set by the Cambridge Report for Grades 7–12, I think it must be found in a new organization of the subject matter. The Report itself suggests this (on p. 7). I do not have the same faith as the Cambridge conferees that better teaching methods (discovery method, spiral method, deemphasis of drill) will make a very great difference in Grades 9–12, whatever they may achieve in Grades K–8. In turning to new organization as the key to the problem, I do not mean just a rearrangement following the elimination of a certain number of subordinate or obsolescent topics, but the kind of reorganization which can only be built around the introduction and exploitation of new fundamental concepts and new points of view. This is why I think the Cambridge Conference should have had a really serious look at what can be done with modern abstract algebra and its applications to geometry (and also to physics) in remodeling and streamlining the school mathematics curriculum. And I submit that the Conference should not have started from scratch to do this, but should have paid serious attention to what others had to say about the matter in the past.

After leading a thorough revision of the entire mathematics offering of the Department of Mathematics at the University of Chicago between 1946 and 1950 and devoting a lot of hard thought to the problems of school mathematics teaching between 1950 and the present time, I have arrived at a fairly clear idea of the kind of reorganization that is needed in mathematics teaching, all the way from kindergarten to the Ph. D. So far as the school mathematics program is concerned, I am in general agreement with those who aim to teach much more mathematics all along the line through Grades K–12. In discussing the Cambridge Report, I have indicated that my criticisms are directed toward individual points, unfortunately very numerous and in some cases absolutely fundamental.

So far as the basic elementary school curriculum is concerned, I believe that it should comprise arithmetic, physical (or intuitive) geometry, the elements of set theory, and the function-concept (for extended remarks concerning the latter, see an article of mine entitled "Learning and Using the Mathematical Concept of a Function"[3]). These subjects should not be taught as isolated topics in mathematics but should be closely interwoven and developed with a wealth of illustration and mathematically interesting detail. The emphasis should be on the concrete operational aspects of mathematics rather than on verbalization, formalization, and proof, although strong emphasis must certainly be laid on the latter at the secondary level. Inevitably, group discussions and classroom exercises will from the beginning force the introduction and precise use of a fairly large number of essential terms and the adoption of suitable symbolism; and disagreements will lead to argument and attempts at demonstration.

In the upper grades (5–6) it would probably be reasonable to start doing some simple semiformal proofs. A beginning could perhaps also be made with the real numbers and some fundamental notions of abstract algebra, probability theory, and mathematical logic, though I see no reason for insisting on initiating any of these topics before Grades 7–8. It is far more important that the program should be designed around a central core which could

[3] *Monographs of the Society for Research in Child Development*, XXX, No. 1 (1965), 5–11.

be handled by all but the very weak pupils, leaving opportunity for the strong pupils to move ahead through special group projects and individual study. Interested pupils with a mathematical bent should be systematically encouraged to explore topics not included in the basic core. In fact, all pupils should be encouraged throughout their elementary school experience to develop individual interests and to do individual work on them with the help of materials specifically provided for the purpose. Successful ways of organizing classroom mathematics along these lines have been developed by Mrs. Lore Rasmussen at the Miquon School (Miquon, Pennsylvania) and have been made the subject of more extensive experiment by the Pennsylvania educational authorities. Our accumulated experience with teaching a broad selection of mathematical topics in a variety of effective ways at the elementary school level points clearly to the possibility of realizing a modern program as an adequate base for the reformed secondary school curriculum which is needed in our times. The major obstacle to introducing such a program is the inadequate preparation of teachers for the elementary school.

In the secondary school program, the most essential innovation that needs to be made is the introduction of basic concepts of abstract algebra and their application to geometry, through an appeal to groups and vector-systems. From both psychological and technical points of view, there are great advantages in thinking operationally about mathematics. This means seeing mathematics as a way of dealing with operations performed on various kinds of objects (either physical objects or mathematical objects, such as numbers, points, lines, functions, and so on) to obtain other objects. The explicit systematic study of operations involves an understanding of the function concept and obviously includes the basic notions of abstract algebra. In fact, abstract algebra can be defined as the theory of finitary operations—that is, operations on a finite number of operands, as opposed to operations (such as the limit operation of analysis) which act on an infinite number of operands. The concrete foundations for teaching abstract algebra are laid in elementary arithmetic (the arithmetic operations, calculations of greatest common denominator and least common multiple, modular or "clock" arithmetic), set theory (the basic concept of function, operation, or mapping) and physical geometry (constructions, transformations, invariant sets). Ways of laying this foundation have been elaborated from both mathematical and pedagogical points of view and have been successfully tried out in a number of places. It seems entirely reasonable to envisage completing the foundations in the elementary school and starting the study of abstract algebra as such in Grade 7.

A way of making this start through generalization of the addition and multiplication tables of arithmetic has been suggested in a contribution I made to the Dubrovnik report.[4] I have seen the first steps in this approach tried with apparent success in an American classroom at one of the Newton, Massachusetts, schools. The study of abstract algebra in the secondary school should include treatment of the basic structures (groups, rings, fields, modules, vector-systems), of some of the basic concepts (homomorphism, isomorphism, endomorphism), and of at least a few simple theorems (for example, the theorem, very useful for geometrical applications, to the effect that the endomorphisms of a commutative group constitute a ring

with unit—and actually one of the most general kind). Many experiments have shown that this much abstract algebra can be taught in the secondary school; Denmark has already undertaken to make a systematic attempt along these lines.

The applications of algebra to geometry begin with the recognition of certain transformations of the plane or of space as basic operations at the physical or intuitive level. The transition to a formal level in terms of groups can be made in various ways (for example, see suggestions for one such way implied by my article on the function concept, cited above). The proposals of Artin for basing the axiomatic treatment of geometry upon a simple theory of parallelism and the study of a related commutative group of transformations[5] appeal to me very strongly as a most promising route to a quick, yet deep understanding of both affine and Euclidean geometries. One important advantage of Artin's approach is that it postpones all problems or order until after an affine coordinate geometry with coordinates from an arbitrary (skew) field has been established (this field emerges as a geometrically distinguished subring of the ring of endomorphisms of the basic group mentioned above). The axioms of order and continuity then enter directly through inspection of the geometrical properties of the line, as coordinatized by the base field. For this field the axioms are just those stated as the characteristic axioms for the real number system in all standard discussions of the latter. Thus, the geometrical basis for the introduction of the real number system emerges in a very clear light without any artificial complications.

[4]See *Synopses for Modern Secondary School Mathematics* (Paris: Organisation for European Economic Co-operation, 1961), pp. 169–71.

[5]See Emil Artin, *Geometric Algebra* (New York: Interscience Publisher's, 1957), and my analysis of its comparative advantages in *L'Enseignement Mathématique*, IX (1963), 45–55.

It is not beyond the bounds of possibility that applications of group theory to physics could be taken up in the final year of high school, or even a little earlier. There would be no difficulty at all in demonstrating the occurrence of groups in crystallography as soon as the group concept is available. Indeed, observations upon crystals could be used even in the elementary grades to help teach the transformation concept and the group concept. The treatment of the polarization-states of monochromatic light[6] in terms of the rotation group in three-space could be adapted with little difficulty to the needs of a senior high school class familiar with the basic mathematical ideas involved. This connection between physics and group theory leads very directly to the formulation of some of the basic concepts of quantum theory and provides by a simple analogy the key to current ideas about the nature of elementary particles (isotopic spin, and the "eightfold way"). It seems to be a fact that physics has at last reached a stage where our everyday intuitions of nature have very little to do with the underlying realities. To grasp these realities we have to think in an abstract space,[7] where the dominant role is played by a certain abstract group acting on it.

There are at least three advantages foreseen for the innovation suggested in these paragraphs: (1) They carry out in detail the operational point of view, which seems to be fundamental in modern mathematics and its applications; (e) they give a rapid, penetrating, and unified approach to the basic concepts of algebra and geometry; and (3) they provide deeper insights into physics as well as into geometry. The advantages would by no means be confined to the secondary school level. Even more bountiful benefits would certainly be harvested in the new college courses in mathematics and physics. I do not want to suggest, except tentatively, that the early introduction and use of the right algebraic concepts would result in economies of time in the secondary program, though quite possibly less time would be needed for the treatment of geometry as a separate topic. At the college level such economies would almost certainly be very great.

The really radical revisions required in secondary school mathematics are these that I have just described—and that are not even discussed in the Cambridge Report. The other changes which have been proposed are extensive but do not go so deep. The introduction of more analysis (real and complex polynomials, elementary functions, calculus, differential equations, approximations), of the elements of probability and statistics, of topics from logic and computation, and so on, are largely a question of providing adequate preparation in the earlier grades and finding time through a skillful organization of the topics to be taken up. Especially important is the early development of the real number system and its connections with geometry and the concept of time.

I do not believe that it is either necessary or desirable to leave the subject surrounded by an aura of mystery and obscurity, as the treatment proposed in the Cambridge Report would almost certainly do. It is not enough to give the student an understanding of the significance and the implications of a set of axioms for the real numbers based on concrete, familiar experiences. This seems to be all that the Cambridge Report proposes, and it is clearly all that I have proposed in the preceding paragraphs. It is necessary to go to the root of the matter and exhibit a way of

[6]See Henri Poincare, *Théorie Mathématique de la Lumière* (Paris, 1892), pp. 275–85.

[7]Richard Phillips Feynman calls it a "crazy" space in *The Theory of Fundamented Processes* (New York: Benjamin, 1962), p. 19.

producing in explicit operational terms a mathematical system satisfying these axioms. Many of the known ways for doing this could be tried in the last years of such a high school mathematics program as I have been describing here, but they are too sophisticated to be taken up earlier. An effective treatment of the real numbers should be started already in Grade 7. What is needed, therefore, is a refinement of the familiar approach through decimal (or dyadic) sequences. The usual discussion evade certain intrinsic difficulties and end up by being nebulous or incomplete. However, a precise treatment suitable for Grades 7–8 has been developed and successfully tried out by Professors Herman Meyer (Chicago) and George Klein (Chicago). An early publication of their ideas would be of general interest, I am sure.

The challenge of the Cambridge Report is real, and it should be accepted by our profession. I hope and believe that a better answer can be given to the challenge than any the Cambridge conferees have themselves offered. I am convinced that such a better answer can be given long before 1990. The real obstacle lies not in our knowledge of mathematics or our knowledge of pedagogy, but in the outmoded and inadequate preparation we are still giving to our future mathematics teachers. It is high time that we stop prating about this obstacle and take counsel as to how we can remove it.

2
Methods

Prior to the revolution in mathematics education there was a tendency by many mathematics educators to consider methods as a set of algorismic procedures—long-established pragmatic ways of teaching specific skills. For example, there was a specific recognized procedure(s) for teaching quadratic equations, one for teaching division of fractions, one for teaching square roots, etc. That is to say, teaching was employing prescribed techniques for teaching specific skills which had built-in, ready-made answers for ready-made questions.

Contemporary school mathematics instruction supports the philosophy that teaching nothing but ready-made answers for ready-made questions is inappropriate. Rather, teachers should be aware of the values of teaching by use of each of several methods and subsequently select a combination of methods appropriate for each teaching situation. The reader will find that the readings included in this chapter are representative of the wide range of materials published on this subject. The articles selected here range from a general philosophical position as described by Professor Jerome S. Bruner, to pro and con positions relative to discovery teaching, to a concern for the relative rigor of a proof, to evaluation of pupils' learning.

On Learning Mathematics

JEROME S. BRUNER

. . . Let me introduce you to my intentions by citing a remark of the English philosopher, Weldon. He noted that one could discriminate between difficulties, puzzles, and problems. A difficulty is a trouble with minimum definition. It is a state in which we know that we want to get from here to there, both points defined rather rawly, and with not much of an idea how to bridge the gap. A puzzle, on the other hand, is a game in which there is a set of givens and a set of procedural constraints, all precisely stated. A puzzle also requires that we get from here to there, and there is at least one admissible route by which we can do so, but the choice of route is governed by definite rules that must not be violated. A typical puzzle is that of the Three Cannibals and Three Missionaries, in which you must get three missionaries and three cannibals across a river in a boat that carries no more than two passengers. You can never have more cannibals than missionaries on one side at a time. Only one cannibal can row; all three missionaries can. Another puzzle, one in which the terminus has not yet been achieved, is the so-called Twin Primes Conjecture. Now, Weldon proposes that

a problem is a difficulty upon which we attempt to impose a puzzle form. A young man, trying to win the favor of a young lady—a difficulty—decides to try out successively and with benefit of correction by experience, a strategy of flattery—an iterative procedure, and a classic puzzle—and thus converts his difficulty into a problem. I rather expect that most young men do all this deciding at the unconscious level; I hope so for the sake of my daughters! But the point of mentioning it is not my fatherly jealousy, but to emphasize that the conversion of difficulties into problems by the imposition of puzzle forms is often not always done with cool awareness, and that part of the task of the mathematician is to work toward an increase in such awareness. But this gets me ahead of my exposition.

Let me urge that the pure mathematician is above all a close student of puzzle forms—puzzles involving the ordering of sets of elements in a manner to fulfill specifications. The puzzles, once grasped, are obvious, so obvious that it is astounding that anybody has difficulty with mathematics at all, as Bertrand Russell once said in exasperation.

Why, the rowing cannibal takes over another cannibal and returns. Then he takes over the other cannibal and returns. Then two missionaries go over, and one of them brings back a nonrowing cannibal. Then a missionary takes the rowing cannibal over and brings back a nonrowing cannibal. Then two missionaries go over and stay, while the rowing cannibal travels back and forth, bringing the remaining

Reprinted from *The Mathematics Teacher*, LIII (December, 1960), 610–19, by permission of the author and the National Council of Teachers of Mathematics. Copyright © 1960 by the National Council of Teachers of Mathematics. This material was originally presented before the National Council of Teachers of Mathematics, Salt Lake City, Utah, August, 1960. Jerome Bruner is Professor of Psychology and Director of the Center for Cognitive Studies, Harvard University.

cannibals over one at a time. And there are never more cannibals than missionaries on either side of the river.

It is simple. If you say that my statement of the solution is clumsy and lacking in generality, even though correct, you are quite right. But now we are talking mathematics.

For the mathematician's job is not pure puzzle-mongering. It is to find the deepest properties of puzzles so that he may recognize that a particular puzzle is an exemplar—trivial, degenerate, or important, as the case may be—of a family of puzzles. He is also a student of the kinship that exists between families of puzzles. So, for example, he sets forth such structural ideas as the commutative, associative, and distributive laws to show the manner in which a whole set of seemingly diverse problems all have a common puzzle form imposed on them.

It is probably the case that there are two ways in which one goes about both learning mathematics and teaching it. One of them is through a technique that I want to call unmasking: discovering the abstracted ordering properties that lie behind certain empirical problem solutions in the manner in which the triangulation techniques used for reconstructing land boundaries in the Nile valley eventually developed into the abstractions of plane geometry, having first been more like surveying than mathematics. Applied mathematics, I would think, is still somewhat similar in spirit, although I do not wish to become embroiled in the prideful conflict over the distinction between pure and applied. The more usual way in which one learns and teaches is to work directly on the nature of puzzles themselves —on mathematics *per se*.

I should like to devote my discussion to four topics related to the teaching or learning of mathematics. The first has to do with the role of *discovery*, wherein it is important or not that the learner discover things for himself. I have been both puzzled (or I should say "difficultied") and intrigued hearing some of you discuss this interesting matter. The second topic is *intuition*, the class of nonrigorous ways by which mathematicians speed toward solutions or cul-de-sacs. The third is mathematics as an analytic language, and I should like to concentrate on the problem of the *translation* of intuitive ideas into mathematics. I hope you will permit me to assume that anything that can be said in mathematical form can also be said in ordinary language, though it may take a tediously long time to say it and there will always be the danger of imprecision of expression. The fourth and final problem is the matter of *readiness:* when is a child "ready" for geometry or topology or a discussion of truth tables? I shall try to argue that readiness is factorable into several more familiar issues.

DISCOVERY

I think it can be said now, after a decade of experimentation, that any average teacher of mathematics can do much to aid his or her pupils to the discovery of mathematical ideas for themselves. Probably we do violence to the subtlety of such technique by labelling it simply the "method of discovery," for it is certainly more than one method, and each teacher has his own tricks and approach to stimulating discovery by the student. These may include the use of a Socratic method, the devising of particularly apt computation problems that permit a student to find regularities, the act of stimulating the student to short cuts by which he discovers for himself certain interesting algorisms, even the projection of an attitude of interest, daring, and excitement. Indeed, I am struck by the fact that certain ideas in teaching mathematics that take a student away from the banal manipulation of natural numbers have the effect of freshening his eye to the possibility of discovery. I interpret such trends as the use of set theory in the early grades partly in this light—so too the Cuisenaire rods, the use of modular arithmetic, and other comparable devices.

I know it is difficult to say when a child has discovered something for himself. How big a leap must he take before we will grant that a discovery has been made? Perhaps it is a vain pursuit to try to define a discovery in terms of what has been discovered by whom. Which is more of a discovery —that $3 + 4 = 7$, that $3x + 4x = 7x$ or that 7 shares with certain other sets the feature that it cannot be arranged in rectangular ranks? Let me propose instead that discovery is better defined not as a product discovered but as a process of working, and that the so-called method of discovery has as its principal virtue the encouragement of such a process of working or, if I may use the term, such an attitude. I must digress for a moment to describe what I mean by an attitude of discovery, and then I shall return to the question of why such an attitude may be desirable not only in mathematics but as an approach to learning generally.

In studying problem solving in children between the ages of eleven and fourteen we have been struck by two approaches that are almost polar opposites. Partly as an analogy, but only partly, we have likened them, respectively, to the approach of a listener and the approach of a speaker toward language. There are several interesting differences between the two. The listener's approach is to take the information he receives in the order in which it comes; he is bound in the context of the flow of speech he is receiving, and his effort is to discern a pattern in what comes to him. Perforce, he lags a bit behind the front edge of the message, trying to put the elements of a moment ago together with those that are coming up right now. The listener is forced into a somewhat passive position since he does not have control of the direction of the message or of its terminus. It is interesting that listeners sometimes fall asleep. It is rare for a speaker to fall asleep. For the speaker is far more active. He, rather than lagging behind the front edge of the message he is emitting, is well out ahead of it so that the words he is speaking lag behind his thoughts. He decides upon sequence and organization.

Now a wise expositor knows that to be effective in holding his auditor he must share some of his role with him, must give him a part in the construction game by avoiding monologue and adopting an interrogative mode when possible. If he does not, the listener either becomes bored or goes off on his own internal speaking tour.

Some children approach problems as a listener, expecting to find an answer or at least some message there. At their best they are receptive, intelligent, orderly, and notably empirical in approach. Others approach problem solving as a speaker. They wish to determine the order of information received and the terminus of their activity and to march ahead of the events they are observing. It is not only children. As a friend of mine put it, a very perceptive psychologist indeed, some men are more interested in their own ideas, others are more interested in nature. The fortunate ones care about the fit between the two. Piaget, for example, speaks of the two processes of accommodation and assimilation, the former being a process of accepting what is presented and changing with it, the latter being the act of converting what one encounters into the already existing categories of one's thought. Each attitude has its excesses. The approach of the listener can become passive and without direction. The approach of the speaker can become assimilative to the point of autistic thinking. As Piaget points out in his brilliant studies of thinking in early childhood, some sort of balance between the two is essential for effective cognitive functioning.

It is in the interest of maintaining this balance that, I would propose, the approach of discovery is centrally important. The overly passive approach to learning, the attitude of the listener, creates a situation in which the person expects order to come from outside, to be in the material that is presented. Mathematical manipulation requires reordering, unmasking, simplification, and other activities akin to the activity of a speaker.

There is one other thing that I would emphasize about discovery: its relation to reward and punishment. I have observed a fair amount of teaching in the classroom—not much, but enough to know that a great deal of the daily activity of the student is not rewarding in its own right. He has few opportunities to carry a cycle of working or thinking to a conclusion, so that he may feel a sense of mastery or of a job well done. At least when he makes a paper airplane, he can complete the cycle almost immediately and know whether or not the thing flies. It is not surprising then that it is necessary to introduce a series of extrinsic rewards and punishments into school activity—competition, gold stars, etc.—and that, in spite of these, there are still problems of discipline and inattention. Discovery, with the understanding and mastery it implies, becomes its own reward, a reward that is intrinsic to the activity of working. I have observed and even taught classes in which the object was to stimulate discovery, and I have seen masterful teachers accomplish it. I am impressed by the fact that, although competitive advantage is still strong in

such a classroom atmosphere, it is nonetheless the case that the experience of discovering something, even if it be a simple short cut in computation, puts reward into the child's own hands.

I need not tell you that there are practical difficulties. One cannot wait forever for discovery. One cannot leave the curriculum entirely open and let discovery flourish willy-nilly wherever it may occur. What kinds of discoveries to encourage? Some students are troubled and left out and have a sense of failure. These are important questions, but they should be treated as technical and not as substantive ones. If emphasis upon discovery has the effect of producing a more active approach to learning and thinking, the technical problems are worth the trouble.

INTUITION

It is particularly when I see a child going through the mechanical process of manipulating numbers without any intuitive sense of what it is all about that I recall the lines of Lewis Carroll: "Reeling and Writhing, of course, to begin with . . . and then the different branches of Arithmetic—Ambition, Distraction, Uglification, and Derision." Or as Max Beberman puts it, much more gently, "Somewhat related to the notion of discovery in teaching is our insistence that the student become aware of a concept before a name has been assigned to the concept."[1] I am quite aware that the issue of intuitive understanding is a very live one among teachers of mathematics and even a casual reading of the Twenty-fourth Year-book[2] of your Council makes it clear that you are also very mindful of

[1] Max Beberman, *An Emerging Program of Secondary School Mathematics* (Cambridge, Mass.: Harvard University Press, 1958), p. 33.
[2] *The Growth of Mathematical Ideas, Grades K-12*, Twenty-fourth Yearbook of the National Council of Teachers of Mathematics (Washington, D.C.: The National Council, 1959).

the gap that exists between proclaiming the importance of such understanding and actually producing it in the classroom.

Intuition implies the act of grasping the meaning or significance or structure of a problem without explicit reliance on the analytic apparatus of one's craft. It is the intuitive mode that yields hypotheses quickly, that produces interesting combinations of ideas before their worth is known. It precedes proof; indeed, it is what the techniques of analysis and proof are designed to test and check. It is founded on a kind of combinatorial playfulness that is only possible when the consequences of error are not overpowering or sinful. Above all, it is a form of activity that depends upon confidence in the worthwhileness of the process of mathematical activity rather than upon the importance of right answers at all times.

I should like to examine briefly what intuition might be from a psychological point of view and to consider what we can possibly do about stimulating it among our students. Perhaps the first thing that can be said about intuition when applied to mathematics is that it involves the embodiment or concretization of an idea, not yet stated, in the form of some sort of operation or example. I watched a ten-year-old playing with snail shells he had gathered, putting them into rectangular arrays. He discovered that there were certain quantities that could not be put into such a rectangular compass, that however arranged there was always "one left out." This of course intrigued him. He also found that two such odd-man-out arrays put together produced an array that was rectangular, that "the left out ones could make a new corner." I am not sure it is fair to say this child was learning a lot about prime numbers. But he most certainly was gaining the intuitive sense that would make it possible for him later to grasp what a prime number is and, indeed, what is the structure of a multiplication table.

I am inclined to think of mental development as involving the construction of a model of the world in the child's head, an internalized set of structures for representing the world around us. These structures are organized in terms of perfectly definite grammars or rules of their own, and in the course of development the structures change and the grammar that governs them also changes in certain systematic ways. The way in which we gain lead time for anticipating what will happen next and what to do about it is to spin our internal models just a bit faster than the world goes.

Now the child whose behavior I was just describing had a model of quantities and order that was implicitly governed by all sorts of seemingly subtle mathematical principles, many of them newly acquired and some of them rather strikingly original. He may not have been able to talk about them, but he was able to do all sorts of things on the basis of them. For example, he had "mastered" the very interesting idea of conservation of quantity across transformations in arrangement or, as you would say, the associative law. Thus, the quantity 6 can be stated as $2 + 2 + 2$, $3 + 3$, and by various "irregular" arrangements, as $2 + 4$, $4 + 2$, $2 + (3 + 1)$, $(2 + 3) + 1$, etc. Inherent in what he was doing was the concept of reversibility, as Piaget calls it, the idea of an operation and its inverse. The child was able to put two sets together and to take them apart; by putting together two prime number arrays, he discovers that they are no longer prime (using our terms now) but can be made so again by separation. He was also capable of mapping one set uniquely on another, as in the construction of two identical sets, etc. This is a formidable amount of highbrow mathematics.

Now what do we do with this rather bright child when he gets to school? Well, in our own way we communicate to him that mathematics is a logical discipline and that it has certain rules, and we often proceed to teach him algorisms that make it seem that what he is doing in arithmetic has no bearing on the way in which one would proceed by nonrigorous means. I am not, mind you, objecting to "social arithmetic" with its interest rates and baseball averages. I am objecting to something far worse, the premature use of the language of mathematics, its end-product formalism, that makes it seem that mathematics is something new rather than something the child already knows. It is forcing the child into the inverse plight of the character in *Le Bourgeois Gentilhomme* who comes to the blazing insight that he has been speaking prose all his life. By interposing formalism, we prevent the child from realizing that he has been thinking mathematics all along. What we do, in essence, is to remove his confidence in his ability to perform the processes of mathematics. At our worst, we offer formal proof (which is necessary for checking) in place of direct intuition. It is good that a student know how to check the conjecture that $8x$ is equivalent to the expression $3x + 5x$ by such a rigorous statement as the following: "By the commutative principle for multiplication, for every x, $3x + 5x = x3 + x5$. By the distributive principle, for every x, $x3 + x5 = x(3 + 5)$. Again by the commutative principle, for every x, $x(3 + 5) = (3 + 5)x$ or $8x$. So, for every x, $3x + 5x = 8x$." But it is hopeless if the student gets the idea that this and this only is *really* arithmetic or algebra or "math" and that other ways of proceeding are really for nonmathematical slobs. Therefore, "mathematics is not for me."

I would suggest, then, that it is important to allow the child to use his natural and intuitive ways of thinking, indeed to encourage him to do so, and to honor him when he does well. I cannot believe that he has to be taught to do so. Rather, we would do well to end our habit of inhibiting the expression of intuitive thinking and then to provide means for helping the child to improve in it. To this subject I turn next.

TRANSLATION

David Page wrote me last year:

When I tell mathematicians that fourth grade students can go a long way into "set theory," a few of them reply, "Of course." Most of them are startled. The latter ones are completely wrong in assuming that set theory is intrinsically difficult. Of course, it may be that nothing is intrinsically difficult—we just have to wait the centuries until the proper point of view and corresponding language is revealed!

How can we state things in such a way that ideas can be understood and converted into mathematical expression?

It seems to me there are three problems here. Let me label them the *problem of structure*, the *problem of sequence*, and the *problem of embodiment*. When we try to get a child to understand a concept, leaving aside now the question of whether he can "say" it, the first and most important problem, obviously, is that we as expositors understand it ourselves. I apologize for making such a banal point, but I must do so, for I think that its implications are not well understood. To understand something well is to sense wherein it is simple, wherein it is an instance of a simpler, general case. I know that there are instances in the development of knowledge in which this may not prove to be the case, as in physics before Mendeleev's table or in contemporary physics where particle theory is for the moment seemingly moving toward divergence rather than convergence of principles. In the main, however, to understand something is to sense the simpler structure that underlies a range of instances, and this is notably true in mathematics.

In seeking to transmit our understanding of such structure to another person —be he a student or someone else— there is the problem of finding the language and ideas that the other person would be able to use if he were attempting to explain the same thing. If we are lucky, it may turn out that the language we would use would be within the grasp of the person we are teaching. This is not, alas, always the case. We may then be faced with the problem of finding a homologue that will contain our own idea moderately well and get it across to the auditor without too much loss of precision, or at least in a form that will permit us to communicate further at a later time.

Let me provide an example. We wish to get across to the first-grade student that much of what we speak of as knowledge in science is indirect, that we talk about such things as pressure or chemical bonds or neural inhibition although we never encounter them directly. They are inferences we draw from certain regularities in our observations. This is all very familiar to us. It is an idea with a simple structure but with complicated implications. To a young student who is used to thinking of things that either exist or do not exist, it is hard to tell the truth in answer to his question of whether pressure "really" exists. We wish to transmit the idea that there are observables that have regularities and constructs that are used for conserving and representing these regularities, that both, in different senses, "exist," and the constructs are not fantasies like gremlins or fairies. That is the structure.

Now there is a sequence. How do we get the child to progress from his present two-value logic of things that exist

and things that do not exist to a more subtle grasp of the matter? Take an example from the work of Inhelder and Piaget. They find that there are necessary sequences or steps in the mastery of a concept. In order for a child to understand the idea of serial ordering, he must first have a firm grasp on the idea of comparison—that one thing includes another or is larger than another. Or, in order for a child to grasp the idea that the angle of incidence is equal to the angle of reflection, he must first grasp the idea that for any angle at which a ball approaches a wall, there is corresponding unique angle by which it departs. Until he grasps this idea, there is no point in talking about the two angles being equal or bearing any particular relationship to each other, just as it is a waste to try to explain transitivity to a child who does not yet have a firm grasp on serial ordering.

The problem of embodiment then arises: How to embody illustratively the middle possibility of something that does not quite exist as a clear and observable datum? Well, one group of chemists working on a new curriculum proposed as a transitional step in the sequence that the child be given a taped box containing an unidentified object. He may do anything he likes to the box: shake it, run wires through it, boil it, anything but open it. What does he make of it? I have no idea whether this gadget will indeed get the child to the point where he can then more easily make the distinction between constructs and data. But the attempt is illustrative and interesting. It is a nice illustration of how one seeks to translate a concept (in this instance the chemical bond) into a simpler homologue, an invisible object whose existence depended upon indirect information, by the use of an embodiment. From there one can go on.

The discussion leads me immediately to two practical points about teaching and curriculum design. The first has to do with the sequence of a curriculum, the second with gadgetry. I noted with pleasure in the introductory essay of the Twenty-fourth Yearbook of the National Council of Teachers of Mathematics that great emphasis was placed upon continuity of understanding:

Theorem 2. Teachers in all grades should view their task in the light of the idea that the understanding of mathematics is a continuum. ... This theorem implies immediately the corollaries that: (1) Teachers should find what ideas have been presented earlier and deliberately use them as much as possible for the teaching of new ideas. (2) Teachers should look to the future and teach some concepts and understandings even if complete mastery cannot be expected.[3]

Alas, it has been a rarity to find such a structure in the curriculum, although the situation is likely to be remedied in a much shorter time than might have been expected through the work of such organizations as the School Mathematics Study Group. More frequently fragments are found here and there: a brilliant idea about teaching co-ordinate systems and graphing, or what not. I have had occasion to look at the list of teaching projects submitted to the National Science Foundation. There is everything from a demonstrational wind tunnel to little Van de Graaff generators, virtually all divorced from any sequence. Our impulse is toward gadgetry. The need instead is for something approximating a spiral curriculum, in which ideas are presented in homologue form, returned to later with more precision and power, and further developed and expanded until, in the end, the student has a sense of mastery over at least some body of knowledge.

There is one part of the picture in the building of mathematical curriculum

now in progress where I see a virtual blank. It has to do with the investigation of the language and concepts that children of various ages use in attempting intuitively to grasp different concepts and sequences in mathematics. This is the language into which mathematics will have to be translated while the child is en route to more precise mastery. The psychologist can help in all this, it seems to me, as a handmaiden to the curriculum builder, by devising ways of bridging the gap between ideas in mathematics and the students' ways of understanding such ideas. His rewards will be rich, for he not only will be helping education toward greater effectiveness, but also will be learning afresh about learning. If I have said little to you... about the formal psychology of learning as it now exists in many of our university centers, it is because most of what exists has little bearing on the complex and ordered learning that you deal with in your teaching.

READINESS

One of the conclusions of the Woods Hole Conference of the National Academy of Sciences on curriculum in science was that any subject can be taught to anybody at any age in some form that is honest.[4] It is a brave assertion, and the evidence on the whole is all on its side. At least there is no evidence to contradict it. I hope that what I have had to say about intuition and translation is also in support of the proposition.

Readiness, I would argue, is a function not so much of maturation—which is not to say that maturation is not important—but rather of our intentions and our skill at translation of ideas into the language and concepts of the age we

[3] *Ibid.*

[4] Jerome S. Bruner, *The Process of Education* (Cambridge, Mass.: Harvard University Press, 1960).

are teaching. But let it be clear to us that our intentions must be plain before we can start deciding what can be taught to children of what age, for life is short and art is long and there is much art yet to be created in the transmission of knowledge. So let me say a word about our intentions as educators.

When one sits down to the task of trying to write a textbook or to prepare a lesson plan, it soon becomes apparent—at whatever level one is teaching—that there is an antinomy between two ideals: coverage and depth. Perhaps this is less of a problem in mathematics than in the field of history or literature, but not by any means is it negligible. In content, positive knowledge is increasing at a rate that, from the point of view of what portion of it one man can know in his lifetime, is, to some, alarming. But at the same time that knowledge increases in its amount, the degree to which it is structured also increases. In Robert Oppenheimer's picturesque phrase, it appears that we live in a "multi-bonded pluriverse" in which, if everything is not related to everything else, at least everything is related to something. The only possible way in which individual knowledge can keep proportional pace with the surge of available knowledge is through a grasp of the relatedness of knowledge. We may well ask of any item of information that is taught or that we lead a child to discover for himself whether it is worth knowing. I can only think of two good criteria and one middling one for deciding such an issue: whether the knowledge gives a sense of delight and whether it bestows the gift of intellectual travel beyond the information given, in the sense of containing within it the basis of generalization. The middling criterion is whether the knowledge is useful. It turns out, on the whole, as Charles Sanders Peirce commented, that useful knowledge looks after itself. So I would urge that we as school men

let it do so and concentrate on the first two criteria. Delight and travel, then.

It seems to me that the implications of this conclusion are that we opt for depth and continuity in our teaching rather than coverage, and that we re-examine afresh what it is that bestows a sense of intellectual delight upon a person who is learning. To do the first of these, we must ask what it is that we wish the man in our times to know, what sort of minimum. What do we mean by an educated man? There is obviously not time now to examine this question in the detail it deserves. But I think we would all agree that, at the very least, an educated man should have a sense of what knowledge is like in some field of inquiry, to know it in its connectedness and with a feeling for how the knowledge is gained. An educated man must not be dazzled by the myth that advanced knowledge is the result of wizardry. The way to battle this myth is in the direct experience of the learner —to give him the experience of going from a primitive and weak grasp of some subject to a stage in which he has a more refined and powerful grasp of it. I do not mean that each man should be carried to the frontiers of knowledge, but I do mean that it is possible to take him far enough so that he himself can see how far he has come and by what means.

If I may take a simple example, let me use the principles of conservation in physics: the conservation of energy, mass, and momentum. Indeed, I would add to the list the idea of invariance across transformation in order to include mathematics more directly. The child is told, by virtue of living in our particular society and speaking our particular language, that he must not waste his energy, fritter it away. In common experience, things disappear, get lost. Bodies "lose" their heat; objects set in motion do not appear to stay in motion as in the pure case of

Newton's law. Yet, the most powerful laws of physics and chemistry are based on the conception of conservation. Only the meanest of purists would argue against the effort to teach the conservation principles to a first-grade student on the grounds that it would be "distorted" in the transmission. We know from the work of Piaget and others that, indeed, the child does not easily agree with notions based on conservation. A six-year-old child will often doubt that there is the same amount of fluid in a tall, thin glass jar as there was in a flat, wide one, even though he has seen the fluid poured from the latter into the former. Yet, with time and with the proper embodiment of the idea—as in the film of the Physical Science Study Committee where a power plant is used as an example—the idea can be presented in its simplest and weakest form.

Let the idea be revisited constantly. It is central to the structure of the sciences of nature. In good time, many things can be derived from it that yield tremendous predictive power. Coverage in this sense, that is, showing the range of things that can be related to this particular and powerful something, serves the ends of depth. But what of delight? If you should ask me as student of the thought processes what produces the most fundamental form of pleasure in man's intellectual life, I think I would reply that it is the reduction of surprise and complexity to predictability and simplicity. Indeed, it is when a person has confidence in his ability to bring off this feat that he comes to enjoy surprise, to enjoy the process of imposing puzzle forms upon difficulties in order to convert them into problems. I think we as educators recognized this idea in our doctrine of the "central subject," the idea of coordinating a year's work around a central theme. But choosing a central theme horizon-

tally, for the year's work, is arbitrary and often artificial. The central themes are longitudinal. The most important central theme is growth in your own sense of mastery, of knowing today that you have more power and control and mastery over a subject than you had last year. If we produce such a sense of growth, I think it produces delight in knowledge as a by-product automatically.

My choice of the conservation theorems as an illustration was not adventitious. I tried to choose one as basic to the natural sciences as one could make it. Similar themes recur and have eventual crescendo value in other fields: the idea of biological continuity whereby giraffes have giraffe babies and not elephant babies, the idea of tragedy in literature, the notion of the unit of measure in mathematics, the idea of chance as a fraction of certainty in statistics, the grammar of truth tables in logic. It would seem to be altogether appropriate to bring about a joining of forces of experienced teachers, our most gifted scholars, and psychologists to see what can be done to structure longitudinal curricula of this order.

When we are clear about what we want to do in this kind of teaching, I feel reasonably sure that we will be able to make rapid strides ahead in dealing with the pseudoproblem of readiness. I urge that we use the unfolding of readiness to our advantage: to give the child a sense of his own growth and his own capacity to leap ahead in mastery. The problem of translating concepts to this or that age level can be solved, the evidence shows, once we decide what it is we want to translate.

I have perhaps sounded optimistic in my remarks. The evidence warrants optimism, and I cannot help but feel that we are on the threshold of a renaissance in education in America. Let me recapitulate my argument briefly.

With the active attitude that an emphasis on discovery can stimulate, with greater emphasis (or fewer restraints) on intuition in our students, and with a courteous and ingenious effort to translate organizing ideas into the available thought forms of our students, we are in a position to construct curricula that have continuity and depth and that carry their own reward in giving a sense of increasing mastery over powerful ideas and concepts that are worth knowing, not because they are interesting in a trivial sense but because they give the ultimate delight of making the world more predictable and less complex. It is this perspective that makes me optimistic and leads me to believe that our present flurry is the beginning not of another fad, but of an educational renaissance.

A Model for
Teaching Mathematical Concepts

KENNETH B. HENDERSON

An activity on which mathematics teachers (and teachers of other subjects, too) spend much time is the teaching of concepts. One may argue that the teaching of concepts is the central objective of academic instruction. It is the purpose of this article to offer a model for teaching mathematical concepts and then to point out how this model may be useful in the education of mathematics teachers and in the direction of research.

In the context of formal (institutionalized) education, one is struck by the fact that just about every case of teaching a concept is also a case of teaching students how to use a term, nounlike in its logic. For example, there is little to distinguish teaching students the concept of an integer from teaching students how to use the term "integer." And if one wants to argue that some teachers teach in such a way that their students discover (in contrast to being told) concepts, there soon comes a time when the students have to give a name to the abstraction they have educed. Whether a student calls his concept "prism whose faces are rectangles," "solids like that" (pointing to a representation of a right rectangular parallelepiped), or "Jack's box," he is learning how to use the appellation he chooses. And if he talks successfully to others about his conceptualization, he is teaching them how to use the term when communicating with him.

It is probably the case that after a short period of use of the idiosyncratic expression, the teacher will encourage the student to adopt a conventional designation. Then the teacher is teaching that the idea the student referred to by his name is referred to by another name. Again, this is a case of teaching

Reprinted from *The Mathematics Teacher*, LX (October, 1967), 573–75, by permission of the author and the National Council of Teachers of Mathematics. Copyright © 1967 by the National Council of Teachers of Mathematics. Kenneth B. Henderson is Professor of Secondary and Continuing Education, University of Illinois, Urbana.

the student how to use a term. Hence it does not seem ill-advised to consider teaching a student a concept and teaching a student how to use a term that designates the abstraction as attaining the same end. The latter not only has the advantage of not being vague; it also lends itself to explication by means of logical theory.

Three uses of terms can be identified. A teacher can talk about objects named by the term. For example, he can use "whole number" to talk about whole numbers—the properties or characteristics they have in common, or the necessary or sufficient conditions for an object to be a whole number. Or the teacher can use "whole number" to identify particular whole numbers. In both of these cases he is using the object language; he is talking about or naming whole numbers. Finally, the teacher can use the metalanguage and talk about the term rather than its referents. For example, he can define "whole number." Or he can give other expressions which connote the same ideas or denote the same objects.

Moves in teaching a concept, outlined at the end of the article, were identified partly by deduction from this theory and partly by a study of the analysis Smith and his coworkers[1] made of those sections of tapes of classroom teaching representing the teaching of concepts. In identifying the moves the expression "referent set" is used. This expression may need explication. We may think of a concept as a set builder. Consider the concept of "even number." The properties of even numbers can be considered conditions which determine the set of objects which are even numbers. It is the set which is determined by the concept, that is, the referent set of the concept. Also, the referent set is the set

denoted by the term designating the concept.[2]

Because of the nature of the concepts in mathematics, e.g., their embodiment in an abstract theory,[3] their precision, the fact that usually the referent set is not empty,[4] and the use of formal definitions to teach them, the set of moves described above is believed to be more useful than Smith's,[5] at least in mathematics education.

A few remarks about the set of moves may be helpful. Any move may be repeated. For example, a teacher may give several characteristics one after another. More than one example can be given. There is another point. The same question may represent different moves. Consider the question, "What is a hexagon?" A teacher who asks this question may be satisfied with the answer, "It is a polygon." In this case the move is a classification move. But if he expects the answer, "It is a polygon of six sides," the move is an identification move. The latter observation leads to another. Not everyone will place a given move in the same category. Consider the move, "Equality, congruence, and similarity are equivalence relations." Is this an analysis move or an exemplification move? One can support either classification.

---

[2]Some theoreticians will want to claim that some concepts do not have referent sets, e.g., consistency, categoricalness, independence, elegance, truth, social security, nationalism, and motivation, among others. Be that as it may, by stepping down the ladder of abstraction, one can conceive, for example, of consistent propositions, independent axioms, elegant proofs, and nationalistic acts. These concepts have referent sets, assuming one is willing to accept sets that are not well defined.

[3]In contrast to concepts in history, literature, art, driver education, and home economics, among others.

[4]The concept of an even prime number greater than 2, for example, has an empty referent set.

[5]*Op. cit.*

[1]B. Othanel Smith *et al., A Tentative Report on the Strategies of Teaching* (Bureau of Educational Research, College of Education, University of Illinois).

USES OF THE MODEL

To be sure, a teacher will employ many of the moves in the model whether or not he has had explicit instruction in teaching mathematics. Many of them "just seem natural"; it is likely that the teacher learned them by imitation of teachers who have taught him. But there are advantages to explicit consideration of the moves in a course in the teaching of mathematics. A discussion of the conditions under which a particular move would or would not be used will lead to the relative advantages and disadvantages of the move. For example, giving a nonexample surely is not effective unless accompanied by other moves, particularly that of giving an example. A counterexample move would seem to be more effective in sustaining thinking in a student than simply telling him that he is wrong, repeating an identification move by means of a question, and then calling on another student. It is likely that for slow students an identification move as a first move is less effective in promoting understanding than giving an example. An identification move in the form of a statement relates two or more concepts. The logic of an exemplification move is simpler. An identification move and a stipulated definition move logically afford precise concepts, hence they seem appropriate for pivotal concepts that are to be used as the basis of other concepts. Moves less rigorous would seem appropriate for concepts less basic.

Another use of the model is for generating hypotheses that can be verified by experimentation. When one studies the tapes of classroom teaching in which concepts are taught, he becomes aware of sequences of moves that are frequently used. Let us call a sequence of moves a "strategy." Illustrative of strategies are (1) a sequence of giving examples, (2) an identification move followed by one or more example moves, (3) one or more examples followed by an identification move, and (4) exemplification accompanied by justification, followed by nonexemplification accompanied by justification.

Is giving an example and then giving a nonexample to demonstrate, at least implicitly, a necessary condition, a more effective strategy than giving several examples? Rollins'[6] research seems to show that it is not. Just what strategies are effective with slow-learning students? Is the effectiveness of some strategies dependent on the nature of the concepts taught? Are some strategies more efficient than others—that is, do some require fewer moves than others to attain the same level of performance by a student? Are some more effective than others for making precise or changing a concept already held by a student? Nuthall[7] tentatively concluded that strategies that contain exemplification moves are most effective and those that make use of comparison moves are least effective. But his study was restricted to teaching by a programmed text the two concepts of cultural symbiosis and ethnocentrism to high school social studies students. Would the same results be obtained by using the same strategies to teach mathematical concepts to comparable groups of students? Even if we find that there is no difference in the effectiveness of several strategies, this knowledge is useful. But whatever the findings are, there will then be some factual basis for the discussions of the moves and strategies in methods classes.

[6]James H. Rollins, *A Comparison of Three Stratagems for Teaching Mathematical Concepts and Generalizations by Guided Discovery* (Ph. D. dissertation, University of Illinois, 1966).
[7]Graham A. Nuthall, *An Experimental Comparison of Alternative Instructional Strategies in the Teaching of Concepts* (Ph. D. dissertation, University of Illinois, 1966).

A Review of Discovery
MARVIN L. BITTINGER

Learning by discovery is the result of a rebellion against the authoritarian, lecture, or tell-to-do method of teaching. In this article learning by discovery is described as any learning situation in which the learner completes a learning task without extensive help from the teacher. In discovery learning the teacher's role may vary from careful guidance to no guidance at all.

Bruner (5) describes discovery as a matter of rearranging or transforming evidence in such a way that one is enabled to go beyond the evidence so reassembled to new insights."

Suchman (33) hypothesizes,

Discovery then can be thought of as the experience associated with the sudden assimilation of perceived data within the framework of a conceptual system regardless of whether this was brought about by a reorganization of the data or of the system.

He describes discovery as a result of inquiry, which will be described later. For purposes of this article it is described as both the process and the result.

Discovery learning is not merely a method of learning, but it entails many methods, some of which will be de-

Reprinted from *The Mathematics Teacher*, LXI (February, 1968), 140–46, by permission of the author and the National Council of Teachers of Mathematics. Copyright © 1968 by the National Council of Teachers of Mathematics. Marvin L. Bittinger is Assistant Professor of Mathematics, Indiana University, Indianapolis.

scribed. These are listed as follows: (1) the inductive method, (2) the nonverbal awareness method, (3) the incidental learning method, (4) the deductive method, and (5) the variation method.

Hendrix (22) describes the first four of these methods. In the inductive method a student is led into the knowledge of a generalization by various examples. This method is characterized by the student's being able to verbalize the generalization he has learned. For instance, by using a rectangle divided into certain size squares a student may learn that

$$\frac{a}{b} \times \frac{c}{d} = \frac{ac}{bd}.$$

Hopefully, he will become verbally aware that for any integers a, b, c, d such that $b \neq 0$ and $d \neq 0$,

$$\frac{a}{b} \times \frac{c}{d} = \frac{ac}{bd}.$$

In the nonverbal awareness method the criterion for a student's learning is lessened to not requiring the student to verbalize the generalization being taught. For instance, a student may have learned the manipulation of multiplying fractions without being able to express verbally what he is doing.

In the incidental method what the student should learn is a by-product of other learning projects; that is, his learning is incidental to other learning projects.

The deductive method is perhaps the most overlooked method in the literature on discovery. Many writers assume discovery is only inductive.

Hendrix (22) describes deduction as "manipulating sentences by logical rules." This method is the most vital to the professional mathematician, but it has less and less use down through college, high school, and elementary school. This method is very much a part of the inquiry method of mathematics. Finding a proof on one's own is discovery.

The method of variation is described in its relation to geometry by Heinke (18):

Variation is defined to mean a process of changing elements of the data, or conclusion, or both, of a geometrical statement, which has been proven to be true or is accepted as true, with a view to obtaining a new set of data, or a new conclusion, or both, resulting in a new statement.

The word "geometrical" could be replaced by "mathematical" in the preceding passage; that is, the process of variation may be applied to any mathematical statement. This can be shown with two examples. First, consider the true statement, "The lengths of the diagonals of a square are equal." Using the process of variation, the student or teacher could replace the word "square" with "parallelogram" and ask if this is still a true statement. The student could then proceed either to prove the statement deductively or to provide a counterexample.

Variation may also be applied to the logical construction of sentences. For instance, if we know the statement $P \rightarrow Q$ is true, we could consider the statement $Q \rightarrow P$.

Clearly these methods are interrelated. For instance, the variation approach uses induction and deduction. Incidental learning may also take place. In the previous example, the process of

considering the diagonals of a parallelogram, the student may discover that the angles formed by the diagonals are different.

THEORETICAL ASPECTS

A comparison of the theoretical aspects of discovery learning will now be considered. Bruner (5) states that "the most uniquely personal of all that he (anyone) knows is that which he has discovered for himself." He goes on to point out the following benefits of discovery: (1) increase in intellectual potency, (2) intrinsic reward, (3) learning the heuristics of discovery, and (4) conservation of memory.

Increase in intellectual potency is the ability to assemble material sensibly. Learning by discovery provides intrinsic pleasure in finding out for one's self. Learning the heuristics of discovery, according to Bruner, is the learning of attitudes and activities that go with inquiry and research and is only achieved through the act of problem solving and the effort of discovery. The heuristics of discovery are "the very attitudes and activities that characterize 'figuring out' or 'discovery,'" Discovering things for one's self also seems to have the effect of making material more readily accessible in memory.

Beberman (3) insists that the student must understand his mathematics. Two things are essential to understanding mathematics: (1) The student's textbook and teacher must use unambiguous language. (2) The student must also be able to discover generalizations by himself.

"Sensible problems and opportunities to invent solutions are the keys to maintaining interest in mathematics."

Suchman (33) describes inquiry as a set of skills and a broad schema for the investigation of causal relationships.

Inquiry involves four types of action: searching, data processing, discovery, and verification. Within the framework of this article inquiry may be interpreted as the process of discovery. Because learning through inquiry (discovery) permits greater self-direction and self-evaluation, the student is more motivated and

freer to pursue knowledge and understanding in accordance with his cognitive needs and his individual level and rate of assimilation. Also, concepts will have greater significance to the child.

Ausubel (2), in almost complete contrast to Bruner and Suchman, feels that "most of what anyone really knows consists of insights discovered by others which have been communicated to him in meaningful fashion." He feels that the use of the discovery method on an all-or-none basis is warranted neither by logic nor evidence. He sees value in rote learning, even though it may have some bad points. Discovery is not essential in the content of mathematical learning materials for the solutions to have meaning and transferability.

Ausubel does not accept Bruner's idea that discovery brings about better organization. According to Ausubel, organized rote learning may bring about better organization. Discovery has its place in the learning of mathematics, and it is this place which will be described later.

Kersh (28) states that when a student learns by "independent" discovery, he develops an interest in the task. He understands what he learns and so is able to remember better and to transfer what is learned; and he learns something the psychologist calls a "learning set" or a strategy for discovering new generalizations.

Cronbach (9) gives an excellent review of discovery learning, and it is with his views that the writer is most closely aligned. Cronbach asserts that discovery

learning has its value in nearly every area of the curriculum, and also that its function is specialized and limited. He feels that the task of research is to define that proper place and function. Discovery has more of a place where the body of knowledge is more rational, e.g., mathematics, but has less of a place in a learning situation which does not fit into any system of mutually supporting propositions, e.g., encoding sentences.

Cronbach and Ausubel both feel that a disadvantage in the use of discovery learning lies in the length of time required. Even Bruner (6) concedes, "One cannot wait forever for discovery. One cannot leave the curriculum and let discovery flourish willy-nilly wherever it may occur."

The place discovery should have in the study of mathematics will be discussed later, as has been said; first a review of discovery studies will be given.

REVIEW OF RESEARCH

In a review of the research on discovery one problem stands out. The didactic (teacher sets forth knowledge) method has not been given a fair chance in the control group. The nondiscovery group should be given the same well-tuned effort as the discovery group.

The review will cover two areas of research. The first is more laboratory in nature, and the second is more classroom in nature.

Ray (32, 1961) made a study of directed discovery (guided discovery) versus the tell-to-do method in the study of micrometer skills. He divided each of two groups into high, average, and low mental abilities. He found that there was no significant difference in initial learning (knowledge of specific facts and principles, ability to solve problems, and actual manipulative performance) between the two groups. There was no significant difference in terms of retention (after one week) of material initially learned. With reference to retention of material initially learned and effective application or transferability, at one week and six weeks of instruction, there was a significant difference in two of the directed-discovery groups. There was no apparent interaction between the teaching method and intellectual level. One may question the quality of the tell-to-do (didactic) approach used in Ray's study. It may have failed to use sound didactic pedagogy, but one cannot be certain of this.

Kersh (26, 1958; 25, 1962) suggests in the first study that the superiority of the discovery method over the tell-to-do method is not adequately explained in terms of "meaningful learning" (understanding or organization), but the discovery learner is more likely to become motivated to continue the learning process or to continue practicing the task after the learning period. As Cronbach (9) remarks, this study begins to make a case for learning by discovery and failing.

In the second study referred to, Kersh found that the guided-discovery group practiced rules more [significantly] and seemed to suggest that the discovery approach is more motivating. There was, though, no significant difference in the scores of the learning groups. The nondiscovery group in the first experiment had a different counterpart in the second. This, he says, resolves the contradiction. It is difficult to completely understand this. Possibly it indicates a contradiction in the two studies.

Haslerud and Meyers (17, 1958) studied discovery learning as applied to encoding of sentences. They argue that the results of this study indicate that independently derived principles are more transferable than those where the principle is given to the group. Cronbach criticizes this study severely. First, because this pattern of discovery learning is not rational; that is, it does not fit into a pattern of propositions. Second, this study suffers from prejudice in its data analysis. Inferences were made on differences in test scores without comparing each test at the discovery-non-discovery level.

Hendrix (21, 1947) did a study using the concept, "The sum of the first n odd integers is n^2." Her results indicated that the students who discovered the concept independently and left it unverbalized exceeded in transfer those who first discovered the concept and then verbalized it. Both discovery groups exceeded in transfer those who had the concept presented to them and exemplified. This nonverbal awareness approach, described earlier, is the basis of the Beberman UICSM project (3).

A questionable contradiction to Hendrix's study is the study of Craig (8, 1956). Two groups of discovery learners were used. One was given guidance, and the other acted independently. After thirty-one days, the group which received the guidance retained a greater proportion of learned relations than the group which proceeded independently. It should be emphasized that both experimental groups were discovering, but one received more help than the other. The subject matter was word relations rather than mathematics and was less rational in approach than the learning situation in the experiment of Hendrix. This may be a reason for the opposite results of the two studies. Also, it should be noted that only one of the groups in Hendrix's study was an actual discovery group.

Gagné and Brown's (15, 1961) experiment on summation of series tasks (finding the formula for the summation of a series) supported the method of guided discovery. Here Cronbach's criticism may be applied. The nondiscovery group was not taught with sound didactic pedagogy. As Cronbach relates,

The guided discovery group was taught to look for a pattern relating the terms of a particular series to its sum; that is, it was taught structural relationships which the nondiscovery group should have been taught.

Expanding upon this further, it would probably be agreed that, in general, teaching mathematics just by stating facts is *not* a good method. A better way might be to point out how the present ideas fit into past and future material and to explicate the structural relationships of the ideas. For example, if one were teaching trigonometry by sound didactic pedagogy, one would not merely state the definitions of the trigonometric functions but would give some reason for their place in our teaching: what they can be used for, as well as the relationships of the different functions.

Wittrock (35, 1963) criticizes the lack of consistent, adequate terminology and labels to describe the stimuli employed in discovery studies. The author attempts to study discovery with an experiment on deciphering sentences using four types of groups. The groups are (1) Rule given, Answer given (Rg-Ag), (2) Rule given, Answer not given, (RgAng), (3) Rule not given, Answer given (RngAg), and (4) Rule not given, Answer not given (RngAng). It was found that the groups which were given the rule decoded more sentences than the groups which were not given the rule. When the rule was not given, giving the answer enhanced learning. The RngAng group required significantly more time to learn than any of the other groups. The RngAng showed a higher retention score than learning score, while the other groups showed lower retention scores than learning scores. This result was also found by Haslerud and Meyers (17, 1958) and Kersh (26, 1958). On retention and/or transfer to new, similar examples, giving of rules was more effective than not giving rules. Giving of rules was more effective than giving both rules and answers or giving neither rules nor answers. One's criticism of this study again would be, as admitted by the author, that the learning did not take place in a rational body of knowledge.

Some classroom-oriented studies will now be reviewed.

Suchman (33) uses physical phenomena in teaching inquiry to elementary school children. An attempt was made to use discoverable material; that is, material within the learner's ability. Teachers were given an eight-week training session, and an attempt was made to use well-qualified teachers. Twelve schools participated in the twenty-four-week study. There were two groups in the study, an inquiry group and a control group. The control group in this experiment did seem to be taught by sound didactic methods. In terms of results it is interesting to note that two of the schools performed significantly higher on a test of content, while in the rest of the schools there was no significant difference. This was interpreted to imply that inquiry training is accompanied by conceptual growth that is equal, if not superior, to that achieved under the traditional expository methods of instruction.

Other results indicated that inquiry-trained children were more fluent. They asked 50 per cent more questions about the test problems. They also asked more analytical questions. But there was no significant difference on "product" tests, those tests which measured such things as principles which underlined the demonstrated phenomena, necessary events occurring in problem solving, and importance of related parameters. This may be attributed to the fact that either the tests were inadequate or that the productivity of inquiry, as measured by the product tests, is a function of more than total fluency and the amount of verification that is done.

Suchman's study seemed well conceived and carried out, but the results do not seem to indicate that learning by discovery is overwhelmingly better than didactic teaching.

Another good classroom study is that by Cummins (11). Discovery was used in teaching first-quarter calculus to freshmen. Two tests were designed to test the outcome of the experiment. Test One was for the discovery group, and Test A was for the traditionally taught group. The scores on Test One for the discovery group were significantly higher than the scores for the traditional group. There was no significant difference in scores on Test A. This may really indicate not that discovery learning is better but only that discovery-trained students will do better on a discovery-type test. Discovery did not seem to be overdone, and a fitting amount of material for a first-quarter course in calculus seemed to be covered.

The Madison Project of Davis (12, 13, 14) seems to be more a project than a study. It is designed to work discovery completely into the mathematics curriculum. Davis admits that this will have to be done with care, not working too much in too quickly. It seems that the care he should take is not to work discovery in completely, but to work it in the proper amount.

The studies do not seem definitely conclusive in view of their possible contradictions. Many of them fail to be convincing because they lack rationality of learning or because they fail to give the didactic method a fair chance.

While surveying the literature, the writer found a wealth of articles (Bolding [4], Willoughby [34], Johnson [23], Ranucci [31], Henderson [20], and Johnson [24]) describing or discussing the philosophy and use of discovery in teaching mathematics. I have to question that this wealth of positive literature really justifies discovery. It seems that this may be an I-support-you-and-you-support-me type of convincing. The writer does feel that discovery has its place, and he will discuss this now.

THE PLACE OF DISCOVERY IN MATHEMATICS

Polya (30) suggests that mathematics actually has two faces. One face is a "systematic, deductive science." This has resulted in presenting mathematics as an axiomatic body of definitions, undefined terms, axioms, and theorems. It is this aspect of mathematics that has been emphasized in the past throughout the Grades 1–12 curriculum and to a greater extent from college through graduate school. What is evolving now is the second aspect of mathematics. Polya describes this by saying, "Mathematics in the making appears as an experimental, inductive science." A report of the Cambridge Conference on School Mathematics (7) states,

Mathematics is something one does, not something that one absorbs passively. One would hope to strengthen the impression that a mathematical idea appeared first as the solution to some problem by some person.

It is this second aspect of mathematics that the discovery method is supposed to illuminate.

Davis (12, 13, 14) with his Madison Project is endeavoring to put this discovery aspect into the mathematics curriculum from Grades 1–12. The writer believes that the amount of discovery used should be a function of the grade in which it is used and of the students to whom it is being taught. It should be used less at first because of the time factor. Students cannot purely discover everything—it would take years to accomplish. The discovery method seems more important for those students planning college or further courses in mathematics because it illuminates the aspect of mathematics which was just described. Is it really esential for the farmers, the businessmen, the milkmen, etc.? Do they really need to discover mathematics to be able to perform the various arithmetic tasks of their work? It is unlikely.

But which students will go on to college mathematics and which will not is an unanswerable question. Discovery should be worked in progressively through the grades because each step along the way gives a better indication of a student's interests and abilities. At the same time we need to be sure that students know the fundamental uses of arithmetic. Cronbach asserts that this discovery attitude should be taught, but that once established it can be sustained in subsequent didactic teaching. Hence discovery should not be overdone.

Cronbach states another aspect concerning the student:

I am tempted by the notion that pupils who are negativistic may blossom under discovery training, whereas pupils who are anxiously dependent may be paralyzed by demands for self-reliance.

REFERENCES

1. Ausubel, D. P., "In Defense of Verbal Learning," in *Readings in the Psychology of Cognition*, eds. R. C. Anderson and D. P. Ausubel. New York: Holt, Rinehart & Winston, 1965, pp. 87–103.
2. ———, *Learning by Discovery: Rationale and Mystique*. Urbana: Bureau of Education Research, University of Illinois, 1961.
3. Beberman, Max, *An Emerging Program of Secondary School Mathematics*. Cambridge, Mass.: Harvard University Press, 1958.
4. Bolding, James. "A Look at Discovery," *The Mathematics Teacher*, LVII (February, 1964), 105–6.
5. Bruner, Jerome S., "The Act of Discovery," *Harvard Educational Review*, XXXI (1961), 21–32.
6. ———, "On Learning Mathematics," *The Mathematics Teacher*, LIII (December, 1960), 610–19.
7. Cambridge Conference on School Mathematics, "Goals for School Mathematics," *American Mathematical Monthly*, LXXI (1964), 196–99.
8. Craig, R. C., "Directed Versus Independent Discovery of Established Relations," *Journal of Educational Psychology*, XLVII (1956), 223–34.
9. Cronbach, Lee J., "The Logic of Experiments on Discovery," in *Learning by Discovery: A Critical Approach*, eds. L. S. Shulman and E. H. Keislar. Chicago: Rand McNally & Co., 1966, 76–92.
10. ———. *Educational Psychology* (2nd ed.). New York: Harcourt, Brace & World, 1963, pp. 378–84.
11. Cummins, Kenneth, "A Student Experience-Discovery Approach to the Teaching of Calculus," *The Mathematics Teacher*, LIII (March, 1960), 162–70.
12. Davis, Robert B., "A Brief Introduction to Materials and Activities," *The Madison Project*, Syracuse University and Webster College, 1963.
13. ———, "The Evolution of School Mathematics." Report of The Madison Project, Syracuse University and Webster College.
14. ———, "The Madison Project of Syracuse University," *The Mathematics Teacher*, LIII (November, 1960), 571–75.
15. Gagné, Robert M., and L. T. Brown, "Some Factors in the Programing of Conceptual Learning," *Journal of Experimental Psychology*, LXII (1961), 313–21.
16. Gibb, E. G., J. R. Mayor, and E. Truenfels, "Mathematics," *The Encyclopedia of Educational Research*, ed. C. H. Harris. 1960, pp. 797–807.
17. Haslerud, G. N., and S. Meyers, "The Transfer Value of Given and Individ-

ually Derived Principles," *Journal of Educational Psychology*, XLIX (1958), 293–98.

18. Heinke, Clarence H., "Variation, a Process of Discovery in Geometry," *The Mathematics Teacher*, L (February, 1957), 146–54.

19. Henderson, Kenneth B., "Research on Teaching Secondary School Mathematics," in *The Handbook of Research on Teaching*, ed. M. L. Gage. (Chicago: Rand McNally & Co., 1963) pp. 1007–31.

20. ——, "Strategies for Teaching by the Discovery Method." *Updating Mathematics*, Section IV, ed. Francis J. Mueller. New London, Conn.: Croft Educational Services, 1964.

21. Hendrix, Gertrude, "Learning by Discovery," *The Mathematics Teacher*, LIV (May, 1961), 290–99.

22. ——, "A New Clue to Transfer of Training," *Elementary School Journal*, XLVIII (1947), 197–208.

23. Johnson, Donovan A., "Enriching Mathematics Instruction with Creative Activities," *The Mathematics Teacher*, LV (April, 1962), 238–42.

24. Johnson, Harry C., "What Do We Mean by Discovery?" *The Arithmetic Teacher*, XI (December, 1964), 538–39.

25. Kersh, Bert Y., "The Adequacy of Meaning as an Explanation for the Superiority of Learning by Directed Discovery," *Journal of Educational Psychology*, XLIX (1958), 282–92.

26. ——, "Learning by Discovery: Instructional Strategies," *The Ariihmetic Teacher*, XII (October, 1965), 414–17.

27. ——, "Learning by Discovery: What Is Learned?" *The Arithmetic Teacher*, XI (April, 1964), 226–32.

28. ——, "The Motivating Effects of Learning by Directed Discovery," *Journal of Educational Psychology*, LIII (1962), 65–71.

29. Kersh, Bert Y., and M. C. Wittrock, "Learning by Discovery: An Interpretation of Recent Research," *Journal of Teacher Education*, XIII (1962), 461–68.

30. Polya, G., *How to Solve It*. New York: Doubleday Anchor Books, 1957, p. vii.

31. Ranucci, Ernest R., "Discovery in Mathematics," *The Arithmetic Teacher*, XII (January, 1965), 14–18.

32. Ray, W. E., "Pupil Discovery vs. Direct Instruction," *Journal of Experimental Education*, XXVI (1961), 271–80.

33. Suchman, J. R., *The Elementary School Training Program in Scientific Inquiry*. Urbana: University of Illinois, 1962.

34. Willoughby, Stephen S. "Discovery," *The Mathematics Teacher*, LVI (January, 1963), 22–25.

35. Wittrock, M. C. "Verbal Stimuli in Concept Formation: Learning by Discovery," *Journal of Educational Psychology*, LIV (1963), 183–90.

Some Psychological and Educational Limitations of Learning by Discovery

DAVID P. AUSUBEL

Learning by discovery has its proper place among the repertoire of accepted techniques available to teachers. For certain purposes and under certan conditions it has a defensible rationale and undoubted advantages. Hence the isssue is not whether it should or should not be used in the classroom, but rather for what purposes and under what conditions. As in the case of many other pedagogic devices, however, some of its proponents have tended to elevate it into a panacea. Thus, because many educators are tempted unwarrantedly to extrapolate the advantages of this technique to all age levels, to all levels of subject-matter sophistication, to all kinds of educational objectives, and to all kinds of educational objectives, and to all kinds of learning tasks, it is important to consider its psychological and educational limitations. What doesn't learning by discovery do? What kinds of objectives can't we hope to accomplish by using it? When isn't its use appropriate or feasible? For what age levels or levels of sophistication isn't it suitable?

Reprinted from *The New York State Mathematics Teachers Journal*, XIII (June, 1963), 90–108, by permission of the author and the publisher. This material was originally presented at the Thirteenth Annual Meeting of the Association of Mathematics Teachers of New York State, Syracuse, May 4, 1963. David P. Ausubel is Professor of Educational Psychology, Doctoral Program, City University of New York, New York City.

PROBLEM-SOLVING IS NOT NECESSARILY MEANINGFUL

The first psychological qualification I wish to propose disputes the widely accepted twin beliefs that, by definition, all problem-solving and laboratory experience is *inherently* and *necessarily* meaningful, and all expository verbal learning consists of rotely memorized glib verbalisms. Both assumptions, of course, are related to the long-standing doctrine that the only knowledge one *really* possesses and understands is knowledge that one discovers by oneself. A much more defensible proposition, I think, is that *both* expository *and* problem-solving techniques can be either rote *or* meaningful depending on the conditions under which learning occurs. In both instances meaningful learning takes place if the learning task can be related in nonarbitrary, substantive fashion to what the learner already knows, and if the learner adopts a corresponding learning set to do so.

It is true that by these criteria much potentially meaningful knowledge taught by verbal exposition results in rotely learned verbalisms. However, this rote outcome is not inherent in the expository method per se, but rather in such abuses of this method as fail to satisfy the criteria of meaningfulness. Some of the more commonly practiced and flagrantly inept of these abuses include

Premature use of verbal techniques with cognitively immature pupils; arbitrary presentation of unrelated facts without any organizing or explanatory principles; failure to integrate new learning tasks with previously presented materials; and the use of evaluation procedures that merely measure ability to recognize discrete facts and to reproduce ideas in the same words or in the identical context as originally encountered [1, pp. 23–24].

Actually, a moment's reflection should convince anyone that most of what he *really* knows and meaningfully understands, consists of insights discovered by *others* which have been communicated to him in meaningful fashion.

Quite apart from its lack of face validity, the proposition that every man must discover for himself every bit of knowledge that he really wishes to possess is, in essence, a repudiation of the very concept of culture. For perhaps the most unique attribute of human culture, which distinguishes it from every other kind of social organization in the animal kingdom, is precisely the fact that the accumulated discoveries of millennia can be transmitted to each succeeding generation in the course of childhood and youth, and need not be discovered anew by each generation. This miracle of culture is made possible only because it is so much less time-consuming to communicate and explain an idea meaningfully to others than to require them to re-discover it by themselves.

There is much greater reluctance, on the other hand, to acknowledge that the aforementioned preconditions for meaningfulness also apply to problem-solving and laboratory methods. It should seem rather self-evident that performing laboratory experiments in cookbook fashion, without understanding the underlying substantive and methodological principles involved, confers precious little meaningful understanding, and that many students studying mathematics and science find it relatively simple to discover correct answers to problems without really understanding what they are doing. They accomplish the latter feat merely by rotely memorizing "type problems" and procedures for manipulating symbols. Nevertheless it is still not generally appreciated that laboratory work and problem-solving are not genuinely meaningful experiences unless they are built on a foundation of clearly understood concepts and principles, and unless the constituent operations are themselves meaningful.

Two related strands of the Progressive Education movement—emphasis on the child's direct experience and spontaneous interests, and insistence on autonomously achieved insight free of all directive manipulation of the learning environment—set the stage for the subsequent deification of problem-solving, laboratory work, and naive emulation of the scientific method. Many mathematics and science teachers were rendered self-conscious about systematically presenting and explaining to their students the basic concepts and principles of their fields, because it was held that this procedure would promote glib verbalism and rote memorization. It was felt that if students worked enough problems and were kept busy pouring reagents into a sufficient number of test tubes, they would somehow spontaneously discover in a meaningful way all of the important concepts and generalizations they needed to know in the fields they were studying.

Of course, one had to take pains to discourage students from rotely memorizing formulas, and then mechanically substituting for the general terms in these formulas the particular values of specified variables in given problems. This would naturally be no less rote than formal didactic exposition. Hence, in accordance with the new emphasis on "meaningful" problem-solving, students ceased memorizing formulas, memorizing instead type problems. They learned how to work exemplars of all of the kinds of problems they were responsible for, and then rotely memorized both the form of each type and its solution. Thus equipped, it was comparatively easy to sort the problems with which they were confronted into their respective categories, and "spontaneously proceed to discover meaningful solutions"—provided, of course, that the teacher played fair and presented recognizable exemplars of the various types.

Similarly, as the terms "laboratory" and "scientific method" became sacrosanct in American high schools and universities, students were coerced into mimicking the externally conspicuous but inherently trivial aspects of scientific method. They wasted many valuable hours collecting empirical data which, at the very worst, belabored the obvious, and at the very best, helped them re-discover or exemplify principles which the teacher could have presented verbally and demonstrated visually in a matter of minutes. Actually, they learned precious little subject matter and even less scientific method from this procedure. The unsophisticated scientific mind is only confused by the natural complexities of raw, unsystematized empirical data, and learns much more from schematic models and diagrams; and following laboratory manuals in cookbook fashion, without adequate knowledge of the relevant methodological and substantive principles involved, confers about as much genuine appreciation of scientific method as putting on a white "lab" coat and doing a TV commercial for "Roll-Aids."

Partly as a result of the superstitious faith of educators in the magical efficacy of problem-solving and laboratory methods, we have produced in the past four decades millions of high school and college graduates who *never* had the foggiest notion of the meaning of a variable, of a function, of an exponent, of calculus, of molecular structure, or of electricity, but who have done all of the prescribed laboratory work, and have successfully solved an acceptable percentage of the required problems in differential and integral calculus, in logarithms, in molar and normal solutions, and in Ohm's Law. It is not at all uncommon, for example, to find students who have successfully completed a problem-solving course in plane geometry who believe that the descriptive adjective "plane" identifies the course as "ordinary" or "not fancy" rather than dealing with two-dimensional figures.

One basic lesson that some modern proponents of the discovery method have drawn from the educational disaster is that problem-solving per se is not conducive to meaningful discovery. Problem-solving can be just as deadening, just as formalistic, just as mechanical, just as passive, and just as rote as the worst form of verbal exposition. The type of learning outcomes that emerges is largely a function of the substance, the organization, and the spirit of the problem-solving experiences one provides. However, an equally important lesson which these same proponents of the discovery method refuse to draw, is that because of the educational logistics involved, even the best program of problem-solving experience is no substitute for a minimally necessary amount of appropriate didactic exposition. But this minimum will never be made available as long as we adhere to the standard university formula of devoting one hour of exposition to every four hours of laboratory work and paper-and-pencil problem-solving.

DEVELOPMENTAL LIMITATIONS

A second psychological limitation of the discovery method is that on developmental grounds this technique is generally unnecessary and inappropriate for teaching subject-matter content, except when pupils are in the concrete stage of cognitive development. During the concrete stage, roughly covering the elementary-school period, children are restricted by their dependence on concrete-empirical experience to a semiabstract, intuitive understanding of abstract propositions. Furthermore, even during these years, the act of discovery is not indispensable for intuitive understanding, and need not constitute a routine part of pedagogic technique. The only essential condition for learning relational concepts during this period is the ready availability of concrete-empirical experience. Thus, for teaching simple and relatively familiar new ideas, either verbal exposition accompanied by concrete-empirical props, or a semiautonomous type of discovery, accelerated by the judicious use of prompts and hints, is adequate enough. When the new ideas to be learned are more difficult and unfamiliar, however, it is quite conceivable that autonomous, inductive discovery enhances intuitive understanding. It presumably does this by bringing the student into more intimate contact both with the necessary concrete experience and with the actual operations of abstracting and generalizing from empirical data.

During the abstract stage of cognitive development, however, the psycholog-

ical rationale for using discovery methods to teach subject-matter content is highly questionable. Students now form most new concepts and learn most new propositions by directly grasping higher-order relationships between abstractions. To do so meaningfully, they need no longer depend on current or recently prior concrete-empirical experience, and hence are able to by-pass completely the intuitive type of understanding reflective of such dependence. Through proper expository teaching they can proceed directly to a level of abstract understanding that is qualitatively superior to the intuitive level in terms of generality, clarity, precision, and explicitness. At this stage of development, therefore, it seems pointless to enhance intuitive understanding by using discovery techniques.

It is true, of course, that secondary-school and older students can also profit sometimes from the use of concrete-empirical props and from discovery techniques in learning subject-matter content on an intuitive basis. This is so because even generally mature students still tend to function at a relatively concrete level when confronted with a new subject-matter area in which they are as yet totally unsophisticated. But since abstract cognitive functioning in this new area is rapidly achieved with the attainment of a minimal degree of subject-matter sophistication, this approach to the teaching of course content need only be employed in the early stages of instruction.

Even when discovery techniques are helpful in teaching subject-matter content, we must realize that they involve a "contrived" type of discovery that is a far cry from the truly autonomous discovery activities of the research scholar and scientist. As a matter of fact, *pure* discovery techniques, as employed by scholars and scientists, could lead only to utter chaos in the classroom. Put a young physics student into a bathtub, and he is just as likely to concentrate on the soap bubbles and on the refraction of light as on the displacement principle that he is supposed to discover. In the UICSM[1] program, therefore, students are given a prearranged sequence of suitable exemplars, and from these they "spontaneously self-discover" the appropriate generalization. Under these conditions pupils are engaging in "true," autonomous discovery in the same sense that a detective independently "solves" a crime after a benevolent Providence kindly gathers together all of the clues and arranges them in the correct sequence.

Nevertheless, if we wish to be pedagogically realistic about discovery techniques, we must concede in advance that before students can "discover" concepts and generalizations reasonably efficiently, problems must be structured for them, and the necessary data and available procedures must be skillfully "arranged" by others, that is, simplified, selectively schematized, and sequentially organized in such a way as to make ultimate discovery almost inevitable. No research scholar or scientist has it quite this easy.

SUBVERBAL AWARENESS AND DISCOVERY

In attempting to provide a sophisticated and systematic pedagogic rationale for the discovery method, Gertrude Hendrix has placed much emphasis on the importance of subverbal awareness. According to her, the achievement of subverbal awareness constitutes the essence of understanding, insight, transfer, and generalization, as well as the basic element of the discovery process; verbalization, on the other hand, is

[1] University of Illinois Committee on School Mathematics.

necessary only for the labeling and communication of subverbally achieved insights. Hendrix (1961) denies that verbal

generalizing is the primary generator of transfer power. . . . As far as transfer power [is] concerned the whole thing [is] there as soon as the nonverbal awareness [dawns]. . . . The separation of discovery phenomena from the process of composing sentences which express those discoveries is the big new breakthrough in pedagogical theory [7, pp. 292, 290].

The "key to transfer," Hendrix (5, p. 200) states, is a "subverval internal process—something which must happen to the organism before it has any knowledge to verbalize." Verbalization, she asserts further, is not only unnecessary for the generation and transfer of ideas and understanding, but is also positively harmful when used for these purposes. Language only enters the picture because of the need to attach symbol or label to the emerging subverbal insight so that it can be recorded, verified, classified, and communicated to others; but the entire substance of the idea inheres in the subverbal insight itself. The resulting problem then, according to Hendrix (7, p. 292), becomes one of how to plan and execute teaching so that language can be used for these necessary secondary functions "*without* damage to the dynamic quality of the learning itself."

How plausible is this proposition? Let us grant at the outset that a subverbal type of awareness or insight exists, and that this type of insight is displayed by rats, monkeys, and chimpanzees in experimental learning situations, and by household pets, saddle horses, barnyard animals, wild beasts, children, and adults in a wide variety of everyday problem solving situations. But is it because of this type of insight that human beings have evolved a culture, and have achieved some progress in such fields as philosophy, chemistry, physics, biology, and mathematics, quite beyond anything yet approached by horses, chickens, or apes? Or is it because of the qualitatively superior transfer power of verbal or symbolic generalization?

The principal fallacy in Gertrude Hendrix's line of argument, in my opinion, lies in her failure to distinguish between the labeling and process functions of language in thought. She writes:

We have been a long time realizing that subverbal awareness of a class, or a property, or a relation had to be in *some*one's mind before anyone could have thought of inventing a word for it anyway. In the natural order of events, the abstraction forms first, and *then* a name for it is invented [6, p. 335].

Now what Hendrix is referring to here is simply the labeling or naming function of language in thought. The choice of a particular arbitrary symbol to represent a *new* abstraction obviously comes *after* the *process* of abstraction, and is not organically related to it. But this is not the *only* role of language in the abstraction process, nor is it the *first* time that it is used in this process. Verbalization, I submit, does more than verbally gild the lily of subverbal insight; it does more than just attach a symbolic handle to an idea so that one can record, verify, classify, and communicate it more readily. It constitutes, rather, an integral part of the very process of abstraction itself. When an individual uses language to express an idea, he is not merely encoding subverbal insight into words. On the contrary, he is engaged in a process of generating a higher level of insight that transcends by far—in clarity, precision, generality and inclusiveness—the previously achieved stage of subverbal awareness.

The old philosophical notion that words merely mirror thought or clothe it in outer garments, is charmingly poetic but has little functional utility

or explanatory value in the modern science of psycholinguistics. Even the seemingly simple act of making a choice of words in developing an idea, involves complex processes of categorization, differentiation, abstraction and generalization; the rejection of alternative possibilities; and the exclusion of less precise or over-inclusive meanings. All of these processes contribute to and help account for the qualitatively superior transfer power of symbolic generalization.

Although the transfer power of symbolic generalization operates at many different levels of complexity and sophistication, even the simplest level transcends the kind of transfer that can be achieved with subverbal insight. Consider, for example, the transfer power of the word "house," which most preschool children can use correctly. Obviously, before the child ever uses this word, he has some unverbalized notion of what a house is. But I submit that once he attains and can meaningfully use the verbal concept of "house," he possesses an emergent new idea that he never possessed before—an idea that is sharper, clearer, more precise, more inclusive, more transferable, and more manipulable for purposes of thinking and comprehension than its crude subverbal precursor. He can now talk about the idea of "house" in the abstract, devoid of all particularity, and can combine this idea with concepts of form, size, color, number, function, etc., to formulate relational propositions that could hitherto be formulated with only the greatest difficulty. That verbal concepts of this nature are more transferable and more manipulable than subverbal insights, is demonstrated by numerous experiments on the effects of verbalization on children's ability to solve transposition problems. Knowledge of underlying verbal principles also enhances the learning of relevant motor performance; and the availability of distinctive verbal responses facilitates rather than inhibits concept formation and conceptual transfer.

Not all ideas, however, are acquired quite as easily as the concept of house. As he enters school the child encounters other concepts of much greater abstractness and complexity, e.g., concepts of addition, multiplication, government, society, force, velocity, digestion, that transcend his immediate experience and language ability. Before he can hope to acquire a meaningful grasp of such abstractions directly, that is, through direct verbal exposition, he must first acquire a minimal level of sophistication in the particular subject-matter area, as well as graduate into the next higher level of intellectual development i.e., the stage of formal logical operations. In the meantime he is limited to an intuitive, subverbal kind of understanding of these concepts; and even though convincing empirical evidence is still lacking, it is reasonable to suppose that preliminary acquisition and utilization of this subverbal level of insight both facilitates learning and transferability, and promotes the eventual emergence of *full* verbal understanding. (Gertrude Hendrix, of course, would say that *full* understanding was already attained in the subverbal phase, and the verbalization merely attaches words to subverbal insight.)

Now, assuming for the moment that Hendrix' experimental findings are valid, how can we explain the fact that immediate verbalization of newly acquired subverbal insight renders that insight less transferable than when verbalization is not attempted [5]? First, it seems likely that verbalization of nonverbal insight, before such insight is adequately consolidated by extensive use, may interfere with consolidation at this level, as well as encourage rote memorization of the ineptly stated verbal proposition. Even more

important, however, is the likelihood that a verbally expressed idea—when ambiguous, unprecise, ineptly formulated, and only marginally competent—possesses less functional utility and transferability than the ordinarily more primitive and less transferable subverbal insight. This is particularly true in the case of children, because of their limited linguistic facility and their relative incompetence in formal propositional logic.

Drawing these various strands of argument together, what can we legitimately conclude at this point? First, verbalization does more than just encode subverbal insight into words. It is part of the very process of thought which makes possible a qualitatively higher level of understanding with greatly enhanced transfer power. Second, direct acquisition of ideas from verbally presented propositions, presupposes both that the learner has attained the stage of formal logical operations, and that he possess minimal sophistication in the particular subject matter in question. The typical elementary-school child, therefore, tends to be limited to an intuitive, subverbal awareness of difficult abstractions. The older, cognitively mature individual, however, who is also unsophisticated in a particular subject-matter area, is able to dispense with the subverbal phase of awareness rather quickly, i.e., as soon as he attains the necessary degree of sophistication; and once he attains it, he probably short-circuits the subverbal phase completely. Lastly, immediate verbalization of a nonverbal insight, when this latter insight is newly acquired and inadequately consolidated, probably decreases its transferability. This phenomenon can be explained by means of the general developmental principle, that an ordinarily higher and more efficient state of development while still embryonic and only marginally competent, is less functional than an ordinarily more primitive and less efficient phase of development. Running, for example, is eventually more efficient than creeping, but if a one-year-old infant had to run for his life, he would make better progress creeping.

Gertrude Hendrix, however, comes out with somewhat different and more sweeping conclusions from the same set of data. First, she regards non-verbal awareness as containing within itself the entire essence of an emerging idea, and insists that language merely adds a convenient symbolic handle to this idea. Second, she generalizes children's dependence on a preliminary subverbal stage of awareness, to all age levels, to all degrees of subject-matter sophistication, and to all levels of ideational difficulty. Actually, this subverbal stage is highly abbreviated, both for young children learning less difficult kinds of abstractions, and for older, cognitively mature individuals working in a particular subject-matter area in which they happen to be unsophisticated; and it is by-passed completely when this latter sophistication is attained. Finally, she interprets her experimental findings regarding the inhibitory effects of immediate verbalization on the transferability of subverbal insight, as providing empirical *proof* of her thesis that both the substance of an idea and the essential basis of its transfer power are present in their entirety as soon as nonverbal awareness emerges. In my opinion, these findings do nothing of the kind. They merely show that a relatively clear subverbal insight, even when only partially consolidated, is more functional and transferable than an ambiguous, inept, and marginally competent verbally expressed idea.

Unlike Gertrude Hendrix, therefore, I would conclude that secondary school and college students, who already possess a sound, meaningful grasp of the rudiments of a discipline like mathematics, can be taught this subject meaningfully and with maximal efficiency, through the method of verbal exposition, supplemented by appropriate problem-solving experience; and that the use of the discovery method in these circumstances is inordinately time-consuming, wasteful, and rarely warranted. Why then do discovery techniques seem to work so well in programs such as the one devised by the University of Illinois Committee on School Mathematics? For one thing, the students entering the program, being victims of conventional arithmetic teaching in the elementary schools, do *not* have a sound, meaningful grasp of the rudiments of mathematics, and have to be reeducated, so to speak, from scratch. For another, I have a very strong impression that as the program develops, the discovery element becomes progressively attenuated, until eventually it is accorded only token recognition. Lastly, stripped of its quite limited discovery aspects, the UICSM approach is a much more systematic, highly organized, self-consistent, carefully programmed, abstractly verbal system of verbal exposition than anything we have known to date in secondary-school mathematics. If it proves anything, the success of this program is a testimonial to the feasibility and value of a good program of didactic verbal exposition in secondary school mathematics, which program is taught by able and enthusiastic instructors, and in its early stages, makes judicious use of inductive and discovery techniques.

TIME-COST CONSIDERATIONS

From a practical standpoint it is impossible to consider the pedagogic feasibility of learning by discovery as a primary means of teaching subject-matter content without taking into account the inordinate time-cost involved. This disadvantage is not only applicable to the type of discovery where the learner is thrown entirely on his own resources, but also applies in lesser degree to the "contrived" or "arranged" type of discovery. Considerations of time-cost are particularly pertinent in view of our aforementioned developmental conclusions, that the discovery approach offers no indispensable learning advantages, except in the very limited case of the more difficult learning task when the learner is either in the concrete stage of cognitive development, or, if generally in the abstract stage, happens to lack minimal sophistication in a particular subject-matter field. Also, once students reach secondary school and university, the time-cost disadvantage can no longer be defended on the dual grounds that the time-consuming concrete-empirical aspects of learning must take place anyway, and that in any case elementary school pupils can't be expected to cover a great deal of subject matter. Thus, simply on a time-cost basis, if secondary-school and university students were obliged to discover for themselves every concept and principle in the syllabus, they would never get much beyond the rudiments of any discipline.

Some discovery enthusiasts (Bruner [2]; Suchman [9]) grudgingly admit that there is not sufficient time for pupils to discover everything they need to know in the various disciplines, and hence concede that there is also room for good expository teaching in the schools. In practice, however, this concession counts for little, because in the very next breath they claim the acquisition of actual knowledge is less important than the acquisition of ability to discover knowledge autonomously, and propose the pedagogy and the curriculum be reorganized accordingly. Thus, in spite of the formal bow they make to didactic exposition, it is clear that they regard the acquisition of problem-solving ability as more basic than the acquisition of subject matter. There is, after all, only so much time in a school day. If the school accepts as its principal function the development of discovery and inquiry skills, even with the best intention in the world, how much time could possibly remain for the teaching of subject-matter content?

Another disadvantage of using a discovery approach for the transmission of subject-matter content is the fact that children are notoriously subjective in their evaluation of external events, and tend to jump to conclusions, to generalize on the basis of limited experience, and to consider only one aspect of a problem at a time. These tendencies increase further the time-cost of discovery learning in the transmission of knowledge. Moreover, children tend to interpret empirical experience in the light of prevailing folklore conceptions that are at variance with modern scientific theories. Lastly, one might reasonably ask how many students are sufficiently brilliant to discover everything they need to know. Most students of average ability can acquire a meaningful grasp of the theory of evolution and gravitation, but how many students can discover these ideas autonomously?

TRAINING IN THE "HEURISTICS OF DISCOVERY"

Some advocates of the discovery method favor a type of guided practice in the "heuristics of discovery" that is reminiscent of the faculty psychology approach to improving overall critical thinking ability through instruction in the general principles of logic. For example, once the heuristics of discovery are mastered, they constitute, according to Bruner (3, p. 31), "a style of problem-solving or inquiry that serves for any kind of task one may encounter." In fact, one of the more fashionable movements in curriculum theory today is the attempt to enhance the critical thinking ability of pupils apart from any systematic consideration of subject-matter content. An entire course of study is pursued in which pupils perform or consider an unrelated series of experiments in depth, and then concentrate solely on the inquiry process itself rather than on this process as it is related to the acquisition of an organized body of knowledge.

One principal difficulty with this approach, apart from the fact that it fails to promote the orderly, sequential growth of knowledge is that critical thinking ability can only be enhanced within the context of a specific discipline. Grand strategies of discovery do not seem to be transferable across disciplinary lines—either when acquired within a given discipline, or when learned in a more general form apart from specific subject-matter content. This principle has been confirmed by countless studies, and is illustrated by the laughable errors of logic and judgment committed by distinguished scientists and scholars who wander outside their own disciplines. From a purely theoretical standpoint alone, it hardly seems plausible that a strategy of inquiry, which must necessarily be broad enough to be applicable to a wide range of disciplines and problems, can ever have, at the same time, sufficient particular relevance to be helpful in the solution of the specific problem at hand.

A second significant difficulty with this approach is that its proponents tend to confuse the goals of the scientist with the goals of the science student. They assert that these objectives are identical, and hence that students can learn science most effectively by enacting the role of junior scientist. The underlying rationale is that all intellectual activity regardless of level is of one piece, and that both creative scientists and elementary-school children rely heavily on intuitive thinking. Bruner (2, p. 14) is an eloquent spokesman for this point of view. According to him,

... intellectual activity anywhere is the same, whether at the frontier of knowledge or in a third-grade classroom. ... The difference is in degree, not in kind. The schoolboy learning physics *is* a physicist, and it is easier for him to learn physics behaving like a physicist than doing something else.

It is also proposed that the ultimate goal of the Inquiry Training Program is for children to discover and formulate explanations which strive for the same universality and unification of concepts achieved by scientists (Suchman [9]).

First, I cannot agree that the goals of the research scientist and of the science student are identical. The scientist is engaged in a full-time search for new general or applied principles in his field. The student, on the other hand, is primarily engaged in an effort to learn the same basic subject matter in this field which the scientist had learned in his student days, and also to learn something of the method and spirit of scientific inquiry. Thus, while it makes perfectly good sense for the scientists to work full-time formulating and testing new hypotheses, it is quite indefensible, in my opinion, for the student to be doing the same thing—either for real, or in the sense of rediscovery. Most of the student's time should be taken up with appropriate expository learning, and the remainder devoted to sampling the flavor and techniques of scientific method. It is the scientist's business to formulate unifying explanatory principles in science. It is the student's business to learn these principles as meaningfully and critically as possible, and *then*, after his background is adequate, to try to improve on them if he can. If he is ever to discover, he must first learn; and he cannot learn adequately by pretending he is a junior scientist.

Second, there is, in my opinion, a world of difference between the intuitive thinking of elementary-school children and the intuitive thinking of scholars and scientists. The elementary school child thinks intuitively or subverbally about many complex, abstract problems, not because he is creative, but because this is the *best he can do* at his particular stage of intellectual development. The intuitive thinking of scientists, on the other hand, consists of tentative and roughly formulated "hunches" which are merely preparatory to more rigorous thought. Furthermore, although the hunches themselves are only make-shift approximations which are not very precisely stated, they presuppose both a high level of abstract verbal ability, as well as sophisticated knowledge of a particular discipline.

DEVELOPMENT OF PROBLEM-SOLVING ABILITY AS THE PRIMARY GOAL OF EDUCATION

In the realm of educational theory, if not in actual practice, exaggerated emphasis on problem-solving still continues to disturb the natural balance between the "transmission of the culture" and the problem-solving objectives of education. Enthusiastic proponents of the discovery method (e.g., Suchman [9]) still assert that

more basic than the attainment of concepts is the ability to inquire and discover them autonomously. . . . The schools must have a new pedagogy with a new set of goals which subordinates retention to thinking. . . . Instead of devoting their efforts to storing information and recalling it on demand, they would be developing cognitive functions needed to seek out and organize information in a way that would be most productive of new concepts.

The development of problem-solving ability, is of course, a legitimate and significant educational objective in its own right. Hence it is highly defensible to utilize a certain proportion of classroom time in developing appreciation of and facility in the use of scientific methods of inquiry and of other empirical, inductive, and deductive problem-solving procedures. But this is a far cry from advocating that the enhancement of problem-solving ability is the *major* function of the school. To acquire facility in problem-solving and scientific method it is also unnecessary for learners to rediscover *every* principle in the syllabus. Since problem-solving ability is itself transferable, at least within a given subject-matter field, facility gained in independently formulating and applying one generalization is transferable to other problem areas in the same discipline. Furthermore, overemphasis on developing problem-solving ability would ultimately defect its own ends. Because of its time-consuming proclivities, it would leave students with insufficient time in which to learn the content of a discipline; and hence, despite their adeptness at problem-solving they would be unable to solve simple problems involving the application of such content.

DISCOVERY AS A UNIQUE GENERATOR OF MOTIVATION AND SELF-CONFIDENCE

Bruner (3, 4) and other discovery enthusiasts (Hendrix [7]; Suchman [9]) perceive learning by discovery as a unique and unexcelled generator of self-confidence, of intellectual excitement, and of motivation for sustained problem-solving and creative thinking. It is undeniable that discovery techniques are valuable for acquiring desirable attitudes toward inquiry, as well as firm convictions about the existence and discoverability of orderliness in the universe. It is also reasonable to suppose that successful discovery experience enhances both these attitudes and convictions, and the individual's feeling of confidence in his own abilities. On the other hand, there is no reason to believe that discovery methods are unique or alone in their ability to effect these outcomes.

As every student who has been exposed to competent teaching knows, the skillful exposition of ideas can also generate considerable intellectual excitement and motivation for genuine inquiry, although admittedly not quite as much perhaps as discovery. Few physics students who learn the principle of displacement through didactic exposition will run half-naked through the streets shrieking, "Eureka." But then again, how many students of Archimedes' ability are enrolled in the typical physics or mathematics class? How comparable to the excitement of Archimedes' purely autonomous and original discovery, is the excitement generated by discovering a general formula for finding the number of diagonals in an n-sided polygon, after working problems one through nine in the textbook? And what happens to Archimedes Junior's motivation and self-confidence if, after seventeen immersions in the tub, he has merely succeeded in getting himself soaking wet?

RESEARCH EVIDENCE

Despite their frequent espousal of discovery principles, the various curriculum reform projects have failed thus far to yield any research evidence in support of the discovery method. This is not to say that the evidence is negative, but rather that there just isn't any evidence, one way or the other—notwithstanding the fact that these projects are often cited in the "discovery" literature under the heading, "research shows." For one thing, the sponsors of some of these projects have not been particularly concerned about *proving* the superior efficacy of their

programs, since they have been thoroughly convinced of this from the outset. Hence in many instances they have not even attempted to obtain comparable achievement test data from matched control groups. And only rarely has any effort been expended to prevent the operation of the crucial "Hawthorne Effect," that is, to make sure that evidence of superior achievement outcomes is attributable to the influence of the new pedagogic techniques or materials in question, rather than to the fact that the experimental group is the recipient of *some* form of conspicuous special attention; that *some*thing new and interesting is being tried; or that the teachers involved are especially competent, dedicated, and enthusiastic, and receive special training, attend expense-free conventions and summer institutes, and are assigned lighter teaching loads.

But even if the sponsors of the curriculum reform movements were all imbued with missionary research zeal, it would still be impossible to test the discovery hypothesis within the context of curriculum research. In the first place, a large number of other significant variables are necessarily operative in such programs. The UICSM program, for example, not only relies heavily on the principle of self-discovery of generalizations, but also on an inductive approach, on nonverbal awareness, on abundant empirical experience, on careful sequential programming, and, above all, on precise, self-consistent, unambiguous, and systematic verbal formulation of basic principles. To which variable, or to which combination of these variables and the "Hawthorne Effect" should the success of this program be attributed? Personally, for reasons enumerated earlier in this paper, I would nominate the factor of precise and systematic verbal formulation rather than the discovery variable. (Students enrolled in the UICSM program learn more mathematics, in my opinion, *not* because they are required to discover generalizations *by themselves*, but because they have at their disposal a systematic body of organizing, explanatory, and integrative principles which are not part of the conventional course in secondary-school mathematics. These principles illuminate the subject for them and make it much more meaningful.)

EVERY CHILD A CREATIVE AND CRITICAL THINKER

One of the currently fashionable educational doctrines giving support to the discovery method movement, is the notion that the school can make every child a creative thinker, and help him discover discontinuously new ideas and ways of looking at things. Creativity, it is alleged, is not the exclusive property of the rare genius among us, but a tender bud that resides in some measure within every child, requiring only the gentle, catalytic influence of sensitive, imaginative teaching to coax it into glorious bloom.

This idea rests on the following questionable assumptions: that one can be creative without necessarily being original; that all discovery activity, irrespective of originality, is qualitatively of one piece—from Einstein's formulation of the theory of relativity to every infant's spontaneous discovery that objects continue to exist even when they are out of sight; that considering the multiplicity of abilities, every person stands a good chance, genically speaking of being creative in at least one area; and that even if heredity is uncooperative, good teachers can take the place of missing genes.

Hohn's (8) use of the term "creativity" is typical of the prevailing tendency in "discovery" circles to "democratize" the meaning of this concept. A child behaves creatively in mathematics,

according to Hohn, when he proposes alternative approaches, grasps concepts intuitively, or displays autonomy, flexibility, and freedom from perseverative rigidity in his discovery efforts. Now one can define words in any way one chooses, and hence can define creativity so that it means nothing more than "autonomous and flexible discovery." But if this is *all* one means, would it not save endless confusion if one used these particular words instead of a term which both connotatively and denotatively implies a rare form of originality?

As a matter of fact, the very same persons who use "creativity" in the more "democratic" sense of the term, also imply in other contexts that the encouragement of *true* creativity (that is, in the sense of original accomplishment) in *every* child, is one of the major functions of the school. This view is implicit in Bruner's (4) position that the school should help every child reach discontinuous realms of experience so that he can create his own interior culture. It is also implicit in the goal of the Inquiry Training Program, namely, that children should be trained to formulate the same kinds of unifying concepts in science which are produced by our most creative scientists (Suchman [9]).

How reasonable now is the goal of "teaching for creativity," that is, in the sense of singularly original achievement? A decent respect for the realities of the human condition would seem to indicate that the training possibilities with respect to creativity are severely limited. The school can obviously help in the realization of existing creative potentialities by providing opportunities for spontaneity, initiative, and individualized expression; by making room in the curriculum for tasks that are sufficiently challenging for pupils with creative gifts; and by rewarding creative achievement. But it cannot actualize potentialities for creativity if these potentialities do not exist in the first place. Hence it is totally unrealistic, in my opinion, to suppose that even the most ingenious kinds of teaching techniques we could devise could stimulate creative accomplishment in children of average endowment.

Even "teaching for *critical* thinking" and "teaching for problem-solving" are somewhat grandiose slogans, although obviously much more realistic than "teaching for creative thinking." To be sure, the critical thinking and problem-solving abilities of most pupils can be improved. But this is a far cry from saying that most pupils can be trained to become good critical thinkers and problem-solvers. Potentialities for developing high levels of these abilities are admittedly much less rare than corresponding potentialities for developing creativity. Nevertheless, there are no good reasons for believing that they are any commoner than potentialities for developing high general intelligence. Also, in my opinion,

... aptitude in problem-solving involves a much different pattern of abilities than those required for understanding and retaining abstract ideas. The ability to solve problems calls for qualities (for example, flexibility, resourcefulness, improvising skill, originality, problem sensitivity, venturesomeness) that are less generously distributed in the population of learners than the ability to comprehend verbally presented materials. Many of these qualities also cannot be taught effectively. Although appropriate pedagogic procedures can improve problem-solving ability, relatively few good problem-solvers can be trained in comparison with the number of persons who can acquire a meaningful grasp of various subject-matter fields [1, p. 23].

From the standpoint of enlightened educational policy in a democracy, therefore, it seems to me that the school should concentrate its major efforts on teaching both what is most important in terms of cultural survival and cultural progress, and what is most teachable to the majority of its clientele. As improved methods of teaching become available, most students will be able to master the basic intellectual skills as well as a reasonable portion of the more important subject-matter content of the major disciplines. Is it not more defensible to shoot for this realistic goal, which lies within our reach, than to focus on educational objectives that presuppose exceptional endowment and are impossible of fulfillment when applied to the generality of mankind? Would it not be more realistic to strive first to have each pupil respond meaningfully, actively, and critically to good expository teaching before we endeavor to make him a good critical thinker and problem-solver?

I am by no means proposing a uniform curriculum and pedagogy for all children irrespective of individual differences. By all means let us provide all feasible special opportunities and facilities for the exceptional child. But in so doing, let us not attempt to structure the learning environment of the *non*-exceptional child in terms of educational objectives and teaching methods that are appropriate for either one child in a hundred or for one child in a million.

REFERENCES

1. Ausubel, D. P., "In Defense of Verbal Learning," *Educational Theory*, XI (1961), 15–25.
2. Bruner, J. S., *The Process of Education.* Cambridge, Mass.: Harvard University Press, 1960.
3. ———, "The Act of Discovery," *Harvard Education Review*, XXXI (1961), 21–32.
4. ———, "After Dewey What?" *Saturday Review* (June 17, 1961), 58–59, 76–78.
5. Hendrix, Gertrude, "A New Clue to

Transfer of Training," *Elementary School Journal*, XLVIII (1947), 197–208.

6. ———, "Prerequisite to Meaning," The Mathematics Teacher, XLIII (1960), 334–39.

7. ———, "Learning by Discovery," The Mathematics Teacher, LIV (1961), 290–99.

8. Hohn, F. E., "Teaching Creativity in Mathematics," *The Arithmetic Teacher*, VIII (1961), 102–6.

9. Suchman, J. R., "Inquiry Training: Building Skills for Autonomous Discovery," *Merrill-Palmer Quarterly of Behavior and Development*, VII (1961), 148–69.

A New Role for the Teacher

G. A. KAYE

Should algebra be introduced in the sixth grade? Should we teach calculus in the twelfth grade? Should geometry be taught from a transformation or vector approach rather than from a Euclidean viewpoint? These and many similar questions are being and have been asked for many years by mathematics educators, and they all miss the point. We have been far too concerned about mathematics and not concerned nearly enough about students!

Before curriculum developments in mathematics and the role of a teacher can be discussed, and before we go any further in any of the developments that are taking place, we need to stop and take stock of what we are doing

We are in danger of losing sight of the fact that education is a total experience and that mathematics education is only a part of that total. It is too easy to lose sight of the student in all our concern about content. Many evidences of this

Reprinted from *The Arithmetic Teacher*, XVI (January, 1969), 39–47, by permission of the author and the National Council of Teachers of Mathematics. Copyright © 1969 by the National Council of Teachers of Mathematics. G. A. Kaye is Associate Superintendent of the Curriculum Section, Ontario Department of Education, Toronto.

overconcern about content can be seen almost anywhere you go. The emphasis we place on testing and examinations is one example. Almost exclusively, examinations and tests are used to discover whether a student has covered a particular block of work—whether he has learned what has been taught. A subtle but important change in emphasis can make the examination or test a significant factor in the learning situation, rather than a hurdle or, in many cases, a block. Should not our testing program be used to tell us what a student is ready to learn, rather than what he has learned? There is a difference! If it is used to tell us what he is ready to learn, then there is no such thing as passing or failing on a test. The more you consider this seemingly minor difference in approach to examinations, the more you realize how wedded we have been to the specific content of a course of study.

Another example of this overconcern about content: Recently I visited a kindergarten, and it disturbed me that the teacher was so concerned about the children being able to talk about "interior regions of simple closed curves." I suppose the instructions to this class for a circle game like dodge ball or "ring around a rosie" would be, "One team will form a simple closed curve, and the other team will stand in the interior region." The word "inside" is a perfectly good word in the language and is very useful at some stage for giving an intuitive meaning to "interior region"—but "interior region" for five-year-olds? Intuitive ideas are basic to mathematics. I'm sure many students have a sound intuitive idea of limits long before they hear or see the formal definition. I'm just as sure that if they don't have a good intuitive "feel" for limits they will be a long time gaining understanding from the formal ϵ, δ definition. The trend indicated by this kindergarten example seems to be to eliminate the intuitive aspects from the learning of the subject and to make a very formal approach to it. Not only does this separate mathematics from the real-life experience of the child, but it imposes additional difficulties in the communication of ideas. The whole approach is alien to the achievement of understanding and enjoyment of mathematics. And thus, if it doesn't actually hinder, this approach does not provide any help in the solution of the main problem in mathematics education.

My main concern in mathematics education is not to produce mathematicians. Certainly, I will have a place in the program for the potential mathematician, but he is the exception, not the rule!

I am not going to tell you what Ontario is doing, because I believe that if you are interested in what we are doing, you will ask or write; but I think it is only fair to point out that in Ontario *all* students study mathematics to the end of the tenth year, about 90 per cent to the end of the twelfth, and about 70 per cent in Grade 13. Yes, we have a thirteen-grade system plus kindergarten for the university-bound group and a twelve-grade program for those going directly to the labor force and to other nonuniversity postsecondary institutions.

Thus part of the reason for saying that my main aim is not to produce mathematicians is because of the environment in which I function—but this is only part of the reason. Another large part of the reason is because of what we, the mathematics teachers, have done over the years as a result of a program based on the production of a few students who will go on to study and use mathematics at the university level. Our main aim at the elmentary level has been to produce (I won't say teach) people who have facility—both speed and accuracy—with arithmetic. The result: 90 per cent (probably more) of our students arrive at the secondary level with a detestation for mathematics. Drill, drill, drill has been their experience with a beautiful subject. "You did it right that time, but not fast enough." This may have been appropriate when the goal of arithmetic teaching was to produce fourteen-, fifteen-, and sixteen-year-olds to work as clerks. We don't send nine-year-olds down into the coal mines any more. Neither should we prepare older students for jobs that don't exist. The only argument that I've heard which could justify the speed-accuracy connection in computation today is that you must work quickly and accurately on examinations—this only proves to me that the examination process is wrong.

There are really only two types of arithmetic. One type is estimation. For example, when I travel by car in your country I want to be able to figure out quickly that sixteen of your gallons make just over twelve of ours; or when I travel to England I want to calculate quickly that £8 is about $18. The second type is accurate arithmetic. When I figure out my expense account I want 327 miles driving at 14 cents a mile to be exactly correct; or when I figure out my income tax I want to pay not one cent more than necessary. When I do this type of arithmetic I either take all the time that is necessary to check and recheck to ensure that it is correct, or I do it by calculator. I doubt that any of us, when we were put through the speed-accuracy hoops, saw any real reason for it; and I am quite sure that pupils after us could not be highly motivated to develop this skill—the hickory stick was a strong motivator, but it has all but disappeared.

Then they came to high school, and we taught them to factor $x^2 - y^2$ by the same drill, drill, drill process. Algebra— that has something to do with letters that I had to learn in high school. It's not like arithmetic because arithmetic is about numbers, and geometry—that's when you want to prove something, or —geometry has to do with propositions. During the early years of secondary school, another large group of students have come to dislike mathematics. The very few people who could take all the trees and build them into a forest are the ones who became mathematicians and mathematics teachers. And we tend to make the gross error of assuming that *our* students will all see the forest because we did, and thus the tendency has been to perpetuate the status quo.

The next trap we are about to fall into is ready and waiting. We have new math programs! The wrongs have been righted! We talk about sets and interior regions, and we're introducing vectors in eighth grade, and now the students will understand. Why? Well, someone said that sets were the unifying concept, so all we have to do is teach sets.

Ask a student to give you an example of a set. Depending on the grade level it will probably be the naturals or the integers or the rationals or the complex numbers. "What about golf clubs?" His reply might be "What have golf clubs got to do with mathematics?" I don't know who the first person was to suggest that the concept of a set could be introduced into our math programs, but I'm sure that if it was a teacher (not someone who calls himself a Teacher but a small "t" teacher), it was because he saw pedagogical value in it. He probably convinced some colleagues to consider his idea and try it, then somebody wrote a textbook and away we went. The pedagogical aspect seemed to disappear, and it soon became sets for sets' sake. You weren't up to date if you didn't teach about sets. Don't talk about the natural numbers, talk about the set of natural numbers. "Set" is the "in" word.

And what have we done? What is the trap that we could be falling into?

The trap is simply that it is assumed that because we have made changes, therefore, there must have been improvements. This is not necessarily the case. I'm afraid that all we have done is to change old content for new content and little else. We have put new trees in the forest and cut down some old ones, but have done little to help make a forest out of all the trees. Content changes alone are not the answer to our problems in mathematics education.

In curriculum development in mathematics we have spent far too much time finding solutions to a problem that has not been clearly enough defined. There has been much more concern whether a solution will sell a textbook, than whether it will help solve the problem.

What is the problem? Is it that we have too few mathematicians? This and similar "problems" are not problems at all, but symptoms of the problem. Often mistaking symptoms for the real illness has led to treatment that has done more harm than good. It is often said that people in the present and near future will need to know more mathematics because the expansion of mathematical knowledge will have a great effect on their lives. This may or may not be true but let's suppose it is. The seemingly logical step to take, then, is to teach more mathematics in a given period of time than we have before. A particular topic is out of date, so we eliminate it and include a new topic which we think is "in-date." By doing this we change nothing. We teach the five-year-old to say "in the interior region" instead of "inside"—four words for one. This has not helped understanding or communication. I'm sure any of us could teach a five-year-old to say "$2x$ is the derivative of x^2," but would this allow us to say we have taught him the calculus? Certainly we must be aware of the symptoms and must attempt to ease the pain caused by them, but let us not feed a starving man cream puffs.

Another symptom is the development over the centuries of reverence for mathematics. If you can claim to be a mathematician you tend to think of yourself as a member of a small intellectual elite. Most people think that one who studies and understands and enjoys mathematics is a bit of a nut and something of a brain. This may be the case, because it probably does take someone with reasonable intellectual power to put together into a cohesive pattern the various bits of mathematics that we have been throwing at our students. I suggest that this is because of the way mathematics has been presented and taught, not because of the nature of mathematics itself.

I have made reference to four symptoms of the problem:

1. Students dislike mathematics.
2. We do not have enough mathematicians.
3. The average citizen will be more directly affected by mathematics in his daily life than in the past.
4. There exists a "mathematics cult."

I think the first two and the fourth are very related, while the third raises another dimension.

Let's look at this third one for a few moments. "The average citizen will be more directly affected by mathematics in his daily life." It is probably incorrect to call this a symptom of the old problem but, I wonder, is it new? I wonder if at most points in time in the past people haven't been concerned about the increasing impact of mathematics on daily life. An examination of this need, I think, leads us to the real problem in mathematics education. It is the average citizen we are concerned about here— not the engineer or physicist or other practitioner of mathematics—but the housewife, the nurse, the English teacher, the factory worker, the bus driver. ... These people are certainly being affected by developments in mathematics, but does this mean that they are using more or different mathematics? I suggest that it does not.

It seems to me that the average person does *not need* to know more mathematics. It is quite possible for him to know even less mathematics—even less arithmetic; cash registers not only total the bill, but some make the proper change. What is needed is for this average person, whoever he is, to have a better *appreciation* of mathematics. He should have some idea of how mathematics is affecting him, how, in fact, it is making his daily life easier. Is it too much to suggest that he should be interested in mathematics to the point of wanting to read about the subject? Does the average, nonmathematics graduate of our high schools have any idea of the mathematics of music, of art, of architecture, of expressway design, of almost anything you want to name? Is he aware that while mathematics can be very abstract, it does emanate from the real world?

I submit that our real problem is to develop an educational process in mathematics which will produce people who are not afraid of mathematics, who will enjoy reading about the subject, who will realize that there is much more to mathematics than arithmetic and Euclid and $x^2 - y^2$.

We must start to develop programs that will produce more people who can find enjoyment in mathematics. This enjoyment will not come by teaching the subject in such a fashion that no one will encounter difficulty, but rather by accepting the idea that the best motivation comes from the student's own interest and from his own world. The problem is not associated so much with the content of our programs as with the structuring of them.

This leads me to three main points that I believe are basic to present and future developments in curriculum design. Before I proceed with these three points, I must clarify my use of the word "curriculum." In my use of it, curriculum is *not* synonymous with course of study or syllabus.

There are three aspects to the development of the learning situation in our schools. First, there is a course of study—this is a printed document of some form, frequently produced and published by a provincial or state department of education. In some cases the course of study may be just a textbook—and I believe this to be one of the worst types of course of study. We put the course of study in some form into the hands of a teacher; the teacher interprets the course and in many cases chooses a textbook and develops a series of lessons. This interpretation and implementation produces a program of studies. Thus we have a mathematics program, a science program, and so on.

Now we put all these programs together and add the many other experiences a child has in the environment of the school, and we have the curriculum. My definition of curriculum, then, is "The totality of the experiences a child has in the environment of the school."

The three phases again:

1. *A printed document: the course of study* (someone's idea of what should be taught)

2. *A teacher's interpretation: the program* (what the teacher feels should be provided by the classroom situation)
3. *The curriculum: the child's experiences* (what actually happens: not what *we* think happens, but what actually happens to the pupil)

Curriculum development, then, is a responsibility of the classroom teacher; anyone else involved is only a resource or an assistance to the teacher in providing the best possible learning situation for the children and young adults in our schools.

The three points that are basic to curriculum design thus require a hard look at our philosophy of what the educational system should provide, rather than a concern about what should be taught when. The three points are:

1. Mathematics courses do not need to be as highly structured as we have believed.
2. Even the structure we have had has been wrong in assuming that a mastery of arithmetic must precede other study of mathematics and science.
3. Programs in mathematics must provide starting points rather than end points.

Even though I see these as three distinct points, it is difficult to discuss any one of them without involving the others, but let's start with the first one. "Mathematics courses do not need to be as highly structured as we have believed." What sort of structure have we imposed on our programs? It seems to me that it is a double restriction; first, the content to be taught, and second, the order in which it is to be taught.

Part of the content restriction has been imposed by courses of study and textbooks, but only part of it. Another part of it exists because we, as teachers, have not been willing to say to our students, "I don't know; why don't you see what you can find out about it." Nor have we accepted the idea that it is more important for the student to study mathematics than to learn what we want him to learn. This last point is one of the real reasons why pupils are led to dislike mathematics. The student has been forced to learn what we think he should learn. We have denied him the chance to go off on a tangent of his own, in a direction that he finds interesting, because *we* know that he won't ever use what he learns, or *we* know that what he learns is not important, or *we* know that he will get out of his depth, or *we* know that if he takes time to do this or that he won't have time to finish the work *we* want him to do. Do we ever stop to think of the advantages of letting him go off on the tangent? He is going to have to research something on his own at his own pace and not struggle to keep up or slow down to wait for the pace *we* know to be the best pace. Of course, he may get out of his depth but he will be the first person to realize this, and maybe the realization that he is out of his depth will be the motivation he needs to acquire the knowledge that will let him go ahead with his own problem.

The official report of the Second Bowling Green Conference of 1958 includes an article entitled "Changing Teachers in a Changing World," by Margaret Mead, in which she says, "If we can't teach every student . . . something we don't know in some form, we haven't a hope of educating the next generation, because what they are going to need is what we don't know." It's quite obvious that we can't take this statement literally. How can we teach others something we don't know? We can prepare our students to learn many things we don't know if we are more concerned about helping them learn to learn than we are about teaching them specific bits of mathematics.

We have imposed a content restriction on our courses which has caused many people to dislike mathematics— not because of the content, but because they were forced to study topics for which they were not motivated. This content restriction, I believe, has led to more people knowing less mathematics than they would have otherwise. The only real motivation has been to pass an examination, and when this is not accompanied by motivation based on the interest of the student, the information "crammed" is forgotten almost immediately after the examination is over.

Associated with this strict definition of content is the parallel definition of order. "This must be learned *and proved* before you can use it and go on to the next step." We deny the student the right to take these undefinable intuitive jumps that occur so frequently. For some reason or other we are unhappy to have a student accept that this or that fact or theorem can be proved and then use the result without going through the proof—and yet in our own reading of mathematics most of us do this much of the time.

Even in the broader sense, until quite recently, it has been accepted that mastery of arithmetic must precede any other study of mathematics. The only motivation we have been able to develop in the majority of pupils has been the same as that for taking medicine—"It tastes terrible but, believe me, it's good for you."

We are now into point 2, that is, we have been wrong in assuming that arithmetic must be the first mathematical experience for the child. Before they reach kindergarten, the experiences most children have are geometrical or scientific and deal with inequality more often than equality.

Children live in a three-dimensional world of buildings of various shapes, backyards, rooms; they play with blocks and balls; they run wheeled toys down slopes; they are constantly concerned with "bigger than," "more than, "less than"; but "equal to" is a relation they are not as familiar with—these are only a very few examples of the experiences of this age group out of which mathematics and science learning can be produced. Most important—these are activities and situations that the children enjoy and are familiar with! Is it not reasonable that our programs should take account of these things? Is it not reasonable that a child could want to learn to add or multiply in order to be able to continue some investigation that interests him? Is there any reason why learning mathematics should not be fun? The learning of arithmetic should come, not as an end in itself, but as a means to an end. The pupil who is faced with a problem that interests him, and is held up because of lack of knowledge of arithmetic, will gain arithmetic skill and competence much faster, and probably at a later age than the pupils of the past. Arithmetic learning can develop from geometry, or science, or a survey of the number of cars and trucks that use the street in front of the school. When you think carefully about it, a good case can be made for not having a specific mathematics program before Grades 5 or 6.

It is very easy for someone who is not interested in investigating the implications of these questions to give supposedly good reasons why a program of this type won't work. We would have students at a great variety of stages in their mathematical development in the same class. We do now, so what's new? We wouldn't be able to give class tests, and thus we wouldn't be able to say whether George stood first in the class or whether Jim did. Quite right, we wouldn't be able to do this, and this would be an improvement. In adult life we choose the fields in which we are going to compete and, obviously, the fields we choose are those in which we have some competence; yet in the schools we have subjected the student to competition in all fields—those in which he has no interest and little

competence as well as the ones that interest him. It is possible to participate and learn without competing!

Some of you will have heard of Miss Edith Biggs of England, who spent most of the fall conducting a series of workshops in Ontario. Miss Biggs and others in England have developed an experience approach to the teaching of mathematics which has been used extensively in Dorest and Leicestershire for a number of years and also, to a lesser extent, in some Ontario schools. Significant success has been met in these experiments. The main difference between this program and most of those that have been developed on this side of the Atlantic is that the emphasis is on methodology rather than on content.

Throughout my remarks I have been discussing our overemphasis on content, so it is not at all surprising that I am interested in a program based on methodology with little or no concern about specific content. But before someone quotes me as saying that I am in favor of a program with no content, let me point out how silly that is. It is like saying that it is possible to learn without learning something. As I have said earlier, it is not the content that concerns me, but rather that our *overemphasis* on content has produced a structuring and a rigidity that is not good. We are still trying to fit the students to the schools and the courses, rather than fitting the schools and the courses to the students. We worry about the dropouts —but I wonder, is it the students who are dropping out or is it the schools?

Before we look at this "experience approach," which has been on trial for eight or ten years in England, let us look at some of the aspects of the structuring of our programs which are, I believe, at the root of the problem.

I have already suggested that we need to take a hard look at sequence. The greatest motivation for a student to learn a particular fact or procedure develops when the student needs to use that fact or procedure to do something he wants to do. Accept this and it means that we should not, for example, postpone the quadratic equation until a student has mastered factoring, but rather let him learn what factoring he needs to know because he wants to solve a quadratic equation. In general, in our traditional programs, we have taught a student all the things he needs to know to solve a problem, and then we have posed the problem and wondered why he couldn't apply his knowledge to the problem. Then, because he had difficulty in solving problems, we set up remedial classes in problem-solving without really analyzing why the student had difficulty. We seem to have made an effort to keep the reason for learning a particular aspect of mathematics a secret from the student. You would almost think that we believed that, because we were teachers, it was unthinkable that our students should question what we were doing or that they should need to know why we were doing it. The fact that *we* did it should be sufficient justification.

Another aspect of the sequence problem that I am glad to say we have broken away from in Ontario is the one year of algebra, one year of geometry type of program. This has caused an unnatural situation with respect to problem-solving. With algebra, synthetic geometry, analytic geometry, and other aspects of mathematics being developed together, there is a far greater chance for a student to bring knowledge from many aspects of mathematics to bear on the solution of a problem.

The major part of our "structure-rigidity" problem is what I shall call the "course-grade situation." Our courses of study and programs specify that this or that shall be covered in a particular period of time in a particular grade. Traditionally we have taken a topic like factoring or permutations and combinations and covered, supposedly, everything that needs to be known about

it in three weeks or in some specific number of lessons. There has been little build-up to the topic and little follow-up afterward. It's quite reasonable that students develop the attitude that each topic is an isolated tree that has no suggestion of forest about it. Even if it were good to take this approach, we haven't done it well. But this approach does not take into account the various speeds of learning and interests of the students, or that the development of mathematical maturity varies tremendously from student to student.

We have established end points and based our programs and lessons on them. I use the term "end point" to refer to a goal or aim that is associated with learning something at a specific time. We have determined that it is best for a student to learn geometry in the tenth grade and have his first course in algebra in the ninth, but intermediate algebra is reserved for the eleventh. This "end-point" attitude carries over right to the individual lesson. Today we are going to teach the formula for solving a quadratic equation—and come hell or high water that's what we do—we teach it, but has anybody learned it? "That's the students' worry. I taught it, and I know how to teach, so they'd better learn it." With this "end-point" philosophy is tied the age-old attitude that the teacher is the fount of all knowledge. All of us like to tell others something they haven't heard before, whether it's a joke or news or information. Because teaching has generally been viewed as the "passing on" of information, the profession has probably gathered together those people who get the greatest enjoyment from informing others, and thus to change from the "handing out of knowledge" to "assisting others to discover"—to change the emphasis from "teaching" to "learning"—poses a major problem for us.

The "experience approach" that is being implemented by Miss Biggs and others is based on "starting points" rather than "end points." A term that is frequently used to describe this approach is "open-ended." Situations that are familiar and interesting to the student are used as jumping-off places for them. Since there is little pattern evident in the activities in classrooms where this approach is used, it is difficult to describe the program. I think you can get an idea of it from some examples that come from these situations.

A reference in a class (ten- and eleven-year-olds) to the various types of vehicles that used the street in front of the school led to a survey to determine what the relationship was between the number of cars, trucks, and buses that used the road. The class discussed the problem of gathering the information, the difference between rush-hour travel and normal travel, and other variables in the traffic flow. Eventually a schedule for a traffic count was set up and the information gathered. This was just the start. Without going into details, some of the developments from this are interesting: Some students became interested in displaying the information and thus got involved in graphing. Some boys were interested in the difference between cars and trucks and got involved with engines, gear ratios, and so on. One boy wondered where the trucks came from and where they were going and thus became involved with economics. Others weren't interested in this problem at all and went to some other situation that did interest them.

In these classes you are constantly surprised. Students may be busy filling whiskey bottles with water in a volume study. They may be trying to discover a relationship between people's height and skin area; they may be timing a toy truck as it goes down an inclined ramp; in fact, they may be doing just about anything. As a teacher gains experience with this approach to learning, he discovers that certain materials and experiences provoke greater learning and interest than others, and thus he provides these materials and experiences for the students, but —and this, I think, is the key—he does not insist that counting cars must lead to graphing.

Two things seem evident to me at this point. In classrooms where this approach is well developed, discipline problems are minimized—the noise level is constantly higher—but the noise is discussion and pupils working together and communicating about their work, rather than a disturbing noise. Secondly, it seems that in this highly student-centered experience approach, the pupils learn more than we would expect, faster than we would expect, and they develop a willingness to tackle a new problem that I was not accustomed to seeing when I was in the classroom.

This approach has been used with much success for children up to twelve or fourteen years of age. It has had less trial at more senior levels. One thing is certain: Students arriving at the secondary school level with this type of elementary school background are not satisfied with the traditional approach of the secondary school. It is quite evident that this type of elementary school approach is rapidly gaining ground on both sides of the Atlantic and, in the near future, students with this background are going to be arriving by the thousands in secondary schools.

Are we going to be ready for them? I hope so. But to be ready for them we must devote large amounts of energy to the study of this type of educational process. We must find the proper balance between student interest and needs, and content. Let us be very careful that we do not spoil the whole development by accepting an open-ended approach and then trying to structure the starting points to various grade levels.

The implementation of the philosophy I have been discussing is up to you. New courses of study and new textbooks cannot do the job. In fact, they can be a hindrance. There can be no overnight change from rigidity to flexibility. The change must be gradual and can only take place as teachers accept their true professional responsibility. I believe that little change will take place as long as the emphasis is on teaching. We must start to accept the fact that the schools exist for the education of our young people.

A new role for the classroom teacher —that's what must develop now. If the teaching profession as a whole, and more important, individual teachers, are willing to accept their real responsibility; if teachers are willing to examine their philosophy of education; if teachers are willing to place the needs and interests of individual students ahead of anything else; if teachers are willing to cease to be the central figure in the classroom all the time, then a truly significant new role for teachers will develop.

This new role will mean that all teachers, not just a few as is now the case, will be doing those things machines can't do. The teacher who does nothing but teach facts can be replaced by a machine. The teacher will be the motivator, the classroom resource center— not necessarily having all the knowledge, but helping the student to dig out the information he needs. The teacher will be an educational counselor.

But most important of all—let's do more than pay lip service to the fact that the educational system exists for the students. Let's stop trying to fit students to the system and start to fit the system to the students!

Revolution, Rigor, and Rigor Mortis
STEPHEN S. WILLOUGHBY

When I first heard the recent changes in mathematics education described as a Revolution, my feeling was that the word was too harsh and implied too much violence—I preferred to omit the "R." Perhaps this is because the word "Revolution" always brings to mind the

Reprinted from *The Mathematics Teacher*, LX (February, 1967), 105–8, by permission of the author and the National Council of Teachers of Mathematics. Copyright © 1967 by the National Council of Teachers of Mathematics. (This article is based on talks given at the National Council of Teachers of Mathematics meeting in Detroit and at meetings in Illinois and Wisconsin.) Stephen S. Willoughby is Professor of Mathematics, Professor of Mathematics Education, and Chairman of the Mathematics Education Department, New York University.

French Revolution and Charles Dickens' *Tale of Two Cities* in which, for some reason, I always identified myself with Sidney Carton (the one who lost his head over a girl).

Upon further thought, however, it occurred to me that perhaps there are some similarities. Prior to 1789 the French Monarchy (notably Louis XIV, and at the end, Louis XVI and Marie Antoinette) had held absolute power. They brooked no difference of opinion, and they allowed no questioning on the part of the people. Prior to 1957, it is reported that some mathematics teachers had been known to insist upon absolute rules. They allowed no thought or questioning on the part of the pupils.

Of course, there were rumblings of discontent before the Revolution, but those in power were too absorbed in their own thoughts to notice them.

Then it came—Bastille Day (July 14, 1789)—or Sputnik Day (October 4, 1957). The French had their States General, their National Assembly, their Committee of Public Salvation. We have our Commission of the College Entrance Examination Board, our National Council of Teachers of Mathematics, our Cambridge Conference.

They had their Robespierre, their Marat, their Danton. We have—well . . . .

Their leaders began fighting among themselves—seeing who could outdo the others in his excesses. Two of them were executed (the need to resist a pun relating the guillotine and Dedekind cuts is obvious) and one was murdered. It seems to me that some of the leaders of our Revolution have been doing a little fighting among themselves lately.

The French Revolution stood for: Liberty, Equality, Fraternity.

Our Revolution stands for: Probability, Inequalities, Sets.

To me the really frightening thing about the French Revolution is that, in the name of freedom, it allowed no freedom. In the name of democracy it was more autocratic and fearsome than the monarchy had been. I hope that future historians will not be able to say the same about our Revolution— that we replaced one dogma by another, and that since the new dogma is one we know less well, we are more dogmatic about it.

Let me hasten to say that this is not an attack upon "modern mathematics." Nor is it a suggestion that we have gone to the same sort of extremes as the French Revolutionists—yet. Rather, I suggest that it is time that we stop for a moment and try to evaluate the Revolution and improve it *without* decapitating any of our esteemed leaders.

A central theme of our Revolution is rigor. One result, either of a revolution or of undue rigor, can be rigor mortis. Surely this is one outcome we want to avoid.

First, let us consider the place of rigor in mathematics. There can be no doubt that mathematics had, and still has, its beginnings in empiricism. Before the Greeks got hold of it, geometry was a very practical, down-to-earth (no pun intended) subject. The Pythagoreans generalized the empirical facts, proved new facts, and continued to study geometry from a more esoteric point of view—virtually as a religion. In many respects, the rigorization of mathematics at the hands of the Greeks reached its culumination with Euclid. And, for some two thousand years, Euclid remained the standard of rigorous reasoning, not only for the mathematical world, but for the entire educated world.

During the past hundred years, however, notable difficulties have come to light because of a lack of rigor in Euclid. Furthermore, the lack of rigor in other subjects, such as analysis, algebra, and early set theory, was more apparent (and to some, more appalling) than any lack of rigor in Euclid.

Let's consider some examples of what can happen when people are not quite so careful as they might be. First, in geometry, there is the well-known theorem that all triangles are isosceles.

Theorem: All triangles are isosceles. *Given:* $\triangle ABC$. *To prove:* $AB = AC$. (See Fig. 1.)

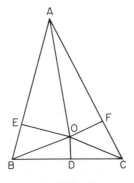

Figure 1

1. Construct perpendicular bisector of $\overline{BC}(\overleftrightarrow{DO})$ and angle bisector of $\angle BAC(\overrightarrow{AO})$. These will meet in some point O (if they are parallel, then $\overleftrightarrow{AO}$ is perpendicular to $\overleftrightarrow{BC}$ and it is easy to show that $\overleftrightarrow{AO}$ and $\overleftrightarrow{DO}$ are the same line, and that $AB = AC$).

2. Construct $\overleftrightarrow{OE}$ and $\overleftrightarrow{OF}$ perpendicular to $\overleftrightarrow{AB}$ and $\overleftrightarrow{AC}$ respectively. Also, draw $\overleftrightarrow{OB}$ and $\overleftrightarrow{OC}$.

3. $\triangle AEO \cong \triangle AFO$. (AAS).

4. $\triangle BEO \cong \triangle CFO$. (Right triangles with two pairs of corresponding sides congruent are congruent; $BO = CO$ because $\overleftrightarrow{DO}$ is a perpendicular bisector, and $EO = FO$ because $\overleftrightarrow{AO}$ is an angle bisector.)

5. $AE = AF$ and $EB = FC$.

6. $AE + EB = AF + FC$. (Equals added to equals are equal.)

7. $AE + EB = AB$, and $AF + FC = AC$. (The whole equals the sum of its parts.)

8. $AB = AC$. (Substitution.)

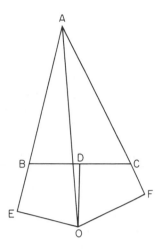

Figure 2

What's wrong with this proof? A common answer is "The picture is drawn incorrectly." But we aren't supposed to rely on the picture for the proof—remember? The picture is meant only to help our intuition along a bit. But suppose we draw the picture differently, as in Figure 2, so that point O falls outside the triangle. Every step of the proof still stands up except that Step 7 must be changed to read $AE - EB = AB$, and $AF - FC = AC$, and the plus signs in Step 6 should be changed to minus signs. Thus, the proof still works.

Of course, the answer to the dilemma is that for any triangle (other than an isosceles triangle) the lines $\overleftrightarrow{AO}$ and $\overleftrightarrow{OD}$ will meet in a point O which is outside the triangle, but is in such a position that precisely one of the points E and F will be a point of the triangle—the other point will be on an extension of a side of the triangle. However, there is nothing in Euclid that allows us to prove where the points E and F are. For most problems of this sort, Euclid (and his followers) would simply have looked at the picture and assumed that points are where they seem to be; and for most situations, such a procedure doesn't get us into trouble. However, it is clear that there are some cases where such a procedure will lead to trouble.

LACK OF RIGOR

The moral of all of this is that Euclid wasn't really very careful about his concept of betweenness. There are also other concepts about which Euclid wasn't very careful. For example, under what circumstances will two arcs meet? This information is needed in his first theorem (construction of an equilateral triangle). Will the angle bisector of an interior angle of a triangle meet a side of the triangle?

There is also the old problem of moving figures (particularly angles). Euclid can be patched up so as to avoid these problems, as shown by Hilbert, but the point is that Euclid's lack of rigor did lead to some rather sticky problems.

Geometry is not the only subject in which a lack of rigor has led to some rather disturbing results.

To consider a trivial example of a problem which might occur if a very naive person applied the procedures of calculus without the appropriate definitions, suppose we find the length of the diagonal of a square in the following way. Consider, in Figure 3, the following paths: *ABC*, *ADEFC*, *AGHIEJKLC*, *AMNOHPQRESTUK-VWXC*, etc. Clearly, the paths are approaching the diagonal. Also, clearly, the length of each path is two times the length of a side of the square. Therefore, the length of the diagonal of a square is equal to twice the length of a side of the square.

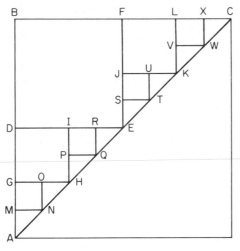

Figure 3

Of course, it is not necessarily true that if all the points of a path approach the points of a line segment, then the length of the path approaches the length of the segment; but some reasonably careful definitions about limits are necessary in order to allow the things we wish to allow while avoiding such problems as this one.

Many other cases could be sighted in which a lack of mathematical rigor can lead to unfortunate results. However, for our discussion here, perhaps the most appropriate such case has to do with set theory. During the latter part of the last century and the early part of this century, mathematicians showed that it is possible to derive all of mathematics from set theory. But they also found that there are certain paradoxes (it is not true that the plural of that word is paradise) which can be derived from set theory. Perhaps the best known of these is Russell's paradox which can be stated as follows: Consider the set, *S*, which has as its members all sets which are not elements of themselves. Is *S* an element of *S*?

Russell's paradox, and others like it, don't happen to be in the main body of set theory, and it is possible to avoid them simply by restricting one's attention to that part of set theory that is useful. However, except for the fact that it leads to contradictions, there is no obvious reason for eliminating a major portion of set theory. We have avoided a weak foundation for our structure not by providing a strong foundation, but by eliminating that part of the structure that is on the weak foundation.

Even more basic than the paradoxes mentioned above are the objections the intuitionists have to certain parts of set theory. In particular, this group of mathematicians objected on philosophic grounds to the concept of general validity and existence which is basic to most proofs in set theory. They felt that one should actually construct a mathematical entity rather than just prove that it must exist, or, in particular, an indirect proof of existence involving infinite sets is not really valid ... a constructive proof would be necessary.

Interestingly enough, mathematicians seem to have accepted the point of view of the intuitionists when it was first proposed. Hilbert even proposed a plan by which it would be shown that traditional mathematics would not lead to contradictions, using the rules laid down by the intuitionists. Then, with the ultimate in rigorous proof, Gödel (distinguishing carefully between objects and their names) showed that we can never prove the consistency or completeness of mathematics without basing the proof on a foundation that is equally shaky. However, to accept the view of the intuitionists would be to eliminate most of topology, measure theory, modern analysis, and indeed, a major portion of modern mathematics. So mathematicians simply ignore the problem and accept these parts of mathematics anyway, because they are useful. Thus, even today, mathematics really has its ultimate justification in empiricism—it is accepted because it works, and because it has some pertinence to the real world, not because it is beautiful and based on a firm foundation.

SIGNIFICANCE TO TEACHERS

What does this mean to the classroom teacher? To begin with, it means that it is just a bit inappropriate for mathematicians to tell teachers that they aren't being rigorous enough. It may be that some mathematics teachers are unnecessarily sloppy in their derivations and proofs, but I contend that this is more a pedagogical question than a mathematical one. Mathematical standards of rigor have changed according to what was needed and appropriate. Surely, the same should be true in the classroom.

Probably the most appropriate action in the classroom is to begin by relying very heavily on the children's intuition. Encourage the children to examine a situation, make conjectures as to what might be true and what is probably not true. Then help them try to convince others that what they believe to be true is true. By asking appropriate questions, and getting the pupils to ask appropriate questions, the teacher can help the pupils to create their own standards of rigor and to change these standards when they become inappropriate. Thus, the pupils will not learn a sterile rigor which they must memorize because somebody else thinks it's important, but rather will develop their own standards of proof.

One of my daughter's favorite songs is entitled "Watch the Doughnut, Not the Hole." Perhaps that can be used to summarize the moral of this article. I am willing to agree that rigor may be central to mathematics. However, when it is simply memorized, without an understanding and appreciation of its need, it is central in the same sense that the hole is central to the doughnut. Sterile rigor is neither more appetizing nor more nutritious to the young mind than the hole of the doughnut is to the young body. Therefore, I leave you with the admonition to "watch the doughnut, not the hole."

The Heart of Teaching

HAROLD C. TRIMBLE

Think about some good mathematics teachers you have known. For the moment don't try to define your usage of the word "good" in a precise way. Perhaps it means "effective." But, then, what is an effective mathematics teacher? You may conclude, as I do, that individual teachers of mathematics may be effective in either of two quite different ways.

Some teachers rate high for efficiency. They give clear explanations. They ask the right questions to lead their students to knowledge quickly and painlessly. They cover the material with time to spare, yet their students master the concepts; that is, they learn to associate the technical terms of mathematics with the corresponding mathematical objects. They can name mathematical objects; they can give suitable examples of objects to which a name refers.

Other teachers may seem quite inefficient, yet they are effective in that their students "learn to learn." A casual observer might wonder whether these students are learning in spite of their teachers. However, the results are clear. The students do well on tests; and they have a hard-to-define "plus" about them. This plus is a combination of freedom from fear, eagerness to continue their study of the subject, and

ability to work independently for surprisingly long periods of time.

As I look about me and listen to what people are saying, I see and hear a lot about the first aspect of good teaching. We are told that programs soon will be built into computers to provide computer-assisted instruction. Much contemporary educational research is dedicated to increasing the efficiency of the teaching of concepts. Professional courses for prospective teachers emphasize concept teaching. And all this seems good to me—at least, so far as it goes.

Again, I look about me and listen. I see and hear that learning to learn is the essential ingredient of an education for living. In a world that changes rapidly, modern man is soon obsolete; and no one knows what knowledges and skills will be in demand as students now in high school become middle-aged workers. I am told that whether students enter the professions or become semiskilled laborers, the one sure thing is that they will need, from time to time, to acquire new knowledges and skills and that it is not possible to predict what new knowledges and skills will be required of them.

What concerns me, then, is the emphasis on a *good* thing, efficient teaching of concepts, and the possible neglect of the *essential thing*, learning to learn. We may be approaching a time when efficient procedures for teaching a specified set of concepts will be known. We might even learn to feed

Reprinted from *The Mathematics Teacher*, LXI (May, 1968), 485–88, by permission of the author and the National Council of Teachers of Mathematics. Copyright © 1968 by the National Council of Teachers of Mathematics. Harold C. Trimble is Professor of Education, Ohio State University, Columbus.

information to students as efficiently as a programmer now feeds data to a computer. And, if this happens, students may become almost as reliable as computers. I suppose that they will sit back and await the next stimulus. (Ask them a question, get the programmed response.)

I recall the days of "progressive education" when boys and girls sometimes asked, "Teacher, do I have to do what I want to do today?" This was the era (should I say error?) when small children were encouraged to tackle broad problems. Under some teachers they focused attention, eventually, on such details as concepts and skills. Some teachers of social studies do this sort of thing still. Perhaps they avoid the excesses of vagueness better than their predecessors did. As a teacher of mathematics, I don't ask young children such questions as this: "What influence do size and shape have upon human happiness?" Perhaps this is a consequence of my training. I wouldn't know how to proceed from such a question to help boys and girls acquire basic concepts of mathematics, let alone to help them learn to learn.

But it seems to me that teachers of mathematics are lucky. It doesn't take much ingenuity to ask a question in mathematics that leads to classroom research. And, I believe, doing research is the vehicle for learning to learn. Let me give one example.

Figurate numbers have interested people at least since the time of Pythagoras. You know the triangular numbers (Fig. 1) and the square numbers (Fig. 2), and perhaps you know the pentagonal numbers (Fig. 3). Now, if you want to do some classroom research, you can define and picture hexagonal numbers, 7-gon numbers, and so on. Of course, other people have done this. But, if you don't peek into the literature for

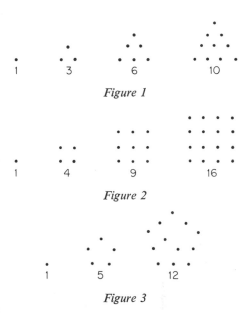

Figure 1

Figure 2

Figure 3

the answers, your investigations will be research for you.

Once you get going, many more questions arise. For example: Are some hexagonal numbers also traingular numbers? You can approach some questions geometrically. You can make dot patterns. When you get boys and girls doing this, some of them may surprise you by their perceptions of patterns. Some boys and girls who do only moderately well with verbal manipulations and, hence, score only moderately well on intelligence tests, are latent geniuses in pattern perception. Some of them later become master craftsmen. Others never get the opportunity in school, or outside, to use their talents. And this may reprsent a serious loss to them and to our society.

You can also organize the information into orderly tables of numbers. Almost any student can be led to do this. The habit of doing it is an important part of learning to learn. It may be critical for solving certain problems of science or accounting. Study Table 1 as an example.

TABLE 1
N-GON NUMBERS

Types of numbers	Numbers										
Counting	1	2	3	4	5	6	7	8	9	10	11 ...
Triangular (3-gon)	1	3	6	10	15	21	28	36	45	55	66 ...
Square (4-gon)	1	4	9	16	25	·	·				
Pentagonal (5-gon)	1	5	12	22	·	·	·				
Hexagonal (6-gon)	1	6	15	·	·	·					
·											
·											
·											
m-tagonal (m-gon)	1	m	·	·	·						
Column Differences	0	1	3	6	10						

You will find lots of patterns. To generate square numbers, you begin with 1; you add 3; to the result you add 5; to this you add 7; and, to continue, you add the next odd number. What about pentagonal numbers? You start with 1, add 4, then 7, then 10, etc. In the columns of the table the differences, going down a column, are 0, then 1, then 3, then 6, etc. So the column differences are zero and the triangular numbers.

There are many other patterns. It is not hard to find the nth triangular number as

$$1 + 2 + 3 + \cdots + n = \frac{n(n+1)}{2}.$$

The nth square number is

$$1 + 3 + 5 + \cdots + (2n - 1) = n^2.$$

The difference is

$$n^2 - \frac{n(n+1)}{2} = \frac{n}{2}[2n - (n+1)]$$

$$= \frac{n}{2}(n - 1).$$

This suggests that the nth pentagonal number is

$$n^2 + \frac{n}{2}(n - 1) = \frac{n}{2}[2n + (n - 1)]$$

$$= \frac{n}{2}(3n - 1)$$

and the nth hexagonal number is

$$\frac{n}{2}(3n - 1) + \frac{n}{2}(n - 1) = \frac{n}{2}(4n - 2)$$

$$= n(2n - 1).$$

Now you can get the nth m-tagonal number as

$$n + (m - 2)\frac{n}{2}(n - 1)$$

$$= \frac{n}{2}[2 + (m - 2)(n - 1)].$$

If you begin to wonder whether your belief in patterns is really justified, you can begin to make proofs. For example, you can use mathematical induction to prove that the nth pentagonal number really is

$$\frac{n}{2}(3n - 1).$$

Now you can attack some of the earlier-raised questions algebraically. For example, the nth triangular number is

$$\frac{n(n+1)}{2};$$

the kth hexagonal number is

$$k(2k - 1).$$

Hence, a choice of n and k such that

$$\frac{n(n+1)}{2} = k(2k - 1)$$

makes the nth triangular number equal to the kth hexagonal number. As you play with this equation you will notice that, for any natural number k, the choice $n = 2k - 1$ makes

$$\frac{n+1}{2} = k.$$

For this choice of n,

$$n\frac{(n+1)}{2} = (2k - 1)k.$$

In other words, each hexagonal number is a triangular number; the kth hexagonal number is the $(2k - 1)$ st triangular number.

This algebraic argument may lead some students to return, in disgust, to geometry. Look again at a typical hexagonal number, the fourth one, for example. (See Fig. 4.) Why is the fourth hexagonal number $(k = 4)$ also the seventh triangular number $(n = 2 \cdot 4 - 1)$? Such questions are the stuff of which research is made.

You will pardon the digression into

Figure 4

which my example led me. Even if you are bored by my example, still you realize that, once you begin on an example of your own, you will find it fascinating. So will boys and girls find discoveries of *their* own fascinating.

Of course, not all students will get the research bug even when you, as a teacher, ask good questions. But it is my expeirence that some students will get this bug, and many students will begin to feel the urgency of questions that some of their classmates are struggling to answer. Thus even these harder-to-reach students may become participants in classroom, group research, even though they fall short of doing somewhat independent, individual research.

I repeat, mathematics teachers are lucky. They can choose from a vast storehouse of rich, readily researchable questions. As they guide students either individually or in groups into the fruitful techniques of research, they will be providing practice in learning to learn.

Finally, then, I am not willing to define "good" teaching to make the "good" apply only to efficient teaching of concepts. I want it to apply also to the plus that I associate with the self-confidence and eagerness of students who are led to do research. This is because I believe that teaching people to learn is the *heart* of teaching and that individual research and group research in mathematics are excellent vehicles for learning to learn.

Is Our Mathematics Inferior?

GEORGE S. CARNETT

The United States has relatively fewer good mathematics students than many other countries.

Our high school youngsters can't compete in mathematics with students their own age elsewhere.

American teachers don't get the results their foreign colleagues do.

Conclusions such as these can easily be read between the lines of *A Comparative Study of Outcomes of Mathematics Instruction*, a five-year evaluation of mathematics teaching in twelve countries. But such conclusions are hasty and will not stand close scrutiny. The project was not designed as an international contest. It will not reveal any educational ranking among the countries taking part.

Readers who try to interpret the results in this way will almost certainly be drawing unjustifiable conclusions. Says Benjamin S. Bloom of the University of Chicago, who is one of the principal U.S. investigators for the study,

The object of the enterprise has been to discern more clearly the interrelationship between aspects of organization, curriculum and teaching, and social factors, on the one hand, and mathematics performance on the other.

Reprinted from *American Education*, III, No. 3 (March, 1967), 1–3, by permission of the author and the publisher. George S. Carnett is Research Associate, Research Training Branch, National Center for Educational Research and Development, U.S. Office of Education, Washington, D.C.

To educators, the interrelationship that was revealed is more startling than the hasty comparisons: No matter what the system of education, or what the preparation of the teacher or the size of the class he teaches, no matter at what age a pupil starts school or what his socioeconomic background, all school systems in all the countries evaluated had almost identical scores on the international test up to the end of the period of universal education. Put another way, students perform equally well under any educational system as far as the point where selective policies enter into secondary schooling.

Table 1 reports the average test scores of representative samples of students in each of the countries studied and the increase in performance between age thirteen and the final year of secondary school.

The report, published by John Wiley & Sons in cooperation with Almqvist & Wiksell of Stockholm, will be released internationally this month. Principal U. S. investigators in addition to Dr. Bloom were C. Arnold Anderson of the University of Chicago and Arthur W. Foshay and Robert L. Thorndike of Teachers College, Columbia University. Financial support was provided in part by the Cooperative Research Program administered by the U. S. Office of Education.

In evaluating what types of schools and what types of mathematics programs produce the best results, the study

TABLE 1
TEST SCORES OF FOUR GROUPS OF STUDENT POPULATIONS

	13-year-old pupils	School grade of most 13-year-olds	Students in final high school year		Increase in test performance
			Taking math	Nonmath	
Australia	20	19	22	—	2.4
Belgium	28	30	35	24	2.9
England	19	24	35	21	3.1
Finland	24	26	25	23	2.6
France	18	21	33	26	3.2
Germany	—	25	29	28	—
Israel	—	32	36	—	—
Japan	31	31	32	25	2.6
The Netherlands	24	21	31	25	2.9
Scotland	19	22	26	21	2.7
Sweden	16	15	27	13	2.8
United States	16	18	14	8	1.8
Total	20	23	26	21	2.6

touched upon a number of topics of particular interest to the American public—questions such as:

Do bright children suffer as a result of a mass education policy? Should high schools specialize? How much homework should be required? How should students be grouped? Are our teachers as good as they should be? How does "new math" stack up against the old?

The principal finding of the study as applied to the United States, says Foshay, is that comprehensive high schools such as we now have "serve the population better than selective secondary schools on the European model." He questions the value of having students devote themselves to a narrow specialization during their last two years of high school. "The study raises serious questions about the wisdom of a national policy of selective education as against comprehensive education," he says.

In the face of the performance levels shown in Table 1, how can such observations be justified? The basic purpose of education in the United States

—education for everyone—provides a ready answer to the question. Retaining larger proportions of students in school for a longer time does lower the average scores, but at the same time increases the "total input" for the age group of that nation. Table 2 shows the percentage of the age group in each

TABLE 2
PERCENTAGE OF AGE GROUP IN SCHOOL; TAKING MATH

	% of age group in last pre-univ. year	% of pre-univ. age group studying math
Australia	23	14
Belgium	13	4
England	12	5
Finland	14	7
France	11	5
Germany	11	5
Japan	57	8
The Netherlands	8	6
Scotland	18	5
Sweden	23	16
United States	70	18

country completing high school and the percentage of final-year high school students taking mathematics (i.e., two of the populations sampled in the international testing program).

Another major finding of the study was that socioeconomic status plays an important part in determining the membership of the preuniversity group. This relationship was very slight in the United States (as well as in Japan and Finland), but is nevertheless significant for its possible bearing on the education of our disadvantaged children: Pupils from lower status homes score higher if they attend school with students from a wide range of family backgrounds—a finding that agrees with a recent OE survey of equal educational opportunities.

"One of the major levers a school has for improving the learning of youngsters from poor families is to put them in association at school with youngsters who come from more-advantaged families," Commissioner Harold Howe II stated in an interview with *U.S. News and World Report* recently. Referring to the OE survey, he said further that "youngsters who come from economically advantaged families don't find themselves handicapped in learning as a result of associating with youngsters who come from poor families." The international mathematics study backs up his observation here, also.

Specifically, it reports that talented students continue to achieve at a high level even when selection barriers are lowered. Table 3 compares students in their last year of secondary school by number of school subjects studied, mean test scores, and mean test scores of the top 4 per cent.

Another controversial subject the research touched on is homework, a subject that finds Americans—educators and parents alike—divided in opinion. Some think class time should be

TABLE 3
SUBJECTS CARRIED AND COMPARISON OF MEAN AND TOP 4% TEST SCORES OF STUDENTS IN PREUNIVERSITY YEAR

	No. of subjects studied	Mean test score	Mean test score of selected upper 4%
Australia	6	22	34
Belgium	9+	35	35
England	3	35	39
Finland	9	25	32
France	9+	33	37
Germany	9	29	32
Israel	8	36	42
Japan	9+	31	44
The Netherlands	9+	32	35
Scotland	4	26	29
Sweden	9	27	44
United States	4	14	33
Range		23	15

given to homework assignments; others feel that homework should be done in study halls under the guidance of qualified teachers; still others feel that homework should be done individually at home. Another group feels that homework is busywork and should be avoided. Research on the subject is inconclusive. Homework assignments therefore tend to differ greatly from school to school, subject to subject, and even from class to class in the same subject in the same school.

More homework and higher scores go hand in hand, this study shows (but it didn't delve into the ratio of homework to classwork or suggest an optimum mix of subjects). Test scores in mathematics rise, both within and between countries, with increases in the amount of homework students reported in mathematics as well as other subjects. Thus, the more homework the student does—and not necessarily in mathematics alone—the better his mathematics performance. And the more homework that students in a particular country do, the better their national performance in comparison with students of other countries. (The U.S. was about average for thirteen-year-olds, but well below average in the final year of preuniversity work. The ratio of mathematics homework to all homework, however, was above average.)

Student attitudes matter. High scores in mathematics are associated with interest in mathematics, the research found, as well as with what the researchers termed "a high regard for the place of math in the society." Boys do better than girls—boys' schools do the best of all. These findings substantiate what Project Talent had previously reported concerning student preferences in occupations: Students are more interested in fields they know most about. Mathematics-related careers show fairly low on prestige and career preference scales; boys frequently check engineering, research, and other fields involving heavy mathematics application, but girls hardly ever indicate even a subsidiary interest in the field.

Teaching preparation matters. There were consistent positive correlations between the mathematics scores of the preuniversity students and the type of training their teachers had received. Table 4 shows the length of training required of teachers in the various countries studied.

In the United States, mathematics is an area of perennial teacher shortage at all levels of instruction. It ranks first among the projected staffing problems of colleges and universities, according to the National Education Association's most recent research report on the subject. Every year it is a major problem of elementary and secondary schools nationwide. At the high school level, for example, last year's college graduates who were qualified for mathematics teaching credentials filled only 70 per cent of the national demand for

TABLE 4
YEARS OF PREPARATION
REQUIRED IN TEACHER PROGRAMS

	Elementary teachers	Secondary teachers
Australia	2 years	2–4 years
Belgium	1	4
England	3	4
Finland	2–4	5–8
France	2	4
Germany	3–4	7
Israel	2	4
Japan	3–4	3–4
The Netherlands	4	6–7
Scotland	3	5
Sweden	2–5	6
United States	4–5	5

new mathematics teachers this school year. Schools that couldn't find qualified teachers took what they could get, which usually meant persons trained in other fields and frequently deficient in mathematics preparation.

"It may not always be possible to schedule classes under fully qualified full-time mathematics teachers," says an OE pamphlet describing the state of science and mathematics teaching in the public schools, "but it is certainly desirable for a pupil to study mathematics under a teacher whose major interest is in that field."

"The supply of mathematics teachers is closely tied in with the whole matter of teaching prestige and professionalism," points out Edwina Deans, one of OE's mathematics specialists. "As long as so many of our best-trained persons choose not to teach, we will have shortages. Salaries, working conditions, and the other factors that make one career desirable in competition with others—all these will have to be improved."

New mathematics or old? That question interested several countries that were adopting or experimenting with "new math" programs. The answer—

students who had been taught new mathematics received slighly higher scores on traditional type mathematics than did other students.

"But it should be remembered that very few of our students were studying under new mathematics programs at the time," says Dr. Deans. U.S. students were tested during the period January–June 1964. "Hardly any of the elementary schools were teaching new mathematics, and the effect on secondary school students at that time was very slight."

Thus, the finding still leaves the value of new math open to question. It does substantiate early research on the "new math" developed by the School Mathematics Study Group, with financial support from the National Science Foundation, to the effect that SMSG classes do just as well on standard tests of mathematical skills as do students taught conventional mathematics while, at the same time, exposing students to a number of concepts not available in conventional courses. But it doesn't solidly refute the anti-new math view, either—the SMSG's long-term evaluation due for release early this year should help clarify the matter for both camps.

These are the bones, then—or a few of them—from the international research project in school mathematics. To understand how they fit into the body of research affecting school curriculums and organization, a bit of the history of the project seems called for.

The story really begins in 1954. Researchers from many countries, meeting at UNESCO's Institute for Education in Hamburg and Office of Economic Cooperation and Development in Paris to compare problems in education, decided that little could be done without some common frame of reference. School structure and organi-

zation, selection processes, school starting age, and achievement differences were so varied between and even within countries that comparison was virtually impossible. Organized cross-cultural, cross national research would be needed, they agreed.

By 1959, twelve countries were ready to undertake a pilot study to see if such research could be carried out in a uniform way and in a meaningful context. The researchers, all heads of important research centers in their respective countries, determined from the outset that the project would be cooperative—each center to contribute fully at every stage of the work and share in all decisions.

The pilot study, "Educational Achievements of Thirteen Year Olds in Twelve Countries" (published as Foshay *et al.*, UNESCO Institute for Education, Hamburg, 1962), was deemed a success. Participants were confident they could get reliable and valid results on pupil achievement that would be applicable for use as an international yardstick. Accordingly, they decided to go ahead with the evaluation of a specific school subject. Mathematics was the area chosen.

The work began on the project itself. The heads of the research centers formed the Council of the International Project for the Evaluation of Educational Achievement (IEA), naming Professor Torsten Husen of Stockholm University as chairman and technical director and Britain's T. N. Postlethwaite as full-time coordinator.

"From the very first, the activities were a cooperative effort in the truest sense," says Howard Hjelm, director of OE's Research Branch. "It wasn't a case of one or two national centers doing the work and the rest passively collaborating."

Bloom amplifies:

The computation center of the University of Chicago carried out the data processing. England supplied an expert in sampling who became responsible for all the sampling plans. Belgium and Sweden supplied mathematics experts to help the test editors, who were drawn from research centers in England, France, and the United States. And special resources from each of the other countries were similarly drawn upon.

As a beginning, each center convened national panels of mathematicians and mathematics teachers to develop national papers. These "position papers" described the mathematics curriculum, objectives, methods of instruction, and the type of tests employed within the country.

Using these papers as a basis, an international panel then determined international specifications for mathematics achievement tests to be used. This process involved considerable liaison with national panels. The international specifications and tests were submitted to the national panels for criticism. Before final printing, the international test materials were tried out in at least five countries.

"One can only imagine the complicated administrative and technical problems the participants had to surmount," says Hjelm.

Researchers with different backgrounds in language and research methodology had to arrive at decisions concerning the advancement of hypotheses and definitions of target populations, uniform sampling procedures, the construction of internationally valid and applicable instruments, uniform coding procedures and data processing, and collective writing and editing.

Complicated and imposing as the process was, the necessary steps were taken in good order. Researchers administered the tests to approximately 130,000 students from over 5,000 schools in the participating countries. In addition to completing mathematics tests, students responded to a series of attitude statements and completed a questionnaire on background information about themselves.

Researchers also collected data about curriculums, the structure of the educational systems, the use of centralized examinations, local practices of selection and streaming, family backgrounds of individual students, and salient economic characteristics of the countries. Additionally, some 13,364 teachers and 5,348 head-teachers contributed data that the computers digested in calculating the "educational yield" of the countries.

Each country paid its national expenses, and a grant of $450,945 under the Cooperative Research Program took care of international costs as well as U.S. expenses.

The international dimension provided by the mathematics research project should benefit teachers, curriculum specialists, and administrators alike. For the first time, they have information from which to evaluate performance on a comparative basis. Literally dozens of correlations were made by the international research group and described in the two-volume report. Additionally, the information collected for the study will be stored in a Data Bank and accessible to researchers who wish to test other hypotheses.

Over and above these benefits, the research provides an important intangible bonus: evidence that educational problems of different countries can be investigated cooperatively, proof that cross-cultural, cross-national evaluation is feasible.

What Does the Secondary-School Teacher of Mathematics Expect from the University?

ANDRÉ DELESSERT

I. INTRODUCTION

For some years many people have been trying to make profound reforms in the teaching of elementary mathematics. The discussions, however, with rare exceptions, have dealt with philosophy, curricula, and textbooks. Such considerations remain strictly academic if we are not simultaneously concerned with the training of the teachers who are to bring about these recommended reforms. No reform in instruction can be realistic if it neglects or underestimates the importance of the teacher. Actually, it is almost impossible to estimate a priori in the abstract the effective value of a system of instruction, for at least two reasons:

1. No teaching plan, however bad, will

Reprinted from *The Mathematics Teacher*, LIX (March, 1966), 279–85, by permission of Howard Fehr and the National Council of Teachers of Mathematics. Copyright © 1966 by the National Council of Teachers of Mathematics. [Translated from the French by Dr. and Mrs. Julius H. Hlavaty; originally published in *L'Enseignement Mathematique* XI (October–December, 1965), 309–20.] André Delessert is Professor of Mathematics, University of Lausanne.
  The following text is based on notes of a talk delivered at the conference on "The Teaching of the Sciences and Economic Progress," held at Dakar, Senegal, January 14–22, 1965. This conference was organized jointly by the Inter-Union Commission on Science Instruction (ICSI) and the International Commission on Mathematics Instruction (ICMI). (The activity of the latter group is concerned essentially with the training of teachers.)

prevent a good teacher from sharing his enthusiasm, nor an intelligent and curious pupil from learning some good mathematics. (Today's great mathematicians were trained under principles and curricula which many of them condemn every day.) On the other hand, despite the best books and the most ingenious methods, the teacher who lacks enthusiasm and a solid foundation in his subject matter will provide instruction that is dull and wearisome and that never reaches most of his pupils.

2. Experiments in the reform of mathematics teaching all succeed, systematically. This is a result of the shared enthusiasm of teacher and pupils who experience together a unique adventure, with the feeling of being in the forefront of progress. Today "experiment" has come to mean a final realization for which the printing of the textbook has been provisionally delayed to permit minor corrections.

If, however, instead of limiting our attention to the few teachers engaged in research on teaching, we turn to the whole teaching staff, we become aware of the great problem of training teachers. This problem can be seen from four angles:

1. *The social aspect:* the role of the school in society; the role of the teacher in school, in life, etc.
2. *The psychological aspect:* a knowledge of oneself, of children, of adults
3. *The cultural aspect:* the place of mathematics in a harmonious education; the personal culture of the teacher who, in

the eyes of his students, must not be a barbarian with one specialty

4. *The technical aspect:* on the one hand, the acquisition of strictly mathematical knowledges and skills; on the other, a paramethematical background including the history of mathematics, philosophic problems raised by mathematics, the psychology of the mathematician, the role and significance of mathematics

Although these aspects are closely related, we shall here limit ourselves to the first part of (4), namely, the strictly technical training of the mathematician teacher.

II. A BRIEF DESCRIPTION OF THE MATHEMATICAL STRUCTURE

For clarity, it may be useful to show graphically the mathematical structure with the hope—or the fear—of finding there a natural division which would permit assigning, without possibility of error, such-and-such a section to secondary school mathematics, and such and such other sections to the university level. Placing oneself at two distinct points of observation, one can set forth what we shall call the "natural ladder" and the "domain of structures." In the interest of prudence, we shall provide a "residue" in which to place those topics in which the mathematician may take an interest, but which are difficult to place, even indirectly, in the two principal charts.

In this diagram (Chart A) we find:

N: set of natural whole numbers (0, 1, 2, 3, . . .)

Z: set of integers (0, 1, -1, 2, -2, . . . , n, $-n$)

Z_n: set of classes of rational whole numbers (modulo n)

Q: set of rational numbers

$Z/_{(10^m)}$: set of rational numbers which can be represented by limited decimal expansion (or the ring of the fractions of Z with respect to the subset of Z formed by the numbers of the form 10^m, where m is in Z.)

R: set of real numbers

E_2: continuous Euclidean plane

E_3: continuous "ordinary" Euclidean space

$GE(2, R)$: set of isometries of E_2

$GE(3, R)$: set of isometries of E_3

C: set of complex numbers

$R[x]$: set of polynomials in one variable x, with real coefficients

$R[x,y]$: set of polynomials in two variables x and y, with real coefficients

R^n: set of sequences of n real numbers, $n = 2, 3, \ldots$

S^{n-1}: real sphere of dimension $n - 1$

P_{n-1}: real projective space of dimension $n - 1$

$GL(n, R)$: complete real linear group of degree n

Var $_{R^n}$: class of real varieties of degree n

G. Lie: class of Lie groups

E. funct.: class of sets of functions with real values, defined on non-empty subsets of R

Distr.: class of distributions

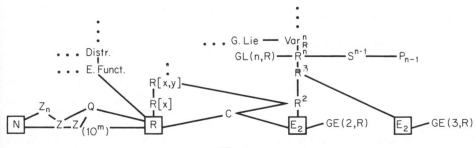

Chart A

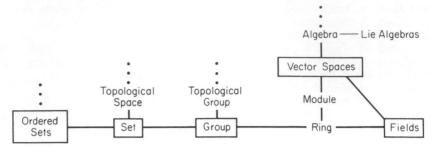

Chart B

C. Residue

1. Ideas and questions of logic.
2. Study of foundations.
3. Problems at present not classifiable (as, for example, this one: Is there a digit which appears only a finite number of times in the decimal expansion of the number π?), etc.

It is well to emphasize that diagrams A and B are merely sketched out. Besides, even if one takes no account of the residual part, C, the union of A and B does not give a complete idea of the mathematical structure. Thus, for example, the notion of metric space (provided with a real distance function) appears in neither. In the domain of structures, it is best to imagine distance in connection with topological spaces. But elsewhere this notion borrows some of its properties from R and in that respect relates to the natural ladder. One might say that diagrams A and B are like complementary projections of the mathematical structure, or if one prefers, that the latter results from the product of diagrams A and B.

III. OBSERVATIONS CONCERNING DIAGRAMS A AND B

1. Diagrams A and B are not essentially independent

Acutually, the links appearing in diagram A symbolize canonical procedures of construction elaborated in the domain of the structures. Reciprocally, a structure appears in B only when it possesses a sufficient number of interesting models in the natural ladder. In this connection, it is appropriate to repeat that there is only a very small number of mathematical notions which are not prefigured in N, R, E_2 or E_3 and the objects which relate to them directly.

2. Diagrams A and B are both monolithic

Let us pass quickly over a "vertical" division like that which consists in distinguishing between algebraic properties and topological properties. It presents an obvious methodological interest, but it does not correspond to a natural division of the mathematical structure. For example, topology makes wide use of algebra, and no algebraist would forego the services of Zariski's topology.

What we seek here is vertical division permitting us to distinguish between elementary mathematics and advanced mathematics. Actually, we must admit that such a split does not appear naturally. Certainly one may note the existence of simple or fundamental notions (set, topological space, R, etc.) and compound or derived notions (vector space, topological group, $Z/10^m$, etc.). But many of the fundamental notions are not elementary, and many of the elementary notions are not simple.

Thus, properly speaking, it appears that there is no "elementary mathematics." Nevertheless, to avoid any misunderstanding, it is important to emphasize an essential point. The mentality of the trained mathematician differs from that of the beginner.[1] Unlike the former, the latter must anchor *visibly*, in the natural ladder, the theory he is studying. For the beginner, for example, *every existence proof must be accompanied by an algorithm of construction*. And it is comforting to think that, faced with a sufficiently novel problem, the professional mathematician often behaves like a beginner. In brief, there certainly exists an elementary approach to, and an advanced study of, mathematics, but this distinction does not reflect a natural partition of the mathematical structure.

3. The ideas in frames (see diagrams) are fundamental.

Actually, either they are in constant use in the building of mathematics (R, topological spaces, etc.), or they appear in all the practical applications (N, R, E_2, etc.), or else they provide vivid terminologies and archetypes in view of more advanced theories (N, R, E_2, E_3) as has already been pointed out in III, 1.

It is remarkable that, eventually, setting aside topological spaces, all these notions are treated at the level of the secondary school, in the course of the ordinary complete curriculum.

In recapitulation, let us say that:

1. If one can imagine an elementary mathematics instruction, then there is no mathematics suitable to secondary school.
2. The role of the secondary school in mathematical education is essential.
3. As a consequence, it is necessary to root out the prejudice that a mathematics teacher is a mathematician who has gone bad.

IV. GENERAL DEMANDS ON THE UNIVERSITY BY THE SECONDARY SCHOOL

Until now the dialogue between the university and the secondary school has been poorly handled. Let us try a metaphor. Mathematical education consists in building in the mind of each pupil a proper model of the mathematical structure. As in every construction, there are temporary parts—scaffoldings—and permanent parts. On the part of the university, the scaffoldings have been generally underestimated; on the part of the secondary school, it has often been foregotten that the scaffoldings must one day disappear, to the advantage of the ultimate structure.

Certain great mathematicians, writing for secondary education, have abandoned themselves to the virtuosity with which they can imagine subtle questions arising from elementary situations. One might think they were trying to attract secondary school teachers by proving to them that today's mathematics has at least as many sadistic brain-twisters as ancient mathematics.

In the world of secondary mathematics, too often the area of sensible teaching has been abandoned in favor of a "pedagogical" attitude, in the worst sense of the word. We mean this: The proper approach consists in determining first the mathematical subjects for study, then finding the appropriate teaching techniques; the "pedagogue," on the contrary, elaborately works out first some more or less clever methods,

---

[1] In this connection, let us quote the remark which M. P. Freyd places in the introduction of his *Abelian Categories* (New York: Harper & Row, 1964), "If topology were publicly defined as the study of sets closed under finite intersection and infinite unions a serious disservice would be perpetrated on embryonic students of topology. The mathematical correctness of such a definition reveals nothing about topology except that its basic axioms can be made quite simple."

and then wonders what he will be able to teach with them; thus he manufactures some pseudomathematics the only merit of which is that it lends itself willingly to preconceived mathematical procedures.

In short, both the university and the secondary school have often forgotten that they are yoked to the same plow.

With a strong interest and clear good will, secondary school teachers are ready to accept from the university a clear description of the mathematical structure. It would be well to present it to them for example in more detailed form—as in diagrams A and B of which we have spoken—and to define the role and the importance of those parts of the diagrams which concern them directly. In a general way, the following questions might appear:

1. Among the ideas dealt with on the secondary level, which are those used by mathematicians and the users of mathematics? Where? In what form?

Thus the teacher will be better prepared to judge the relative importance which he should assign to each topic.

2. What are the natural generalizations of the topics seen in the secondary school?

The answer to this question permits the choice of elementary expositions which lend themselves to such generalizations.

3. In the mathematics dealt with in the secondary school, what are the *internal connections* which are seen in the light of higher-level mathematics?

For example, the theory of the classical groups, the theory of groups, and Lie algebras make it possible to clarify Euclidean geometry.

4. What are the present-day trends in mathematics?

Thirty years ago, one could state that mathematics was being reorganized around the theory of sets and the idea of structure. It is unfortunate that secondary education has taken so long to come to grips with these new forms of thought. Otherwise we could have avoided transforming into a revolution what should have been a normal evolution. Today the ideas of category and of morphism are probably about to influence the mathematics education of tomorrow.

V. THE NECESSARY INSTITUTIONS

Let us point out right now that it does not seem desirable to create a complete mathematics curriculum specifically designed for future teachers. Actually, since the *Faculté des Sciences*[2] is not in principle a professional school, there would be the risk that the mathematical education of the teaching corps would be entrusted sooner or later to autonomous institutes of mathematical pedagogy. Among mathematicians, there would thus be reintroduced, in an aggravated state, a division which, as we have seen, does not correspond to the nature of things. It is, moreover, a good idea to facilitate contacts among future teachers, future researchers, and future users of mathematics.

On the other hand, in the framework of a normal mathematical education provided by the university, and in other areas where the curriculum designed for teachers does not yet exist, it would be well to plan seriously the following measures:

1. In the courses in mathematics
   a. Increase the number of examples of applications to elementary problems.
   b. Indicate systematically the elementary situations which serve as

[2]The *Faculté des Sciences* in Europe is similar to a Faculty of Pure Science (e.g., Mathematics) in the American university.

points of departure for advanced generalizations.

Mathematicians have often been reproached for their secretiveness and the coyness with which they conceal the sometimes ingenious models that serve as their guides in the elaboration of very subtle theories. We suggest to them here that they give up these characteristics, at least in courses of general interest.

2. To create a course on "elementary questions in mathematics seen from an advanced viewpoint"

The subject matter for such a course is not lacking—it is enough to think of the contributions of Klein, Hilbert, Lebesgue, Choquet, Dieudonné, Artin, Polya and many others.

3. To create a course on "mathematical techniques of users of mathematics"

Among these users, we must count mathematicians themselves, physicists, chemists, engineers, biologists, statisticians, architects, musicians, etc.

For instance, it might be useful to know that, despite appearances, there is a certain relationship between the ideas evoked by the word "tensor" in the mind of a mathematician and that of a physicist.

4. To create a seminar for the teaching of mathematics

In rotation, there would be studied, in depth, elementary questions of mathematics following this plan:

a. Mathematical exposition.
b. Different elementary presentations possible; comparisons.
c. Difficulties of essential order of presentation.
d. Exercises with a real interest for the question being dealt with, or its extension...

Let us take a concise example. Let us suppose that it is a question of presenting the set $R[x, y]$ of polynomials with real coefficients, and with two variables, x and y. One would examine successively:

a. The graduated symmetric algebra $\zeta(R^2)$ on vector space R^2
b. Some classic presentations of $R[x, y]$ without forgetting the following sequence: the algebra $R[x]$ of polynomials in x with real coefficients; the ring $Z[x]$ considered as a Z module; polynomials in x with rational whole-number coefficients; the ring $(R[y])$ $[x]$ considered as $R[y]$-module.
c. The possible confusion between the notions of "polynomials in 2 variables" and "polynomial functions with 2 variables" which find their source in the isomorphism of $\zeta(R^2)$ and $\zeta((R^2)^*)$ where $(R^2)^*$ is the dual of R^2.
d. Besides the classic exercises based on the use of operations existing in algebra $R[x, y]$, the formal composition of polynomials, diverse derivations, the permutation of x and y, linear substitutions bearing on x and y, etc.

5. To create courses and supplementary seminars for in service teachers

More precisely:

a. To devote periodically, once a semester or once a year, one week to university courses on the subject-matter mentioned under the headings 1, 2, 3, and 4. The theoretic expositions would necessarily be accompanied by exercise-sessions. Let us point out that there is already such an institution, in Holland, for example.
b. To organize, in every secondary school district, a weekly or semi-monthly seminar in which all who teach mathematics would participate. The university would have charge of the technical part: editing of texts, preparation and correction of problems. In each interested insti-

tution, a responsible teacher would attend to the liaison with the university of the area. (An arrangement similar to this now exists, in the canton of Vaud, centered in the University of Lausanne.)

These proposals have two aims: to make it immoral for a teacher to be able to stop studying mathematics, after he has his degree, and to oblige the administration to provide time and money for the continuing education of in-service teachers.

6. To create, at each university, a joint council of university and secondary school personnel for the accomplishment of tasks 1 through 5

The existence of such an institution is self-justifying. But, in addition, it would provide reciprocity of information which would dissolve many misunderstandings.

VI. CONCLUSION

The continuing education of teachers is necessary for the continuing development of mathematics instruction. To fail to provide it is deliberately to choose the régime of periodic revolution with which we are familiar: Every twenty or thirty years, there will be an uncertain war between the "old school" and the supporters of the "new movement," a battle during which several groups of students will be reduced to the role of guinea pigs.

Morevoer, when we neglect the continuous adaptation of the teaching corps to its task, we find it necessary to "condition" teachers and pupils simultaneously to the "modern" ideas. Instead of planning curricula sufficiently flexible so that the properly informed teacher can harmoniously develop his own abilities, we end up by elaborating systems of an exacerbated dogmatism. The more variations possible, the more divisions are conceivable. Whatever is not forbidden is obligatory. Many of the doctrines proposed today are strikingly inflexible and intolerant, and they cause feelings of isolation and frustration among the teachers who are their victims.

I have tried, primarily, to show that it is in the nature of things that the university and the secondary school share the responsibility for mathematics teaching, and for the continuing training of teachers. I have then sketched out an organization, a plan, which will permit the accomplishment of these important tasks.

What Can the Classroom Teacher Do about Evaluation?

DONOVAN A. JOHNSON

One of the continuous activities which we face as classroom teachers is the evaluation of the achievement of our students. It is a time-consuming activity which may frequently be tedious as we work out our test questions, score papers, record marks, and make out grades. It is frequently a discouraging task when we find out how little our students have apparently learned from our carefully planned instruction. But it is an important, reoccurring task which is becoming increasingly important when we are committed to having each of our pupils achieve to the maximum of his potential. And with the current need for developing our intellectual resources to a maximum it becomes an essential activity for every mathematics teacher.

The evaluation of achievement in mathematics is important because it plays many roles in the classroom. One of the most important of these is the improvement of instruction. It is through evaluation activities that you locate your present status and measure the progress you make in the direction you wish to go. It is evaluation which will determine the effectiveness of the techniques, materials, or content you are teaching. Thus, it is the basis for selecting topics and methods of teaching these topics.

Another major function of evaluation is its potential for improving the progress of individual students. We need to use tests to determine the readiness for instruction, to diagnose weaknesses and strengths, to locate difficulties and faulty mental processes. Remedial instruction is then planned to fit the needs of individual students. The measures of mathematical aptitude and achievement can then be used to guide the student into courses and vocations suited to his aptitude.

With the current ferment involving the mathematics curriculum and the criticism of education, evaluation can furnish data to answer questions being asked. Test results furnish data on which to render judgment as to the quality of a particular mathematics program. The need for accurate, extensive data for research projects now and in the future should stimulate us to collect as much data as possible about our students. The increasing standards for admission to colleges and employment further emphasize the need for accurate records of the potential and the actual achievement of our students.

Of course evaluation activities in themselves are of value to the student participating in them. Competition with one's own record, the class record, or national norms can be a stimulating experience, at least for the successful student. Completing a test is an intense learning experience in itself. Discussing

Reprinted from *The Bulletin of the National Association of Secondary School Principals*, XLIII, No. 247 (May, 1959), 154–61, by permission of the author and the publisher. Donovan Johnson is Professor of Education, University High School, University of Minnesota, St. Paul.

and correcting errors on a test help to locate errors, misunderstandings, and wrong procedures as well as to reinforce correct learnings.

A basic consideration for us to have in mind in evaluating our students is the goals of our instruction. We must be clear as to what our goals are so that we can measure the progress we have made toward attaining these goals. This means that we need to measure in terms of *all* our goals. In general it is easy to measure the progress or growth of our students in building computational skills or in learning facts and rules. As we do this however, we need to be reminded of the importance of measuring understanding as well as accuracy and efficiency. But evaluation of achievement in mathematics must be more than measuring skills and knowledge. If we accept goals such as attitudes and appreciations, we need to measure our students' status relative to these goals.

If we are teaching how to study mathematics or how to read mathematics, we should test our students' progress in learning these skills. If we are attempting to teach how to apply mathematical learning to new situations, we need to devise tests of this ability. If we are building skill in thinking logically and critically in non-mathematical situations as well as mathematical ones, we will need to build test situations or items in which the student can exhibit his ability to do thse things. Thus, it is apparent that we shall need to use a variety of evaluation instruments in our classrooms. In the way of tests and examinations it means not only the typical test with computational problems, but also reading tests, vocabulary tests, open-book tests, take-home tests, performance tests, attitude tests, and tests of logical analysis or problem solving. We shall need to use a variety of test items similar to the following:

The meaning of a process

1. In the problem 54×23, what is the mathematical explanation of the reason we write the 8 under the 6?
   A. We write the product under the multiplier.
   B. We write the product in the ten's place because the multiplier is a ten.
   C. We move over one place when multiplying by the second figure.
   D. We are using a short cut that works.

$$\begin{array}{r} 54 \\ 23 \\ \hline 162 \\ 108 \\ \hline 1242 \end{array}$$

2. The multiplication of 24 by $3\frac{1}{2}$ is the same as 24 multiplied by 3.5. Why do we not indent the partial product 72 in the second example as is done in the first example?

$$\begin{array}{r} 24 \\ 3.5 \\ \hline 120 \\ 72 \\ \hline 84.0 \end{array} \qquad \begin{array}{r} 24 \\ 3\frac{1}{2} \\ \hline 12 \\ 72 \\ \hline 84 \end{array}$$

   A. The multiplier 3 has a different place value in each example.
   B. The multiplier .5 and $\frac{1}{2}$ are not equivalent.

C. The fraction $\frac{1}{2}$ does not have place value.
D. The multiplier 3 and $\frac{1}{2}$ have the same place value.

The meaning of numbers

1. In the number 842, the 8 has a value that is
   A. twice the value of the 4
   B. four times the value of the 2
   C. twenty times the value of the 4
   D. forty times the value of the 2
   E. two hundred times the value of the 4
2. A fraction with a large denominator may be larger than a fraction with a small denominator.

Visualizing a proccess

1. The line given for each example below is $2\frac{1}{2}$ inches long. Show how you can get the answers to these examples by dividing the lines into fractional parts. Label your diagram, so that the process is explained.

   A. $1\frac{1}{4} + 1\frac{1}{4} = 2\frac{1}{2}$

   B. $2\frac{1}{2} - \frac{3}{4} = 1\frac{3}{4}$

   C. $\frac{1}{2} \times 5 = 2\frac{1}{2}$

   D. $2\frac{1}{2} \div \frac{1}{4} = 10$

2. The line given for each example below is 10 centimeters long. Divide the line into fractional parts and label your diagram to show the meaning of the answers to these examples

   A. $.4 + .5 = .9$

   B. $.75 - .20 = .55$

   C. $.8 \div .2 = 4$

   D. $.2 \times 3 = .6$

3. Label the four parts of this rectangle to show the partial products of $(x + 2)(x + 3)$

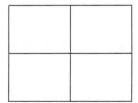

Performance test

1. Materials: Irregularly shaped paper; carpenter's square; compass; ruler; shears.

   Station No. 1—At this station you are given irregularly shaped pieces of paper and several devices to aid you in performing the required tasks.

_____1. Construct a triangle containing two 45 degree angles by folding a piece of paper.

_____2. Construct a 30–60 degree right triangle by folding.

_____3. Fold and cut a scalene triangle. Locate the three altitudes of the triangle by folding.

2. Materials: Container of damp sand-cement mixture; home-made height gauge; graph paper—5 sqs. to an inch.

Station No. 2—The sand-cement mixture has been poured in the shape of a cone on the graph paper. The graph paper has been marked off in inches.

_____1. Assuming the base of the pile to be circular, what is the area of the base?

$$(A) \ A = \frac{169''}{16} \quad (B) \ 36'' \quad (C) \ \frac{169''}{4} \quad (D) \ 9''$$

_____2. What is the height of the pile?

_____3. The formula for finding the volume of a cone is $V = \frac{1}{3}\pi r^2 h$. What is the volume of this cone?

Finding information—Select the answer for each of the following items, that is the best source of the information needed.

1. The best place to find page references about a specific topic in a textbook is to look for the topic in the
   A. Preface   B. Table of Contents   C. Chapter Summaries   D. Index
2. You are unable to recall the name of the author of the book *Makers of Mathematics*. Where would you look to find whether this book is in your school library?
   A. in the *Readers Guide to Periodical Literature*.
   B. in the card catalog under *Makers*
   C. in the card catalog under *Mathematics*
   D. among the books in the "M" shelves of the library.
3. In which could you find the most data concerning the athletic contests in the United States during the last decade?
   A. A World Almanac
   B. A geography textbook
   C. An encyclopedia
   D. A world atlas

Applications and interpretations

1. In which one of the following schools does the largest proportion of the pupils have bicycles?
   A. 80 bicycles for 240 pupils.
   B. 24 bicycles for 96 pupils.
   C. 120 bicycles for 540 pupils.
   D. 6 bicycles for 15 pupils.
   E. 18 bicycles for 63 pupils.
2. Which one of these is the best buy?
   A. 12 for $1.00
   B. 10¢ each

C. 5 for 38¢
D. 7 for 55¢

3. Which of the figures shown below is an exception to the statement: If the diagonals of a quadrilateral are equal, it is a parallelogram.

Mathematics reading test

A number that has been of great interest to mathematicians is a prime number. A whole number greater than one is called a prime number if it can be divided evenly only by itself and one. The smallest prime numbers are 2, 3, 5, 7, 11, 13, etc. The number 1 might be considered prime, but this is not the custom. To do so would force us to state exceptions to many statements about prime numbers. For this reason 2 is considered the smallest prime number. Information about prime numbers is important because they are the building blocks of all numbers. Many statements in the study of numbers are based on whether or not a number is prime. More than 2,000 years ago, Euclid, who is most famous for his book on geometry, proved that the number of primes is infinite.

Another interesting group of numbers has been named perfect numbers. These numbers are the whole numbers which are exactly equal to the sum of all their divisors except themselves. The smallest perfect number is 6 for the divisors of 6 are 1, 2, 3, and $6 = 1 + 2 + 3$. Some numbers, such as 10, have divisors that add to less than themselves. $5 + 2 + 1 = 8$. These integers are called "deficient" numbers. Some numbers, like 12, are called "excess" numbers because the sum of the divisors is more than themselves.

1. Which one of the following is a prime number?
    A. 51
    B. 55
    C. 57
    D. 59
2. The number of even primes is
    A. infinite
    B. unknown
    C. equal to the number of odd primes
    D. one
3. Which one of the following statements is true?
    A. The decimal .6 is a perfect number since $.1 + .2 + .3 = .6$
    B. The decimal .5 is a prime number.
    C. The number 36 is an excess number.
    D. The smallest prime number is 1.

Methods of reasoning

Directions: In each answer space, write the letter of the method of reasoning that is there illustrated. Any letter may be used as often as it is needed.
(a) stating a generalization by examining particular cases (b) reasoning from a general statement to a particular case (c) arranging a proof in orderly fashion (d) analysis (e) method of analogy (f) indirect method (g) none of these

_____1. If a girl can sew, she will save money on clothes. Mary can sew. Therefore, Mary will save money on clothes.

_____2. When a mechanic attempts to determine why a car will not start, he may begin by checking in order, the spark plugs, wiring, battery, and continuing in this way until he locates the trouble

_____3. I can prove that two arcs of a circle are equal, if I can prove that the chords are equal. Each cord is 5 inches from the center of the circle. Therefore, I can prove that the two arcs are equal.

_____4. A robin has feathers; a sparrow has feathers; an oriole has feathers, and many other birds have feathers. Thus one might conclude that all birds may have feathers.

Relationships in problems

From the problem, table, and diagram, decide which of the following equations are true. Mark the true statements below with a plus the false with a zero and the unknown with a question mark.

A. "Two friends, Bill and Joe, live in towns M miles apart. Deciding to meet at the earliest possible time, they leave their own homes at the same time and drive toward each other. Bill travels b miles per hour and Joe travels y miles per hour. How long will it take them to meet?"

	Distance	Rate	Time
Bill	a	b	c
Joe	x	y	z

Bill $\longrightarrow$ $\longleftarrow$ Joe

1. $ab = c$ 4. $a = x$ 7. $a + x = bc + yz$
2. $a + b = c$ 5. $b = y$ 8. $a + x = M$
3. $x = yz$ 6. $c = z$ 9. $ax = M$

B. "When a golf ball is thrown to a height of 24 feet it rebounds one fourth the height from which it fell. How far has the ball traveled when it strikes the sixth time?"

_____1. This will be a geometric progression.

_____2. The first term is 24.

_____3. It is impossible for a golf ball to rebound this much.

_____4. $n = 5$

_____5. $d = \frac{1}{4}$

_____6. The distance the ball travels is found by finding the last term of a progression.

_____7. The ball travels about 40 feet.

Of course the evaluation of all of our objectives cannot be done by tests alone. Work habits, curiosity, creativeness, communication skills will need to be evaluated with so-called non-testing appraisal instruments. These include such devices as questionnaires, checklists, progress charts, rating scales, interviews, and diaries. In addition, there are completed student products such as assignments, projects, and reports to be examined and rated. Here one must consider communication skill, craftmanship, organization, and creativeness in judging the quality of the product. There are the daily observations of classroom performance to record and evaluate. However, we need to be careful to distinguish between learning activities and evaluation activities. Most assignments should be for the purpose of promoting learning rather than for the purpose of establishing a mark. An assignment is worth while because of the learning it promotes, not as a means of getting a grade.

Besides teacher-made appraisal instruments, we need to capitalize on the wealth of available published evaluation materials. These tests are constructed by experts, are based on extensive experimentation, and have established norms. These published tests include tests such as prognostic tests, diagnostic tests, unit tests, and long-range achievement tests. Some of them emphasize the manipulative aspects of mathematics but some of them emphasize interpretive items or application situations. Some of them can be used to measure year-to-year progress in mathematics, while others measure achievement in specific topics or subjects. Published tests usually furnish norms such as grade equivalents or percentile ranks or standard scores. These norms can be very useful if interpreted intelligently in terms of the sample on which the norms are based. To be "up" to the norm also means that you are "down" to the norm. The norms may be unsatisfactory as a standard or measure of a class because the class may be very different in aptitude than the norm sample.

Thus, measurement in the mathematics classroom is a highly technical task for which we need adequate materials and original ideas. It becomes a highly satisfying experience for the learner and the teacher when it is done in an accurate and comprehensive manner.

A Time for Testing

PETER K. GURAU

I like the teaching profession. I enjoy my students, my subject, and the general atmosphere. My work gives me a sense of accomplishment.

Until it comes to grading tests. Then, all of a sudden, I don't have the vaguest idea of what I am doing. Please don't misunderstand me. I can hand out

Reprinted from *The Mathematics Teacher*, LX (February, 1967), 133–36, by permission of the author and the National Council of Teachers of Mathematics. Copyright © 1967 by the National Council of Teachers of Mathematics. Peter K. Gurau is Assistant Professor of Education, Springfield College, Springfield, Massachusetts.

grades with the best of them. I do it regularly. The trouble is that I always get a creepy feeling running down my spine when I am grading test papers— I know that the grades are meaningless.

There was a time, early in my teaching, when I felt that if I could only make a study of evaluation, and revamp the entire system, I could bring some order out of the chaos. Then, for a time, I got furious at some students for being so appallingly stupid, thick, lazy, careless, and obtuse. Indeed, in weaker moments, especially when I am tired, this feeling recurs.

But such feelings do not solve problems. The only thing to do was to seek improvements.

First came the matter of how much each question on a given test should be worth. Originally, I adhered to the philosophy that the harder a problem is, the more credit it should carry. The results were usually catastrophic. The good students did very well, while the slow students did appallingly badly. So I switched to a different system. I gave each question the same value, regardless of how easy or difficult it was. Now the slow student picked up slightly, since he got more credit for the easy questions, which he answered correctly. However. I still had many failures, and more modifications seemed in order.

Hence I adopted a system whereby the slow student could, in principle, answer 70 per cent of the questions, if he studied. Besides, 15 per cent more were geared for the student of average ability, and the last 15 per cent aimed to challenge the best students. Naturally the mathematical purist in me cringed, but he found consolation in hoping that the slow student would be weeded out of the mathematical curriculum in short order.

Of course, implicit in these "humanitarian" efforts on my part were some unusual assumptions: Firstly, I could decide which questions a slow student could answer in principle. Secondly, I could create a test that covered the ground and at the same time would break down into the 70–15–15 division. Thirdly, I could categorize my students and actually precondemn them to a given grade.

Of course, my students did not always live up to my expectations. Indeed, in some cases, they did not live down to them! Yet, for better or worse, I had at least found a format with which I could balance those ambivalent feelings that always crop up at test-grading time.

I had thus sought refuge in a highly involved system of marking. Before I began to check the papers, I usually figured out how much I would take off for each type of error. The trouble with this system, however, was that students are so highly imaginative that they always managed to come up with new errors that I could not have thought of in my wildest dreams!

A second device I have resorted to is to hide the names of the students from myself, so there can be no possibility of my prejudices' having some effect upon the number of points I take off. I have noticed that if a bright student makes a mistake, I am likely to say, "Oh, how careless of him! But at least he knows the work. I'll take one point off." On the other hand, if one of the more obtuse or lazy members of the class makes similar mistakes I am inclined to say, "There he goes again! He simply has to learn! I'll teach him a lesson. Five points off." Who hasn't reacted in this way at some point?

So, with the names hidden, I began the grading process. But despite my best efforts, the slower, lazier, less capable members of the class identified themselves by an excess of incorrect answers. Aside from recognizing their handwriting, I recognized their patterns of work. My system of hiding the student's identity from myself went down the drain.

HOW MUCH OFF?

Thus I was left with only a chart beside me, telling me how much to take off for each type of error. Each question was now worth the same number of credits, regardless of its difficulty.

But soon the pupils wreaked havoc with my carefully worked out system. Here are some results for the test item

"Factor, completely, $16a^4 - 16a^2$":

$$16a^4 - 16a^2 = \\ (4a^2 + 4a)(4a^2 - 4a). \quad (1)$$

This was not factored completely, so I take off two points.

$$16a^4 - 16a^2 = 4a^2(4a^2 - 4). \quad (2)$$

Is the answer worse? Should I take off three points?

$$16a^4 - 16a^2 = \\ 16(a^2 + a)(a^2 - a). \quad (3)$$

Here, our hero did not recognize the GCF of $16a^2$ But he did do both distributive factoring *and* conjugate factoring. Should it be three points off, or should it be two and one-half? At least, so far we haven't run across any mistakes in factoring.

$$16a^4 - 16a^2 = 8a^2(2a^2 - 2a) \\ = 16a^2(a^2 - a)16a^2[a(a - 1)]. \quad (4)$$

This one I was totally unprepared for. Here was an error in distributive factoring. Take off full credit? Or four points?

$$16a^4 - 16a^2 = \\ 2a2a2a2a - 2 \cdot 2 \cdot aa \cdot 2 \cdot 2. \quad (5)$$

Now we know that this is incorrect. Our student should know that in factoring an algebraic expression, he must give it a principal operator of multiplication. Full credit off?

$$16a^4 - 16a^2 = (2a^2 - 2a)(8a^2 + 8a) \\ = (2a + 2a)(a - a)8a(a + 1). \quad (6)$$

Imaginative enough? Now that first step certainly shows that he knows how to factor. Four off? Five?

$$16a^4 - 16a^2 = 16[(a^2)^2 - (a^2)] \\ = (a^2 - a)(a^2 - a). \quad (7)$$

I was caught napping again. I wasn't prepared for this one. Good student, though. Oh, I forgot, that isn't supposed to matter. Four off? No credit at all?

$$16a^4 - 16a^2 = 4(4a^4 - 4a^2) \\ = 4(2a^2 2a)(2a^2 2a). \quad (8)$$

What do you say? Let's just take five off and forget the whole thing! I'm getting tired, and this is only the first question.

$$16a^4 - 16a^2 = 16(a^4 - a^2) \\ = 16(a \quad)(\quad). \quad (9)$$

Now if he hadn't written that last part, I could give him a little credit for some distributive factoring. Four off?

I could go on with this. But you have the idea. How do *you* handle this sort of thing? Right or wrong only? Part credit, with lots of little notes to explain the whole thing? Now please don't tell me that one point more or less is not important. With twenty problems, that could add up to twenty points.

Let's get to the heart of the matter. What should we do? Extra help sessions? Of course. More drill? Certainly. But this is only one class, and most of us have five classes to teach. There just aren't enough hours after school to take care of all the problems.

A BETTER SYSTEM

Suppose we look for a different solution. Quite possibly this is not the only way, nor the best way, of educating youngsters. Indeed, there *is* a better system. Better for the teacher, and far superior for helping the student to understand.

But we may have to scrap much of the system of education as we now know it. Let us get some good programmed texts. We can start by testing our students at the beginning of the semester, and finding out what they *do not know*. Then we can send them to that portion of the programmed materials where their understanding stopped. Each one may, of course, be in a different place, but that is not bad. Instead of preparing today's lesson, we now begin to answer questions as they arise. And when a student is finished with a section of the programmed text, he takes an achievement test.

If he has any questions about the problems on the achievement test, he simply brings them up and asks. Right in the middle of the test! And we explain them to him. Obviously, the best time to explain something to a student is when he wants to know, and when he needs to know. And what better time to help a student than during a test?

Of course, that terminates the test. Instead of letting him go on, we now send him back to his seat with some previously prepared drill problems and let him practice. After he completes the drill work, he continues with the achievement test. Then he and we mark the achievement test *together*, and we explain his mistakes to him at the time of the grading. And for each mistake, we immediately assign him some more work which has been prepared just for this occasion.

Now, what about his grade? Well, now we can afford to be strict again. Only completely correct answers can be accepted, and the passing mark is now 85 per cent.

Of course, the student can take an achievement test on this section as many times as he needs to pass it, because these are several different versions prepared for just such an occasion. The student doesn't have to be nervous about failing a test any more. He is just slowed down until he can finally pass the test. But at least we know that he will have mastered the materials before going on to the next steps.

Now our bright students can go as fast as they like, without being held up by the slowpokes. In addition, all papers are marked immediately after the student finishes them. That way, the student still has the material fresh in his mind. We don't have to take home a lot of papers to mark. We don't have to write endless notes on the tests. We don't have to quibble with students about grades any more.

DOES IT WORK?

Now there must be readers who are shaking their heads and saying: "It won't work."

But it does. I have been working with such materials, and the fact is that the students are doing better. They get more individual attention. They do more mathematics, because they aren't sitting around 70 percent of the time listening to me. They are actually working on mathematics. And, automatically, each student gets the amount of drill he individually needs. The fast students who can catch on the first time get relatively little drill, while the slower student may go through the process three or four times before he catches on. In addition, I apportion my time in relation to the individual's needs.

True, a lot of work still has to be done to prepare the necessary materials, but that isn't unreasonable. What we need is plenty of testing devices, and plenty of drill materials especially coordinated to these tests. And, of course a good programmed text.

Admittedly, I am a very busy teacher during the class period. But I get to know the students better, and I can help them individually. Also, I don't have to be King Solomon every time I have to grade tests. And the bright ones, the sharp mathematicians, are now able to finish a year's work in half a year or less!

By contrast, in the conventional system I wasn't at all sure about what the test-grade numbers meant. All I knew at the end of a conventional test was that there were still many students who didn't know what I *thought* I had taught. For a while I even sought a bell-shaped curve. If I could get the class to behave as predicted by some statistical norm, wouldn't that suffice? Of course, if I did not have a normally distributed class then it would have taken an unusual test to make a normal distribution.

Now, with this new method of conducting my classroom, I don't worry about grades any more. Nor do my students. Consequently, they can expend their energies learning and understanding instead of seeking to impress me. Better still, I am now a person who can be turned to for help and information.

The meaning of grades has constantly eluded me. What was it I was quantifying "scientifically"? Carelessness? Intelligence? Maturity? The ability to function under pressure?

No! The only thing I was really quantifying was achievement, and it seems that if the achievement of an individual is not up to our expectation, we have no right to proceed with further courses.

Accordingly, there will always be a time for testing. But why do we stick to an archaic system of education when, close at hand, we have a newer and more humane system, ready to do a superior job?

3
Curriculum

Historically, curricular changes in school mathematics in this country have occurred very slowly. In fact, it has been stated that the changes in high school geometry have been so minor that Euclid would have been at home in most classes until recently. Because the curricular metamorphosis has developed slowly, changes in textbooks and other instructional materials have also been gradual. Therefore, teachers of mathematics have simply taught from one of the few books which were available, with the result that students throughout the country experienced little variation in mathematics instruction.

Today teachers are faced with an increasing variety of instructional materials from which to choose, and it will undoubtedly become more difficult to make choices as the range of possibilities increases. This section of readings is designed to help the teacher make such decisions.

Some of the articles which follow represent major curricular concerns involved in selecting materials for instruction. Other selections provide specific examples of dramatic curricular changes which are being considered and incorporated in some forward-looking mathematics departments. The remaining articles present a few of the issues involved in selecting textbooks and evaluating the preparation of mathematics teachers in the United States and abroad.

Through additional investigation of these kinds of issues the teacher of school mathematics can begin to formulate more consistently his philosophy about the mathematics curriculum.

The New World of Mathematics
JAMES H. ZANT

A revolution is underway in the field of mathematics and mathematics teaching. This involves the amount of mathematics known and used in the modern world and it also affects the content and point of view from which mathematics is, or should be, taught at the elementary level, at the secondary level and at the college level. There is a new world of mathematics and the revolution has been going in the content of the field with ever increasing rapidity so that now the new mathematics forms the bulk of the total accumulation.

Though mathematics has been developing for 5,000 years the subject has never been as lively as it is today. The pace of mathematical discovery and invention has accelerated amazingly during the last twenty years. It has been said that mathematics is the only branch of learning in which all of the theories of two thousand years ago are still valid. Hence there is little that is basically wrong with the mathematics of the past and the vitality and vigor of present day mathematical research indicates that the sheer bulk of mathematical developments is staggering.

While mathematics is basically a logical structure which has no need for applications to justify its existence, applications are well known and numerous. This is true of the most abstract parts of the subject as well as

Reprinted from *The Mathematics Magazine*, XXXIII, (March–April, 1960), 211–17, by permission of the author and the publisher. James H. Zant is Professor Emeritus of Mathematics, Oklahoma State University, Stillwater, Oklahoma.

many sections which may seem, at the time of their creation, to be mere playthings invented purely for the mathematician's enjoyment. For example, the decimal number system with the base ten using the ten digits 0, 1, 2, 3, . . . , 9 has been used by nearly all people all over the world. Humans were born with ten fingers and almost universally they have counted to ten and started over. But number systems to other bases have been invented by mathematicians. One of these, to the base two, is called the binary number system and may have been invented for the pleasure of the mathematicians. This system uses only two digits, 0 and 1. Numbers are then 1, 10, 11, 100, 101 instead of 1, 2, 3, 4, 5. This number system is not practical for counting things in ordinary life or for writing numbers. However, it is not a fad. It has a new importance and has made a terrific impact on the modern world because this method of counting is of necessity that used by the powerful modern digital computers. The reason is that they count on electrical relays, which have only two *"fingers,"* "off" and "on."

We find mathematics being applied to all sorts of situations: in the social sciences; to the distribution of manufactured products; to traffic flow; bacterial growth is expressed as an exponential function; the same function is used to determine the half-life of radio-active substances. It is now thought that the area of topology can be used in describing the surface of the living cell. A new kind of algebra to represent the thinking process is being sought by neurophysiologists. This process is by no means random, but is not entirely methodical. Instances of applications of mathematics and sought-for applications could be continued indefinitely.

From all of this it is clear that the world of today demands more mathematical knowledge than in the past. No one can predict with accuracy his future profession or how much mathematics will be demanded in a particular profession 25 years from now. It is important to learn mathematics with understanding so that students of today will be able in later life to learn the new mathematical skills which the future will surely demand of many of them.

A language barrier exists here, however. The language for the communication of mathematical ideas is largely in terms of symbols and words which the public cannot understand and therefore does not listen. This is not true in the other sciences as was illustrated in 1956 when two theoretical physicists, Chen Ning Yang and Tsung Dao Lee demolished the principle of parity. The press did a commendable job of describing the abstruse physical ideas and the implications involved, but said nothing about the mathematical theory of groups on which the conclusions were based. Physicists, with tongue in the cheek reservations, talk about atoms and subatomic particles as if they were little marbles, but there is no popular terminology for talking *about* mathematics.

However, some mathematicians have always been able to communicate—often better to children than to adults. The late Dr. Edward Kasner of Columbia University regularly lectured to kindergarten classes on infinite sets. The children easily reconciled themselves to the notion of infinity and got the fundamental ideas of set theory faster than some of his undergraduate students. Children seem naturally attuned to mathematical abstractions, perhaps because it is not unlike pure fantasy. One of the best-loved of all children's books is *Alice's Adventures in Wonderland*, first conceived as stories told to children by a professional mathematician, Charles Lutwidge Dodgson, who used the pen name, Lewis Carroll. Presently one of our outstanding young mathematicians, Dr. Paul C. Rosenbloom of the University of Minnesota, is successfully introducing mathematical concepts, particularly in the field of number theory, to grade school children.

The Great Teacher said "Except ye become as a little child, ye shall in no wise enter the Kingdom of Heaven." Perhaps this is the key to teaching real and exciting mathematics to the young students in our schools.

THE NEW MATHEMATICS IN THE SCHOOLS

By some curious coincidence the field of mathematics, which has expanded continuously over a period of 5,000 years, became a static, almost stagnant, subject in the classrooms of both the high schools and colleges of this country. Subject matter for courses in algebra, geometry, trigonometry, analytical geometry and the calculus extending from grade 9 through undergraduate college curriculum was crystallized into its present form approximately 60 years ago and has changed little since that time. The subject matter, which was developed for the most part over 300 years ago (in the case of plane and solid geometry it was over 2,000 years ago), was chosen and its presentation organized in accordance with an attitude toward mathematics which no longer holds and which has been discarded by present day mathematicians. With this curriculum and point of view mathematics is presented mainly as a collection of slightly related techniques and manipulations. The profound, yet simple concepts get little attention. It has been said that "if art appreciation were taught in the same way, it would consist mostly of learning how to chip stone and mix paint."

The type of mathematics and mathematics courses referred to above are all too common in high school and college today. We shall refer to this as *Traditional Mathematics*. This will be in contrast to the terms *Modern Mathematics* or *Contemporary Mathematics* now coming into common use for courses and curricula which include new concepts and which are taught from a different point of view.

Thus the whole field of mathematics, traditional and modern, is very large and all of it basically good mathematics. We cannot teach all of it in high school and college. It is also almost impossible to separate this subject matter into high school and college mathematics at this stage in the development of mathematical curricula; there will always be an overlap. We hope that by the use of both new concepts and conscious emphasis on the point of view that mathematics is concerned with abstract patterns of thought or a mathematical structure that students will acquire an understanding of and an interest in mathematics as a cultural as well as an applied subject.

It should be noted at once that there is no sharp dividing line between "traditional" mathematics and "modern" mathematics. The development of mathematics has been continuous; the newer ideas have grown out of the older; and many teachers have been presenting traditional content from a point of view accurately described as modern.

The approach of considering the concepts of mathematics from many points of view is one of the characteristics of modern mathematics that has made it a powerful tool for understanding mathematics and also in applying it to different situations. We can solve problems in new ways, solve some problems that we have been unable to solve before and discover properties that have eluded us before.

The case for modern mathematics rests on a number of points. Mathematics is a dynamic, growing field and has far outrun the curriculum both at the school and college level. The traditional curriculum has not resulted in our students learning enough mathematics or good mathematics and does not emphasize the fact that the developments and applications of mathematics are not only important but indispensable to human progress. The use of newer concepts not only increases the power of the students in applying mathematics, but also enhances his understanding of the subject. The necessity for a thoroughly reorganized program oriented to the needs of the second half of the twentieth century is dictated by the immediate and urgent needs for mathematicians as well as scientists and engineers who understand basic modern mathematics and know how to use it to solve the problems incident to a wide variety of the aspects of modern civilization.

TRENDS IN MATHEMATICS AND MATHEMATICS TEACHING

Mathematics is a basic element in the whole program of revised science education. The crisis in science education is a real one. It is not an invention of the newspapers or the scientists or the Pentagon. While the U.S.S.R. is not the "cause" of the crisis, it has served as a rude stimulus to awaken us to reality. The cause of the crisis is our breath-taking movement into a new technological era. This movement into a new phase of man's long struggle to control his environment involving the use of nuclear energy, exploration of outer space, revolutionary creations and applications of both mathematics and science can test to the utmost our adaptive capacities. Education, at all levels, must meet this challenge. We need a well trained citizenry, but we need, perhaps more, an ample supply of high caliber scientists, mathematicians and engineers.

To meet this basic need two trends in mathematics curricula and teaching are significant. This represents the revolution in mathematics teaching. The trends are acceleration and modernization of content and point of view.

ACCELERATION

Generally acceleration is taking place in the secondary schools independently of any change in the curriculum. Perhaps the most common sort of acceleration now underway consists of allowing or requiring students to start algebra in the eighth grade and then proceed with other traditional mathematics courses in order. Administratively this is the easiest way to do it and it is becoming almost a national trend. Other methods of acceleration are to encourage students to take courses in mathematics during the summer and to separate the class according to ability and allow the better students to proceed through the courses at a faster rate.

All of these and other methods are in use and have some merit. There are also certain disadvantages. One of these is that secondary mathematics is organized as a four year sequence at most and acceleration allows the student to complete this sequence by the end of the junior year. This makes it necessary to offer a course in analytics and calculus during the senior year or provide no mathematics for the students during the last year in high school. Few committees or groups of professional mathematicians recommend that calculus be taught in high school, but it is being done in a great many schools. It is almost a national trend. The fact is that there is no other available course or textbook with which teachers are familiar.

A second disadvantage of accelerating students is that it is usually assumed that the present curriculum in high school mathematics is a good one. This is contrary, of course, to the contention of this discussion. I feel that secondary mathematics from the first grade up, but especially from grade 7 through 12, should be reorganized to include a number of modern concepts and that it should be taught from the point of view that mathematics is concerned with abstract patterns of thought. If the mathematics curriculum is so organized and taught, then it will be possible to have enough material in all grades through the twelfth to give the students a broad understanding of the true meaning of the subjects and to furnish him an understanding of the processes and skills necessary to live and work in the modern world.

MODERNIZATION OF THE MATHEMATICS CURRICULUM

Certain characteristic features of a modern mathematics program may be stated briefly as follows: Courses are designed for college capable students, but may be used with less talented students if they are given more time. New concepts and a different point of view are used because such knowledge is needed by the students. Modern concepts lead to a clarification of the subject. Changes will not be radical enough to cause a great disturbance with teachers or students. While changes will help students meet present needs, they also provide an understanding of mathematics for future change and development.

While it is not possible to give a complete outline of modern mathematics for the five grades under discussion here, such outlines have been made and one set of textbooks in preliminary form is being used on an experimental basis this year in 22 Oklahoma schools. In this series of books grades 7 and 8 deal with the structure of arithmetic and the real number system as a progressing development and with metric and non-metric relations in geometry. Though these ideas are associated with their applications, materials [involve] experience with and appreciation of *abstract concepts*, the role of *definition*, the development of *precise vocabulary* and *thought, experimentation* and *proof.* Notable for its absence is the area of socialized arithmetic dealing with paying bills, insurance, taxes and the like. These latter situations are not real to students at this age level, but they are capable of learning the more fundamental concepts of number and measurement.

The ninth grade is basically algebra. Students will explore the behavior of numbers and invent new numbers to describe new situations. They will find that all the manipulations with symbols can be made understandable and that they "hang together" in a very satisfactory way. The mathematics is sound; it will not be necessary to unlearn parts of it later. It is this emphasis on a clear cut and mathematically sound picture of the structure of algebra which distinguishes this course from the more traditional ones.

New concepts introduced are simple, but extremely useful in getting a better understanding of algebra. They include sets and operations on sets of numbers, phrases and sentences (for expressions and equations), the properties (commutative, associative and distributive) of numbers, the real number line, order and the coordinate (rectangular) system.

In like manner, the tenth grade is concerned entirely with geometry, but designed in such a way that the algebra studied in the ninth grade becomes a more useful tool. The course includes a few chapters on solid geometry (no separate course in solid geometry is recommended) and a single chapter on analytic geometry. The conviction is that the traditional content of Euclidean geometry deserves the prominent place it has always held in the high school. Changes have been made only when the need for them appears compelling. The postulates used (they are those of G. D. Birkhoff rather than the more sophisticated system devised by Hilbert) assumes a knowledge of the number system treated adequately in the ninth grade. After the first few chapters, which teachers must learn the first time with the students, it is not anticipated that there will be a great difference from the traditional course. It will, however, be more precise and more logically presented.

The eleventh grade course will consist of topics which usually appear in intermediate algebra and trigonometry, but it is not a course in "mathematics made easy" wherein the students learn how to *do* certain things. Since this is usually an elective course in high school, some selection of the students can be assumed. Hence inherent difficulties in understanding are candidly appraised and forthrightly explained in terms appropriate for students at this level. A controlling consideration is the desire to advance the students' understanding of the number system. Mathematical proofs are used, but it is not necessary that they be unduly rigorous.

An appeal is often made to the student's intuition and he is led by an inductive approach to make and test conjectures about the nature of the principles to be proved. New symbolism is used only when it serves to convey meaning more accurately and succinctly than could be done by other means.

The material for the twelfth grade, traditionally solid geometry and college algebra or college algebra and trigonometry, departs more radically from the traditional than for the other courses. While some of the so-called modern concepts are used, the subject matter itself can probably be more accurately described as "traditional mathematics which is developed from a more up-to-date point of view."

The title of this course is usually *Elementary Functions*, which may be thought of as a more sophisticated term for *Algebra*. It deals with polynomial functions, exponential and logarithmic functions, trigonometric functions, algebra of matrices, and perhaps an introduction to abstract algebra.

Alternative subject matter has been and is being written. There is a book on *Introductory Probability and Statistical Inference* which is suggested for the second semester of the twelfth grade. Generally the recommendations as to the content of the twelfth grade course are much more flexible than for the other grades. However, as has been said, none of the recommendations include a course in calculus.

SUMMARY AND IMPLICATIONS

1. There is a new world of mathematics. This affects us in our daily lives, not only for people who use mathematics in the many ramifications of our scientific age, but also in what we should be teaching in our schools to prepare present day students to live and work in the world of the future.
2. The mathematics curriculum of the schools must be revised to meet this challenge.
3. This revision process is already well underway so that schools in Oklahoma

are now teaching courses involving the new mathematics.
4. This revision is not drastic in terms of courses and topics included. However, it is fundamental in terms of the use of new concepts and point of view in teaching and learning mathematics.
5. All possible help must be provided both for teachers now in service and for those who are preparing to teach this new and exciting material.

The future in the field of mathematics and through it all of the new developments of our modern scientific age, was never brighter. Fundamental research is progressing at an amazing rate. The center of much of this activity is shifting to the United States. In like manner the reorganization of the curriculum in mathematics is being pursued with vigor and enthusiasm and from a most realistic point of view. This reorganization is being supported and contributed to by many of our finest mathematicians. They are working cooperatively and in equal numbers with outstanding teachers of mathematics in the schools. Administrators realize the importance and significance of this effort and are supporting it with enthusiasm. Finally, perhaps the most important characteristic of the whole movement is the direct involvement of teachers in the classroom at local levels. Those of us who are familiar with what appeared to be promising efforts over the last 50 years realize that success is often less than anticipated. Perhaps the closer involvement of administrators and teachers in a cooperative effort at local levels may be the difference which will insure the success of this program.

On the Meaning of Structure in Mathematics
HOWARD E. TAYLOR/THOMAS L. WADE

In recent years, the word "structure" has appeared frequently in mathematical literature,[1] first at the college level, then at the high school level, and now at the elementary school level. Recommendations of various groups considering mathematics education at levels from kindergarten through college have laid heavy emphasis on the introduction of the concept of structure in mathematics early in the curriculum. In December, 1963, the United States Department of Education made available a bulletin[2] in which there were listed four familiar goals of elementary school mathematics, along with two new additional goals, one of the latter two being "To

Reprinted from *The Mathematics Teacher*, LVIII (March, 1965), 226–31, by permission of the authors and the National Council of Teachers of Mathematics. Copyright © 1965 by the National Council of Teachers of Mathematics. Howard Taylor is Callaway Professor of Mathematics, West Georgia College, Carrollton. Thomas L. Wade is Professor of Mathematics, Florida State University, Tallahassee.

[1] For example: Mary P. Dolciani, Simon L. Berman, and Julius Frelick, *Modern Algebra, Structure and Method*, Book 1 (Boston: Houghton Mifflin Company, 1962); May Hickey Maria, *The Structure of Arithmetic and Algebra* (New York: John Wiley & Sons, Inc., 1958); Goerge D. Mostow, Joseph H. Sampson, and Jean-Pierre Meyer, *Fundamental Structures of Algebra* (New York: McGraw-Hill Book Company, Inc., 1963); Francis J. Mueller, *Arithmetic, Its Structure and Concepts* (Englewood Cliffs, N. J.: Prentice-Hall, Inc., 1956).

[2] Edwina Deans, *Elementary School Mathematics: New Directions* (Washington, D. C.: United States Department of Education, OE-29042, Bulletin 1963, No. 13).

help each child understand the structure of mathematics, its laws and principles, its sequence and order, and the ways in which mathematics as a system expands to meet these needs." Indeed, if we were to select one emphasis that is characteristic of the new curricula in mathematics at all levels, that emphasis would likely be the emphasis on structure in mathematics. Quite probably, each of us has his own notion of the meaning of "structure" in mathematics. If we were asked to appraise an interesting book titled *An Introduction to Algebra* by John Bonnycastle, published in England in 1815, we would most likely agree that, while it has extensive and interesting treatments of surds and the rule of three, it contains little of what we might call "structure." Many of us probably feel very much the same way regarding the texts which were in use in high school in the period 1910 to 1950.

It appears that, at present, the concept of "structure" in mathematics has a status somewhat like the status of the concept of "function" in mathematics a decade or so ago; namely, that it means different things to different people. Is "structure" a thing or a concept—does it have a definition—just what is "structure"? Just as there may be advantages in having a straightforward, explicit definition of a mathematical function, there may be advantages in having a straightforward, explicit definition of a mathematical structure. We shall endeavor to formulate a definition of a structure[3] in elementary mathematics, where by elementary mathematics we will mean mathematics that precedes a thorough course in calculus at the university level.

In mathematics dictionaries available to us we find no mention of structure; in English dictionaries we may discover that, generally speaking, a structure "denotes the formation, arrangement, and articulation of parts in anything built up by nature or art."[4] It seems reasonable to assume, then, that a "mathematical structure" should be some sort of formation, arrangement, or result of putting together of parts. What are these parts to be?

We take as the fundamental building units of a structure the members a, b, c, ... of some nonempty set S. The mortar which we shall use to hold together these building units will consist of one or more *operations*. Let us recall some facts about the meaning of an operation.

A (binary) operation on a nonempty set S associates with each ordered pair (a, b) of members of S one and only one member of S. We use the symbol $\circ$ to denote an operation on a set. The member of S that is associated with the ordered pair (a, b) is denoted by $a \circ b$. An operation $\circ$ is defined on a set S whenever, for any members a, $b \in$ S, we are able to decide which particular member of S the symbol $a \circ b$ represents. To illustrate, if

$$S = \{a, b, c, d\},$$

we may define an operation $\circ$ on S by the use of the following table.

$\circ$	a	b	c	d
a	a	b	c	d
b	b	c	d	b
c	c	d	a	b
d	d	b	b	c

In this table we understand that the element which appears in the row with c at the left and in the column with b at the top is to be identified as $c \circ b$, and so on. From this table we are able to infer that

$$c \circ b \text{ is } d, \quad d \circ c \text{ is } b, \quad a \circ d \text{ is } d,$$

and so on.

The familiar operations of addition, denoted by $+$, and multiplication, denoted by $\cdot$, of natural numbers are operations on the set N of natural numbers. According to the definition given above, subtraction is not an operation on the set of natural numbers, since the difference of two natural numbers may not be a natural number. But subtraction is an operation on the set I of all integers.

Most of us would agree that a jumble of bricks put together with just any type of mortar and lacking in architectural and aesthetic design would be lacking in appeal. Similarly, a set S = $\{a, b, c, ...\}$ with just any old kind of operation and without any "nice" mathematical properties would lack mathematical appeal. In order to create an entity which is mathematically attractive, we may begin by requiring that an operation be "uniquely defined with respect to an equivalence relation"; let us recall what this means.

We remember that if a universe U is given, then a *relation* in U is a set of ordered pairs whose entries are members of U, and that a relation is an equivalence relation if it is *reflexive*, *symmetric*, and *transitive*.

The concept of an equivalence relation is one of the most basic and most useful of mathematical concepts. Until

---

[3] Note that in this paper we are concerned with "structure *in* mathematics"; in particular, we consider some elementary algebraic structures. We do not believe it is fruitful to talk about "*the* structure of mathematics."

[4] See *Webster's Dictionary of Synonyms* (Springfield, Mass.: G. & C. Merriam Company, 1942), p. 797.

several years ago, a student of mathematics usually had first contact with this concept in an upper division or graduate course.[5] Lately, several books have appeared which present the concept of an equivalence relation in a setting suitable for study by high school seniors and college freshmen.[6]

Let $\mathscr{E}$ denote an equivalence relation, and let us indicate

$$(a, b) \in \mathscr{E} \text{ by writing } a \mathscr{E} b.$$

We read $a \mathscr{E} b$ as "a is equivalent to b" (under the equivalence relation $\mathscr{E}$). For an equivalence relation $\mathscr{E}$, the following statements are true:

$a \mathscr{E} a$ (the reflexibe property);

$a \mathscr{E} b \longrightarrow b \mathscr{E} a$ (the symmetric property);

$a \mathscr{E} b$ and $b \mathscr{E} c \longrightarrow a \mathscr{E} c$ (the transitive property).

A familiar equivalence relation is the relation in a set U of numbers defined by the concept of arithmetic equality, that is, the relation

$$E = \{(x, y) \mid y = x\}.$$

Other familiar equivalence relations are the congruence relation and the similarity relation in the set Y of all triangles.

Suppose that $\circ$ is a binary operation on a set S and that $\mathscr{E}$ is an equivalence relation in S. The operation $\circ$ on S is uniquely defined with respect to the equivalence relation $\mathscr{E}$ if and only if

$$a \mathscr{E} a' \text{ and } b \mathscr{E} b'$$
$$\longrightarrow a \circ b \mathscr{E} a' \circ b'. \quad (1)$$

We may read (1) as "If a is equivalent to a' and b is equivalent to b', then $a \circ b$

[5] With a text such as *Introduction to the Foundations of Mathematics*, by R. L. Wilder (New York: John Wiley & Sons, Inc., 1952), see especially p. 46.

[6] For example, Howard E. Taylor and Thomas L. Wade. *University Freshman Mathematics* (New York: John Wiley & Sons, Inc., 1963), see especially pp. 13–20.

is equivalent to $a' \circ b'$. As an illustration consider the equality relation $\mathscr{E} = \{(x, y) \mid y = x\}$ in the set I of all integers. The operation of addition on the set I, denoted by $+$, is uniquely defined with respect to the equality relation, since, for $a, a', b, b' \in$ I, it is true that

$$a = a' \text{ and } b = b'$$
$$\longrightarrow a + b = a' + b'.$$

Similarly the operation of multiplication on the set I, denoted by $\cdot$, is uniquely defined with respect to the equality relation; that is, for $a, a', b, b' \in$ I, it is true that

$$a = a' \text{ and } b = b'$$
$$\longrightarrow a \cdot b = a' \cdot b'.$$

Let us return to the consideration of the operation $\circ$ on the set $S = \{a, b, c, d\}$ which is defined in the table. It can be shown that the relation

$$\mathscr{E} = \{(a, a), (b, b), (c, c), (d, d),$$
$$(a, c), (c, a), (b, d), (d, b)\} \quad (2)$$

is an equivalence relation in the set S. Since

$$(b, b) \in \mathscr{E} \text{ and } (d, b) \in \mathscr{E}$$

we have, respectively,

$$b \mathscr{E} b \text{ and } d \mathscr{E} b.$$

Also, from the table, we have

$$b \circ d \text{ is } b \text{ and } b \circ b \text{ is } c.$$

Now $(b, c) \notin \mathscr{E}$, that is, b is not equivalent to c, and therefore it is *not* true that

$$b \mathscr{E} b \text{ and } d \mathscr{E} b \longrightarrow b \circ d \mathscr{E} b \circ b.$$

That is, the operation $\circ$ on the set S $= \{a, b, c, d\}$ defined by the table is not uniquely defined with respect to the equivalence relation $\mathscr{E}$ defined by (2).

Subsequently, whenever we consider one or more operations on a set S, we shall assume that the operation or operations are uniquely defined with respect to an equivalence relation in S. Frequently, the equivalence relation is the "identity" relation, that is, the relation whose members are the ordered pairs of the form (x, x) where $x \in S$. To illustrate the "identity" relation in the set $S = \{a, b, c, d\}$ is

$$\{(a, a), (b, b), (c, c), (d, d)\},$$

and with respect to this equivalence relation the operation $\circ$ on S specified in the table is uniquely defined.

It must be clearly understood that an equivalence relation in a set need not be the usual equality relation. However, since the idea of an equivalence relation is a generalization of the idea of equality, it is frequently convenient for simplicity of notation to use the symbol $=$ to indicate that two members of a set are equivalent with respect to an equivalence relation $\mathscr{E}$. We agree that subsequently when $\mathscr{E}$ is an equivalence relation in a set S and $a \mathscr{E} b$, that is, when $(a, b) \in \mathscr{E}$, we will write

$$a = b \quad \text{to mean } a \mathscr{E} b,$$

unless specifically stated to the contrary.

If S is a nonempty set on which one or more operations have been uniquely defined with respect to an equivalence relation, then the set S together with the operation or operations is called a *mathematical system*. We will denote such a system consisting of a set S and an operation $\circ$ by $\langle S; \circ \rangle$. A system consisting of a set S and two operations $\circ_1$ and $\circ_2$ will be denoted by $\langle S; \circ_1, \circ_2 \rangle$.

A (mathematical) *structure* is a mathematical system with one or more explicitly recognized (mathematical) properties. To illustrate, let us recall some examples of properties that mathematicians have thought it desirable for mathematical structures to possess.

Let $=$ denote an equivalence relation $\mathscr{E}$ in a set S and let $\circ$ be an operation on S which is uniquely defined with respect

to $\mathscr{E}$. If, whenever $a, b, \in S$, it is true that

$$a \circ b = b \circ a,$$

the operation is *commutative*. If, whenever $a, b, c, \in S$, it is true that

$$(a \circ b) \circ c = a \circ (b \circ c),$$

the operation is *associative*.

Let $\circ_1$ and $\circ_2$ be two operations on S which are uniquely defined with respect to $\mathscr{E}$. If, whenever $a, b, c, \in S$, it is true that

$$a \circ_2 (b \circ_1 c) = (a \circ_2 b) \circ_1 (a \circ_2 c)$$

and

$$(b \circ_1 c) \circ_2 a = (b \circ_2 a) \circ_1 (c \circ_2 a),$$

the operation $\circ_2$ is distributive with respect to $\circ_1$. Observe that if $\circ_2$ is commutative and one of these statements is true, then the other statement is true. However, if $\circ_2$ is not commutative, one of these statements may be true and the other false.

To illustrate, the operations of addition and multiplication on the set I of all integers are both commutative and associative. For if $a, b, c, \in I$, then

$$a + b = b + a,$$
$$a \cdot b = b \cdot a,$$
$$a + (b + c) = (a + b) + c,$$
$$a \cdot (b \cdot c) = (a \cdot b) \cdot c.$$

Moreover, multiplication is distributive with respect to addition.

We may create a structure from a mathematical system by making specific recognition of one or more of the commutative, associative, or distributive properties that the system may have.

A structure which consists of a mathematical system $\langle S; \circ \rangle$, with one operation, in which the operation $\circ$ is associative, is called a *semigroup*. To illustrate, the set of positive integers under addition is a semigroup, as is also the set of positive integers under multiplication.

A structure which consists of a mathematical system $\langle S; \circ_1, \circ_2 \rangle$, with two operations, in which each of the operations $\circ_1$ and $\circ_2$ is commutative and associative, and in which one of the operations is distributive with respect to the other, is called a *number system*. A *number* is a member of the set S in a number system. Among the familiar number systems are the following three: the natural number system $\langle N; +, \cdot \rangle$, the nonnegative integral number system $\langle N_0; +, \cdot \rangle$ (here N_0 denotes the set of nonnegative integers), and the integral number system $\langle I; +, \cdot \rangle$.

If in a mathematical system consisting of a set S and at least one operation $\circ$ there is a member $i \in S$ with the property that

$$i \circ a = a \circ i = a, \qquad (3)$$

whenever $a \in S$, we call i an identity member of S under the operation $\circ$. To illustrate, a semigroup with an identity member is called a *monoid*. The semigroup of positive integers under multiplication is a monoid, for 1 is an identity member of N under multiplication. On the contrary, the semigroup of positive integers under addition is not a monoid, for the set N has no identity member under addition.

In addition to the structures mentioned above (number systems, semigroups, monoids) there are many others such as fields,[7] vector spaces,[8] groups, rings, and algebras.[9]

With one or more basic structures at hand, one may construct other structures. Since plane analytic geometry is the study of subsets of the Cartesian set Re × Re, where Re is the set of real numbers, plane analytic geometry may be considered as a superstructure based upon the structure known as the real number system.

While a basic structure $\mathscr{S}$ consists of a mathematical system with certain specifically recognized properties, we are usually interested in a more complete structure $\bar{\mathscr{S}}$, which consists of $\mathscr{S}$ together with one or more theorems which are logical consequences of the specifically recognized characteristics or properties of $\mathscr{S}$. To illustrate, let S be a given set, $\circ$ an operation on S which is uniquely defined with respect to an equivalence relation in S, so that we have a mathematical system $\langle S; \circ \rangle$. Consider the basic structure $\mathscr{S}_1$ consisting of the mathematical system $\langle S; \circ \rangle$ and the property that S has an identity member i under the operation $\circ$. The following theorem is readily established.[10]

Theorem A. *If i is an identity member of the set S under the operation $\circ$ in a structure $\mathscr{S}_1$ then i is unique.*

Let us denote by $\bar{\mathscr{S}}_1$ the structure which consists of the basic structure $\mathscr{S}_1$ and Theorem A. Although this seems to be a very simple structure, a knowledge of it will serve us very well. Any time we have an $\mathscr{S}_1$ structure we know that Theorem A is valid and that we have an $\bar{\mathscr{S}}_1$ structure. To illustrate, in considering complex numbers, as soon as we have shown that we have an identity complex number under multiplication, we are assured that it is the only such identity. Similarly, in considering square matrices of a given order n, as soon as we have shown we have an identity matrix under multiplication, we are assured that it is the only such identity.

Let us take structure $\bar{\mathscr{S}}_1$ and add the property that $\circ$ is associative: we will call this structure $\mathscr{S}_2$. If, corresponding to a member $a \in S$, there is a member $a' \in S$ for which

$$a \circ a' = i \quad \text{and} \quad a' \circ a = i, \qquad (4)$$

we call a' an inverse of a under the operation $\circ$. The following theorem can

---

[7] *Ibid.*, p. 33.
[8] *Ibid.*, p. 151.
[9] *Ibid.*, pp. 166–68.

[10] *Ibid.*, p. 21.

now be proved[11] about the structure $\mathscr{S}^2$.

Theorem B. *If in a $\mathscr{S}_2$ structure, a member* a ϵ S *has an inverse a' under the operation* ∘, *then a' is unique.*

Again, a knowledge of the structure which consists of $\mathscr{S}_2$ and Theorem B will serve us well. To illustrate, in considering square matrices of a given order n, having shown that multiplication of such matrices is associative, then if a given matrix has an inverse (an identity under multiplication), Theorem B assures us that such an inverse is unique.

A *group* is a structure which consists of the mathematical system $\langle S; \circ \rangle$ and which has the following three properties.

1. The operation ∘ is associative,
2. There is an identity member under the operation ∘,
3. Each member $a \epsilon$ S has an inverse under the operation ∘.

From Theorems A and B we have at once that the identity member in a group is unique and that the inverse a' of a is unique.

A natural question now is: "How should we endeavor to teach structure?" We believe that such teaching should be done very, very gently. A student should be led gradually to an awareness of certain basic structures such as number systems, fields, and groups before such structures are studied from

a rigid postulational viewpoint. Certainly, as the fundamental operations with integers are considered, the commutative and associative properties should be recognized and discussed, and the use of the distributive law emphasized. Numerous books dealing with arithmetic and elementary algebra have appeared recently with such emphases.

We believe that the teacher should know more about structures than he teaches, and that he should teach more than he expects all of his students to learn. He should consciously and consistently seek opportunities and ways to lead his students to an awareness of structures and an appreciation of their value and importance. This is consistent with the viewpoint that a good teacher of any subject will know and practice numerous precepts and principles which should serve as guidelines for his students, with the goal that as many of his students as possible will grow in sensitivity to those precepts and in practice of those principles.

We would do well to keep in mind the enjoinder of the distinguished teacher and mathematician, Professor Angus E. Taylor, namely,

In mathematics we have not only ideas and thories, but techniques. ... The best results, for teacher and student alike, will come from a measure of care and balance in preservation of what is good in the old ways, along with the adoption of new ideas and new ways.

[11] *Ibid.*, p. 33.

Some Comments on General Mathematics

IRVING ALLEN DODES

In order to place a discussion of "general mathematics" in its proper frame of reference, let us note that there are at least three main "tracks" in the teaching and learning of mathematics:

1. The Honors Track. This track is for students who are able to proceed quickly and confidently because of high ability, *and* who are well-prepared, *and* who are so interested that only a minimum of motivational technique is needed to assure success. The students in this category are usually regarded as *honors students*. Courses designed for these students are usually accelerated in pace and deepened in concept. Lecture lessons are quite suitable for these students.

2. First Track. This track is for students who have less ability, *or* who are not sufficiently well-prepared, *or* who require distinct motivation. This motivation may, in fact, be only a reflection of the interest of the teacher, or it may be success, or it may rest on the solution of puzzle-type problems, or it may be based upon a display of practical or (more typically) pseudo-practical uses for the material to be discussed. Courses

Reprinted from *The Mathematics Teacher*, LX (March, 1967), 246–51, by permission of the author and the National Council of Teachers of Mathematics. Copyright © 1967 by the National Council of Teachers of Mathematics. This reading is from a talk given at the Joint Meeting of the Association of Teachers of Mathematics and the Mathematics Chairmen's Association in New York City, May 15, 1965. Irving A. Dodes is Professor of Mathematics, Kingsborough Community College, City University of New York.

designed for these students are usually called *regular academic* courses. These courses vary in pace and depth, depending upon the school, the teacher, and the class. Developmental lessons are very suitable for this group.

3. Second Track. This track is for students who, by reason of low ability, *or* poor preparation, *or* low interest level, *or* miscellaneous difficulties (psychological, reading, language, etc.), are not suited to academic courses and the developmental lesson. It should be emphasized that this is a mixed group. A student may have good ability and good preparation, but very low interest; or he may be very interested, but have insufficient ability and preparation. These students are ordinarily grouped into classes in *second-track mathematics*. In the ninth and tenth years, the courses are usually called *general mathematics*. A mixture of developmental, discussion, and experimental lessons is recommended for this group of students.

THE PROBLEM

Any student who does not fit into the demanding categories of "honors" and "first-track" courses is ordinarily assigned into a "second-track" class. It should be clear that *this group is not necessarily dull*, and that a program based upon such a hypothesis is doomed at the outset. It is common knowledge that courses in general mathematics are, and almost always have been, unwelcome to teachers and students, with results ranging from a mild discomfort to a species of torture. The problem, in short, is to determine what kind of course can be devised to serve the students in second-track courses, keeping in mind the important fact that these students vary greatly in ability, preparation, and interest.

We really are asking, "What is *general mathematics?*"

A PHILOSOPHY

As teachers of mathematics, we should agree that the content of a "second-track" course in mathematics includes topics and concepts in two overlapping and interwoven categories:

1. Some ideas in mathematics are important from the viewpoint of *culture*, designed to enable the citizen to understand and appreciate the mechanism and the background of his environment. *Appreciation* is the aim for the topics in this category, although it may be desirable to develop skill in some instances, if only as a teaching device. Topics often included in this category are the following: why and how a formula is developed, why and how an equation is solved, the meaning of a graph, the use of locus to solve position problems, the use of indirect measurement with instruments, and how to unravel certain problems involving simple set-theoretic ideas, e.g., problems in finite probability.

2. Certain skills are important for the adequate participation of a citizen in his technological, commercial, and industrial civilization. We emphasize that, while some degree of skill is desirable in this category, *skill is never the primary aim of any second-track* course. In fact, teachers will often find it impossible to develop skill and they must not be unhappy about this.

It will be noticed that *interest* has not been mentioned as an antecedent to the selection of course material for general mathematics. This is a deliberate omission. My viewpoint is that *interest is a result of teaching skill, not of course material.* The art of teaching is precisely this: to make important materials interesting. It is *not* to make interesting materials important. Any expert teacher can make any topic interesting, provided the topic is within the ability of the student.

The philosophy expressed here can be condensed into the single statement that second-track mathematics, including general mathematics, is a *liberal-arts subject*, with all the aims and objectives of any liberal-arts subjects. Second-track mathematics should open the eyes of the students to the beauty and wonder of mathematics, without attempting to make the student into a half-mathematician. I shall be more specific later.

HISTORY OF GENERAL MATHEMATICS

I have already mentioned that courses in general mathematics have not enjoyed great popularity among students and teachers. My thought is that the wrong questions have been asked in designing these courses.

The *first* question has usually been, "What do the students want?" This was a doomed approach because the students do not know what they want (how could they?). Ordinarily the authors of the courses assumed that boys would be interested in something like the computation of baseball batting-averages (which they do not compute—they read these averages in the newspaper if they are interested). The authors often assumed that girls were interested in computing the number of stitches in a line of knitting (which they do not compute—they read from an instruction sheet). The authors often assumed that everyone wanted to know how to fill out an income tax blank (which no one really wants to do).

The *second* question has usually been, "What will the student enjoy?" This approach was equally doomed because no adult has retained enough wisdom to know what students enjoy. Anyhow, all teachers of mathematics are, by definition, specialists and lovers of pure mathematics. The students in general mathematics, again by definition, are different from us, and do not enjoy pure mathematics.

A broad observation which may be inaccurate in many specific instances is that the authors of courses in general mathematics often did not know what the students wanted, nor did they know what the students would enjoy. One result of this "child-centered" approach to the design of courses in general mathematics was the so-called *flexible course of study*, an abomination which no serious course in any subject on any level would abide. In this situation, the teacher could decide, on the spur of the moment, which topic to take up. (Syllabi for general mathematics often offered a choice, but the teacher was not restricted even to this choice.) This often led to ludicrous situations, particularly in schools where the first half was taught by one teacher, and the other half (to a reshuffled group) by another. In one school, the entire first half was spent in plotting the sewer system in a set of city blocks. In another school, the entire first half was spent in making scale models by cutting and pasting cardboard. One wonders (1) what the teacher in the second half found to build upon, and (2) what the students would say if they were asked what they learned in mathematics.

The proper question to ask in any course is always, *"What do the students need?"* It may be difficult or almost impossible to reach a decision about this, but it is certainly the professional question. A physician does not ask, "What medicine does the patient want?" nor does he ask, "What medicine will the patient enjoy?" He tries to satisfy a need, whether or not the patient thinks he needs it.

WHAT DO THE STUDENTS NEED?

Even when the proper question is asked, the answer may be inadequate. Many different courses in second-track mathematics have been devised upon an estimate of need. Here are some of them:

1. *Diluted algebra and geometry.* These courses are, in effect, the regular academic courses "watered down" so that some of the basic concepts could be taught, at least on a mechanical level. An example of such a course is the so-called *one-year intermediate algebra* course taught in some schools. Typical of these courses is the removal of some difficult mathematical ideas, and lengthening of the time devoted to the course. These courses are defensible when the difficulty lies in preparation and ability, *and* when there is a chance that the student will continue in mathematics, after the upgrading procedure. Some general mathematics courses are, in reality, diluted ninth-year algebra and tenth-year geometry with the minimum skill requirement and even less concept requirement. These are indefensible.

2. *Rehabilitation courses.* These are the hodge-podge ad hoc courses mentioned previously as the "flexible course of study," but shored up with some skills and minor concepts from the regular academic courses. A teacher might, for example, try to awaken interest in mathematics by lengthy units on paper-folding, paste-ups, working in clay, and weaving, with the thought that eventually the students would become so interested in mathematics (if this is mathematics!) that they would be able and willing to apply themselves to the regular academic topics. In my own mind, I call this "Advanced Sandbox."

3. *Remedial courses.* Nothing good can be said about remedial courses. Typically, they are "more of the same." There is more work with fractions, decimals, ratio and proportion, done the same way they were done previously. An important objection to this kind of course is that there is absolutely no reason to believe that students who did not learn from such an approach the first time will learn by the same approach the second, third or n^{th} time. Remedial *clinics* can, of course, be very useful.

4. *Accounting and bookkeeping courses.* These courses arose when departments of mathematics confessed failure and turned the unsolved problem over to the business department. The business department typically taught the children to write checks, balance books, construct budgets, and write income tax forms. All of this may be useful, particularly when taught by a person who knows something about them other than the bare arithmetic, but no one will claim that it is mathematics. In effect, this move deprived the student of an important facet of our culture: mathematics.

5. *The liberal-arts approach.* Here, teachers make a professional decision as to the important concepts of mathematics. Then ways and means are devised for teaching these concepts.

THE LIBERAL-ARTS APPROACH

Not all mathematicians will agree on what are the important things to be taught in a liberal-arts course in mathematics. This is a difficult decision precisely because the things which are fascinating to us, e.g., the relation between the roots and coefficients of an equation, the nth term of a Fibonacci sequence, the inversion of a matrix, are of doubtful importance or concern to a non-mathematician.

For a moment, transfer the question to the field of *art* taught as a liberal-arts subject. What does the non-artist need to know about art, if he is to consider himself cultured in today's civilization?

Well, among other things, he might need to know something about the great artists, at least for the purpose of removing certain stereotyped ideas (not all artists starved in garrets; some artists were revered by their contemporaries and forgotten by their followers, some quite the reverse; some were excellent in many fields, others illiterate except in art). The non-artist would need to know something about the materials and instruments of art: the media, the brushes, the sculpting tools, silk-screening. The non-artist would need to know some of the basic principles used by the artist: perspective, design, color balance. The non-artist would need to know something about the interpretation of art; in particular, he would need to know why professional artists regard certain paintings as great, and others as mediocre or bad. The non-artist might never be able to paint an acceptable picture or an acceptable design, but he would have an *appreciation* for art. After this exposure, it is even possible that some non-artists would discover an interest and an ability and become artists.

This is what I mean by a liberal-arts approach: a course based on the work of the professional, the place of the professional in civilization, some knowledge of materials and instruments some knowledge of basic principles and some insight into interpretation. In working out a liberal-arts approach to mathematics, it should be kept firmly in mind that general mathematics is a part of secondary mathematics. It is not advanced kindergarten, playtime, elementary arithmetic twice-cooked, or business arithmetic. It is a subject whose content should be decided by professionals, taught with dignity, and learned with respect.

Among the "big ideas" which seem to me to be important are those illustrated by the following:[1]

1. Mathematicians: who, what, when, why?
Bhaskara was a great mathematician for his times, but in some respects he did not show much common sense. Explain.
2. The basic nature and laws of numbers
   a. Use the distributive principle to find 8×999.
   b. Decide whether the uses of the numbers in the following are *exact* or *approximate:* (1) I weigh 120 pounds. (2) There are 5,280 feet in 1 mile.
3. Illustrations of mathematics in science and technology
   a. Find the wattage of a TV set that takes 112 volts and draws 14.2 amperes. (Formula given.)
   b. What is the SAE horsepower of a 6-cylinder car with cylinders of 3.25 inch diameter? (Formula given.)
4. Interpretation of graphs
   a. Given a sketch of a flower, "code" it in terms of coordinates.
   b. Given a statistical graph, interpret it.
   c. Given a time-change graph, interpolate and extrapolate.
   d. Draw a graph for $y > 2x - 1$.
5. Making and solving formulas and open sentences
   a. Translate into English: $3x + 8 = 2x - 10$.
   b. The sum of five consecutive odd numbers is 30. Find the numbers.
   c. Graph a set of simultaneous relations.

d. Given a set of coordinates, find a "visual line of best fit."
6. Experimental techniques: sampling, inference
   a. The producer of a television show wanted to measure its popularity. He called 25 people in various occupations: one teacher, one doctor, one plumber, one housewife, and so on. He collected their opinions and drew conclusions. Discuss.
   b. A food product advertises a butter fat content of 4.0. Tests on a sample show 3.8, 4.0, 4.2, 3.8. Discuss the validity of the claim.
7. Experimental geometry, including simple locus
   a. (Map given.) A manufacturer wishes to establish a factory equidistant form Elephant Creek and Fox Creek, and also equidistant from Indian City and Jeremiah City. Where should the factory be located?
   b. Draw any triangle *ABC*. Find the midpoint of *AB*. Call this *M*. Through *M*, draw a line parallel to *BC*, cutting *AC* at *N*. Compare *MN* and *BC*, also *AN* and *NC*. (In the book, the diagram is given.)
8. Indirect measurement
   (Using a home-made "transit.") Measure the width of your classroom, and check by direct measurement.
9. Logic
   a. Point out the word or words that need definition: Mrs. Rich said, "This hat is not expensive."
   b. Discuss: In an argument about doing the dishes, Leon said to Alice, "You should do the dishes, Alice. After all, you're a girl."
   c. Draw a diagram for: If *X* is a skree, then *X* is a zilch.
   d. Discuss: Every good baseball player must have good muscular

---

[1]The questions following each topic are taken from the author's *Mathematics—A Liberal Arts Approach* (New York: Hayden Book Co., 1964), with the kind permission of the publisher.

coordination. John has excellent muscular coordination. He should be a good ball player.

e. Discuss: A safety device was put on this machine a year ago. It was a waste of time, because we have not had a accident since it was put on.

f. Discuss: Lyons is in France, and Paris is in France. Therefore, Paris is in Lyons.

10. Topics associated with simple set theory, e.g., probability

a. A questionnaire study showed that 19 people liked Brand A, 18 liked Brand B, and 20 liked Brand C. Five of these people liked A and B, 9 liked B and C, and 7 liked A and C. Two people liked all three. How many people were there? (Done by diagram.)

b. Mary has been told that she must take pills for an illness. In each month, she needs at least 20 units of X but not more than 50 units. She needs 10 units of Y but not more than 40 units. She should have at least 40 units of X and Y together. If X costs $1.00 per unit and Y costs $2.00 per unit, what is the cheapest satisfactory combination? (Done graphically.)

c. What is the probability of rolling either 5 or 7 with a pair of "fair" dice? (Done by Kemeny tree.)

d. You roll a pair of dice. If you get a 7, you roll the dice again and win on a 5. If you do not get a 7 on the first roll, you roll again and win on a 4. What is your chance of winning? (Done by Kemeny tree.)

An Approach to Vector Geometry

ROBERT J. TROYER

The mathematics curriculum is undergoing many exciting changes, and geometry is no exception. However, it seems very difficult to obtain general agreement concerning changes in geometry. Many high schools are faced

Reprinted from *The Mathematics Teacher*, LVI (May, 1963), 290–97, by permission of the author and the National Council of Teachers of Mathematics. Copyright © 1963 by the National Council of Teachers of Mathematics. This article is based on a sequence of three lectures given at the Summer Meeting of the National Council of Teachers of Mathematics in Madison, Wisconsin, August 15–17, 1962. Robert J. Troyer is Associate Professor of Mathematics, Lake Forest College, Lake Forest Illinois.

with the following questions: Should the traditional one-semester course in solid geometry be dropped from the curriculum? If this is done, what should be taught in its place and how does this affect the plane geometry course?

There is little doubt that it is desirable to integrate parts of plane and solid geometry. But is not the development of a closer tie between algebra and geometry, whereby an individual no longer regards them as two unrelated disciplines, of even greater importance? Vector geometry affords one excellent opportunity for such a development. A one-semester course in vector geometry would be a suitable replacement for the twelfth-grade solid geometry course. For a complete discussion of such a course, let me recommend the article, "If Not Solid Geometry, Then What?" found in *The Mathematics Teacher,* May, 1961.

Let us now focus our attention on the tenth-grade geometry course, under the assumption it is desirable to integrate parts of plane and solid geometry. A considerable amount of coordinate geometry, in one form or another, has been included in many recently published geometry textbooks as well as in much of the experimental geometry material produced by various writing groups. From the Report of the Commission on Mathematics (College Entrance Examination Board), *Program for College Preparatory Mathematics,* one finds some pertinent remarks. First, the objectives given for the study of geometry are:

1. The acquisition of information about geometric figures in the plane and in space;
2. The development of an understanding of the deductive method as a way of thinking, and a reasonable skill in applying this method to mathematical situations;
3. The provision of opportunities for original and creative thinking by students.

Second, some proposals are made as to how these objectives might be attained. Among the proposals are:

1. A reduction in the number of theorems proved by the formal method;
2. An introduction of coordinate geometry;
3. Once coordinate geometry has been introduced, the use of analytic (algebraic) as well as synthetic methods in proving geometric theorems and exercises.

Articles 14 and 15 of the *Appendices* (Report of the Commission on Mathe-

matics) give a detailed exposition relative to the above proposals.

Since the plane and solid geometries are being integrated, should not whatever coordinate geometry that is introduced be done in such a manner that the plane coordinate geometry be easily generalized to solid coordinate geometry? One satisfactory method of doing this is by means of a vector approach. In order to prove geometric theorems and exercises by analytic techniques, one would need the following concepts:

1. length of a line segment;
2. division of a segment in a given ratio;
3. the concept of parallelism and perpendicularity.

The presentation that follows is not intended to be a complete or strictly logical approach to vector analytic geometry, for indeed it is not. It is hoped that the presentation will give the reader a greater appreciation for the connection between algebra and geometry and provide him with some idea how vector analytic geometry might be developed.

MOTIVATION

It is important to see the overall picture before starting the details, so let us detour momentarily to motivate what will be done. We say "two points determine a line." However, we also know that a point and a direction also determine a line. In plane geometry this direction is usually given by a number called the slope (with the exception of the vertical line). Given two points $X = (x_1, x_2)$ and $Y = (y_1, y_2)$ in the plane, we know that the slope is given by the formula $m = (y_2 - x_2)/(y_1 - x_1)$, $y_1 - x_1 \neq 0$. Have you ever asked yourself why you divide these numbers? Division always necessitates the consideration of the special case when $y_1 - x_1 \neq$

0. Observe that the slope is given in terms of the two real numbers $y_1 - x_1$ and $y_2 - x_2$. But these numbers are respectively the differences of the first coordinates and the second coordinates of the points X and Y. In other words, the direction seems to be determined by the two numbers $y_2 - x_2$ and $y_1 - x_1$. These numbers, which we might venture to write in the form $Y - X = [y_1 - x_1, y_2 - x_2]$, lead us into the notion of vectors. It is clear that by this technique each ordered pair of points in the plane gives rise to an ordered pair of real numbers, and every ordered pair of real numbers is obtained in this manner. (In fact, each ordered pair of real numbers is obtained from an ordered pair of points in the plane in many ways.)

VECTORS

Assuming the algebraic properties of the real numbers, we begin the formal presentation.

1.1 Definition. A plane vector X is an ordered pair of real numbers and is denoted by $X = [x_1, x_2]$. A space vector X is an ordered triple of real numbers and is denoted by $X = [x_1, x_2, x_3]$.

The real numbers x_1 and x_2 are repsectively called the first and second components of the vector X. For a space vector, x_3 is called the third component.

1.2 Definition. (Equality of vectors.) If $X = [x_1, x_2]$ and $Y = [y_1, y_2]$ are plane vectors, then $X = Y$ iff (if and only if) $x_1 = y_1$ and $x_2 = y_2$. If $X = [x_1, x_2, x_3]$ and $Y = [y_1, y_2, y_3]$ are space vectors, then $X = Y$ iff $x_1 = y_1$, $x_2 = y_2$ and $x_3 = y_3$.

1.3 Remark. A geometric model (see Fig. 1) for the plane vectors is obtained as follows: To each vector $X = [x_1, x_2]$ we associate the directed line segment beginning at the origin and terminating at the point (x_1, x_2). A similar model is used for space vectors.

Figure 1

1.4 Definition. (Vector addition.) If $X = [x_1, x_2]$ and $Y = [y_1, y_2]$ are plane vectors, then $X + Y = [x_1 + y_1, x_2 + y_2]$. If $X = [x_1, x_2, x_3]$ and $Y = [y_1, y_2, y_3]$ are space vectors, then

$$X + Y = [x_1 + y_1, x_2 + y_2, x_3 + y_3].$$

For those who have a background in physics, a few examples (see Fig. 2)

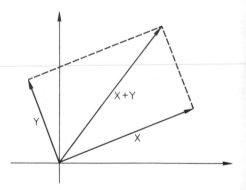

Figure 2

will quickly show that a model for the geometry of addition of vectors is none other than the parallelogram law used in elementary physics.

1.5 Definition. (Scalar multiplication.) For any real number t and any plane vector $X = [x_1, x_2]$, we define

$$tX = [tx_1, tx_2]$$

If $X = [x_1, x_2, x_3]$ is any space vector, we define $tX = [tx_1, tx_2, tx_3]$. In mathematical slang, we say the vector X is "stretched" by an amount t.

1.6 Definition. (Special vectors.)
a. The vector $[0, 0]$ (or $[0, 0, 0]$) is the zero vector and is denoted by 0.
b. The negative of a plane vector

$$X = [x_1, x_2]$$

is defined to be the vector

$$(-X) = [-x_1, -x_2].$$

The negative of a space vector

$$X = [x_1, x_2, x_3]$$

is defined to be the vector

$$(-X) = [-x_1, -x_2, -x_3].$$

1.7 Definition. Using the procedure suggested by real numbers, we define subtraction of vectors by the formula $X - Y = X + (-Y)$.

1.8 Theorem. The following rules of operation hold for plane and space vectors.

A_1 If X, Y are vectors, then $X + Y$ is a vector.

A_2 For any three vectors X, Y, and Z, $(X + Y) + Z = X + (Y + Z)$.

A_3 For any vector X, $0 + X = X = X + 0$.

A_4 For any vector X, $X + (-X) = 0 = (-X) + X$.

A_5 For any two vectors X and Y, $X + Y = Y + X$.

S_1 For any vector X and any real number t, tX is a vector.

S_2 For any real numbers s and t and any vector X, $(st)X = s(tX)$.

S_3 For any real numbers s and t and any vector X, $(s + t)X = sX + tX$.

S_4 For any real number t and any vectors X and Y, $t(X + Y) = tX + tY$.

S_5 For any vector X, $1 \cdot X = X$.

Proof: Only A_2 will be proved. The remaining properties are proved in a

similar manner. Let $X = [x_1, x_2]$, $Y = [y_1, y_2]$, $Z = [z_1, z_2]$. Then

$(X + Y) + Z$
$= ([x_1, x_2] + [y_1, y_2]) + [z_1, z_2]$
$= [x_1 + y_1, x_2 + y_2] + [z_1, z_2]$

by *1.4*

$= [(x_1 + y_1) + z_1, (x_2 + y_2) + z_2]$

by *1.4*

$X + (Y + Z)$
$= [x_1, x_2] + ([y_1, y_2] + [z_1, z_2])$
$= [x_1, x_2] + [y_1 + z_1, y_2 + z_2]$

by *1.4*

$= [x_1 + (y_1 + z_1), x_2 + (y_2 + z_2)]$

by *1.4*

$= [(x_1 + y_1) + z_1, (x_2 + y_2) + z_2]$

Associative law of real numbers.

Hence $(X + Y) + Z = X + (Y + Z)$ by *1.2*.

1.9 Observations.
a. One can extend properties A_2, S_2, S_3, and S_4 to what is usually referred to as general associativity and general distributivity. Moreover, because of general associativity and A_5, we may omit parentheses (in a manner analogous to that of real numbers).
b. The proofs of the above properties do not depend on "dimension" two or three and hence would be true of any dimension.

Let E_2 denote the rectangular cartesian coordinate system of plane analytic geometry, i.e., the points of E_2 are ordered pairs of real numbers. Clearly there is a one-to-one correspondence between points of E_2 and plane vectors; namely, the point (x_1, x_2) corresponds to the vector $[x_1, x_2]$. It is through this correspondence that we may study vector coordinate geometry. More generally, to each ordered pair of points (X, Y), where $X = (x_1, x_2)$ and $Y = (y_1, y_2)$, we associate the vector $Y - X = [y_1 - x_1, y_2 - x_2]$. (See Fig. 3.)

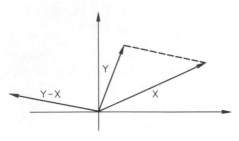

Figure 3

Suppose $X = [x_1, x_2]$ is a nonzero vector, and one considers the set of all points of E_2 corresponding to vectors tX, for each real value of t, i.e., all possible stretches of X. One would expect to obtain the straight line through the origin and the point (x_1, x_2). All such vectors would have the form $Z = tX$ or $[z_1, z_2] = [tx_1, tx_2]$. This is equivalent to, by *definition 1.2*,

$$z_1 = tx_1$$
$$z_2 = tx_2,$$

which are just the parametric equations for a straight line. Now x_1 or x_2 is not zero since X was assumed to be distinct from the zero vector, say $x_1 \neq 0$. Hence $t = z_1/x_1$, which upon substitution in the second equation yields $z_2 = (x_2/x_1)z_1$. But this is just the equation of the line through the origin and the point (x_1, x_2). If $x_1 = 0$ we easily see that one obtains the *y*-axis. With this as motivation we are ready for the definition of a straight line.

1.10 Definition. Let $X = (x_1, x_2)$ and $Y = (y_1, y_2)$ be two distinct points in E_2. The straight line *l* determined by the points X and Y is the set of ordered pairs

$$Z = (z_1, z_2)$$

whose corresponding vector Z satisfies the vector equation $Z = X + t(Y - X)$, where t is any real number.

It seems appropriate to justify that *l*:
a. passes through the points X and Y,
b. has an equation of the form $y = x$, or $y - y_1 = m(x - x_1)$ where

$$m = (y_2 - x_2)/(y_1 - x_1).$$

Part (*a*) is verified by taking $t = 0$ and $t = 1$, respectively. We proceed with part (*b*) by noting that the equation of the straight line as given in *1.10* becomes, when written out in component form,

$$[z_1, z_2] = [x_1, x_2]$$
$$+ t[y_1 - x_1, y_2 - x_2].$$

By scalar multiplication and vector addition, one obtains

$$[z_1, z_2] = [x_1 + t(y_1 - x_1),$$
$$x_2 + t(y_2 - x_2)].$$

By equality of vectors we have the two equations

$$z_1 = x_1 + t(y_1 - x_1)$$

and

$$z_2 = x_2 + t(y_2 - x_2).$$

Assuming $y_1 - x_1 \neq 0$, we can solve the first equation for t and obtain

$$t = (z_1 - x_1)/(y_1 - x_1).$$

Substitution of this value for t into the second equation yields the second equation in part (*b*), which is just the two-point form of the equation through the points X and Y. If $y_1 - x_1 = 0$, one obtains the equation $z_1 = x_1$. As an example, for the points $X = (3, 2)$ and $Y = (-1, 6)$ one obtains the vector equation $Z = [3, 2] + t[-4, 4]$.

The vector equation as given in *1.10* seems to distinguish between the points X and Y. Is this really necessary? The answer is no, and, in fact, the line *l* is also determined by the vector equations

$$Z = X + t(X - Y)$$
$$Z = Y + t(Y - X)$$
$$Z = Y + t(X - Y).$$

This is proved by showing that any point Z whose corresponding vector Z satisfies one of the above four vector equations must also satisfy each of the other three. Suppose Z is a point on line l: then by *1.10* there is a real number t_1 such that $Z = X + t_1(Y - X)$. Using the properties of *1.8*, this vector equation can be rewritten in the three forms

$$Z = X + (-t_1)(X - Y)$$
$$Z = Y + (t_1 - 1)(Y - X)$$
$$Z = Y + (1 - t_1)(X - Y).$$

Thus any vector Z which satisfies the vector equation of *1.10* also satisfies the other three vector equations. The remaining cases are proved in a similar manner.

Moreover, if l is the straight line determined by the points X and Y, and if P and Q are any two points of l, one easily verifies that l is also given by the vector equation $Z = Q + t(P - Q)$, where t is any real number. This is expressed by saying that the vector equation for l is independent of the choice of points which determine l.

Observe that no special consideration need be given to vertical lines. This alone, although attractive, is hardly sufficient reason to prefer the vector to the usual approach to coordinate geometry. The advantage is seen when one seeks the vector equation for a straight line through two points X and Y in space; for the equation again becomes $Z = X + t(Y - X)$. However, a little thought will convince you that the notion of slope cannot directly be generalized.

We now consider the notion of parallelism. Two non-vertical lines l and l' are usually defined to be parallel iff their slopes are equal. Suppose m and m' are the slopes of l and l', respectively. If $X = (x_1, x_2)$ and $Y = (y_1, y_2)$ are points of l, and if $P = (p_1, p_2)$ and $Q = (q_1, q_2)$ are points of l', then $m = (y_2 - x_2)/(y_1 - x_1)$ and $m' = (q_2 - p_2)/(q_1 - p_1)$. Hence $m = m'$ iff $y_2 - x_2 = m(q_2 - p_2)$ and $y_1 - x_1 = m(q_1 - p_1)$. In terms of vectors, this is equivalent to saying that the vector $Y - X$ is a scalar multiple of the vector $Q - P$. This suggests a definition for parallelism, but is this relationship valid, independent of our choice of points X, Y, P, Q? (We know this to be the case for m and m'.) This question is now answered in the affirmative.

1.11 Theorem. Let l be the line determined by the two points X and Y, i.e., given by the vector equation

$$Z = X + t(Y - X).$$

If A and B are any two points of l, the vector $B - A$ is a scalar multiple of $Y - X$.

Proof. Since A and B belong to line l, there exist real numbers t_1 and t_2 such that $A = X + t_1(Y - X)$ and $B = X + t_2(Y - X)$. Hence $B - A = (t_2 - t_1)(Y - X)$, i.e., the scalar is the number $t_2 - t_1$.

We are now ready for the definition.

1.12 Definition. Line l is parallel to line l' iff for any two points X, Y of l and any two points X', Y' of l', the vector $Y - X$ is a scalar multiple of $Y' - X'$.

If line l is parallel to line l', then line l' is also parallel to line l. Again, it is interesting to note that no special attention need be given to vertical lines.

THE DOT PRODUCT

In this section we investigate a concept which is found in many branches of mathematics and which will be used to define the distance between two points and the notion of perpendicularity. It is called the dot product.

2.1 Definition. If $X = [x_1, x_2]$ and $Y = [y_1, y_2]$ the dot product of X and Y is defined to be the real number given by the formula $X \cdot Y = x_1 y_1 + x_2 y_2$. If

$$X = [x_1, x_2, x_3]$$

and

$$Y = [y_1, y_2, y_3]$$

are space vectors, then

$$X \cdot Y = x_1y_1 + x_2y_2 + x_3y_3.$$

A word of warning is in order here. The terms "inner product" and "scalar product" are often used in place of the term "dot product" as defined in *2.1*. If the term "scalar product" is used in *2.1*, one must be careful not to confuse it with the term "scalar multiplication" as defined in *1.5*.

2.2 Theorem. The dot product satisfies the following laws of calculation. If X, Y, Z are any vectors and t is any real number, then

a. $X \cdot Y = Y \cdot X$
b. $(X + Y) \cdot Z = X \cdot Z + Y \cdot Z$ and $Z \cdot (X + Y) = Z \cdot X + Z \cdot Y$
c. $t(X \cdot Y) = (tX) \cdot Y = X \cdot (tY)$
d. $X \cdot X \geq 0$ and $X \cdot X = 0$ iff $X = 0$.

The proof of this theorem is an immediate consequence of *2.1* and the properties of real numbers; it will be omitted.

2.3 Definition. The length of a vector X is defined by the formula

$$\text{length } X = [X \cdot X]^{1/2}.$$

2.4 Definition. The distance from the point X to the point Y is the real number given by the formula

$$d(X, Y) = \text{length } (Y - X).$$

If $X = (x_1, x_2)$ and $Y = (y_1, y_2)$, then $d(X, Y) = [(y_1 - x_1)^2 + (y_2 - x_2)^2]^{1/2}$, which is just the usual formula for the distance between two points. (You didn't really expect anything different, did you?) Moreover, this definition yields the usual formula for the distance between two points $X = (x_1, x_2, x_3)$ and $Y = (y_1, y_2, y_3)$ in space; namely, $d(X, Y) = [(y_1 - x_1)^2 + (y_2 - x_2)^2 + (y_3 - x_3)^2]^{1/2}$.

What about perpendicularity? Let us consider some examples.

Example I (see Fig. 4) Let l and l' be straight lines given respectively by the equations $2x - y = 3$ and $x + 2y =$

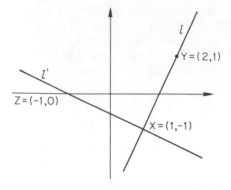

Figure 4

-1. These two lines are perpendicular. Consider the points X, Y, Z as given in the diagram. For the vectors $Y - X$ and $Z - X$, we observe that $(Y - X) \cdot (Z - X) = 0$. Is this just a coincidence? The answer is no, as the next example proves.

Example II. Two non-vertical lines l and l' are usually defined to be perpendicular iff the slope of one is the negative reciprocal of the other. Consider Figure 5 and assume l is perpendicular

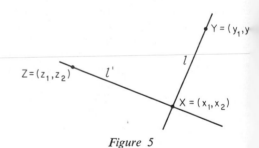

Figure 5

to l'. The slopes of l and l' are $m = (y_2 - x_2)/(y_1 - x_1)$ and $m' = (z_2 - x_2)/(z_1 - x_1)$. Now

$$m = -1/m' \text{ iff } mm' = -1.$$

An easy computation shows this is equivalent to

$$(y_1 - x_1)(z_1 - x_1)$$
$$+ (y_2 - x_2)(z_2 - x_2) = 0.$$

But this is just the dot product of $Y - X$ and $Z - X$. Each step in this calculation is reversible; consequently, if the dot product of the vectors $Y - X$ and $Z - X$ is zero, line l is perpendicular to line l'.

Example III. Let l and l' be two straight lines that intersect at a point A. With the notation of the diagram (see Fig. 6), from the law of cosines we have

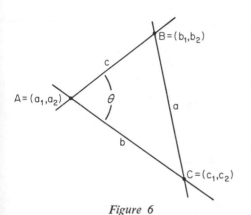

Figure 6

$$a^2 = b^2 + c^2 - 2bc \cos \theta,$$

or

$$\cos \theta = (b^2 + c^2 - a^2)/2bc.$$

If we use the coordinates of A, B, C to compute the lengths of a, b, c, and apply a little high-powered seventh-grade arithmetic we obtain:

$$\cos \theta = \frac{(c_1 - a_1)(b_1 - a_1)}{[(c_1 - a_1)^2 + (c_2 - a_2)^2]^{1/2}} \\ + \frac{(c_2 - a_2)(b_2 - a_2)}{[(b_1 - a_1)^2 + (b_2 - a_2)^2]^{1/2}}$$

or

$$\cos \theta = \frac{(C - A) \cdot (B - A)}{\text{length}(C-A)\,\text{length}(B-A)}.$$

Hence $\theta = \pi/2$ iff the dot product

$$(C - A) \cdot (B - A) = 0.$$

Thus we see that the angle between the two lines l and l' can be defined in terms of the angle between the vectors $C - A$ and $B - A$. Moreover, if s and t are

positive real numbers, the angle between the vectors $s(C - A)$ and $t(B - A)$ is the came as the angle between the vectors $C - A$ and $B - A$.

In view of these examples, and in particular the expression for $\cos \theta$ in Example III, we give the following definition.

2.5 Definition. Two non-zero vectors X and Y are perpendicular iff $X \cdot Y = 0$.

Here again we see an advantage to the vector approach. For, although the motivation for *2.5* comes from plane geometry and plane vectors, this definition gives us the notion of perpendicularity for space vectors as well as for plane vectors. Indeed, even in the "higher dimensions," two non-zero vectors X and Y are defined to be perpendicular if $X \cdot Y = 0$.

2.6 Definition. Let X, Y be any two points of a line l and X', Y' any two points of a line l'. Then l is perpendicular to l' iff the vectors $Y - X$ and $Y' - X'$ are perpendicular, i.e., iff $(Y - X) \cdot (Y' - X') = 0$.

We need one more concept before we are ready to prove theorems of plane geometry by techniques of vector analytic geometry, namely, division of a segment into a given ratio. But first, a segment must be defined.

2.7 Definition. The line segment determined by the points X and Y of the line l is the set of points Z satisfying the vector equation $Z = X + t(Y - X)$, $0 \le t \le 1$.

By methods similar to those used in the remarks following *1.10*, it can be shown that the line segment determined by the points X and Y of the line l can also be given as the set of points Z satisfying the vector equation $Z = Y + t(X - Y)$, $0 \le t \le 1$.

2.8 Definition. If Z lies on the line segment determined by the points X and Y, and $Z = X + r(Y - X)$, then

$$d(X, Z)/d(X, Y) = r.$$

Proof. From 2.3 and 2.4 we have

$$\frac{d(X, Z)}{d(X, Y)} = \frac{[(Z - X) \cdot (Z - X)]^{1/2}}{[(Y - X) \cdot (Y - X)]^{1/2}}$$

$$= \frac{[r(Y - X) \cdot r(Y - X)]^{1/2}}{[(Y - X) \cdot (Y - X)]^{1/2}}$$

$$= r.$$

2.9 Corollary. The coordinates of the midpoint (z_1, z_2) of the segment determined by the points $X = (x_1, x_2)$ and $Y = (y_1, y_2)$ are given by $z_1 = (x_1 + y_1)/2$ and $z_2 = (x_2 + y_2)/2$.

THEOREMS PROVED BY VECTOR METHODS

In this concluding section, vector techniques are used to prove two theorems of plane geometry.

Theorem I. A line segment joining the midpoints of two sides of a triangle is parallel to the third side and equal to one-half of it.

Proof. Let us assume a diagram as given (Fig. 7). (Here some justification

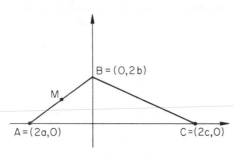

Figure 7

for this choice is necessary.) By *2.9*, $M = (a, b)$ and $N = (c, b)$. Using *2.3* and *2.4*, we obtain $d(M, N) = |c - a|$ and $d(A, C) = 2|c - a|$. Moreover, $N - M = \frac{1}{2}(C - A)$ and hence the

segment *MN* is parallel to side *AC* by *1.10*.

Theorem II. The medians of a triangle are concurrent in a point that lies two thirds of the distance from each vertex to the midpoint of the opposite side.

Proof. Let us assume a diagram as given (Fig. 8). By *2.9*, $M = (a, b)$, $N =$

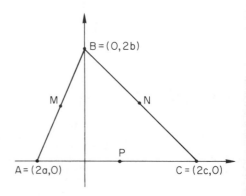

Figure 8

(c, b) and $P = (a + c, O)$. Let Q, R, S denote the points which lie two thirds of the distance from A, B, C, respectively, to the midpoint of the opposite side. Applying *2.8* to each of the segments *AN*, *CM*, and *BP* with $r = 2/3$, we have

$$Q = A + 2/3(N - A)$$
$$\text{or } Q = 2/3[c + a, b]$$
$$R = B + 2/3(P - B)$$
$$\text{or } R = 2/3[c + a, b]$$
$$S = C + 2/3(M - C)$$
$$\text{or } S = 2/3[c + a, b].$$

This shows Q, R, and S are concurrent and concludes the proof of the theorem.

The Dilemma in Geometry

CARL B. ALLENDOERFER

The mathematical curriculum in our elementary and secondary schools faces a serious dilemma when it comes to geometry. It is easy to find fault with the traditional course in geometry, but sound advice on how to remedy these difficulties is hard to come by. The Commission on Mathematics of the CEEB, the School Mathematics Study Group, the Illinois Project, and many other curricular reform groups at home and abroad have tackled the problem, but with singular lack of success or agreement. On the other hand, the "new math" has made great strides in arithmetic and algebra that seem to be acceptable to all except the congenital standpatters who resist change of any kind. We are, therefore, under pressure to "do something" about geometry; but what shall we do? In this article I shall discuss the reasons for the present state of confusion and make suggestions for modest first steps toward clearing it up.

ALGEBRA VERSUS GEOMETRY

Why was it possible to reform arithmetic and algebra with relative agreement on all sides, when geometry raises so many problems? The answer here is quite simple: The objective of algebra is the development of the properties of

Reprinted from *The Mathematics Teacher*, LXII (March, 1969), 165–69, by permission of the author and the National Council of Teachers of Mathematics. Copyright © 1969 by the National Council of Teachers of Mathematics. Carl B. Allendoerfer is Professor of Mathematics, University of Washington, Seattle.

the fields of rational, real, and complex numbers. The notion of a field is easy to grasp, and its importance is unquestioned. The only room for discussion and innovation is that of the pedagogy involved.

In geometry, however, there is not even agreement as to what the subject is about. Oswald Veblen said, quite seriously, that "geometry is what geometers do." Felix Klein thought of it as the study of the invariants of transformation groups. To some it is the study of geometric figures, while in the minds of others it is almost identified with a method of proof. In addition, there are many geometries such as Euclidean, affine, non-Euclidean, projective, algebraic, and differential. And each of these may be studied in two, three, or, indeed, in *n* dimensions. There is enough material here for a lifetime of study—how do we select a portion of this for our elementary and secondary schools? There is no agreement on the answer.

OBJECTIVES OF GEOMETRY

Presumably, in designing a curriculum we should start by stating our objectives. Even at this step there are troubles with geometry. Let me give my list of the major objectives of geometry in our schools:

1. *An understanding of the basic facts about geometric figures in the plane and geometric solids in space:* This information is needed by craftsmen in practical arts, by students of science and engineering, by students of art and architecture—indeed, by everyone with normal mental capacity.

2. *An understanding of the basic facts about geometric transformations such as reflections, rotations, and translations:* These ideas occur in science (for example, in connection with the symmetries in space and time) but also are of great importance in art, architecture, and design.

3. *An appreciation of the deductive method:* For two thousand years geometry has been the chief vehicle for the teaching of the deductive method. In our civilization we have learned to reason from premises to conclusions in nearly every aspect of our lives. Geometry has, then, been an essential element in the education of every intelligent man in our Western civilization. Until and unless this aspect of our culture is to be introduced in other portions of the school curriculum, the deductive method must be an essential objective of our courses in geometry.

4. *An introduction to imaginative thinking:* We wish to stimulate our pupils to be creative, to have ideas of their own, to be more than just memorizing machines. The problem material in geometry can assist greatly in this direction, for the solution of "originals" is quite different from merely turning the crank on routine algebraic algorithms.

5. *Integration of geometric ideas with other parts of mathematics:* Geometry should not be isolated from algebra and analysis, with its separate content and method, but should become an essential part of the mainstream of modern mathematics.

To meet all of these objectives is a large order, and we can certainly not hope to do so in a single course in one year of high school. Either we must abandon some of these objectives or we must find ways of spreading instruction in geometry throughout the whole school program, just as we have done traditionally for algebra and arithmetic.

APPROACHES TO GEOMETRY

Our problem is complicated by the fact that there are three basically different approaches to geometry.

1. *Synthetic:* This is the method used by Euclid and so familiar to all of us. It is based on a rather complicated and difficult system of axioms, some of which escaped attention by the Greeks. To most people this *is* geometry.

2. *Analytic:* Invented by Descartes, this method solves geometric problems by means of algebra through the use of coordinate systems. Its logical foundations are based on those of algebra but include other axioms that are largely unknown to those who use the method. This type of geometry is of great importance in modern science and in the notations used in calculus and higher mathematics.

3. *Vector:* In this approach vectors are used to develop the theory through the use of standard vector algebra. This approach is "coordinate-free," and its methods are the same as those employed widely in physics. It is also closely allied with the notion of a vector space, which is one of the principal concepts in modern algebra.

The discussion of the relative advantages of these three approaches is not likely to result in any conclusion that is widely acceptable. There is heavy pressure these days for coordinate methods in geometry. But at the same time the fashion in higher mathematics has turned sharply in the direction of "coordinate-free" synthetic and vector methods. Thus the users of coordinates in schools may be "modern," but if they persist in this way to college they are sure to become "back numbers."

I take a tolerant view toward this controversy. After all, these approaches are merely tools, and all three of them are useful in their own way, so that students may wish to learn them all. Again, however, this multitude of approaches certainly complicates our curriculum problem, for there is hardly time for them all.

PROBLEMS OF RIGOR

In contrast to arithmetic and algebra, geometry is plagued with problems of rigor. Virtually every modern treatment seeks to find a set of axioms that will fix the weaknesses of Euclid, and then everything must be proved on this basis. This leads to enormous tedium, and there is no escape if rigor is to be preserved. Even so, most of these schemes are bogus, for they assume the completeness properties of the real numbers, which are seldom if ever taught in the schools. Good teachers know how to compromise at this stage, and I encourage them to do so. We must not bury the geometry under an avalanche of rigor.

I think well of another suggestion that has been around a long time. This is that we abandon the goal of proving everything from our axioms. When intuition suffices, let us use it. Then we can develop small, self-contained, deductive systems within which everything can be proved.

ADVICE FROM ABROAD

In our dilemma we shall do well to look at what other countries are doing about geometry. This is very helpful, for all kinds of trends exist that we can evaluate.

One trend is the complete abandonment of traditional deductive geometry; I find this view especially prevalent in countries with a system of national examinations that effectively determine the future of each young person. In these countries the examinations in geometry had become very stereotyped, so that there was a fixed list of theorems to be memorized word for word and in a prescribed order. Geometry then became an awful chore of memorization

and was a hated subject. So—away with it! Fortunately for us, the CEEB long ago gave up this method of examination, so we are not so plagued; but in many countries the old system is still in effect.

When the method of Euclid was displaced in some of these countries, they turned to transformation geometry. Textbooks exist which are based on these ideas, and they deserve widespread attention in the United States.

It is easy, however, to overestimate the trend of European countries away from classical Euclid. At the Montreal meeting I listened to the enthusiastic presentation of vector geometry by Professor Papy, of Belgium. He was so convincing that I supposed that all of Belgium was following him! A few weeks later I was favored with a visit from the chief inspector for mathematics in Belgium, and I asked him about Papy. In effect, he said that Papy had interesting ideas, but that well over 90 per cent of the Belgian schools teach geometry from the classical textbook of Lagrange (1736–1813). I am told that the same is true in France in spite of the efforts of Dieudonne and Choquet, two of the most prominent French mathematicians, who favor the vector approach with slogans such as "Down with triangles, long live the parallelogram!" So when you read about experiments abroad, take the ideas seriously; but do not suppose that, as a nation, we are behind other nations in the teaching of geometry.

ADVICE FROM COLLEGE PROFESSORS

Another apparently sensible thing for you to do is to ask college professors about the curriculum in geometry. You will not get much help, and you may get undeserved abuse for not doing a better job. The algebraists could not care less about geometry, and they know precious little geometry anyhow. The analysts believe in geometry just so long as it does not take time away from the teaching of analysis. The geometers are badly divided, each favoring his own specialty as the one and only true geometry. College-level courses in geometry reflect this disarray, and so I fear that you will get little help from above and must solve your problems yourselves.

POSSIBLE COURSES OF ACTION

After hearing this dismal array of problems, controversies, and confusions you may well wonder how society can expect you to do your job when it gives you so little help. So let us examine a number of possible courses of action for you to take.

1. *Give up geometry entirely:* There are those who favor this, but I deplore this attitude. Geometry is of very great importance—we must seek to solve the problem of teaching it.

2. *Stand pat:* Since there is so much confusion, the safe position is to do nothing—then your neck will not be out. But this is the program of the ostrich, and when his head is in the sand his neck is very vulnerable.

3. *Proceed slowly with small changes:* This is the intelligent approach to any curricular reform, the emphasis being on the word *proceed*. In fact there is much that can be and is being accomplished in this area:

a. Introduction of informal geometry in the elementary schools. Here you can teach many of the facts of plane and solid geometry and introduce the children to simple geometric transformations. There are many opportunities for using geometric ideas in connection with art, geography (maps, great circles, etc.), and science. Geometric facts can be discovered through the use of construction problems. In this connection we should not be limited to the

classic ruler-and-compass constructions, but should use any drawing instrument that will do the job. By the time the youngster reaches the tenth grade he should have a good working knowledge of elementary geometry. This idea is already being implemented in better schools in the United States and in some foreign countries. It still, however, has to penetrate into the boondocks at home and abroad.

b. Revive the teaching of solid geometry, but in an informal fashion. When the curriculum reformers of the forties and fifties urged that solid geometry be dropped, they were badly misunderstood. What was to be dropped was the deductive treatment of this subject; the discussion of space was to be maintained on an informal basis. Unfortunately it, too, was often dropped. We cannot get along without a knowledge of the properties of lines, planes, angles, spheres, etc., in space. Students also need practice with space perception and perspective. We must bring these back. One possibility is for us to cooperate with teachers of mechanical drawing who are skilled in three-dimensional drawings. Experience with a T square and a triangle at a drawing board may well teach more space geometry than an equal time spent on theorems or equations.

c. Begin introducing geometric transformations. There are simple ways of doing this in the plane through the use of coordinates and pairs of linear equations, and the informal ideas can be given in the elementary school.

4. *Think seriously about more drastic long range changes:* First of all, we should discuss our objectives in geometry. Do we agree with those that I have stated earlier? If not, how should they be modified? Then when an idea for change arises which might meet our objectives, a small group should try to work this out as a practical course of

instruction. Some mathematicians in this country (such as the group at Wesleyan University) and abroad have conducted projects of this kind. These materials should be taught in selected classes by adventuresome teachers, criticized, and refined until they are as polished as possible. Finally, they should be evaluated on two grounds: (*a*) Are they generally teachable? (*b*) Do they meet our objectives more successfully than was true of older materials? If the answer to both questions is "Yes," then we are ready for a major change.

This is a long and exhausting process, but it must be carried foward. I hope that more college and school teachers of mathematics will become involved in it.

A SCHOOL CURRICULUM IN GEOMETRY

As a summary, let me extend my own neck and outline what I think is a reasonable curriculum for geometry in the schools at the present time:

1. *Elementary school:* Informal plane and solid geometry and geometric transformations.

2. *Junior high:* More informal geometry, use of coordinates in algebra, graphing, elements of deductive proofs.

3. *Tenth grade:* Formal deductive plane geometry with informal solid geometry. Possible inclusion of brief analytic geometry.

4. *Eleventh or twelfth grade:* Full semester of plane and solid analytic geometry and geometric transformations in preparation for use in calculus. If this is not taught in the high school, the students will never get it; for this material is very rapidly dropping out of the colleges. Conclude with a brief treatment of non-Euclidean geometry.

CONCLUSION

I am an incurable optimist concerning the future of geometry in our schools. In spite of the confusions and controversies that I have discussed, geometry is so beautiful and so important that it is certain to enjoy a healthy existence. Nevertheless, those who love it must repeatedly examine its objectives rethink its details, state its virtues, and fight for an appropriate allocation of time for it in the curriculum. We must strive to teach our geometry courses with a truly *geometric* flavor, and not merely as an exercise in algebra or in logic. We must apply our geometry to algebra, calculus, science, art, architecture, and elsewhere. In these ways we can keep geometry fresh and exciting for all our students and maintain it as one of the most fundamental subjects in our schools.

A Case for Applications of Linear Algebra
and Group Theory

R. K. JARVIS

This is an appeal for help. Briefly, I am a physicist with the usual sort of background in mathematics, but teaching mathematics extensively at the high school level. I make no claims as a mathematician, nor many as a physicist, but I have had extensive experience in teaching mathematics and science to high school students and college freshmen.

My problem concerns the applications of mathematics in general, but in particular the applications of linear algebra and group theory. To particularise still further, it is especially the application of matrices in linear algebra which concerns me most. It is a matter of the utmost concern to me, in whatever I teach, to show the power of mathematics in addition to its inherent fascination and beauty, and I am always very grateful to hear from any professional, whatever may be his field, of some new and interesting way in which he has put some mathematics to work. Many of the applications most commonly exhibited at the school level are certainly dated and new ones are badly needed.

In linear algebra, especially matrices, which has just begun to creep down into the schools in a significant way, I have been unable to find more than a very few significant applications which do not

require extensive training in other disciplines in order to be appreciated. Perhaps I am asking too much and it is indeed impossible to satisfy the requirements of real significance and comprehension without extensive extra-mathematical training, but I hope not. There are a great many very bright men and women in science and applied mathematics, and matrices are extensively used. I have been encouraged to think by one university professor, who unfortunately does not have the time to work on this himself, that such applications as I could make use of in teaching bright high-school students are available. My question is, "Where?"

Two or three mathematicians I have spoken to think I am too concerned with the applications. "The subjects stands on its own feet." It is not that I do not appreciate this point of view, but there are high-school and beginning college students, too intelligent to be ignored, for whom "pure mathematics is to applied mathematics, as crossword puzzles are to literature." A mathematician may disagree with this attitude, but it cannot be proved wrong. I recently attended a set of undergraduate lectures and it was clear both during class and from conversation afterwards, that a large percentage of the audience were left untouched, were baffled and frustrated by what for them was not meaningful or useful and purely academic. I have been approached by a few undergraduates and some of the boys I teach, all of them doing linear algebra, with the same complaint; "So what?" I

Reprinted from *The American Mathematics Monthly*, LXXIII, No. 6 (June–July, 1966), 654–56, by permission of the author and the publisher. R. K. Jarvis is a member of the Mathematics Department and the Science Department, Groton School, Groton, Massachusetts.

think that the fact has to be accepted that not all students are inspired by linear algebra *per se* and their lack of appreciation is not overcome by the all too numerous purely abstract presentations of the subject in current texts. If I may quote one professor, albeit talking of some presentations of the calculus: "Too much purity does not lead to fertility." There are many potential users of mathematics passing through teachers' hands, who need to see mathematics work if they are to apply it. I reject the idea that if any student cannot appreciate the linear algebra of itself then that is his own bad luck. Mathematicians who insist on the "pure approach" and the pure approach alone for their recommendations as to what should be taught, particularly at my level, are, in my opinion, doing this country a great disservice which could have tragic consequences. There always will be more users than creators of mathematics and using mathematics does not simply come naturally once a student has some mathematics. He needs to be trained. To be sure he should understand what is mathematics and what is not in any application, but that is another problem. Men and women with a real command of mathematics, whether their viewpoint is pure or applied, are too valuable for us to reject any, simply because they are asking for a different point of view.

Perhaps people may ask, "Why worry with linear algebra at the high-school level anyway?" My reason comes from a few very able students, now on their way to degrees and graduate degrees in science who insist that I should teach some. They claim that an early introduction to it would have been a great help to them. Who am I to argue? They are a part of the new generation of scientists, applied mathematicians and engineers and they ought to know.

You may ask what I regard as a significant application of mathematics. I draw the following from physics for obvious reasons but I have no prejudice as to field of application, scientific or otherwise. This example does not need extensive preparation in another field. A simple harmonic motion is not difficult to understand nor to demonstrate. Most twelfth grade students have dealt with Newton's law in their physics, or even if they have not, $F = ma$ is not difficult to accept on an intuitive basis, particularly at this age. It needs no detailed explanation to describe how the equation of a simple harmonic motion follows from here with a little integration, but that is not all. One of the best devices in the teaching of mathematics is prediction, and consideration of a point moving subject to two such motions superposed at right angles allows one to predict its paths given certain changes in amplitude, frequency and phase. Now show precisely this using an oscilloscope and, judging by reactions I have had, this is a really significant application. There is some excitement, there is some suspense, there is a sense of accomplishment.

And so I make an appeal to anyone who can find a moment, to do a little hard thinking and come up with some problems they have dealt with, particularly ones where matrices were used, which will show the power of the mathematics. The problems should be easy to introduce without extensive digression into other fields (it would be unrealistic to expect that no digression will be necessary) and, if possible, should create some excitement. Matrices, one tells the student, are indispensable in many fields to avoid a quagmire of symbols. Can this be shown in any reasonably easily understood application? How can I convey to the beginning student in linear algebra that, beautiful as it is mathematically, the algebra of matrices is much more than an interesting mental exercise, indeed more than one of the foundation stones of mathematics?

References to sources would be useful, but better still, something from a person's own work, maybe just a small piece of something much larger, but thought out in some detail as to introduction, significance and possible presentation. I hope that this is not so much of a chore that no one will feel inclined to undertake it. Will anyone help?

Opinions of College Teachers of Mathematics regarding Content of the Twelfth-year Course in Mathematics

O. LEXTON BUCHANAN, JR.

During the spring of 1964, a survey was made to determine the opinions of college teachers of mathematics regarding the content of the twelfth-year course in mathematics and to determine, in particular, their opinions regarding the inclusion of a unit on limits. A questionnaire was sent to the chairman of each of the 233 departments of mathematics, applied mathematics, and statistics of those colleges and universities which were located in the United States and which offered a graduate program (and financial assistance) to graduate students in those departments.

PURPOSES OF THE SURVEY

During the school year 1963–64, the writer conducted a study of the teaching of a unit on limits for the twelfth-year course.[1] For this purpose, a unit on

Reprinted from *The Mathematics Teacher*, LVIII (March, 1965), 223–25, by permission of the author and the National Council of Teachers of Mathematics. Copyright © 1965 by the National Council of Teachers of Mathematics. O. Lexton Buchanan, Jr., is Assistant Professor of Mathematics, University of South Carolina, Columbia.

[1] O. Lexton Buchanan, Jr., "A Unit on

limits was written and was taught experimentally to twenty-five classes. The experimentation provided information as to how such a unit might best be constructed and taught and also as to its effectiveness. In addition to the experimentation, there existed the pertinent value judgment, *"Should such a unit be taught in the twelfth grade?"* To help answer this question, the survey of college teachers of mathematics was conducted.

Since there has been a great deal of controversy recently regarding a unit on calculus for the twelfth-year course, it was hoped that the survey would yield some indication of the prevalence of similar controversy regarding a unit on limits.

ASSUMPTIONS

In planning the survey, it was deemed inappropriate to simply pose the question, "Do you approve of a unit on limits for the twelfth-year course?" since answers to that question would often depend on the particular topics being taught in the course. On the other hand, since a great many combinations of

Limits for the Twelfth-Year Course in Mathematics" (unpublished doctoral dissertation, University of Kansas, 1964).

two one-semester courses were possible for the twelfth-year course, the number of combinations to be referred to had to be minimized. Hence, the following assumptions were stated:

In answering this questionnaire, it should be assumed that students in the classes involved are college-capable, twelfth-grade students whose previous three years of study in mathematics has consisted of two years of algebra and one year of deductive geometry (plane and solid); a substantial portion of trigonometry will have been included. It should be assumed further that the first semester of the twelfth-grade course is a course in Elementary Functions of the type recommended by the Commission on Mathematics of the College Entrance Examination Board.

THE QUESTIONNAIRE

Accompanying the questionnaire was a two-page summary of the unit on limits.

The questionnaire included a postcard, which was all that the respondent needed to return (Fig. 1). The following instructions were given for filling out the card:

In Column A on the postcard, please mark with a double-check (√ √) the course you most prefer for the second semester of the twelfth grade. If there are two courses which you prefer equally well for a first choice, you may double-check both of these courses. Of the remaining courses, mark with a single-check (√) your second-choice preferences. You may have as many second-choice preferences as you wish; you may wish to mark no second choice.

For each of the courses checked in Column A, please decide whether or not you would be in favor of including a unit on limits. If you are in favor of this, write "Yes" in Column B. If you are not in favor of this, write "No" in Column B.

For each of the courses checked in Column A (except calculus), please decide whether or not you would be in favor of including a unit on calculus. If you are in favor of this, write "Yes" in Column C. If you are not in favor of this, write "No" in Column C.

RESULTS OF THE SURVEY

Table 1 shows the number and percentage of respondents who chose each course. There were 169 respondents—a

COURSES	A	B	C	Comments:
Anal Geom				
Matrix Alg				
Mod Alg				
Prob,Stat				
More El Fns				
Calc				
Combination*				
Other**				Name, position, and school:

    * Specify which topics:

    ** Specify:

Figure 1   Postcard Used for Responses in Survey

TABLE 1

NUMBER AND PERCENTAGE OF RESPONDENTS WHO CHOSE EACH COURSE

Courses	First and second choices combined N	%	Rank	First choices N	%	Rank	Second choices N	%	Rank
Analytic geometry	139	82	1	103	61	1	36	21	4
Additional elementary functions	87	51	2	24	14	2	63	37	1
Probability and statistics	78	46	3	21	12	4	57	34	2
Matrix algebra	68	40	4	24	14	2	44	26	3
Modern algebra	38	23	5	11	7	6	27	16	5
Calculus	31	18	6	12	8	5	19	11	6
Combination	14	8	7	9	5	7	5	3	7

TABLE 2

PERCENTAGES OF RESPONDENTS FAVORING THE INCLUSION OF A UNIT ON LIMITS AND A UNIT ON CALCULUS FOR EACH COURSE

If the course to be taught during the second semester is the following one:	Then, of the respondents who chose this course as either a first or a second choice, the following percentage favored the inclusion of a unit on:	
	limits	calculus
Analytic geometry	48	28
Additional elementary functions	68	24
Probability and statistics	24	13
Matrix algebra	15	2
Modern algebra	19	9
Calculus	90	Not applicable
Combination	64	50

response of 73 per cent. Table 2 shows the percentages of respondents favoring the inclusion of a unit on limits and a unit on calculus for each course.

Analysis of the data

For the second-semester course, analytic geometry was by far the most popular course, and additional elemen-

tary functions was clearly the second most popular course. Probability and statistics, and matrix algebra were the third and fourth choices, respectively, and were favored almost equally. These four courses were the most popular; each was selected by at least 40 per cent of the respondents as either a first or a second choice.

The remaining three courses ranked as follows: modern algebra, calculus, and a combination course. Each was selected by no more than 23 per cent of the respondents.

A unit on limits was more favored than a unit on calculus in the following ways:

1. A unit on limits was favored for inclusion in analytic geometry, additional elementary functions, calculus, and a combination course, whereas a unit on calculus was favored for inclusion only in a combination course.
2. For every course, the percentage of respondents who favored a unit on limits was higher than the percentage who favored a unit on calculus.
3. Sixty-five per cent of the respondents favored a unit on limits for at least one course, whereas 61 per cent of the respondents were opposed to both a unit on calculus in any course and a semester course in calculus.
4. If a respondent was opposed to a unit on limits for a given course, the probability that he would be opposed to a unit on calculus for that course was

very high (.93), whereas if he was in favor of a unit on limits, the probability that he would favor a unit on calculus was equal to chance (.48).

CONCLUSIONS

A unit on limits for the twelfth-year course in mathematics was favored by a majority of the college teachers of mathematics, whereas a unit on calculus was not favored. Consequently, the teaching of a unit on limits in the twelfth year does not appear to be nearly as controversial among college teachers of mathematics as is the teaching of a unit on calculus. Moreover, if the first semester of the twelfth year is to be devoted to elementary functions, then the colleges would prefer that the second-semester course be analytic geometry, additional elementary functions, probability and statistics, or matrix algebra, in that order.

Mathematics at St. Mark's School of Texas
W. K. MC NABB

St. Mark's School of Texas is an independent day school with selective admissions. It has a maximum enrollment of 688 boys in grades 1 to 12. The school is separated into three administrative divisions. The Lower School includes grades 1 to 4, with a maximum of 128 boys and a separate faculty. The Middle School contains grades 5 to 8 with a maximum of 240 boys, and the Upper School has grades 9 to 12 with a maximum of 320 boys.

Mathematics in grade 1 is taught within self-contained class rooms, but mathematics in grades 2 to 4 is taught by mathematics specialists. One of these mathematics teachers coordinates the mathematics program of the Lower School under the direction of the head of the mathematics department. The nine members of the mathematics department teach all mathematics courses for grades 5 to 12 on a two-year rotation of course assignments. New men in the department usually begin at grades 11 and 12 and then work their way down through the curriculum. After reaching grade 5, they begin the cycle again at grade 12.

The mathematics program of grades 1 to 6 follows the Singer Series *Sets and Numbers* by Suppes, supplemented by some locally prepared materials and by introductory work with a slide rule in grades 5 and 6. Grades 7 to 11 follow an integrated spiral sequence of elementary mathematics materials. Currently these consist of a locally prepared text for grade 7, followed by the grades 9 and 10 texts of the Copp-Clark Canadian series in grades 8 and 9, the SMSG text *Geometry With Coordinates* in grade 10, and SMSG *Intermediate Mathematics* in grade 11. Present plans are to phase out the SMSG texts during the next two years, replacing them with the grade 11 and 12 texts of the Copp-Clark series.

Reprinted from *The Bulletin of the National Association of Secondary School Principals* vol. 52 (April, 1968), 48–54, by permission of the author and the publisher. R. K. McNabb is Chairman of the Mathematics Department, St. Mark's School of Texas, Dallas.

HONORS WORK OFFERED

Two levels of courses are offered. Each year one or two of the five sections in each course for grades 5 to 12, depending upon available students, become honors sections. These classes study the same materials as do other students and take the same examinations, but the depth and tone of treatment is different and a few extra topics are introduced, particularly in grade 11.

Mathematics is not required of St. Mark's students in grade 12. Students of grade 11 honors sections are eligible for the APP mathematics course of the CEEB in grade 12. These students are also eligible for two one-semester courses, one in Matrix Algebra and the other in the SMSG Analytic Geometry. The grade 11 nonhonors students or others not selected for the grade 12 honors courses take in the twelfth grade an elementary functions course using the SMSG texts, *Elementary Functions* and *Intermediate Mathematics* (chapters 11 to 15). For 1968–69 it is planned to shift these students to the new AB-level course of the APP of the CEEB.

For those students who do not plan to take any college mathematics, an introductory calculus course of one semester is offered. A one-semester probability and statistical inference course is also available, and it is planned to add one-semester courses in numerical analysis and number theory within several years. Also in 1968–69 we plan to change our present APP calculus course to the new BC-level course of the APP.

For students particularly interested in mathematics, Problems Seminars are offered for both Middle and Upper School students. These seminars consider more difficult problems than those that can be used in course work. The Upper School group makes considerable use of the Olympiad problems of Eastern Europe and others of related

difficulty. Materials for the Middle School group are much more difficult to obtain.

A wide range of mathematics content is available in the central library of the school with over 150 volumes excluding mathematics textbooks kept for reference in one of the mathematics office areas. The school also has a chapter of Mu Alpha Theta, the national honorary society for high school and junior college mathematics students, and each year approximately 150 students participate in the Annual High School Mathematics Contest sponsored by MAA, the Society of Actuaries, Mu Alpha Theta, and the NCTM. The school also sends entries each year to the Hockaday and Andrews Mathematics Contests, and it sponsors a Junior High School Mathematics Contest for students in the Dallas metropolitan area. Midyear and end-of-year papers are required of students in grade 12 honors courses.

ENTRY TEST IN MATH

As a part of the general admission process for students applying for entrance to grades 5 to 12, a mathematics test is given. The result of this test is reviewed by a committee of the department to determine the student's ability and background. A recommendation concerning possible admission is then made to the school admissions committee. If a student is accepted for admission, he is then placed at an appropriate level of the mathematics sequence by the mathematics department regardless of his general grade placement. A summer school program is available and recommended for new students as a means for making early adjustment to the mathematics program of the school.

Each spring a standardized achievement test is given to all students in grades 3 to 11 in order to relate local students' achievement to that of other schools. The results of these tests are also used to develop local norms which are used with the mathematics admissions test. Also, each spring a detailed questionnaire is sent to all of our previous year's graduates in order to check their secondary mathematics training against their college mathematics experiences.

The mathematics department is housed in two wings of the Mathematics-Science Quadrangle. Six members of the department have individual offices around a central common room in one wing, while four others share a large office area in the other wing. Electric typewriters with interchangeable keys for special symbols are available in each office area, and a supply room contains duplicating equipment: mimeograph, spirit duplicator, and photo copy. Other equipment includes a six-stage collator, electric stapler, Thermofax copier, two portable overhead projectors, and file cabinets containing specially prepared overhead projector transparencies. The hall outside one office area contains two large bulletin boards and twelve framed pictures of famous mathematicians, together with a brief bibliography.

LOGISTICS AND ORGANIZATION

Eight classrooms and a seminar room are contained in the mathematics wings and all mathematics classes for grades 5 to 12 meet in these rooms. Each room is fully carpeted, has four walls of chalkboard, and has separate desks and chairs for flexible seating arrangements. At one end of each classroom is a three-deep set of sliding chalkboard panels including both rectangular and polar grids. A projection screen, large demonstration slide rule, and closed circuit television system are also available in each class room. The seminar room contains two large conference tables. The department also has nine Monroe Educator desk calculators which are kept at the rear of one classroom for student use during any free time when the machines are not in class use.

In the common room of the mathematics department a statistical-type rotary calculator and a printing calculator are available for faculty and student use. Present plans are to extend the use of calculators, which now begins in the Lower School, by the addition of a four-terminal, high-speed electric calculator and a small computer in the very near future. Work with computers is not a part of the mathematics program, although several short courses in programing have been given on Saturdays by staff personnel of local commercial firms.

The teaching load of a department member is four sections of not more than sixteen students, each meeting daily five times a week. An effort is made to split the courses of each teacher into two closely related grade areas. In addition to this, a teacher is expected to carry some special department duty as well as an assignment involving a general school activity, such as sports or special interest groups. Special department activities involve handling problems seminars, contests, library, bulletin boards, and audiovisual materials.

Teaching assignments are made each year so that two or three teachers are involved in each course having more than one section. One of these teachers is designated as course coordinator and is responsible for the preparation of lists of daily assignments, which are printed and distributed to the students, and for preparation of the unit examinations. A full-period examination is given at least once within each two-week period. This examination is cooperatively prepared by all those teaching the course. A common scoring process and grading scale is agreed upon for each examination and is used for all sections. Copies of the assignment sheets and examination, together with grading methods, grade scales, and error summaries are filed for future reference.

Every second week that does not coincide with a school grade report time, a departmental checklist report is turned in to the department head for all students having difficulty or working below their capacity. Copies of these reports are kept in the mathematics office, and the reports are given to the heads of the Middle and Upper School for information. They in turn pass these on to the students' advisers for information and action.

IN-SERVICE TRAINING

So that teachers continue to develop professionally, a departmental seminar is held periodically with faculty from both public and independent schools in the area invited. These meetings usually consist of an informal presentation of some topic in mathematics which is of special interest to one of the group, or a discussion of new materials, new equipment, or new methods. Participation is voluntary and open to other department members also. In past years formal study of a topic or text was tried, but it was not as successful as the current practice. An effort is made to send each department member to at least one regional or annual meeting of the NCTM during the year, particularly outside of the local region. This has been a great help in keeping department members aware and informed about new materials, curricula, and methods.

This program in mathematics has gradually evolved, and is continuing to change each year even more rapidly, from a rather drastic change made in 1960–61. At that time, the full impact of the new program in mathematics was being felt and a decision was made, chiefly on the basis of the availability of a person familiar with the SMSG program, to create a department of mathematics specialists and to move immediately into a "new" mathematics program. Up to then, a traditional sequence of algebra, geometry, and trigonometry had been taught by science teachers, administrators, coaches, and only two teachers prepared as mathematics teachers.

In the fall of 1960–61, grades 7 to 9 moved immediately to SMSG texts, with grades 10 and 11 both doing a traditional geometry course in order to change the following year from the algebra-algebra-geometry sequence then used in grades 9 to 11. The APP mathematics course of the CEEB was begun this first year, with the compromise that those students would also take an elementary functions course. Trigonometry and solid geometry were dropped from the program. The excitement of new materials and both the enthusiasm and hard work of the faculty managed to carry off this drastic change. During the past six years, changes in the Lower School mathematics program began affecting later courses severely. The SMSG program for grades 4 to 6 was adopted the second year (1961–62) and this change soon put pressure for change with the grade 7 material. Similarly, the introduction of the Singer materials in grades 1 to 3 soon forced out the grades 4 to 6 SMSG texts. By 1965–66, the SMSG program in grades 7 to 9 began to be phased out due to the strong preparation of students in the lower grades.

IN REVIEW

In considering the changes since 1960–61 in the St. Mark's School of Texas mathematics program, it is very difficult to find any clear-cut basis for the many decisions that were made for change. For the most part changes seem to hinge more strongly on the personalities involved than on logical or scientific bases. However, a few general points seem evident in relation to these changes and those still in progress:

1. Current mathematics programs demand highly trained specialists with strong mathematics background at all levels.
2. Students can develop a thorough understanding of much more sophisticated mathematics content if it is presented in a spiral manner with emphasis on structure and relation to previous material.
3. Continual adjustment of the curric-

ulum is necessary as new materials and methods appear.
4. The enthusiasm and interest of students in mathematics is not dependent upon the use of social or scientific applications.

In 1967–68, a five-year plan for modification of the St. Mark's mathematics program was projected; now, one year later, much of it has already been changed considerably. It appears that mathematics education at the elementary and secondary level has now reached a continuing state of change, so that curriculum and methods studies have become an important part of the mathematics department operation.

Aids for Evaluators of Mathematics Textbooks
PHILIP PEAK

The National Council of Teachers of Mathematics continually tries to bring to its membership various types of material which will be beneficial to the mathematics teacher in his day-to-day activities. Due to the rapidly changing nature of the mathematics being taught in the elementary and secondary school, it seems wise to provide at this time a

Reprinted from *The Mathematics Teacher*, LVIII (May, 1965), 467–73, by permission of Philip Peak, Chairman, the Committee on Aids for Evaluators of Textbooks, and the National Council of Teachers of Mathematics. Copyright © 1965 by the National Council of Teachers of Mathematics. Other members of the Committee are William Chinn, Alice Hach, Kenneth Henderson, Maurice Kingston, and Zeke Loflin. Philip Peak is Associate Dean in the School of Education, Indiana University, Bloomington.

set of criteria which will aid the teacher in the selection of the textbook which will best meet his needs.

A committee of Council members was chosen and charged with this responsibility. Throughout its deliberation, this committee felt that it must guard against a set of criteria which would tend to establish a national curriculum. At all times the local community's particular characteristics must be considered.

The committee first gave careful consideration to existing sets of criteria and circulated to the Council membership a request for suggestions and methods which have proven helpful.

This report is an instrument to aid in making qualitative judgments, not in quantifying the characteristics of texts.

Therefore, there are no numerical rankings or quantifying numbers associated with any element. The report is designed to help the user in his decision-making process, but will not make the decision for him. It is not possible to use a single number to measure the quality of a textbook for use in a single institution. It is, rather, a subjective judgment based on careful consideration of criteria which are relevant to the evaluation. It is this type of criteria we have tried to establish. The report includes criteria applicable for grades K–12, but in any one situation not all criteria may be applicable. Neither will each criterion necessarily be of equal value to all groups evaluating texts.

For the effective use of this instrument there must be some prior preparation on the part of the group making the text selection. The group must first arrive at a consensus as to the contribution of mathematics to the total educational program of their system. They must also recognize the mathematical competence of the teachers who will be using the text. They must be conscious of the philosophy of the school system and the direction its program is to take. They must be aware of the varying programs provided for range of student ability. The formulation of a mathematics program for the school system is the responsibility of the teachers and administrators in the system. The program should be formalized prior to the investigation of textbooks. The textbooks are selected as aids in carrying out established programs for a particular school. The selection is likely better to satisfy the needs of a school if the opinions of the teachers who are to use the text are considered in its selection. If these steps are taken prior to active investigation of texts, a better selection will result.

No special mention is made of series of texts. The committee feels that general principles of sequence, structure, compatibility, etc., which apply to one text also apply to a series, only in greater degree. Therefore, it is recommended that the evaluators of a series study the total body of material as they would a single text.

In order that the report may be as functional as possible, it has been divided into sections. These sections are not intended to follow any particular books' organization. The first part of the report deals with criteria applicable to content, presentation, and organization of texts. The criteria have been brought together under headings that are closely related to large ideas. These headings are: "Structure"; "Rigor"; "Vocabulary"; "Definitions and undefined terms"; "Correctness"; "Theorems and proofs"; "Generalizations"; "Ordering"; "Tests, exercises, and reviews"; "Illustrative examples"; "Teachability"; "Optional topics." The criteria are in the form of questions, which it is hoped will help the selector in making his decision.

Each section has an introductory statement which either clarifies what the committee means by the heading or indicates the significance of the ideas encompassed by it. These statements are applicable to both the elementary and secondary level. Following each general statement is a set of criteria and an accompanying illustrative example to aid the evaluator when considering the area covered by the topic. In cases where a criterion is not applicable to both elementary and secondary, it will be so indicated. In cases where a criterion is sufficiently clear, no examples appear.

In the second part are found criteria relating to physical characteristics of the text and to services provided by the publisher. These criteria have been separated into sections on general format, index, and references, usability, services, and teachers' manual.

CRITERIA RELATING TO PRESENTATION AND CONTENT

I. Structure

A. Mathematics is a body of organized knowledge. Each element which is a part of this body must fit into a properly established structure.
1. Does the presentation assist the student in understanding the structure of this particular area of mathematics?
   a. *Elementary:* If the commutative property has been verified for addition, then is the student asked to test this property for other operations?
   b. *Secondary:* Does the text point out that $y = 3x + 6$ describes a set of ordered pairs, determines a function and defines a line?
2. As an extension of a topic is made, does the development show clearly how the extension is related to the structure under consideration?
   a. *Elementary:* Is it shown that when the natural numbers are extended to rationals, the set is closed under addition and multiplication?
   b. *Secondary:* As natural numbers are extended to real numbers, does the material show that the multiplicative identity exists in each extension?

II. Rigor

A. Rigor in a text refers to the nature of the development of the arguments and the kind of justification that is used in proof. Few presentations are entirely rigorous or completely without rigor. The level of rigor in a text may have much to do with the future understanding of the subject by its reader.

1. Is the development of the topic made on appropriate levels of rigor?
   a. *Elementary:* To what extent are reasons presented for principles and procedures?
   b. *Secondary:* To what extent are reasons presented for principles and procedures?
2. Does the author attempt to cultivate and capitalize on the reader's intuitive understanding while pointing out the dangers and limitations of dependence on intuition?
   a. *Elementary:* Are students led to see that multiplication doesn't always result in a larger number than the product?
   b. *Secondary:* Since $1 + 3 = 4$, $1 + 3 + 5 = 9, 1 + 3 + 5 + 7 = 16$; does it appear that $1 + 3 + 5 + 7 + \ldots + (2N \pm 1) = N^2$?
3. Is the material presented in such a way that the student is expected to make conjectures and test their truth?
   a. *Elementary:* If the sum of two even numbers is even, is the sum of two odd numbers odd?
   b. *Secondary:* The student learns that the diagonals of a rectangle bisect each other. Does this condition hold for diagonals of all quadrilaterals? If not, does it hold for any quadrilaterals other than rectangles?
4. Are the proofs appropriate for the maturity of the student?
5. If insufficient reasons are given for some of the steps of a development, is this justified to the student and are the omissions indicated?
   a. *Elementary:* Not applicable.
   b. *Secondary:* We probably

would accept the Pythagorean theorem without proof in Grade 7, whereas in a subsequent grade we would require proof before use.

6. Does the text point out the dangers of such common errors as circular proof, assuming truth of converses, assuming uniqueness and using theorems as evidence before they have been demonstrated or stated as exercises?

   a. *Elementary:* Not applicable.

   b. *Secondary:* Trying to prove the base angles of a triangle congruent by dropping a perpendicular to the base before having proved it is always possible to construct such a perpendicular.

III. *Vocabulary*

A. Most of the terms which are introduced are names of significant ideas. Since these ideas are an important part of the structure, it is essential that the terms be presented effectively.

   1. Is the vocabulary appropriate for the level of the student?

   2. Is the rate of introducing new terms appropriate to the mathematical maturity of the student?

   3. Once a term has been defined, is it used?

   4. In order to strengthen understanding, are ideas restated in different language rather than by mere verbatim repetition?

IV. *Definitions and undefined terms*

A. Basically, definitions amount to symbol substitutions; that is, the stipulation that a simple symbol, for example, one word, can be used instead of a complex symbol like a long phrase. In the context of teaching, giving a definition amounts to teaching a student how to use a symbol; viz., (1) by stating the conditions which are necessary and sufficient for something to be called by the symbol being defined, (2) by naming objects which are called by the symbol being defined, or (3) by stating what symbol or symbols can be used to replace the symbol being defined.

1. Do all definitions in the text contain in the defining expression only those terms which can reasonably be expected to be understood by the student at his stage of development in the subject?

   a. *Elementary:* If simple closed curve is used to define a polygon, is "simple closed curve" understood?

   b. *Secondary:* Defining a quadrilateral as a geometric configuration consisting of four sides when "geometric configuration" is not understood.

2. For the object to be named by the term being defined, are the stated conditions necessary and sufficient?

   a. *Elementary:* A triangle is formed by three line segments is not a satisfactory definition.

   b. *Secondary:* Defining a regular polygon as a polygon with congruent segments for sides is not satisfactory.

3. Has the defining expression avoided using the term being defined or a term directly derived from it which has not been defined?

4. Does the content make clear the particular usage of a term which may have a different meaning in another context?

   a. *Elementary:* Divide evenly as it relates to sharing as opposed to a division problem where the remainder is zero.

b. *Secondary:* "Equivalent" as used with set as compared to its use with equations.

5. Is there a clear distinction between terms taken as undefined and those defined?

a. *Elementary:* Not applicable.

b. *Secondary:* "Two figures are said to be congruent if they can be made to coincide" is not a satisfactory definition of congruent figures.

V. Correctness

A. There are some statements which practically every mathematician would agree are errors. There are other statements which some mathematicians would regard as errors but others would not.

1. Is the text free of statements most mathematicians would agree are false?

a. *Elementary*
   (1) Implying there are more points on a line 10 units long than on a line one unit long.
   (2) Confusing the area of a polygon with the interior of a polygon.

b. *Secondary*
   (1) Giving the solution of a quadratic equation $x^2 + 5x + 24 = 0$ as $x = 3$ and $x = -8$.
   (2) Failure to specify the domain when it is stated that 37 cannot be factored and similarly, at a later stage,
   $$x^2 + 4\sqrt{4} = \pm 2, \sqrt{x^2} = x.$$
   $$\sqrt{x^2 - 2ax + a^2} = x - a.$$
   (3) Referring to the function $f(x)$ instead of the function f evaluated at x.

VI. Theorems and proofs

A. Here we are concerned with major generalizations which form the essential structure of the text and the arguments by which the formal conclusions are established.

1. Is it made clear that the demonstration of many instances of a mathematical generalization does not prove it although it does increase its plausibility?

a. *Elementary:* Testing the divisibility of a number by three by dividing the sum of its digits by three any number of times would not prove the rule.

b. *Secondary:* "3, 5, 7, 11, 13 ... are prime numbers; therefore, all prime numbers are odd" is not a valid statement because 5 or 50 instances do not mathematically prove a generalization.

2. Are the steps in the proof sufficiently "short" so that the normal reader can bridge the gap?

3. Are counterexamples used wherever they may be employed to an advantage?

a. *Elementary:* $18 \div 4$ and $4 \div 18$ or $16 - 3$ and $3 - 16$ shows by counterexample that natural numbers are not closed under subtraction.

b. *Secondary:* Using 41 as a counterexample for $N^2 - N + 41$ generates prime numbers but does not hold for $N = 41$.

4. Are all postulates which are used stated explicitly, including those that are plausible and often implicitly assumed?

5. Is it pointed out that there may be other proofs of a theorem (not applicable to elementary textbooks)?

6. Is it quite clearly indicated in each case where a proof or demonstration ends (not applicable to elementary textbooks)?
7. Is the appropriate logic available before proofs of theorems are introduced (not applicable to elementary textbooks)?
8. Has a foundation been laid for indirect proofs before it is used? Are fewer theorems presented for acceptance on faith as the material is developed (not applicable to elementary textbooks)?
9. Is there ever an attempt to show why the hypotheses of a theorem are as stated and how the conclusion would be changed if a hypothesis was altered (not applicable to elementary textbooks)?

VII. Generalizations

A. Generalizations are statements of relationship and together with concepts serve to portray structure.
   1. Are opportunities to generalize provided?
      a. *Elementary:* If $5 \times 7 = 35$, $5 \times 4 = 20$, and $5 \times 9 = 45$, then is it true that any number whose decimal numeral ends in 0 or 5 is divisible by 5?
      b. *Secondary:* When certain geometric properties are established in two space, are the students encouraged to consider whether these properties can be generalized to three space?
   2. Are instances that lead to generalizations appropriate in sequence and number?
   3. Are intermediate generalizations brought in when necessary to establish a continuity in generalization?

VIII. Ordering

A. Ordering refers to the sequence of topics and the steps within topics either within the text or throughout the series of texts from grade to grade.
   1. Is the material presented in a way which develops various topics on an elementary level and returns to the development at intervals exploring each topic more deeply with each repetition?
      a. *Elementary:* The commutative property of addition for counting numbers holds for whole numbers and also rational numbers.
      b. *Secondary:* Factorability depends on the universe $X^4 - 25$ factored over integers is $(X^2 - 5)(X^2 + 5)$; over the reals is $(X^2 + 5)(X - \sqrt{5})(X + \sqrt{5})$ and over the complex numbers is
      $$(X - i\sqrt{5})(X + i\sqrt{5}) \times (X - \sqrt{5})(X + \sqrt{5}).$$
   2. Are reasons given for choosing any unusual arrangement of material or for using a particular approach?

IX. Tests, exercises, and reviews

A. Exercises, whether appearing as part of a topic, in a review, or in a test, secure a response from the student. They provide a deepening of his understanding and an evaluation of his progress. They furnish the teacher a means for assessing the student's understanding.
   1. Are there adequate materials to permit a valid evaluation?
   2. Are there materials to help the pupil develop the power and habit of self-evaluation?

3. Are there periodic tests to assist in evaluating?

4. Do the tests provide a means for the evaluation of the entire range of abilities?

5. Are questions clearly and concisely stated to avoid their being misinterpreted?

6. Are there some exercises that require the student to generalize, to discover, to consolidate concepts, to improve skills, and to apply what he has learned to new situations?

7. Are exercises of varying difficulty identified?

8. Are there exercises designed to challenge the student?

9. Are there exercises designed to encourage thinking?

10. Do the review exercises make it possible to identify specific instructional needs?

11. Does the review direct attention to the significant elements and their relationship to each other?

X. *Illustrative examples*

A. Frequently, illustrative examples may be designed to anticipate the development of some concepts, illustrative examples may also be used to reinforce some of the concepts which have been previously established.

1. Do the examples clarify the concepts presented?

2. Are examples used to lead into similar problems in the set of exercises without being merely duplications?

3. Are examples used to indicate the area of application of generalizations?

4. The implications of a generalization may sometimes be lost unless various examples of its applications are cited to illustrate its extensiveness.

5. Are examples appropriate for the grade level?

XI. *Teachability*

A. Textbooks are used by the student both with and without the direction of the teacher. Insofar as the text can be used by the student on his own, its effectiveness is enhanced.

1. Are ideas developed by raising questions, considering alternatives, and encouraging conjectures which may be verified later?

2. Are references made to topics which precede and follow so that the student may see a problem in a better perspective?

XII. *Optional topics*

A. It should be recognized that a text is written to satisfy many readers and the suggestions of many critics are incorporated into its final form. It is, therefore, not absolutely imperative that a teacher consider every topic equally essential and hence feel compelled to devote time to all of them.

1. Is the text written in such a manner that those items considered to be optional can be deleted without destroying the continuity of the presentation?

CRITERIA RELATING TO PHYSICAL CHARACTERISTICS AND SERVICES

The mechanical features of a text and the services provided by the publisher are, of course, important, but only if the criteria of content and presentation have been met. Impressions of quality of print, paper, page organization, etc., should not become the major factor in making the final decision.

I. General format

A. The purpose is to attract and sustain the students' attention.
   1. Does the cover of the text identify it as one on mathematics?
   2. Do the symbols and pictures raise mathematical questions related to the textural material?
   3. Does the page arrangement generally give a feeling of continuity?
   4. Do the headings clearly portray the sequence of the subject matter?
   5. Are the type size and style suitable for the group for whom the book is intended?
   6. Is the book of a convenient size and shape for the group for which it is intended?
   7. Is the paging and paragraphing such that references, ordering of ideas, and class discussion can be easily carried out?
   8. When color is used, does it contribute to the presentation?
   9. Is the quality of paper, binding, print, and cover such that the text will maintain its functionality under reasonable use?

II. Index and references

A. Does the index facilitate referral to related ideas?
B. Is the table of contents detailed enough to be used for reference and an initial estimate of the scope of the book?
C. Does the text contain a glossary of the essential symbols and their definitions?
D. Are cross-references provided as part of the textual material?

III. Usability

A. Are definitions, theorems, axioms and other important items presented in a manner appropriate to their importance and purpose in the text?
B. Does the text require the purchase of additional material to teach the mathematics effectively?
C. Is the text equipped with sufficient tables to provide adequate support for the presentation and are they located conveniently?
D. Is the text relatively free of typographical errors?

IV. Services

A. Is the sales-promotion material accurate and informative?
B. Are the educational services provided by the publisher useful?
C. If there are supplementary tests and materials, do they aid in the effective use of the text?
D. Is the buyer clearly informed of major changes when there are revisions?
E. Does the publisher have a record of fulfilling its agreements?

V. Teachers' manuals

A. Does the format provide for convenient and effective use?
B. Does the manual provide clarification of the text material?
C. Are there materials and suggestions to aid in diagnosis, remediation, and evaluation?
D. Does the manual assist the teacher in selecting a suitable sequence of topics, methods of presentation, and in determining time to be spent on a particular topic?
E. Does the manual contain background material that is helpful to teachers?

F. Does the manual provide help in the solution of problems?

G. Are the pages keyed to the related text materials?

H. Does the manual indicate that there

may be different approaches to solving a problem and that there may be different but equally desirable ways of expressing the answers?

Recommendations of the Mathematical Association of America for the Training of Mathematics Teachers

The Committee on the Undergraduate Program in Mathematics (CUPM)[1] is a committee of the Mathematical Association of America and is supported in part by the National Science Foundation. The general purpose of this committee is to develop a broad program of improvement in the undergraduate mathematics curriculum of the nation's colleges and universities.

As part of its mandate, CUPM established a Panel on Teacher Training.[2] This panel was instructed to prepare for CUPM a set of recommendations of minimum standards for the training of teachers on all levels. The following report is the result of the work

Reprinted from *The American Mathematics Monthly*, LXVII (December, 1960), 982–91, by permission of the publisher.

[1] Members of CUPM: R. C. Buck (*Chairman*), E. G. Begle, L. W. Cohen, W. T. Guy, Jr., R. D. James, J. L. Kelley, J. G. Kemeny, E. E. Moise, J. C. Moore, Frederick Mosteller, H. O. Pollak, G. B. Price, Patrick Suppes, Henry Van Engen, R. J. Walker, A. D. Wallace, R. J. Wisner (*Executive Director*).

[2] Members of the Panel on Teacher Training: J. G. Kemeny (*Chairman*), E. G. Begle, W. T. Guy, Jr., P. S. Jones, J. L. Kelley, E. B. Meserve, E. E. Moise, Rothwell Stephens, Henry Van Engen, R. C. Buck (*ex officio*), R. J. Wisner (*ex officio*).

of the Panel on Teacher Training, and has received the endorsement of the Committee on the Undergraduate Program in Mathematics and of the Board of Governors of the Mathematical Association of America.

The Panel on Teacher Training has been further charged with the implementation of these recommendations and hopes to issue supplementary reports as well as to hold various regional conferences, to make these minimum standards a reality.

The report consists of the following: General Recommendations, The Five Levels, Recommendations for the Five Levels, Summary of Recommendations, Curriculum-study Courses, Training of Supervisors, Sample Course Descriptions.

Further information and reprints of this report may be obtained by writing to CUPM, P. O. Box 1024, Berkeley, California.

GENERAL RECOMMENDATIONS

The purpose of this report is to present a preliminary outline of the panel's recommendations for the minimal college training program for teachers of mathematics. We have found it a most useful device to arrive at a classification of mathematics teachers which does not, as far as we know, depend on any present scheme of training teachers for their various tasks. The existing classifications seem to have arisen from a series of historical accidents and from fundamental psychological considerations. We hope this report reflects our feeling that we have made a serious attempt to classify teachers according to their position in an over-all sequential schedule of presenting the main ideas of mathematics.

For each classification presented, we give a recommendation as to the type and minimum amount of mathematics which should be taken by the student preparing for a career in teaching. Further, we spell out in some detail the *types* of courses—included as an Appendix—which we recommend to implement the goals described. The courses we describe which are specifically designed for prospective teachers should be taught by persons who are masters of their subject matter and who have, in addition, a knowledge of the problems which teachers face.

These sample courses are given solely for illustrative purposes to explain the type of courses and the levels of advancement desirable for prospective teachers. It should be clearly understood that different institutions will wish to exercise considerable freedom in implementing these recommendations, both as to the way topics are combined into courses and as to the exact choice of topics for individual courses.

There are several very sincere words of warning to be put forth in regard to the reading and interpretation of this report.

First, the classifications are to be taken in the rather loose fashion in which they are described. Their exact delineations will of course depend upon local conditions of school and curricular organization. It should be noted that the various classifications overlap: this is done deliberately in an attempt to meet just such local conditions.

Second, the recommendations are not motivated by a desire to meet the demands of any special program of mathematics education; nor do the descriptions or outlines of courses to be taken by prospective teachers represent an attempt on the part of this committee to further the goals of any particular school curriculum planning organization. The recommendations are meant to be the minimum which should be required of teachers in any reasonable educational program, and the course descriptions are presented only to illustrate what is meant by the course titles.

Third, it is to be hoped that everyone recognizes good mathematics education to be a sequential experience. Thus, the teacher at any particular level should have an understanding of the mathematics which will confront the student in subsequent courses; and as a consequence, it is desirable that a teacher at a given level be prepared to teach at least some succeeding courses. Ideally, a person preparing for teaching should meet, in addition to the minimal requirements set forth here, as many of the requirements for the next level as his or her college program permits.

Fourth, this report is meant as a guide to the preparation of people who will be teaching any mathematics whatsoever. The suggestions apply, within each level, to all people who teach any mathematics. The recommendations do not in any sense exclude the teacher who is assigned classes scheduled primarily for students of low aptitude.

Fifth, every good teacher knows that mathematics must begin at the concrete level before it can proceed to the more technical or abstract formulation. Motivation for new concepts must be derived and later application of the theory to nature must be included. In each of the outlines to follow, it is assumed that topics will contain a judicious mixture of motivation, theory, and application. A purely abstract course for teachers would be madness, and a course in calculation with no theory would not be mathematics.

Sixth, the phrase "a course" occurs in several places in this report. For purposes of fixing ideas, this phrase is employed in the sense of a three-semester-hour presentation of the subject matter described, and it is not meant to exclude integrated programs or other curricular arrangements.

Finally, the reader should note that the training for Level I teaching is a separate program, while the curricula for the further levels form a cumulative sequence, in which each program is a continuation of the preceding one.

The committee benefited greatly from previous studies on teacher preparation, such as that of the Cooperative Committee on the Teaching of Science and Mathematics, a committee of the American Association for the Advancement of Science. The committee was also guided by discussions with a variety of professional organizations. It is pleased to note the considerable degree of agreement common to all proposals.

It should be emphasized that these recommendations are minimal in nature and that some institutions have already met and exceeded these recommendations. It is expected that as high school curricula are strengthened, these minimum recommendations will be revised.

THE FIVE LEVELS

I. *Teachers of elementary school mathematics*. This level consists of teachers confronted with the problem of presenting the elements of arithmetic and the associated material now commonly taught in grades K through 6. The committee recognizes that special pedagogical problems may be connected with grades K through 2, and so a special program may be appropriate for teachers of such grades.

II. *Teachers of the elements of algebra and geometry*. Included here are teachers who are assigned the task of giving introductory year courses in either algebra or geometry, or the less formal preliminary material in these fields. These introductory courses are now commonly taught in grades 7 through 10.

III. *Teachers of high school mathematics*. These teachers are qualified to teach a modern high school mathematics sequence[3] in grades 9 through 12.

IV. *Teachers of the elements of calculus, linear algebra, probability, etc.* This is a mixed level, consisting of teachers of advanced programs in high school, junior college teachers, and staff members employed by universities to teach in the first two years. These teachers should be qualified to present a modern two-year college mathematics program.

V. *Teachers of college mathematics*. These teachers should be qualified to teach all basic courses offered in a strong undergraduate college curriculum.

The levels having been presented, we are now ready to proceed to a description of our recommendations of the minimal college training requirements for entry into the teaching profession at each level.

RECOMMENDATIONS FOR LEVEL I (TEACHERS OF ELEMENTARY SCHOOL MATHEMATICS)

As a prerequisite for the college training

---

[3] Such sequences have been recommended by the Commission on Mathematics, the School Mathematics Study Group, the University of Illinois Committee on School Mathematics, and others.

of elementary school teachers, we recommend at least two years of college preparatory mathematics, consisting of a year of algebra and a year of geometry, or the same material in integrated courses. It must also be assured that these teachers are competent in the basic techniques of arithmetic. The exact length of the training program will depend on the strength of their preparation. For their college training, we recommend the equivalent of the following courses:

A. A two-course sequence devoted to the structure of the real number system and its subsystems. (See course-sequence 1.)[4]
B. A course devoted to the basic concepts of algebra. (See course 2.)
C. A course in informal geometry. (See course 3.)

The material in these courses might, in a sense, duplicate material studied in high school by the prospective teacher, but we urge that this material be covered again, this time from a more sophisticated, college-level point of view.

Whether the material suggested in (A) above can be covered in one or two courses will clearly depend upon the previous preparation of the student.

We strongly recommend that at least 20 per cent of the Level I teachers in each school have stronger preparation in mathematics, comparable to Level II preparation but not necessarily including calculus. Such teachers would clearly strengthen the elementary program by their very presence within the school faculty. This additional preparation is certainly required for elementary teachers who are called upon to teach an introduction to algebra or geometry.

[4]Sample courses, by numbers, are to be found in the Appendix.

RECOMMENDATIONS FOR LEVEL II (TEACHERS OF THE ELEMENTS OF ALGEBRA AND GEOMETRY)

Prospective teachers should enter this program ready for a mathematics course at the level of a beginning course in analytic geometry and calculus (requiring a minimum of three years in college preparatory mathematics). It is recognized that many students will have to correct high school deficiencies in college. (However, such courses as trigonometry and college algebra should not count toward the fulfillment of minimum requirements at the college level.) Their college mathematics training should then include:

A. Three courses in elementary analysis (including or pre-supposing the fundamentals of analytic geometry). (See course-sequence 4.)

This introduction to analysis should stress basic concepts. However, prospective teachers should be qualified to take more advanced mathematics courses requiring a year of the calculus, and hence calculus courses especially designed for teachers are normally not desirable.

B. Four other courses: a course in abstract algebra, a course in geometry, a course in probability from a set-theoretic point of view, and one elective. One of these courses should contain an introduction to the language of logic and sets. (See courses 5–7.)

RECOMMENDATIONS FOR LEVEL III (TEACHERS OF HIGH SCHOOL MATHEMATICS)

Prospective teachers of mathematics beyond the elements of algebra and geometry should complete a major in mathematics and a minor in some field in which a substantial amount of mathematics is used. This latter should be selected from areas in the physical sciences, biological sciences, and the social studies, but the minor should in each case be pursued to the extent that the student will have encountered substantial applications of mathematics.

The major in mathematics should include, in addition to the work listed under Level II, at least an additional course in each of algebra, geometry, and probability-statistics, and one more elective.

Thus, the minimum requirements for high school mathematics teachers should consist of the following:[5]

A. Three courses in analysis. (See course-sequence 4.)
B. Two courses in abstract algebra. (See course-sequence 5.)
C. Two courses in geometry beyond analytic geometry. (See course-sequence 6.)
D. Two courses in probability and statistics. (See course-sequence 7.)
E. Two upper-class elective courses, e.g., introduction to real variables, number theory, topology, history of mathematics, or numerical analysis (including use of high-speed computing machines).

One of these courses should contain an introduction to the language of logic and sets, which can be used in a variety of courses.

RECOMMENDATIONS FOR LEVEL IV (TEACHERS OF THE ELEMENTS OF CALCULUS, LINEAR ALGEBRA, PROBABILITY, ETC.)

On this level we recommend a Master's degree with at least two-thirds of the

[5] The requirements for Level II preparation have been included in this list.

courses being in mathematics, and for which an undergraduate program at least as strong as Level III training is a prerequisite. A teacher who has completed the recommendations for Level III should use the additional mathematics courses to acquire greater mathematical breadth.

Since these teachers will be called upon to teach calculus, we recommend that the program include the equivalent of at least two courses of theoretical analysis in the spirit of the theory of functions of real and complex variables.

It is important that universities have graduate programs available which can be entered with Level III preparation, recognizing that these students substitute greater breadth for lack of depth in analysis as compared with an ordinary B.A. with a major in mathematics. In other respects, graduate schools should have great freedom in designing the M. A. program for teachers.

RECOMMENDATIONS FOR LEVEL V (COLLEGE MATHEMATICS TEACHERS)

We recognize the tremendous problems created by the shortage of qualified college mathematics teachers. A recommendation for the alleviation of this problem is now receiving serious attention.

CURRICULUM-STUDY COURSES

The above recommendations have dealt in detail with the subject-matter training of mathematics teachers. There are many other facets to the education of the scholarly, vigorous, and enthusiastic persons to whom we wish to entrust the education of our youth. One of these merits special mention by us. Effective

SUMMARY OF RECOMMENDATIONS

Level	Description	Degree	High school prerequisites	Minimum number college courses
I	Elementary School	B.A.	Two Years of College Preparatory Mathematics	4
II	Elements of Algebra and Geometry	B.A., Mathematics Minor	Preparation for Analytic Geometry and Calculus	7
III	High School	B.A., Mathematics Major	Preparation for Analytic Geometry and Calculus	11
IV	Elements of Calculus, Linear Algebra, Probability, etc.	M.A. in Mathematics	Preparation for Analytic Geometry and Calculus	18 (approx.)

BREAKDOWN BY SUBJECTS

Level	Numbers	Analysis	Algebra	Geometry*	Probability-Statistics	Elective
I	2		1	1		
II		2	1	2	1†	1‡
III		2	2	3	2†	2‡
IV§		4	2	3	2	7

* Including analytic geometry.
† An introduction to the language of logic and sets should appear in some one course.
‡ Preferably from the areas specified.
§ The numbers in this row indicate the approximate number of courses.

mathematics teachers must be familiar with such items as:

A. The objectives and content of the many proposals for change in our curriculum and texts.
B. The techniques, relative merits, and roles of such teaching procedures as the inductive and deductive approaches to new ideas.
C. The literature of mathematics and its teaching.
D. The underlying ideas of elementary mathematics and the manner in which they may provide a rational basis for teaching, unless taken care of by mathematics courses especially designed for teachers.
E. The chief applications which have given rise to various mathematical subjects. These applications will depend upon the level of mathematics to be taught and are an essential part of the equipment of all mathematics teachers.

Such topics are properly taught in so-called "methods" courses. We would like to stress that adequate teaching of these can be done only by persons who are well informed *both* as to the basic mathematical concepts and as to the nature of American public schools, and as to the concepts, problems, and literature of mathematics education. In particular, we do not feel that this can be done effectively at either the elementary or secondary level in the context of "general" methods courses, or by persons who have not had at least the training of Level IV.

TRAINING OF SUPERVISORS

There is a great need for providing adequately trained supervisors of mathematics, Grades K–12, for our public schools. At present, administrators find no ready supply of such individuals and, hence, are through necessity making appointments which are highly questionable, if not indefensible. For this reason, it is urgent to develop a program for supervisors and to seek adequate support for those individuals who have the desired qualities for supervision and the ability to benefit from advanced training. Such training would prepare the "leaders of teachers" in the local system, (A) to make sound judgments concerning mathematics programs for the schools, (B) to understand thoroughly the recommendations made by national committees, and (C) to enable schools better to articulate school mathematics with college mathematics.

Prerequisite to this program should be a regular Master's degree in mathematics or a Master's degree given as a result of participation in an Academic Year Institute. The program should consist of additional graduate courses in abstract algebra, analysis, and geometry, with courses selected from logic, statistics, theory of numbers, philosophy of education, history of education, history of mathematics, seminar courses on the program of the elementary school and secondary school mathematics, and additional elective courses in algebra, analysis, or geometry to provide some degree of concentration.

The committee feels that action must be taken to fill the need for supervisory personnel, and we recommend such action to the appropriate authorities.

APPENDIX:
COURSE DESCRIPTIONS

We list below sample courses that might be used to fulfill the minimum requirements for Levels I through III, and the undergraduate requirements of Levels IV and V. These brief descriptions are included to clarify the meaning of course titles but are not intended as syllabi for actual courses. It must be recognized that there are other equally good ways of combining various recommended topics, and colleges should be encouraged to work out detailed curricula to suit their own tastes and local conditions. However, the committee hopes that these very brief descriptions will help in indicating the types of courses desirable and the level of advancement.

Level I

1. *Algebraic structure of the number system* (2-course sequence). This is a study of the numbers used in elementary school—whole numbers, common fractions, decimal fractions, irrational numbers.

Emphasis should be on the basic concepts and techniques: properties of addition, multiplication, inverses, systems of numeration, and the number line. The techniques for computation with numbers should be derived from the properties and structure of the number system, and some attention should be paid to approximation. Some elementary number theory, including prime numbers, properties of even and odd numbers, and some arithmetic with congruences should be included.

2. *Algebra.* Basic ideas and structure of algebra, including equations, inequalities, positive and negative numbers, absolute value, graphing of truth sets of equations and inequalities, examples of other algebraic systems—definitely including finite ones—to emphasize the structure of algebra as well as simple concepts and language of sets.

3. *Intuitive foundations of geometry.* A study of space, plane, and line as sets of points, considering separation prop-

erties and simple closed curves; the triangle, rectangle, circle, sphere, and the other figures in the plane and space considered as sets of points with their properties developed intuitively; the concept of deduction and the beginning of deductive theory based on the properties that have been identified in the intuitive development; concepts of measurement in the plane and space, angle measurement, measurement of the circle, volumes of familiar solids; treatment of coordinate geometry through graphs of simple equations.

Levels II–V

4. *Analytic geometry and calculus* (3-course sequence). Approximately one-third of the sequence should be devoted to analytic geometry, taught either in coordination with calculus or after the calculus sequence. This should include the coordinate plane, functions, polar coordinates, the algebraic description of subsets of the plane—related to solutions of equations—and parametrically as the range of a function, change of coordinates, and brief treatment of conic sections.

The sequence should also give a thorough treatment of the calculus for functions of one variable, with stress on the basic ideas, but with adequate attention to manipulative skills. The course should introduce differentiation, integration, the rational, trigonometric, and exponential functions, as well as a brief treatment of series and some very elementary differential equations.

5. *Abstract algebra* (2-course sequence). One course in this sequence constitutes an introduction to algebraic structures, such as groups, rings, fields, etc. The basic approach is to proceed from the concrete to the abstract. Use should be made of algebraic systems familiar to the student in order to motivate the abstract axioms. On the one hand, stress should be placed on rigor-

ous algebraic proofs to convince the student that geometry is not the only area for axiomatic treatment. On the other hand, to keep the abstract procedure tied to the student's experience, various "concrete" applications should be given for theorems. Examples should be drawn from number systems, geometry, and other areas.

The other course should be devoted to linear algebra, restricted to real, finite-dimensional cases. This can be introduced by concrete manipulation of vectors and matrices, after which the student should be motivated to free himself from the accident of the choice of a basis. The student should be taught the handling of vector equations and inequalities along with an intuitive introduction to linear programming and games. A good treatment of linear functions and transformations is needed, including a thorough understanding of the solution of m equations in n unknowns.

6. *Geometry* (2-course sequence). These recommendations have in general been based on the idea that advanced courses for teachers should be designed in such a way as to deepen understanding of the material which they will be teaching. In geometry, such a program involves special problems, because here some of the appropriate background material is not ordinarily thought of as being geometry at all, and much of it is not ordinarily taught on the undergraduate level.

The foundations of geometry, in the sense of Hilbert, is only one among many topics. Some further examples are as follows:

a. Generalization of the idea of congruence to include rigid motions, that is, one-to-one correspondences preserving distances.
b. A corresponding generalization of the idea of similarity.
c. Enough measure theory to turn the familiar area and volume formulas into

theorems, and to justify Cavalieri's Principle.

d. "Pure analytic geometry," in which points, lines, and so on are defined and treated in terms of a coordinate system, without the use of any synthetic postulates at all. This is quite different from conventional analytic geometry in which the synthetic postulates are used in the very construction of coordinate systems. The "purely analytic" treatment can be used to give a consistency proof for the synthetic postulates.

These topics are given merely as illustrations of the sort of material that is needed. The choice of topics and the order of priority may require considerable study. The course might well take the form of a series of fairly long digressions from an outline of a high school course, with each advanced topic taken up at the point where it seems most relevant.

7. *Probability and statistics* (2-course sequence). The purpose of this sequence is to introduce the student to probability theory from a set-theoretic point of view, and to apply basic probability theory to problems of statistical inference.

The first course should be an introduction to random variables on a finite space. It must include motivation, axiomatic treatment of a measure on a finite space, and the proof of a few key theorems. There should be numerous applications from elementary statistics, stochastic processes, and everyday life.

In the second course more stress should be placed on stochastic processes, and probabilities on a continuous sample space should be treated. A substantial amount of time could be devoted to the development of principles of statistical inference.

Note: One of the course sequences, 4 through 7, should include an introduction to the language of logic and sets, so that these concepts may be used wherever appropriate. This introduction could be restricted to a brief treatment of the propositional calculus and of Boolean algebra, stressing the isomorphism between the two structures.

Electives (For Levels II–V)

8. *Introduction to real variables.*
9. *Number theory.*
10. *Elementary topology.*
11. *History of mathematics.*
12. *Numerical analysis, with the use of machines.*

The Education of Mathematics Teachers in Other Countries

HOWARD F. FEHR

To give an entire account of the teacher preparation in all countries would indeed be a lengthy process, the writing of which would require several volumes. In this report the educational program for a selected set of developed countries is examined by indicating:

The school organization
The selection and education of elementary school teachers
The selection and education of secondary school teachers
The actual situation as it exists in practice
The in-service or continued education of teachers

From this review a number of significant differences and similarities will be recognized that can permit a comparison with the training of mathematics instructors in the schools of the United States.

Since today all elementary school teachers are in a real sense also teachers of mathematics, this report includes the education of elementary school teachers as well as the training of secondary school teachers of mathematics.

FRANCE

In France, education is compulsory for

Reprinted from *The Mathematics Teacher*, LXII (January, 1969), 48–56, by permission of the author and the National Council of Teachers of Mathematics. Copyright © 1969 by the National Council of Teachers of Mathematics. Howard Fehr is Professor Emeritus of Mathematics, Teachers College, Columbia University.

all children aged six to fifteen years. Corresponding to our nursery and kindergarten schools there is a state-administered *Ecole Maternelle* for children from two and a half to six years old. While attendance is optional, most children of this age attend this preformal schooling. The formal elementary school called Forms 11, 10, 9, 8, and 7, is of five years' duration, for ages six to eleven, and contains the same curriculum for all pupils. The mathematics program is largely arithmetic and problem solving, and recently geometric ideas have been included. While all children follow the same curriculum, the instruction is geared to the upper level of intelligence. For example, all multiplication facts have been taught in Form 10 (age seven).

Then children attend the lower cycle of the secondary school. It is of four years' duration, with Forms 6, 5, 4, and 3, for children aged eleven to fifteen. For pupils who take the "long" course, that is, express an intention of preparing for university or higher study, this instruction is given in the lycée. For those who take the "short" course, that is, express an intention of going into work or leaving school at age fifteen, the instruction is given in a continuation of career school. At the end of this period of schooling, there is an official state examination called the *brevet* (certificate examination) which, once required, is now optional in all the commonly taught subjects. If, however, pupils intended to continue in the lycée, where the number of places is limited, or if they intend to enter into elementary school teaching, they had better take the brevet and get a good grade!

The upper cycle of secondary school is the continuation of the "long" course and consists of Forms 2, 1, and terminal. It is for students aged fifteen to eighteen. At the end of the terminal year the students take a *baccalauréat* examination in the subjects of the line followed in the lycée. The lines presently offered are Latin-Greek, technical, social-economic, modern, and scientific. All these lines require mathematics for one year, but only the technical and scientific require mathematics study every year. For those who desire skilled careers there is another type of lycée with an upper cycle of a practical nature (secretarial, technical, business, etc.) where students may earn various certificates of aptitude.

To enter the university or any liberal or civil service careers, passing the *baccalauréat* is a requirement. University study is of three years' duration; passing the required courses leads to the licentiate, or degree in arts, in law, in science, etc. This degree is approximately equivalent to the master's degree in universities in the United States. The mathematics major in this program includes the equivalent of 51 semester hours of study.[1]

We now ask the question, "How do mathematics teachers emerge from this program?"

The elementary school teacher usually selects his career at the age of *fifteen years*, upon completing the lower secondary cycle and passing the *brevet*. (Actually, it would be more appropriate to say "her" rather than "his," but we continue with the masculine form.) He enters a teacher-train-

ing institution called an *école normale* and studies for three years, taking the equivalent of a *baccalauréat* program except that no mathematics study is required. After about age eighteen, the intending teacher continues with two years of practical training—psychology, history of education, general pedagogy, methods of teaching the disciplines, and observation and practice teaching in a school. If, as is the case for more than half the aspirants, he does this study satisfactorily, he receives a certificate of aptitude and begins his professional career at age twenty. Note that for the majority of these persons, outside of a review of the elementary mathematics they must teach, their mathematics study ended with the *brevet*—equivalent to the first course in algebra and some plane geometry. These teachers have the same fear of mathematics that is felt by teachers here who have a similar lack of adequate preparation.

Alternately, a graduate of the lycée with the baccalaureate can enter the elementary school teaching profession either by entering the *école normale* at an advanced level and doing the practical study or (without this practical study) begin teaching at a little more than eighteen and, under an inspector's supervision for six years, gain the certificate of aptitude.

To qualify for the lower cycle of the secondary school (with students aged eleven to fifteen), the intending teacher must be a graduate of the lycée. Then he must attend a university for three years to obtain his licentiate in mathematics and follow this with another year of study at the university in practical training—psychology, philosophy and history of education, and pedagogy—and, if successful, he obtains his certificate of aptitude to teach mathematics in the lower cycle.

To teach in the upper cycle of the lycée, an aspiring teacher must take one of the most arduous training programs

---

[1] This study is outlined in a booklet entitled "European Students Record," attainable from the mathematics department of any European university.

in existence. Having received his *baccalauréat*, he first pursues two years of preparatory study in classes called *élémentaire* and *supérieure*. He then takes the *concours*, a competitive examination for places in university study. After this study he receives a "license" degree and then takes further competitive examinations to enter the *Normale Supérieure*. All students admitted to this school are paid complete expenses plus a living allowance. At the end of the second year a final examination, called the aggregation, is given. This is an examination in actual teaching, evaluated by observers, and a written examination in pure mathematics of the level of certification for Ph.D. candidates in our country. The number of candidates who pass this examination is controlled by the number of positions that are to be filled in the following school year. Those who pass the examination become *Elèves Anciens de Normales Supérieures*, the highest professional rating except that of Ph.D., and have permanent teaching positions.

However, due to the great shortage of teachers and the lack of persons qualifying to teach, many elementary school teachers, through one, or at most two, further years of mathematics study are teaching in the lower cycle of the secondary school—and many lower-cycle teachers have now moved up to teaching in the upper cycle without any further study.

BELGIUM

The school system of Belgium is similar in structure to that of the United States. However, education is compulsory only from ages six to fourteen. After age fourteen it is optional for those who care to continue for two or more years in study or career preparation, but of course it is obligatory for students intending to attend a university.

In outline form, the system consists of the following:

1. Nursery school, ages three to six, at the parents' pleasure and mostly private.
2. Primary instruction, ages six to twelve. This six years of instruction is the same for all children.
3. Lower secondary, ages twelve to fifteen. Children intending to go to university study take the "long" course and select a line of study among technical, Greek-Latin, Latin-mathematics, Latin-science, or scientific, the last-named being separated into A, mathematics, and B, science. (Note the selection at age eleven of a future commitment.) There is also a three-year continuation of common education in schools for those intending to enter the working world at age fourteen or fifteen.
4. Upper secondary, ages fifteen to eighteen. This three years is a continuation of the lower secondary study.
5. University study, ages eighteen to twenty-two. This four years of study leads to the licentiate.

Teachers for the elementary schools are trained in normal schools. To enter the normal school, an aspirant must be a graduate of the upper secondary cycle of the lycée (age eighteen). The study in the normal school is very practical—two years of psychology, history, philosophy, pedagogy, and practice-teaching. There is no mathematical study during these two years, except for a little on methods of teaching elementary school mathematics. At age twenty these teachers begin their professional careers.

The teachers in the lower cycle of the secondary school receive the same training as those for the elementary school with the exception that they must include one year of study of mathematics beyond that of the lycée in the two-year practice program.

To qualify for teaching in the upper cycle of the secondary school the intending teacher must be a graduate, with the licentiate, of the four-year university. In this period the student studies only two (or at most three) subjects— for example, mathematics and physics, or mathematics, physics, and another science or a language. After graduation he takes one year of study, called aggregation, for secondary instruction. This study is done in a department of education associated with the university but under the control of the National Ministry of Education. Observation and practice-teaching are included in this year of study. Upon the successful completion of this study, a teaching certificate in the major subjects is granted. This is made permanent upon successful teaching for a period of five years in a private secondary school or three years in a public secondary school.

Recently a genuinely modern program in mathematics has been created for the six-year secondary school, ages eleven-plus to eighteen. To compensate for the lack of education in the modern aspects of this mathematics, in-service courses have been given to over five thousand teachers.

SWEDEN

The school structure and the training of teachers in the Nordic countries (Norway, Sweden, and Denmark) are similar. These countries experienced a reorganization of the school programs in 1959 and another in 1967, aimed at a so-called greater democratization of instruction. The formal schooling begins at age seven and is compulsory for a nine-year elementary school administered as outlined:

1. Lower elementary or primary, ages seven through nine, Grades 1—3.
2. Middle elementary, ages ten through twelve, Grades 4—6.
3. High elementary, ages thirteen through fifteen-plus, Grades 7—9.

All pupils graduate from elementary school and receive a leaving certificate. Continuation of schooling beyond Grade 9 is in two streams:

1. Gymnasium, ages sixteen through eighteen or nineteen, for professional careers and university-intending students; three years.
2. Fach's school (vocational school), ages sixteen and seventeen, for those who desire more schooling before entering the working world; two years.

Young persons intending to teach in elementary school Grades 1—3, enter a teacher-training college upon attaining the age of seventeen and graduating successfully (that is, receiving high grades) from either the Fach's school or the gymnasium. Fach's school graduates study two and a half years and take a five-week summer school to make up the last year of gymnasium work, while gymnasium graduates study only two more years. The only mathematics in the two years of preparation for teaching is a review of the material they must teach. The rest of the study is psychology, pedagogy, observation, and practice-teaching.

To teach in Grades 4–6 of the elementary school the same admission requirements hold, but the teacher-training period is extended to three years. No more mathematics is required than a review and pedagogy of what the candidates are expected to teach.

Those who intend to teach in the higher elementary school, Grades 7–9, must attend the university for three years after graduation from the gymnasium. In this period they study two subjects as major fields, and they may elect to complement this study with a third subject. Upon successful completion of this disciplinary study they receive the degree of "Magister," equivalent to our B.A. degree. Then the aspirants attend a teacher-training college for one year of practical study—

mostly pedagogical—and are certified to teach. Despite the three-year concentration on mathematical study at the university, authorities in mathematics feel that these teachers do not have sufficient mathematical knowledge to do the teaching the syllabus demands.

For teaching in the gymnasium there are two levels of training. Teachers at the lower level (in rank and salary) have the same preparation as the teachers for the higher level elementary school and are called "adjuncts."

The higher level teachers are called "lektors." These teachers, upon graduation from the university, spend two or three additional years of mathematics study at the graduate level, rivaling the study of Ph.D.'s in mathematics. After one year of additional practical training under the supervision of the teacher-training college, they are certified to teach. These are the highest-paid teachers in the country.

As is the case elsewhere, so it is in the Nordic countries where there is a shortage of qualified teachers. Teacher-training-school graduates who taught in Grades 4–6, by additional study of twenty hours (one year) in two subjects can be classified as adjuncts and allowed to teach in the higher elementary school, Grades 7–9. Once a teacher has been certified and has had two probationary years of teaching, for the most part a formality, a permanent license is issued; and nothing more of study is required the rest of his teaching career.

Teachers are occasionally inspected by the board of education.

Recently short courses, on a voluntary basis, have been organized for teachers to help them interpret the new programs.

GERMANY

In Western Germany there are nine lands, or states, and the educational structure varies from state to state. A typical structure is the following:

1. All children begin school at age six in a common elementary school, the *Volksschule* of four years' duration. At the end of this period there is a separation of the children into three distinct types of secondary schooling.

2. About 50 per cent of the population enter the second part of the *Volksschule* for a period of five years, ages ten to fifteen. This is the end of the compulsory general education period. However, these children are compelled to take an apprenticeship in some vocation and attend a corresponding vocational school full or part-time.

3. About 20 per cent of the population enter the "middle school" of six years' duration, ages ten to sixteen. Admission is by examination. These children usually proceed to a technical or higher commercial school.

4. The remaining 30 per cent, by passing examinations, enter the gymnasium of nine years' duration, separated into three three-year sequences. The first three years are spent in the lower school (*Unterstufe*), and the instruction is a common academic one. After that, in the *Mittelstufe*, the students select one of three or more lines—classical, modern languages, or mathematics-science. At the end of the nine-year gymnasium, there is a severe examination (the *Abitur*) in all the subjects studied, which must be passed by all students who wish to continue their education.

The intending teachers of the *Volksschule* (for ages six to ten) must have attended the gymnasium and passed the *Abitur*. At this time they are nineteen years of age. They attend a *Pedagogische Hochschule* (normal school) for three years. During this period they must attend two one-semester seminars on the teaching of arithmetic and/or geometry. In addition, all teachers must select one field to deepen their performance in this field. About 5 per cent of the students select mathematics, and the other 95 per cent select other fields. Thus the mathematical knowledge of most common elementary school teachers is that which they learned in the gymnasium—approximately that which corresponds to a first course in algebra and a course in plane geometry in our schools.

These teachers may also teach in the continuation of the common school, ages ten to fifteen, but must pursue a two-year study of a discipline, such as mathematics, in the normal school. This study is equivalent to the *Mittlestufe* program of the gymnasium.

The training of a middle-school teacher varies greatly. At the maximum it is the same as that of a gymnasium teacher, to be explained next. At the minimum it is the same as that of a teacher in the second part of the *Volksschule*, as explained before.

A prospective gymnasium teacher (at age nineteen, on entering the university) has to select two or possibly three subjects he desires to teach and study only these subjects for five or six years. These must be subjects that are taught in the gymnasium. It is usually six or seven years before the study is completed and certified by examination. The student must also attend lectures and seminars in philosophy and pedagogy. At the end of this period (usually at age twenty-six) the intending teacher takes his "First State Examination." This consists of (1) writing a thesis of 80 to 100 pages on a special mathematical topic, showing up-to-date complete mastery of the topic, (2) taking two written examinations in each of his selected fields, each examination requiring four to five hours, (3) taking one-hour oral examinations, one in each of his selected fields, and (4) taking

a written and oral examination (the *Philosophicum*) in philosophy and pedagogy.

Having passed this examination, he enters a two-year period of teacher preparation, in the first year being an intern in a gymnasium and in the second year a member of a seminar in which the practice and theory of school life and of teaching are combined. At the end of these two years, (now age twenty-eight) the aspirant takes the "Second State Examination." During this time the *Referendar*—as the candidate is called during these two years—has to write a report on a certain period of his own class-teaching, to analyze the mathematical and didactical structure of the topics taught, to describe the reactions of the pupils and his work with the pupils, to identify individual characteristics of some pupils, and to evaluate his teaching. Furthermore, he has to present two demonstration lessons in front of an examination board, one in a class known to him and the other in a class not familiar to him. Finally, there is an oral examination in pedagogy and methodology of teaching.

If he fails, he has a second chance after one more year of internship. If he passes, he has a life position as a gymnasium teacher. His salary at the start is equal to that of a lawyer, doctor, engineer, or other professional worker of this category. His standing in the community is the highest. As you might expect, there is a real scarcity of fully certified gymnasium teachers.

The training in Holland is of similar severe nature.

ENGLAND

In England, children begin formal schooling at age five in a three-year "infant school" and continue their elementary school education in a junior school to the age of eleven. Then they attend a secondary school to a compulsory age of fifteen.

The secondary schools are of four types: the so-called public schools, which are highly selective private schools with tuition; the so-called grammar schools, which are solely preparatory schools for university study; secondary modern; and comprehensive. The latter two types of schools are tuition-free schools financed by the government and are similar to secondary schools in this country.

The first four years of secondary school, for ages eleven to fifteen, are called Forms 1–4. School-leaving examinations called "O-level" (for "ordinary education") are given at the end of this time. For these examinations the candidate chooses three, or at the most four, subjects that he has studied during the four years. Mathematics need not be selected, and frequently it is not.

The upper level of secondary school is only university preparation, for ages sixteen to nineteen. It consists of Form 5 (one year) and Form 6 (two years). At the end of this period all students take an "A-level" (for "advanced education") examination in two subjects, or at the most three. Passing this examination is a requirement for entrance to all universities except Oxford and Cambridge, which give their own admission examinations.

Intending teachers for elementary school (ages five to eleven) must pass the O-level examination and spend at least one more year in grammar school, Form 5. Attaining age seventeen, they enter a teacher-training college for a three-year training program that includes the barest minimum of mathematical study required for understanding what they must teach. Most entrants have omitted the O-level mathematics examination. Thus what they study is equivalent to O-level

school mathematics for the equivalent of three to six semester hours. However, each teacher must select a major and a subsidiary-level study, which may be mathematics. The major study is 300 hours (eighteen semester hours), and the subsidiary is 200 hours (twelve semester hours). Very few teachers select mathematics as a major study. The rest of the program is given over to pedagogy and practical teaching. These candidates are ready to begin teaching at age twenty.

To teach in the secondary school, the aspirant must pass the O-level examinations, including the subject or subjects he wishes to teach, and in addition pursue successful study in Form 5 and the first year of Form 6. The intending teacher then enters a four year program of study in a college of education. The syllabi and examinations in this study are under the control of a university to which the college is associated. The teachers college must be recognized, inspected, approved, and accepted by the university. Those who major in mathematics may teach in Forms 1, 2, and 3, but note that they may teach *any subject* in these forms. The same is true for the other major subjects, i.e., a physical education major may teach mathematics in these forms, as may language majors or any other non-mathematics majors.

In the grammar schools, where Forms 5 and 6 are crucial for passing A-level examinations and obtaining university entrance, mathematics teachers are graduates of a three-year university with one further year of pedagogical training taken in a college of education. At the university the entire study is in mathematics except for a few related courses in physics. The teacher begins his career at age twenty three.

However, as in other countries, there is a shortage of fully qualified and certified teachers. Hence in the secondary modern schools the majority of teachers are three-year graduates of a teachers college.

In the new projects for grammar school mathematics, the older in-service teachers find much material they never studied in their training. Many teachers have attended voluntary short courses, at their own expense in money and time, to update themselves.

CONCLUSIONS

Elementary teachers formation

Looking at the training of teachers for elementary schools, involving children of ages five to thirteen, one is immediately startled by the fact that except for a small proportion of these teachers, 10 per cent at the most, their mathematical knowledge is exceptionally meager—approximately no higher than a first high school course in algebra. Added to this is the fact that their post-high-school education averages about two years, most of which is given over to practical matters of pedagogy and methodology. They begin their teaching at about age twenty years, two years earlier than in elementary schools here, and with two years less study. Their salaries are much lower than those paid secondary school teachers who are university-trained. Observation in their classes shows that, except for recently innovated activities related to the so-called new maths, the teaching is authoritative. It consists of rote learning of computation and its applications to business and social affairs—not as problem solving, but as how you do it.

These elementary teachers, except in Germany, do not usually graduate from the elite secondary schools (grammar, gymnasium, lycée) but enter a career school at the end of the lower cycle of secondary school, as other pupils enter certain vocational schools.

It is approximately fair to say that generally, in the countries reviewed, elementary teaching is a vocation—a job—and not a profession in the usual sense of the word.

However, in the international Assessment of Mathematical Achievement, at the thirteen-year-old level all these countries achieved as high as (or higher than) the same age group in the United States. One may well ask: With the added two years of teacher preparation given to our elementary school teachers, what advantages or gains do we obtain compared with these other countries? Surely it is not an increased knowledge of mathematics, or an interest in it, on the part of our students.

Middle-school teachers formation

The training of mathematics teachers for the lower cycle of secondary school, children eleven to fifteen years old, poses one of the serious problems of education in all countries. In general these teachers receive the same pedagogical training as that of the elementary school teachers. In many cases, but far from the majority, these teachers had a higher training in the secondary school than did the elementary school teachers, and presumably if the teacher is to teach only mathematics, a provision exists for more extensive study of mathematics than that obtained in the secondary school. However, the shortage of qualified teachers is greatest at this level—one reason being that those genuinely qualified have moved up to higher teaching and another the feeling that still exists that at this level of instruction anyone pedagogically trained can teach any subject without having a college or university major in the subject.

Another cause of concern is the new programs proposed for this level of mathematics education, which include a completely new approach to mathematics learning as well as much substance that used to be considered upper-secondary or collegiate mathematics. The in-service or veteran teachers are not equipped to teach the new programs and the problem of reeducation while on the job is far more difficult than that in our own country because of the lack of government support for such programs.

In general these middle-school teachers are graduates or near graduates of the elite secondary schools; they may or may not have majored in mathematics. They have an average of three years of college training plus one year of practical teaching education and begin their professional careers when they meet full qualifications, at about twenty-two years of age.

Senior high school teachers

While elementary school teachers abroad have less training than those here, the senior high school teachers of mathematics who are qualified have much more training. They are, first of all, graduates of the elite schools in which they teach, that is to say the grammar school, gymnasium, or lycée. This places the teachers certainly in the upper 5 to 10 per cent of the intellectual attainment of the country.

Secondly, their university work consists entirely of the study of mathematics and one or two closely allied subjects. This university study involves four to six years of study and the accumulation of knowledge well beyond that for the M.A. degree in pure mathematics of our good universities.

The pedagogical training is much less than that required of the lower-level teachers, and it stresses classroom methodology in the subject taught, rather than general pedagogy. Thus, at this level subject-matter mastery appears far more significant than so-called teaching procedures. In fact, at this level, internship with a vetaran teacher is considered the best practical pedagogy.

These teachers not only study longer, but they enter the profession later, generally at over twenty-five years of age. Their compensation is generally much higher than that for lower-level teachers and is comparable to that for other high professions. However, these teachers are not taking in-service courses or updating their knowledge; on the contrary, they are giving such courses for lower-level teachers and setting the pace in innovating new programs in their classes. There is no problem of introducing "new math" in the elite secondary schools abroad.

4

Research

Research is characterized as a systematic investigation of questions relevant to a specific area. Only as classroom teachers actively participate in evaluating these kinds of questions can enough solutions be found to make significant changes in mathematics education. Based on the assumption that the impact of research is only as great as the involvement of classroom teachers in it, the following readings were selected to provide the teacher with a sampling of the variety of research in mathematics education. Because teachers differ in individual capabilities, uniqueness of teaching assignments, administrative attitude toward research, and other problems, both the sophistication and nature of the research which they will investigate, and the research results which they will utilize will vary. Nevertheless, regardless of the level of research carried out by the teacher, the fact that he has a part in the investigation of significant issues in the field will deepen his sense of involvement in the development of mathematics education.

Teaching, Discovery, and the Problems of Transfer of Training in Mathematics

JERRY P. BECKER / GORDON K. MC LEOD

Learning transfer (or transfer of training) is an important topic in many branches of psychology. The topic receives extensive coverage in texts of general experimental psychology and in treatments of learning. As one may expect, it is especially important in the psychology of human learning and in educational psychology.

In its broader sense, something like transfer of learning is basic to the whole notion of schooling. Those who support schools, like those who conduct them, must assume that the thing being taught at this particular moment will have some value at a later moment and in a somewhat different situation. For example, we assume that today's lesson in geometry will surely help in tomorrow's lesson in the same subject, that it may be of use in later study of analytic geometry, and, more ambitiously, that it may induce an appreciation of logic so profoundly that it affects the student's entire way of life. Clearly, without some degree of reliance on transfer, teaching would be hopelessly specific. It would be necessary to train each student in every specific situation he might ever encounter.

We believe most teachers of mathe-

matics make the assumption that the skills and understanding which they endeavor to impart to their students will influence the behavior of the students beyond the classroom setting in which the learning takes place. We expect specific learning in mathematics to transfer to ensuing situations both inside and outside school. When one takes account of the evidence, however, our assumption is not necessarily borne out in practice. This is, indeed, discouraging to teachers of mathematics. But what is more discouraging is the fact that students seem to have difficulty in effecting learning transfer from one situation to another even within the mathematics curriculum itself.

It seems reasonable to inquire into the degree of validity of the conjecture that there is a broad transfer power in the study of mathematics. For example, it is commonly stated that a significant outcome of the study of mathematics is the ability to think more logically. What we propose to ask as educators in mathematics is whether psychological theory can give us a basis for a hopeful view of the problem of learning transfer. This is, in fact, the objective of this paper. With psychological theory as our guide, we propose to consider the problem of structuring the learning situation in mathematics so that maximum transfer of learning can occur.

DEFINITIONS AND MODEL OF TRANSFER

It seems appropriate to inquire about a definition of transfer at this point.

Reprinted from *Research in Mathematics Education* (National Council of Teachers of Mathematics Publication, 1967), 93–107, by permission of the authors and the National Council of Teachers of Mathematics. Jerry P. Becker is Associate Professor of Mathematics Education at Rutgers University, New Brunswick, New Jersey. Gordon K. McLeod is Associate Research Scientist in Curriculum Planning, American Institute for Research, Palo Alto, California.

It turns out that few people have actually defined the term. Consequently, we have concluded that transfer of learning can be thought of as a broad, inclusive phenomenon. Let us consider a few examples.

"Learning how to learn" to solve a class of problems is considered to involve an important type of transfer. Mathematics teachers consider the application of logical processes of analysis learned in geometry to non-mathematical situations to be a very desirable example of transfer. Experimenters in psychology consider as evidence of transfer the application of a principle in a test situation, where the test situation may differ only slightly from the training session in which the principle was learned. We submit that every learning situation involves transfer to some extent, since a learner brings his past learning experiences and attitudes to any new learning situation.

We think it would be useful to examine a model suggested by Ferguson (1956) in order to bring into focus the consideration of the problem of transfer. His transfer model, in its simplest form, is a mathematical function of three variables. If y is the dependent variable representing a measure of performance on some particular task, then $y = f(x, t_x, t_y)$, where x is a measure of performance on another task, while t_y and t_x represent the amount of practice on each of the two tasks. Here x is also a function of t_x; that is, $x = \phi(t_x)$, so that $y = f(\phi(t_x), t_x, t_y)$. Ferguson (1956) used this model to describe a formulation of the concept of transfer and we propose to consider it in more detail.

When two tasks are the same, so that the measures of performance are identical, the expression for y reduces to a function of one variable, since $x \equiv y$ implies that $t_x \equiv t_y$. Therefore we find $y = g(t_y)$. Clearly, this expression relates a measure of performance on a task to a measure of the amount of practice on the task and the result is a representation of the traditional learning curve. Thus, Ferguson's model suggests that learning is a special case of the more general phenomenon of transfer.

Looking at it another way, if no practice is allowed on the task represented by y, then y reduces to a function of two variables so that $y = h(x, t_x)$. This case represents a transfer experiment where measurement is made of the effect of practicing one task upon the performance of another nonpracticed task.

Consideration of this model enables one to obtain a broad, general view of the problem of transfer. Further, it suggests the following definition: "Transfer of learning occurs whenever the existence of a previously established habit has an influence on the acquisition, performance, or relearning of a second habit" (McGeoch and Irion, 1952, p. 299).

There are many phenomena which are consequences of learning; among them are skills and understandings. In light of Ferguson's model, we will focus attention on these in this paper. Therefore, the term "habits" as used in the definition above will refer to skills and understandings in subsequent pages. It seems clear that an implication of the definition and the model is that *transfer can be positive or negative.*

THEORIES OF TRANSFER

Before proceeding to a consideration of transfer of learning in the educational setting, we think it is appropriate to examine briefly some general theories which deal with the mechanism of transfer. Man's first theory of transfer proclaimed that formal study in school subjects was the best way to secure the ability to apply sound judgment and logical reasoning to problems outside of school. It held that the more difficult the formal study, the more exercise for the mind and the better its training for transfer. For example, this theory held that the development of logical thinking in geometry would transfer automatically to sound logical reasoning in social studies.

The investigations of Thorndike and Woodworth (1901) at the turn of the century proved this theory inaccurate. In a series of experiments, the influence of special training in estimating magnitudes (lengths, areas, etc.) on the ability to estimate magnitudes of a more general nature was tested. The conclusion was that performance on the more general tests was not significantly influenced by the special training.

Later Thorndike (Thorndike and Woodworth, 1901) formulated his doctrine of identical elements to explain the phenomenon of transfer. It stated that transfer occurs only when identical elements are involved in the influencing and influenced function. McGeoch and Irion (1952, p. 343) claimed that by two identical elements, Thorndike seemed to mean any clearly discriminable aspect of two activities which is the same in each. It was further suggested by McGeoch and Irion (1952) that Thorndike wrote as if he intended the theory to cover more than strict identity. In the light of Ferguson's model, Thorndike's view would claim that performance on any task is largely reduced to the case $y = f(t_y)$. In words, practice must be specific to the performance being sought. Other writers have concluded that Thorndike's view on transfer was an extremely pessimistic one.

Travers (1963, p. 193) states the opinion that Thorndike's theory is thought of today as an oversimplification of the phenomenon of transfer. The famous experiment of Judd suggested the theory of generalization which has come to supplement Thorndike's theory. Modern day Gestalt psychologists talk about essentially the same phenomenon in terms of meaningful organization of learning or the reorganization of experience.

It has been demonstrated that this kind of learning leads to transfer power. Bruner states ". . . massive general transfer can be achieved by appropriate learning, even to the degree that learning properly under optimum conditions leads one to 'learn how to learn'" (1962, p. 6). We propose to devote much of the remainder of this paper to dealing with the following two questions: What is *appropriate learning* for transfer? What might be considered *optimum conditions* for such learning? We will not confine our discussion to the area of mathematics, although what is discussed is certainly relevant to learning transfer in mathematics.

THE ROLE OF PRINCIPLES

Judd (1908) conducted an experiment on maximizing transfer of learning. This experiment consisted of throwing darts at a submerged target. Judd reached the conclusion that the best way to guarantee transfer is to teach principles. However, he believed that a principle must be exercised in practice while it is being learned, since he found his experimental group, which had been supplied with the principle of refraction, to be not significantly better than the control group in the first test; therefore, he contended that knowing the principle was not a substitute for direct experience. However, having organized their experiences using the principle as a frame, the subjects in the experimental group readily worked out necessary adjustments in succeeding tests with the target at different depths. Judd (1908) also found that experiences *alone* led to confusion on succeeding tests. The control group was not able to adjust readily to changes in depth.

It is not possible to critically evaluate

the research design of Judd's experiment since many details are not available. We do know that the groups of boys were equated on the basis of the teacher's judgments of their brightness; however, such things as the number of subjects, the apparatus details, the procedure used in teaching the principle to the experimental group, and the quantitative results are not reported. For these reasons, it is significant to mention that Hendrickson and Schroeder (1941) conducted an experiment in which they modified Judd's experiment so that the skill being tested was shooting an air gun at a submerged target. Their conclusions confirmed the main result of Judd, although the differences between the three groups in the study were not large.

The transfer measured in Judd's experiment can be represented in terms of Ferguson's model. The performance of the control group in throwing darts at the target, submerged to a particular depth, may have been dependent only on the group's practice at that depth. If we let this performance be represented by y_c and let the amount of practice at this depth be t_y, then $y_c = f_1(t_y)$. Thus, this situation reduces to the usual learning curve. However, the performance of the experimental group was dependent not only on practice at a particular depth, but also on knowledge of the principle of refraction and on practice in its application at a previous depth. Thus, for the experimental group, if we let x represent a measure of knowledge of the principle and let t_x represent the amount of practice in applying this knowledge, then $y_c = f_2(x, t_x, t_y)$.

There is another way of looking at the transfer involved in Judd's experiment, and that is to attempt to provide an explanation for the poor performance of the control group in terms of negative transfer. We could conjecture that training at the first depth interfered with performance at the second depth. If we let w represent a measure of performance at the first depth, then, for the control group, $y_c = g_1(w, t_w, t_y)$. Now in order to represent the performance of the experimental group, it is necessary to extend the model so that it is a function of five variables instead of three. We could conjecture that knowledge of the principle and practice with it in some way mediated the performance of the experimental group at the first depth so that the transfer effect of that experience is positive. Thus, we get that $y_c = g_2(x, t_x, w, t_w, t_y)$, where, as before, x represents a measure of knowledge of the principle.

THE ROLE OF DISCOVERY

Let us again refer to the study done by Hendrickson and Schroeder (1941). A significant observation reported in that study was the apparent importance of *discovery* of the solution by individual subjects. Knowledge of the refraction principle seemed to hasten this discovery for the subjects in the experimental group. Therefore, we see that discovery enters the picture in transfer of learning.

Ervin (1960) used third- and fourth-grade pupils to investigate transfer effects of learning a verbal generalization. She led pupils to discover the principle of reflection by means of experiments in ejecting a marble from a tube against a barrier. One experimental group worked out the verbal principle from its observations while the other was given nonverbal aid in observing relevant facts. All instruction was individual. While there were no overall differences between the two experimental groups and a control group in performance on the transfer criteria, one test item was a key one. Here a flashlight was to be aimed upwards towards a mirror so that it would reflect on a target. The mirror was tipped sharply, and the target was low, near the flashlight. The usual error is to aim the flashlight too high, thus sending the beam up to the ceiling (Ervin, 1960, p. 547). On other test items, subjects could achieve success by aiming at a point somewhere between the vertical projections of the target and flashlight. But this doesn't work when the mirror is tipped steeply; only subjects who adjusted the incidence angle could be correct. Striking differences were found on this transfer item, with superior performance for those subjects who arrived at the correct verbal rule during training. Finally, it should be noted that both groups in the study had been guided toward discovery.

In another study of discovery, Gagné and Brown (1961) prepared programs to instruct ninth- and tenth-grade boys in deriving formulas for summing various number series [e.g., $1 + 3 + 5 + \ldots + (2n - 1)$]. Then, instead of testing transfer by summing series of the same type, they tested ability to develop new formulas for summing new series (e.g., $1 + 3 + 9 + \ldots + 3^{n-1}$). They constructed three programs: The first (R and E) gave the *rule* (formula) for finding the sum of n terms of each training series and taught subjects to apply it to *examples;* a second (GD) divided the task into forty steps of *guided discovery*, each step requiring an analysis of a small part of the series; finally, a third (D) demanded *discovery* of the formula and provided hints as needed. All groups showed improvement from one training series to another. The transfer test required subjects to find rules for new series utilizing a few hints as needed. Guided discovery was found to be superior to each of the other groups. It should be mentioned that the tasks selected by Gagné and Brown appear to be well chosen. Not only are they representative of series problems, but insofar as one task can be,

they are representative of all mathematics (Cronbach, 1965b, p. 4).

Gagné (1959) and Cronbach (1965a) report that claims for discovery, as a method of learning, have had widespread influence on mathematics educators. At the same time, they state that the answer to the question "What kind of training will make a student capable of discovery?" has not been given. Consequently, Gagné and Cronbach and others have called for more research in this area.

Even so, mathematics educators should be aware of the attention that has been given to the effect that "discovery" of principles has upon transfer of learning. In a study of the effect of external direction during learning on the transfer of principles, Kittell (1957) used 132 sixth-grade students, divided into three experimental groups, who were trained by different methods to select one word that did not belong in a set of five given words. During the training process, the subjects in the "minimum" treatment group were told when correct responses were made, but they were required to discover principles independent of other help. The appropriate principle was briefly stated in general terms for the "intermediate" treatment group for each task, but they had to discover how to apply it in each case. The "maximum" treatment group was given not only the principles but also correct responses. The design of the research was of the following type:

$$O_1 \, T_1 \, O_1 \, O_2 \, O_3$$
$$O_1 \, T_2 \, O_1 \, O_2 \, O_3$$
$$O_1 \, T_3 \, O_1 \, O_2 \, O_3$$

where $T_i(i = 1, 2, 3)$ represent the treatments and $O_i(i = 1, 2, 3)$ represent the observations. (In this experiment, the observations which preceded and immediately followed the treatments were made with the same test instrument.)

The second observation measured the application of principles, learned during the training period, to new items. The third observation measured the ability to discover and use new unpracticed principles. Kittell (1957) concluded that superiority of the "intermediate" group, which received a certain amount of direction in discovering the principles, was established at a statistically significant level for both observations. At the same time, the "maximum" help group was also significantly superior to the group which derived principles independently.

The technique utilized by Kittell (1957) to train his "intermediate" group could be thought of as a type of learning in which principles are taught by examples. Katona (1940) in several interesting transfer experiments compared the effectiveness of learning by means of examples with learning by rote. He thought of the former as meaningful learning and the latter as senseless learning. His conclusions indicated superior results for the method of meaningful learning when transfer of learning was tested. Also, there was substantial transfer for the groups that learned by examples and practically none for the groups that memorized.

Although most educators would not find Katona's conclusions surprising, his experiments were weak in several respects. For example, he used a very small number of tasks and questionable statistical controls. According to Melton (1941), Katona's major results were unreliable. He observed that "understanding" and "transfer" were not independently defined words; hence, the hypothesis that learning by understanding leads to greater transfer was not actually tested. Melton further suggests that a more defensible explanation of the results might be to attribute the difference in performance to a *shift from a rote-learning attitude to a problem-solving attitude.*

Melton's conjecture is supported by the results of an experiment by Kersh (1958) in which the effects of independent discovery, as compared to directed discovery, of a generalization were tested. He concluded that "the superiority of the independent discovery procedure may be better explained in terms of motivation than in terms of understanding" (Kersh, p. 290). He goes on to say that the independent learner is more likely to become motivated to continue the learning process or to continue practicing a task after the learning period. However, in a later study, Kersh (1964) found that neither of the discovery groups employed the learned material more frequently after instruction that did the third group in the experiment. This suggests that his previous findings may be unique to the particular instructional setting or to the learning materials used in the earlier study.

The same contrast in approaches to the learning of mathematics is emphasized in a book by Bruner (1960). He points out that an overly passive approach to learning creates a situation in which the learner expects order to come from the outside, that is, from the material which is presented. Mathematical reasoning, however, requires unmasking, simplification, reordering, etc. Therefore, the role of attitudes is recognized here as important in learning and hence to transfer of learning.

Hilgard, Irvine, and Whipple (1953) repeated and extended Katona's card trick experiment using sixty high school students in an attempt to counter Melton's (1941) criticisms of poor research design. The conclusions supported the hypothesis that transfer to new related tasks is greater after learning by understanding than after learning by rote. However, these authors felt that "the failures of the understanding group were more impressive than their successes, in view of the logical advantages inherent in the methods they were taught" (1953, p. 290). Consequently, a second study was undertaken in an attempt to reduce the number of errors (Hilgard, Irvine, and Whipple, 1954). Subjects in the understanding group were taught by five different methods, but the overall differences in success among the methods were slight. Hence the complex nature of transfer was brought into focus.

Wittrock (1963) used college students to study the effect of different schedules of help and statement of rules in learning on the following criteria: initial learning, retention, transfer to new examples. Wittrock's results indicate that explicit and detailed direction appear to be most effective and efficient when the criterion is initial learning. An "intermediate" amount of direction, however, appears to produce the best results when retention and transfer are the criteria.

Craig (1956) also used college students to test the effect of giving the rule and providing help on the criteria of initial learning, retention, and discovery of new principles. The group which was given the principle was superior in the number of rules learned initially and retained many more items after thirty-one days. A test for discovery of new principles, however, did not reveal reliable differences.

A study by Haslerud and Meyers (1958) also compared the transfer power of a principle which was derived by the subject with the transfer power of a principle presented by the experimenter in the form of a statement and an example. The researchers concluded that independently derived principles transferred more readily than given principles. However, other researchers have questioned the interpretation of the results and the conclusions drawn by Haslerud and Meyers (see Cronbach, 1965b, pp. 6–7; Wittrock, 1965, p. 41).

THE ROLE OF VERBALIZATION

As suggested earlier, another important consideration in the transfer of learning is the question: "What role does verbalization play in transfer?" In a study previously cited, Katona concluded that "the ability to solve the tasks can be acquired without verbal formulation of what has been learned and successfully performed" (1940, p. 101). Several people have pursued this observation in research.

In one of these experiments, Hendrix (1947) tested three hypotheses. They were (1) the nonverbalized awareness method of learning a generalization is superior to the method in which an authoritative statement of the generalization comes first; (2) verbalizing a generalization immediately after discovery does not increase transfer power; and (3) the possibility exists that transfer power may decrease as a result of verbalization. We found no trace of statistical controls in the study and the type of transfer tested was somewhat limited in scope. This is borne out by the fact that only one principle was considered for the three methods of training. Hendrix suggests, in conclusion, that the "flash" of *nonverbalized awareness* is the phenomenon that accounts for transfer power. This conjecture, we believe, should be tested under an improved design.

The University of Illinois Committee on School Mathematics (UICSM) also has something to say on the question of verbalization. This group believes that the student should become aware of a concept before a name is assigned to the concept. Many mathematics educators share this view.

TRANSFER IN GEOMETRY

In all of the research studies we have examined, the tasks performed in the experiments were not unlike the analysis of relationships encountered in mathematical problem solving. Thus, we accept the conclusions as being relevant to learning in mathematics. Under careful scrutiny, however, it will be realized that the tasks to which the learning was transferred were only slightly different from the training tasks. Mathematics teachers have long felt that there might be a more general type of transfer to be gained from the study of mathematics, namely, an improvement in reasoning ability outside of mathematics.

Several studies we have examined have dealt with the hypothesis that training to think logically in geometry can transfer to nongeometric situations. Parker (1924), Perry (1925), Fawcett (1938), and Ulmer (1939) conducted such studies. The study of Ulmer virtually entailed the others, and hence we will consider it alone.

Ulmer's (1939) experiment was designed to evaluate the results achieved by a number of high school geometry teachers in different communities who utilized a method of teaching in which emphasis was placed on the cultivation of critical thinking. Ten teachers and 1,239 students in seven high schools were used. The subjects were divided into three groups: the experimental group with 638 students, the nongeometry control group with 575 students, and the geometry group (traditional courses) with 416 students. The nongeometry control group was composed of sophomores from schools having geometry as a junior course. Only the most capable teachers were used for both the experimental and traditional geometry courses. In the experimental group, definite emphasis was placed on concise, logical thought and application of critical thinking to nongeometric situations.

The evaluation instruments were reasoning tests prepared at The Ohio State University. The results indicated significant gains in critical thinking at all levels of intelligence for the experimental group at no loss in the learning of geometry content. The geometry control group showed a slight gain and the nongeometry group displayed no gain. We agree that the study illustrated very vividly that even highly competent geometry teaching offers little hope for the transfer of critical thinking *unless* definite provision is made for it in the teaching act. On the other hand, if such provision is made, the results can be rewarding indeed.

DISCUSSION OF THE RESEARCH

The preceding review of studies dealing with various teaching methods reveals the lack of consistent empirical evidence on the relative efficacy of these methods and points to the need for more carefully controlled research. The hypotheses which precede these studies frequently focus on the extent to which discovery activity should be guided.

We submit that this may not be the critical variable and that possibly these studies can be better understood if we separate *what* happened from *why* it happened. In the experiments in which the subjects who were given the principle performed best, these subjects comprised the *group that had the most practice in using the principle.* They were practicing the principle on trials when the others were trying, sometimes unsuccessfully, to discover it.

Particularly in the instances when the transfer task was recognition of *new examples of a learned principle*, practice in using the principle may be the most important variable. Of the groups which were tested for ability to discover *new principles*, only the discovery groups in Gagné and Brown's (1961) study were more successful than the nondiscovery group. In the studies by Wittrock (1963), Craig (1956), and Kittell (1957), the subjects in the principle-given groups had the higher scores in discovering new principles. It is difficult to equate these studies, but the weight of this evidence does not appear to give an advantage to learning by discovery.

It is more difficult to attribute differences to practice in those experiments in which the guided discovery group performed best. We would hypothesize that it was a combination of practice, increased attention, and reflection upon what was learned that was responsible for the differences in results in these cases.

In regard to transfer, the argument appears to be that learning by discovery helps a student to organize knowledge and the knowledge therefore is more susceptible to transfer (Baskin, 1962; Bruner, 1961). Hilgard states, "Transfer to new tasks will be better if, in learning, the learner can discover relationships for himself, and if he has experience during learning of applying the principles within a variety of tasks" (1956, p. 487). However, Travers (1963) sees no advantage to learning by discovery and prefers the learning of principles and *overlearning* as the superior preparation for transfer.

In the experiments by Wittrock (1963), Craig (1956), and Kittell (1957) described above, the superior group had more opportunity for overlearning than any other groups in the same experiment. Mandler (1962, p. 425) cites evidence to the effect that "there is an initial negative transfer effect followed by a reversal to a positive direction after the organism has had longer experience with the original task." Thus Mandler's results would appear to argue for overlearning on specific tasks. But in an experiment by Duncan (1958), where one series of groups had different schedules of overlearning on a single problem task

and another series of groups learned the responses to varied stimuli, the group with experience in "learning to learn" was superior on transfer tasks. Hence, the role of overlearning in transfer remains unclear.

SUMMARY

It is acknowledged that some aspects of the problem of transfer of learning have not been discussed in this paper. Much of the paper has been devoted to the best way to learn principles in order to maximize transfer. The conclusions of Haslerud and Meyers (1958) and of Kersh (1958, 1964) contradicted those of Kittell (1957) so that it is not clear whether principles should be derived independently by the learner or learned through a certain amount of direction from the teacher. Kersh (1958) is of the opinion that this is exactly the teacher's dilemma. The teacher has to decide whether the most important outcome of a learning experience should be maximum understanding or maximum motivation to continue learning. In our judgment, both outcomes are essential to maximum transfer. Thus, the teacher is confronted with the task of striking the proper balance.

Ausubel (1961) claims: "Learning by discovery has its proper place among the repertoire of accepted pedagogic techniques available to teachers. For certain designated purposes and for certain carefully specified learning situations, its rationale is clear and defensible" (1961, p. 53). On the other hand, he argues that discovery methods are not unique in their ability to generate self-confidence, intellectual excitement, and sustained motivation for learning. Finally, he states his position that available research does not provide a basis for generalizing to any one position.

We have concluded from this investigation what other writers have concluded in the past; namely, that transfer of learning is not automatic. The objectives of the methodology must be carefully formulated with transfer as a primary goal and with provision for various learning experiences as a means to the goal. Also, we believe that the learning of principles increases positive transfer in most situations and that principles *discovered* by the learner are more susceptible to transfer than those learned by *rote*. Finally, it is not completely clear whether principles should be discovered relatively independently by the learner or through close direction from the teacher in order to increase transfer. A crucial question that needs to be answered here is whether the increased expenditure of time required for independent discovery warrants its use. Similarly, the role which verbalization plays in transfer of mathematics learning remains unclear. Consequently, specific additional research is needed in these areas.

Ausubel (1961), in reviewing a sample of research studies, states that such relevant learning variables as rote-meaningful, inductive-deductive, verbal-nonverbal, and intramaterial organization were not controlled. Thus, the generalizability of such studies is limited. Ausubel's observations should be considered in future research in teaching, discovery, and the problem of transfer of training in mathematics.

REFERENCES

1. Ausubel, D. P., "Learning by Discovery: Rationale and Mystique," *Bulletin of the National Association of Secondary School Principals*, XLV (December, 1961), 18–58.
2. Baskin, S., "Experiment in Independent Study." *Journal of Experimental Education*, XXXI (1962), 183–86.
3. Bruner, J.S. "The Act of Discovery," *Harvard Educational Review*, XXXI (1961), 21–32.
4. ———, "On Learning Mathematics," *The Mathematics Teacher*, LIII (December, 1960), 610–19.
5. ———, *The Process of Education.* Cambridge, Mass.: Harvard University Press, 1960.
6. Campbell, D. T., and J. C. Stanley, "Experimental and Quasi-Experimental Design for Research on Teaching," in *Handbook of Research on Teaching*, ed. N. L. Gage. Chicago: Rand McNally, 1963.
7. Craig, R. C., "Directed Versus Independent Discovery of Established Relations," *Journal of Educational Psychology*, XLVII (1956), 223–34.
8. Cronbach, L. J., *Educational Psychology.* New York: Harcourt, Brace & World, Inc., 1954, pp. 245–68.
9. ———, "Issues Current in Educational Psychology," in *Mathematical Learning*, eds. L. N. Morrisett and J. Vinsonhaler. (Monographs of the Society for Research in Child Development.) Chicago: University of Chicago Press, 1965 (a).
10. ———, "The Logic of Experiments on Discovery." Paper prepared for the Conference on Learning by Discovery, New York, N.Y., January 28–29, 1965 (b).
11. Duncan, C. P., "Transfer After Training with Single Versus Multiple Tasks," *Journal of Experimental Psychology*, LV (1958), 63–73.
12. Ervin, S. M., "Transfer Effects of Learning a Generalization," *Child Development*, XXXI (1960), 537–54.
13. Fawcett, H. P., *The Nature of Proof*, Thirteenth Yearbook, National Council of Teachers of Mathematics. New York: Columbia University, 1938.
14. Ferguson, G. A., "On Learning and Human Ability," *Canadian Journal of Psychology*, VIII (1954), 95–112.
15. ———, "On Transfer and the Abilities of Man," *Canadian Journal of Psychology*, X (1956), 121–31.
16. Gagné, R. M., "Implications of Some Doctrines of Mathematics Teaching for Research in Human Learning," in *Psychological Problems and Research Methods in Mathematics Training*, eds. R. L. Feierabend and P.H. DuBois. U.S. Office of Education. St. Louis: Washington University, 1959.

17. Gagné, R. M., and L. T. Brown, "Some Factors in the Programing of Conceptual Learning." *Journal of Experimental Psychology*, LXII (1961), 313–21.

18. Gagné, R. M., *et al.* "Factors in Acquiring Knowledge of a Mathematical Task," *Psychological Monographs*, LXXVI (7 [Whole No. 526], 1962).

19. Haslerud, G. M., and S. Meyers, "The Transfer Value of Given and Individually Derived Principles," *Journal of Educational Psychology*, XLIX (1958), 293–98.

20. Henderson, K. B. "Research on Teaching Secondary School Mathematics," in *Handbook of Research on Teaching*, ed. N. L. Gage. Chicago: Rand McNally, 1963.

21. Hendrickson, G., and W. H. Schroeder, "Transfer of Training in Learning to Hit a Submerged Target," *Journal of Educational Psychology*, XXXII (1941), 205–13.

22. Hendrix, G. "A New Clue to Transfer of Training," *Elementary School Journal*, XLVIII (1947), 197–208.

23. Hilgard, E. R. *Theories of Learning*. New York: Appleton-Century-Crofts, 1956.

24. ———, R. P. Irvine, and J. E. Whipple, "Errors in Transfer Learning with Understanding: Further Studies with Katona's Card Trick Experiment." *Journal of Experimental Psychology*, XLVII (1954), 457–64.

25. ———, "Rote Memorization, Understanding, and Transfer: An Extension of Katona's Card Trick Experiment." *Journal of Experimental Psychology*, XLVI (1953), 288–91.

26. Judd, C. H., "The Relation of Special Training to General Intelligence," *Educational Review*, XXXV (1908), 28–42.

27. Katona, G., *Organizing and Memorizing*. New York: Columbia University Press, 1940.

28. Kendler, H. H., and R. Vinebeig, "The Acquisition of Compound Concepts as a Function of Previous Training." *Journal of Experimental Psychology*, XLVIII (1954), 252–58.

29. Kersh, B. Y., "The Adequacy of 'Meaning' as an Explanation for the Superiority of Learning by Independent Discovery." *Journal of Educational Psychology*, XLIX (1958), 282–92.

30. ———, "Directed Discovery Versus Programmed Instruction: A Test of a Theoretical Position Involving Educational Technology." Final report. Title VII, Project No. 907. Monmouth, Oreg.: Oregon State System of Higher Education, 1964.

31. Kittell, J. E., "The Effect of External Direction During Learning on Transfer and Retention of Principles," *Journal of Educational Psychology*, XLVIII (1957), 391–405.

32. Kolesnik, W. B., "Note on Transfer of Training Research," *Peabody Journal of Education*, XXXIV (1957), 215–19.

33. Mandler, G., "From Association to Structure," *Psychological Review*, LXIX (1962). 415–27.

34. McDonald, F. J., *Educational Psychology*. Belmont, Calif.: Wadsworth Publishing Co., 1959.

35. McGeoch, J. A., and A. L. Irion, *The Psychology of Human Learning*. New York: Longmans, Green, 1952.

36. Melton, A. W. "Review of Katona, Organizing and Memorizing," *American Journal of Psychology*, LIV (1941), 455–57.

37. Murdock, B. B., Jr., "Transfer Designs and Formulas," *Psychological Bulletin*, LIV (1957), 313–26.

38. Parker, E., "Teaching Pupils the Conscious Use of a Technique of Thinking," *The Mathematics Teacher*, XVII (1924), 191–201.

39. Perry, W., *A Study in the Psychology of Learning Geometry*. New York: Columbia University Press, 1925.

40. Thorndike, E. L., and R. S. Woodworth. "I. The Influence of Improvement in One Mental Function upon the Efficiency of Other Functions; II. The Estimation of Magnitudes," *Psychological Review*, VIII (1901), 247–61; 384–95.

41. Travers, R. M. W., *Essentials of Learning*. New York: The Macmillan Company, 1963, pp. 187–216.

42. Ulmer, G., "Teaching Geometry to Cultivate Reflective Thinking: An Experimental Study with 1239 High

School Pupils," *Journal of Experimental Psychology*, VIII (1939), 18–25.

43. Wittrock, M. C., "The Learning by Discovery Hypothesis." Paper prepared for The Conference on Learning by Discovery, New York, N.Y., January 28–29, 1965.

44. ———, "Verbal Stimuli in Concept Formation: Learning by Discovery,"

Journal of Educational Psychology, LIV (1963), 183–90.

45. Young, R. K., and B. J. Underwood. "Transfer in Verbal Materials with Dissimilar Stimuli and Response Similarity Varied," *Journal of Experimental Psychology*, XLVII (1943), 153–59.

Individual Differences: Does Research Have Any Answers for Junior High Mathematics Teachers?

ROBERT E. WILLCUTT

Individual academic differences have always been a challenge to the junior high school mathematics teacher. Most teachers accept this thesis as a true one and many think the degree of these individual differences is increasing. A great deal of written evidence exists concerning individual academic differences; an example is the following statement by Jarvis:

[A] wide range of individual differences in the area of arithmetic is an incontestable fact. The teacher cannot and should not seek to eliminate them. But what he does to meet these individual needs once they have been identified is the important issue and should be the goal to which good arithmetic teaching is directed. . . . It is common knowledge among teachers of arithmetic that individual pupil differences in the elementary school are very pronounced at every grade level. It is equally apparent that the range of individual differences increases from grade level to grade level. [These differences reach]

. . . between six and seven years at the sixth-grade level. . . .[1]

It is recognized that the existence of these individual differences is not unique to the mathematics curriculum, but Gane states: "In no other school subject is the matter of individual differences so apparent as in arithmetic,"[2] Whether individual differences in arithmetic are more pronounced than in other curricular areas and whether these arithmetic individual differences are increasing through the years is not, however, the major point at this time. What is important is that the problem of individual difference in mathematics is a realistic one today just as it has been for many years.

Different methods of grouping students have been attempted in an effort to minimize some of the problems inherent in a class with a wide range of individual differences. These types of

Reprinted from *School Science and Mathematics*, LXIX (March, 1969), 217–25, by permission of the author and the publisher. Robert E. Willcutt is Assistant Professor of Education, Boston University.

[1] O. T. Jarvis, "Analysis of Individual Differences in Arithmetic," *Arithmetic Teacher*, XI (November, 1964), 471–73.

[2] J. T. Gane, "Research Should Guide Us," *Arithmetic Teacher*, IX (December, 1962), 441–45.

ability grouping have taken on many forms and apparently have met with varying forms of success. On one end of this continuum is the intra-class grouping or ability grouping within a self-contained heterogeneous class whereby a teacher attempts the herculean task of teaching two or three or more groups within a single class of thirty students. On the other end of this ability grouping continuum is the complete ability-grouped homogeneous class which moves together on its special track for a year or two years or even longer. These two examples as well as the many degrees of grouping between them have all been attempts to meet the problem of individual differences.

Many basic questions can be raised with regard to ability-grouping and in fact, many questions have been brought forth. A review of the research literature from the past fifteen years suggest the following questions may be the most basic ones.

1. Can you get homogeneous groups?
2. How do you prevent homogeneous grouping from being an end in itself?
3. Must there be curriculum changes before the grouping can be effective?
4. Must ability grouping be flexible?
5. Should ability grouping involve acceleration or enrichment?
6. What happens to attitudes toward mathematics of students involved in ability grouping?
7. Does ability grouping bring academic gains?
8. Does ability grouping lead to sociological problems?

These questions do not lend themselves to any concrete yes or no answers. However, some general trends and patterns may be found and it is on this premise and hope that this report is based.

The first question concerns the entire process of grouping by ability.

Franseth poses this dilemma:

Can children be grouped according to ability? It is becoming increasingly difficult to accept that they can. Although grouping children according to ability may be possible to a limited extent for short periods, the number of different interrelated factors make it difficult if not impossible to achieve. Evidence indicates that changes within individuals take place continually so that homogeneity—which might have been obtained when a group was first formed—will continue to move toward heterogeneity.[3]

This same view is expressed by Balow when he concludes that one cannot create homogeneous groups, and, if one could, such groups would not remain homogeneous.[4] Thus, it appears to be a deception to think that a homogeneous group can be attained; perhaps a dangerous deception.

Questions two and three deal with one of the major criticisms of ability grouping in that educators often tend to treat ability grouping as an end in itself. In their recent doctoral dissertations, Moses,[5] Tobin,[6] and Wilcox[7] echo this point and conclude that curriculum changes must take place before grouping can be effective. Vergason summarizes this view as follows.

As we realize that different curricula offer a far more promising attack to the facilitation of instruction, grouping will be used as an aid rather than as an answer in itself. Such grouping should be con-

[3] J. Franseth, "Does Grouping Make a Difference?" *Education Digest*, XXVIII (January, 1963), 15–17.

[4] I. H. Balow, "Effects of Homogeneous Grouping in Seventh-Grade Arithmetic," *Arithmetic Teacher*, XI (March, 1964), 186–91.

[5] J. P. Moses, "A Study of the Effect of Inter-Class Ability Grouping on Achievement in Reading," *Dissertation Abstracts*, XXVI, 4342.

[6] J. T. Tobin, "An Eight Year Study of Classes Grouped Within Grade Levels on the Basis of Reading Ability," *Dissertation Abstracts*, XXVI, 5141.

[7] J. Wilcox, "A Search for the Multiple Effects of Grouping Upon the Growth and Behavior of Junior-High School Pupils," *Dissertation Abstracts*, XXIV, 205.

sidered as instructional grouping and be divorced from the idea of there being anything homogeneous about it or that spectacular results can be expected from instructional grouping without differential curricula.[8]

Another major criticism that appears throughout the literature is the lack of flexibility in grouping programs. Too often we expect children to learn on a stair-step theory when we should know that children seldom if ever follow such an approach. The following diagram is an oversimplified pattern of a normal curriculum track for ability grouping in junior high school.

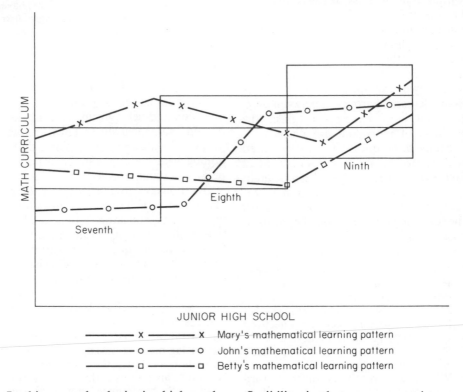

In this example, the junior high mathematics classes have been grouped on a three-track approach but neither Mary, a bright student, Betty, an average student, or John, a slow student "fit this mold." A specific fallacy of this system might be that Betty, who is assigned to the middle track for the three-year period, really doesn't fit that track much of the time.

Leland points out that about the only flexibility is that some grouping programs allow students to be in different ability-level classes in different subject areas[9]. Within the mathematics class, however, grouping is usually far from flexible, a condition believed to be unhealthy by the following writers. Moench states: "Yet when rigid grouping is observed in the total arithmetic program, the ability gaps widen rapidly and the more difficult a return to hetero-

[8]G. A. Vergason, "Critical Review of Grouping," *High School Journal*, XLVIII (April, 1965), 427–33.

[9]R. D. Leland, "Grouping Practices Providing Differentiated Education in California Junior-High Schools," *Dissertation Abstracts*, XXIV, 200.

geneity becomes."[10] Hart believes: "Flexibility [in grouping] is an essential ingredient in any arithmetic program if teachers entertain the hope of meeting the challenge of tomorrow—or even of today."[11] Brewer adds: "Flexibility in grouping should be maintained so that each pupil can work with the group which will most appropriately serve his needs, interests, and abilities."[12] Perhaps the strongest statement concerning flexibility comes from Lerch when he concludes: "Grouping for arithmetic instruction ought to ... involve some continuous regrouping procedure in which pupils are grouped and regrouped as new topics, areas, or units are studied and as varying degrees of ability are displayed by pupils."[13]

It is usually agreed that grouping is designed to help reduce the range of individual differences within a classroom, but it is not so easily agreed as to what happens to the students after they are grouped. Oftentimes, as was pointed out in the above paragraphs, nothing happens to the students that is any different than that found in normal heterogeneous classrooms. When changes are made in mathematics curriculums, they are many times of an accelerated nature. Echternacht and Gordon[14] as well as Townsend[15] found that such acceleration

procedures produce significant results, but, as often happens, these men do not ask or answer the questions, "What happens to them the next year?" and/or "Sure they can do it, but should they?" Thus the dilemma of a need for different ability levels and the concern of an accelerated versus a depth approach for such a special curriculum raises many penetrating questions.

Still another area of major concern with regard to ability grouping in mathematics is that of relationship of grouping with attitudes. There is a great deal of evidence; including dissertations by Girgis[16] and Ernatt,[17] and articles by Lyda,[18] Bassham,[19] and Brown[20]; that the classroom organization and its corresponding curriculum does have a major effect on the students' attitudes. McDermott points out the importance of the students' arithmetic experiences in the elementary school when he states: "Most students in high school having fear and dislike of mathematics met with frustration in the elementary grades."[21] Dutton also observes: "Apparently lasting attitudes toward arithmetic are developed at each grade level. Grades V and VII

[10] Laurel Moench, "Individualized Practice in Arithmetic—A Pilot Study," *Arithmetic Teacher*, IX (October, 1962), 311–29.

[11] R. H. Hart, "The Non-Graded Primary School and Arithmetic," *Arithmetic Teacher*, IX (March, 1962), 130–33.

[12] E. Brewer, "Survey of Arithmetic Intraclass Grouping Practices," *Arithmetic Teacher*, XIII (April, 1966), 310–14.

[13] H. H. Lerch, "Intra-Class Grouping for Arithmetic Instruction: Critique and Criteria," *Arithmetic Teacher*, VIII (December, 1961), 404–7.

[14] C. Echternacht, and V. Gordon, "Breaking the Lock Step in Arithmetic," *Arithmetic Teacher*, IX (February, 1962), 86–89.

[15] R. C. Townsend, "An Experiment in Arithmetic Acceleration," *Arithmetic Teacher*, VII (December, 1960), 409–11.

[16] M. M. M. Girgis, "Relationship Between Individual Values and Curriculum Organization in Junior-High Schools," *Dissertation Abstracts*, XXV, 3201.

[17] R. Ernatt, "A Survey of Pupils' Attitudes Toward Intergrade Ability Grouping for Reading Instruction," *Dissertation Abstracts*, XXV, 1651.

[18] Wesley Lyda, Jr., and E. C. Morse, "Attitudes, Teaching Methods, and Arithmetic Achievement," *Arithmetic Teacher*, X (March, 1963), 136–38.

[19] Harrel Bassham, Michael Murphy, and Katherine Murphy, "Attitude and Achievement in Arithmetic," *Arithmetic Teacher*, XI (February, 1964), 66–72.

[20] K. E. Brown and T. L. Abell, "Research in the Teaching of Elementary School Mathematics," *Arithmetic Teacher*, XII (November, 1965), 547–49.

[21] L. A. McDermott, "A Study of Some Factors That Cause Fear and Dislike of Mathematics," *Dissertation Abstracts*, XIX, 71.

were pronounced most crucial."[22] If the type of organization does play such an important role and if the early years are such vital ones with regard to attitude, then the type of grouping implemented in the junior high, whether heterogeneous or homogeneous, is of major interest to mathematics educators. Lerch summarizes this point:

Thus, classroom organizational procedures and teaching methods should be ones which assure each pupil a measure of success at his own level of ability and understanding, and which at the same time encourage the development and maintenance of favorable attitudes toward arithmetic.[23]

Additional positive arguments point to some signs of student academic gains and positive attitudes toward mathematics while other negative arguments cite that only an exceptional teacher can handle intraclass grouping and that complete ability grouping can lead to many sociological problems. Also present on the negative side is the constant reminder that individual differences within a class are never eliminated and that deception to believe otherwise can be very dangerous.

A discussion of ability grouping can continue to great lengths and one can continually probe for a better understanding of this intriguing educational device. In the judgment of this writer, the theory of ability grouping in junior high school mathematics is sound, but, in reality, the practices do not reflect the theory. Yet these ideas are intriguing ones and in an effort to find some answers to some of these questions, a research project was conducted. Seventh graders provided the population for

[22]W. H. Dutton, "Attitudes of Junior High School Pupils Toward Arithmetic," *School Review*, LXIV (January, 1956), 18–22.

[23]H. H. Lerch, "Arithmetic Instruction Changes Pupils' Attitudes Toward Arithmetic," *Arithmetic Teacher*, VIII (March, 1961), 117–19.

the basic question, "Is there a better way, a way that has not been tried before?" It seemed from past experiences that students showed wide variations during a year and that specifically, these variations seemed to have some correlation with the topic being studied. Therefore, a research design was created to see what effect grouping of seventh graders on the basis of proficiency tests before each new unit or topic might have on academic achievement as well as on mathematical attitudes.

Thus, this study was concerned with two different methods of assigning seventh-grade students to their mathematics classes. In one case, students were assigned at the beginning of the year to one teacher and remained with that teacher throughout the year. These classes were heterogeneous and each class operated independently of all other seventh-grade mathematics classes. In the second method, seventh-grade students were assigned to their mathematics classes on the basis of test results which indicated the students' proficiency in a subject unit. These proficiency tests were taken and assignments made eight different times throughout the year, once for each of the eight different subject units studied throughout the year.

This study was therefore made to answer two basic questions:

1. Are there any significant differences in the mathematical academic achievement of the students involved in the two different classroom assignment methods?
2. Are there any significant differences in the attitudes toward mathematics of the students involved in the two different classroom assignment methods?

The value of this study lies in the information it can give to junior high school mathematics teachers and administrators. It is hoped that these teachers and administrators can use the results of this project to help them determine if either of the two types of classroom organizational methods described in this study would have value in their particular school system. Briefly stated, it is hoped that this study can help answer the following oversimplified question: Which of the following two classroom organizational methods would be best for the teaching of mathematics in our junior high school:

1. Self-contained heterogeneous classes with each individual teacher handling the individual differences within his class as he so desires, or
2. Classes which are ability grouped by subject-matter proficiency, such classes being determined before each new mathematics topic, and teachers working together as a team, attempting to handle individual differences as they so desire.

The major purpose of this research project was to compare the mathematical achievement and attitudinal changes toward mathematics of students in seventh-grade mathematics classes. Half of the total number of students were involved in a method of ability grouping while the other half were not involved in ability grouping. The entire seventh-grade class (240 students) was assigned to mathematics classes by the guidance department. One-half of the total seventh-grade class was assigned into four first-period classes and acted as the control group. The other half of the seventh-grade class was assigned into four second-period classes and became the experimental group.

The four control classes operated as independent classes in that no students were moved from one class or teacher to another class or teacher. Each teacher organized and presented the material to his class as he so desired. All classes used the same textbook and covered the same basic material, but the decisions as to the order of the material,

the method of teaching, and the degree of emphasis on any particular content were made by the individual teacher. Student progress was reported to parents on school report cards at normal six-week grading periods. Therefore, the four control classes were constructed to represent "typical" self-contained classes with four teachers operating independently.

The four experimental classes were taught by the same four teachers who taught the control classes, but the experimental classes were organized and operated on an ability-grouping plan throughout the year. The students in the experimental classes received a proficiency examination before entering each new subject unit. Results of these hour examinations determined ability-group assignments for that particular unit topic. The proficiency examinations were prepared by a committee of the four teachers and were designed to cover the basic content that was to be studied in each forthcoming topic, i.e., "What should they know after they finish with the unit on common fractions?"

The four experimental classes were classified in the following levels: one review class, two standard classes, and one depth class. All the experimental classes covered the same basic subject content, but the degree of emphasis and the depth of study varied according to the abilities of the three levels of classes. The depth class was designed for those students who demonstrated the highest degree of ability on the proficiency test, the standard classes for those students who performed at an expected seventh-grade level of ability and the review level class for those students who demonstrated a very low level of performance on the proficiency test. The decision was made by the four teachers as to which proficiency test scores determined the different ability class assignments. There were always four ability-grouped classes and an attempt was made to keep class sizes approximately the same although the number fluctuated with each subject unit. The teachers of the four experimental classes exchanged the teaching of the different ability levels so that one teacher did not stay with one ability level throughout the year. The progress of the students in the experimental classes was reported to parents at the end of each subject unit by a special mathematics department from which showed the topic studied, the class level assigned, the teacher instructing, and the student evaluated by the instructing teacher. Before the experiment began, the four teachers agreed on some basic rules of operations so that transitions from class to class and teacher to teacher would be somewhat easier for the students involved. Classroom behavioral rules and expectations, homework, testing procedures, and grading system were included in this unified approach.

Throughout the year, the four teachers involved in the experiment were encouraged to offer their experimental class a curriculum different from that being followed in their control class. Thus, for example, it was hoped that the teacher operating with the review class would follow different methods and content in his experimental class than he would in his control class. The depth classes were expected to work within the particular subject unit on common fractions; the depth classes worked with applications of common fractions in more sophisticated and abstract ways than did their peers who were in the standard and review classes. Difficult word problems and common fractions in other numeration systems are two examples of topics that the students in the depth classes encountered which were not covered in the standard and review classes.

The purpose of this investigation was to compare the students taught in a traditional self-contained classroom organization with students taught in a flexible ability-grouped type of classroom organization. The students were compared on the basis of mathematical achievement at the end of the 1965–66 academic year. The students were also compared for attitudinal changes toward their mathematics classes during the year in which the experiment took place.

The experimental and the control groups were formed by matching students from the self-contained classes with students from the ability-grouped classes. All students were matched by sex and the results of two standardized tests administered just prior to the start of the experiment. Seventy-eight matched pairs of students made up the total control and experiment groups.

Mathematical achievement was measured at the conclusion of the experiment by comparing test results from two standardized tests and one original test. The three tests measured computation skills, knowledge of the structure of mathematics, and the actual mathematical content covered by the students during the academic year. The results of all three tests failed to show any significant differences between the scores of those students in the control group and those students in the experimental group.

Attitudinal changes, as measured by response to a questionnaire which was administered just before the experiment and at the conclusion of it were of significant interest. There was a general positive change in the attitudes toward mathematics of those students in the experimental classes, especially with those students who at the beginning of the year considered mathematics with very negative thoughts. Specifically, these positive changes occurred at significant levels in the areas of (1) least favorite subject, (2) hardest subject,

(3) most boring subject, and (4) subject that was too difficult. The experimental groups also indicated mathematics to be a challenging subject whereas the control groups indicated mathematics to be unchallenging. Again on the positive side, the students who made up the experimental class indicated significant levels of endorsement of the experimental procedures involving several changes of teachers, classes, and classmates. At no point in the questionnaire did the results indicate a more positive attitude for the students in the control classes. There were some neutral results, i.e., those questions dealing with (1) subject with which they worked the hardest, (2) favorite year and favorite year of mathematics in school, (3) desire to study new and challenging ideas as opposed to studying the same subjects again, (4) affirmation that each

year has been more exciting and (5) desirability of being in classes with students who make similar grades.

If one accepts the widely held premise that attitudes do play a significant role in the learning process, then the experimental nature of this research project has produced significant results for mathematics education in the junior high school.

The findings from this experiment are the basis for the following conclusions. First, the experimental treatment of flexibly grouping students on the basis of a proficiency test before each new topic has not caused significant differences in academic achievement. Secondly, the experimental treatment of flexibly grouping students on the basis of a proficiency test before each new topic has resulted in significant degrees of positive attitudinal changes.

Effect of Teaching Concepts of Logic on Verbalization of Discovered Mathematical Generalizations

KENNETH A. RETZER / KENNETH B. HENDERSON

A method of teaching that is lauded by many mathematics educators is the method of guided discovery. Among the advocators of this method, there are some who believe that asking the stu-

Reprinted from *The Mathematics Teacher*, LX, No. 7 (November, 1967), 707–10, by permission of the authors and the National Council of Teachers of Mathematics. Copyright © 1967 by the National Council of Teachers of Mathematics. Kenneth B. Henderson is Professor of Secondary and Continuing Education, University of Illinois, Urbana, Illinois. Kenneth A. Retzer is Associate Professor of Mathematics, Illinois State University, Normal, Illinois.

dent to verbalize what he has discovered as soon as he has made the discovery is ineffective because he does not have the linguistic capacity.[1] Moreover, some argue that if the premature verbalization is incorrect, the basic insight may actually be multilated.[2] Others doubt this and question the adequacy of the

[1] Max Beberman, *An Emerging Program for Secondary School Mathematics*, Inglis Lecture for 1958 (Cambridge, Mass.: Harvard University Press, 1958).

[2] Gertrude Hendrix, "Learning by Discovery," *The Mathematics Teacher*, LIV (May, 1961), 290–99.

evidence advanced by the former group to support their contention.[3]

The purpose of the present article is not to debate this issue, but to conjecture that if a group of students are taught concepts such as variable, open sentence, universal quantifier, universal set, universal statement (generalization), instance of a generalization, and counter-instance and are given practice in applying these concepts in writing generalizations and making judgments about the truth of the generalizations, they will be able to state correctly the relations they discover when taught by the method of guided discovery. This conjecture seems plausible when one considers the difficulty of using the vernacular and the ease of using a technical language. In using the latter to report discoveries about numbers, for example, one begins with a true statement in which constants appear, replaces one or more constants by variables, and binds these variables by universal quantifiers operating over some designated sets. For example, suppose a student has considered the true statements

$$\text{If } 2 < 6, \text{ then } 2 \cdot 10 < 6 \cdot 10$$
$$\text{If } 2 < 6, \text{ then } 2(\tfrac{1}{4}) < 6(\tfrac{1}{4})$$
$$\text{If } -1 < 0, \text{ then } -1 \cdot 5 < 0 \cdot 5$$
$$\text{If } -1 < 0, \text{ then } -1(\tfrac{1}{2}) < 0(\tfrac{1}{2})$$

among others of the same form and has sensed the pattern and has also considered the true statements

$$\text{If } 2 < 6, \text{ then } 2 \cdot 0 \not< 6 \cdot 0$$
$$\text{If } 2 < 6, \text{ then } 2 \cdot -10 \not< 6 \cdot -10$$
$$\text{If } 2 < 6, \text{ then } 2(-\tfrac{1}{4}) \not< 6(-\tfrac{1}{4})$$

among others of the same form and has sensed this pattern. He can state his discovery readily by substituting vari-

ables for constants and appending quantifiers: "For all the numbers x and y we know and for all the positive numbers z we know, if $x < y$, then $xz < yz$." Whether the generalization reached is true depends partly on the skill of the director of the guided discovery (the teacher or the student himself) and partly on the care of the student in choosing the set or sets over which the respective quantifiers operate. But if a false generalization is stated, a counterinstance will indicate the need for restriction of the domain of one or more of the variables.

DESCRIPTION OF THE EXPERIMENT

The design of an experiment to test this conjecture was a two-way analysis of variance. The dependent variable was the ability of a group of college-capable junior high school students to verbalize precisely mathematical generalizations they discovered. The independent variables were the following two, with their indicated partitions.

Factor A: Study of selected logical concepts, or lack thereof.

A_1: Completion of the programmed unit *Sentences of Logic*.

A_2: Not having studied the programmed unit *Sentences of Logic*.

Factor B: Ability level.

B_1: Gifted (IQ 135 and above).

B_2: College-capable but not gifted (IQ 116–128).

The *Sentences of Logic* unit used in this experiment contained the concepts described in formulating the conjecture of this article.

The hypotheses tested were as follows:

H_1: Completion of the *Sentences of Logic* unit has no effect on the ability of college-capable junior high school students to verbalize discovered mathematical generalizations.

[3]David P. Ausubel, *Learning by Discovery: Rationale and Mystique* (Urbana, Ill.: Bureau of Educational Research, University of Illinois, 1961), and Lee J. Cronbach, *Educational Psychology* (2nd Ed.). (New York: Harcourt, Brace & World, Inc., 1963).

H_2: The ability level of college-capable junior high school students has no effect on their ability to verbalize discovered mathematical generalizations.

H_3: The effect of completion of the *Sentences of Logic* unit on verbalization is independent of the ability level of college-capable junior high school students.

The research population consisted of 80 junior high school students (20 in each cell of the research design), which permitted each hypothesis to be tested by comparing two sets of 40 subjects each. There were 37 male and 43 female students; 44 were in the eighth grade and 36 in the seventh grade.

The treatment group completed the *Sentences of Logic* unit. Both the treatment and control groups were led to discover three generalizations about vectors by means of a programmed unit; within this unit each student was asked to verbalize his discoveries. Following each frame that asked for verbalization was a series of frames that gave hints designed to improve precision.

Specifically, each student was led to discover the generalizations that may be expressed in the following three sentences:

1. For each vector (a, b), for each vector (c, d), $(a, b) + (c, d) = (a + c, b + d)$.
2. For each vector (a, b), $(0, 0) + (a, b) = (a, b)$.
3. For each scalar m, for each vector (a, b), $m(a, b) = (ma, mb)$.

The fact that each subject was getting correct answers as he did vector operations indicated that he had discovered these generalizations. Following each subject's attempt to state one of these generalizations was a hint designed to improve his precision of expression on subsequent attempts. One hint outlined some common mistakes that a student makes in attempting to state a generalization precisely, so that he might avoid them; another gave an overview of the information contained in a complete correct statement of a generalization, so that he would check his attempt for omissions. Other hints led him, step by step to a correct expression of a *part* of a complete, correct sentence, and subsequent hints attempted to lead him to other parts. Each attempt at verbalization was awarded precision points according to a key developed for use in the experiment, and these precision scores were weighted so that a subject got a higher verbalization score if he could state a sentence at a given degree of precision with fewer hints.

Two standards for awarding verbalization scores were used. The strict standard called for a complete, correct declarative sentence; the lenient standard allowed points for sentences that are technically incorrect but are accepted and used by mathematicians who are not meticulous. Three mathematics professors served as judges; each subject's verbalization score was the mean of the points awarded by the judges.

A test described by Winer,[4] using analysis of variance to estimate reliability of scores assigned by the judges, indicated that if the experiment were to be repeated with another random sample of three judges but with the same subjects the correlation between the mean ratings obtained from the two sets of data would be 0.99. This same correlation was obtained with the scores assigned according to the strict scoring key and the lenient one. A split-half reliability test was used to check the evaluation unit for internal consistency, and the Spearman-Brown formula was used to estimate what the reliability would have been for the entire test. This resulted in a reliability coefficient of 0.96 for both strict scoring and lenient scoring.

[4] B. J. Winer, *Statistical Principles in Experimental Design* (New York: McGraw-Hill Book Co., 1962). p. 124.

The assumption of independent observations, which underlies use of analysis of variance to test the experimental hypotheses, was met. One may question a second assumption; that of the experimental population's being randomly selected from a normal population. The research population contained students with a minimum IQ of 116 and was randomly selected only to the extent that students are randomly assigned to one of 34 mathematics classes in a school that attempts to group the students according to IQ and general achievement. However, Hays states that inferences made about means are valid even when the forms of population distributions depart considerably from normal, provided that the number in each sample is relatively large,[5] it was felt that 40 subjects used in each level of this experiment gave a sample sufficiently large to satisfy this condition. Even though the assumption of homogeneity of variance was violated, Hays states that this assumption can be violated without serious risk, provided that the number of cases in each sample is the same.[6] In this experiment there were exactly 40 subjects in each factor, 20 in each of the four cells.

The subjects who studied the *Sentences of Logic* unit did significantly (0.005 level) better than the control group in verbalizing universal generalizations precisely; the gifted students verbalized significantly (0.005 level) better than the other college-capable

group. The null hypothesis concerning interaction of the main effects was rejected at the 0.05 level under the strict standard and at the 0.10 level under the lenient standard; this indicates that the verbalization of the gifted was aided more by studying the logic concepts than that of the others.

This experiment does support the conjecture of this article. It offers an instance in which the following things happened:

1. Students were taught concepts, including those of variable, open sentence, universal quantifier, universal set, universal statement (generalization), instance of a generalization, and counterinstance.
2. They were given practice in applying these concepts in writing generalizations and making judgments about the truth of the generalizations.
3. They were guided to make discoveries.
4. And they were able to state their discoveries precisely.

Currently, at least one author has advised teachers to postpone verbalization of discoveries until linguistic formulation can be undertaken as an end in itself.[7]

This research suggests an alternative. Teachers could teach logical components of universal generalizations as an explicit part of the curriculum. Then they could ask for immediate verbalization of a newly discovered generalization with an increased expectancy that the students will be able to respond precisely.

[5]William L. Hays, *Statistics for Psychologists* (New York: Holt, Rinehart & Winston, 1963), p. 378.
[6]*Ibid.*, p. 379.

[7]Hendrix, *op. cit.*, p. 292.

The Case for Information-oriented (Basic) Research in Mathematics Education

PATRICK SUPPES

The marvelously clear and definite structure that is characteristic of most parts of modern mathematics can be misleading when problems of mathematical instruction are considered. The very clarity of the structure of mathematics itself can lead to the mistaken view that nothing beyond this structure need be considered in analyzing and deciding how mathematics should be taught.

Yet anybody who has taught mathematics knows how far from the truth this claim is. It is not a straightforward or simple matter for the average student to learn mathematics! And there is no doubt that the ordinary student finds that he has to think harder in learning mathematics than in learning just about any other subject in the curriculum.

The case for basic research in mathematics education can be stated quite simply in terms of these well-known difficulties of students. It is the ultimate objective of basic research in mathematics education to understand how students learn mathematics, and to use this understanding to outline more effective ways of organizing the curriculum. It is probably also agreed, on all sides, that we are still very far

Reprinted from *Research in Mathematics Education* (National Council of Teachers of Mathematics Publication, 1967), pp. 1–5, by permission of the author and the National Council of Teachers of Mathematics. Patrick Suppes is Professor of Philosophy and Statistics, Stanford University, Stanford, California.

from realizing this objective. Without question, we do not yet understand in any reasonable degree of scientific detail what goes on when a student learns a piece of mathematics, whether the mathematics in question be first-grade arithmetic, undergraduate calculus, or graduate-school algebraic topology.

In this brief article I want to survey some of the more important reasons for having a vigorous program in basic research in mathematics education.

DEFECTS OF INTUITION

Many teachers, who would admit that the logical structure of mathematics alone is not sufficient to determine the mathematics curriculum and how it is to be presented to students, would still maintain that the remaining gaps can be closed by appropriate use of intuition.

The first puzzling thing about this claim for intuition is that most of us have only a vague idea of what another person means when he talks about knowing something by intuition. What is intuition? We all recognize the role of experience in the training of teachers. As a rule, the teacher who has taught several years is able to do a better job than the beginner. Intuition is involved —intuition as the acquisition of knowledge and information in an inexplicit and nonformalized way on the basis of teaching experience. No one faced with the complex problems of teaching mathematics or any other part of the

233

curriculum would want to belittle the importance of experience and practice in the training of good teachers.

Yet many examples exist in the mathematics curriculum to show that it is not sufficient to leave the curriculum to the intuition of curriculum writers and the experience of teachers. The extensive research by Brownell and others on methods of subtraction has made everyone dealing with the curriculum in arithmetic sensitive to the analysis of the actual steps that must be taught children in learning the subtraction algorithm. Another example is the evidence that in the learning of a sequence of mathematical concepts, the important problem is often to minimize negative transfer rather than to facilitate positive transfer. The existence of negative transfer in passing from one concept to another is the sort of thing that is noticed by the very good teacher; it is also the kind of phenomenon that needs to be pinned down, in terms of research, and made part of the objective evidence presented to all teachers in telling them about learning difficulties. Another example that goes contrary to the formal structure of our standard teaching of geometry is found in the clear results concerning children's perceptions of rotations and stretches of standard geometrical figures in the plane. Although Euclidean geometry uses the fundamental notion of congruence that is invariant under rotations of figures, but not under stretches in their size, at the perceptual level this notion of congruence is more difficult for young children than perceiving the relation of similarity between figures that have the same orientation and shape but different sizes. Because teachers have themselves been taught Euclidean geometry and are familiar with the concept of congruence, it is all too easy for them to infer that this is the more natural concept for children. Without supporting research, it would

be difficult to convince many teachers of the true state of affairs.

DEFECTS OF SHEER EMPIRICISM

It is also important to emphasize, in discussing the role of basic research in mathematics education, that simple applied empirical research will not answer all the many questions that confront us. For example, if we hope to determine by experimental research the optimum sequence of topics in the first two grades of elementary school (or, with equal pertinence, in the first two years of university mathematics), it is easy enough to show for either of these cases that the mathematical constraints that are placed on the possible sequences of topics are not sufficient to reduce the number of *possible* sequences of concepts to a manageable number of experiments. The number would be greater than all persons now working in mathematics education could perform in the next ten or fifteen years, even if they devoted themselves wholly to this question. The sort of mathematical constraint I have in mind is that the introduction of multiplication would, from a mathematical standpoint, have to be preceded by the introduction of addition, if multiplication is initially to be talked about in terms of repeated addition. On the other hand, there is no real reason why we could not experiment with the introduction of subtraction before addition.

Examples of a more practical nature center around questions of the following sort. Should addition and subtraction be introduced simultaneously? If not, should addition be carried to sums not greater than five, not greater than six, not greater than seven, etc., before subtraction (or at least the notation for subtraction) is introduced? Such purely empirical questions are endless in number, and I emphasize once again, there is no purely mathematical answer to them. Because there is no purely mathematical answer, the importance of a psychological theory of mathematics-learning is crucial, in order ultimately to provide appropriate answers to problems of curriculum organization.

Another way of putting the matter is that purely empirical research lacks conceptual power, because the absence of any theory prohibits us from making extensive generalizations to other situations and broader classes of problems.

From this standpoint, I would emphasize that the demands for a psychological theory of mathematics-learning, and thus for theoretical basic research as well as empirical basic research, are practical demands. Without such theory it is impossible for us to anwer in any scientific way many substantive questions of curriculum organization. The vast literature on readiness, drills, practice, and overlearning in arithmetic and other subjects has made all of us aware of the complex and subtle nature of the empirical problems. Anyone who thinks that he can answer these problems either by intuition or by any simple experimental program, without facing the theoretical problems of weaving into one coherent theoretical pattern the many kinds of results already obtained, is surely daydreaming.

In this discussion of empirical problems I have emphasized the kind of questions that have arisen in elementary-school mathematics. The reason for this is simply that a greater body of research already exists in this area. The problems of mathematics-learning at the university level are certainly more complex and difficult, and may demand even more of an effort in basic research in order to begin to understand them.

ANALYSIS OF LEARNING DIFFICULTIES

Given a particular organization of the curriculum in terms of the concepts to be taught and the sequence in which

these concepts will be presented, it is still a major task of basic research to analyze and provide a theory for the kind of learning difficulties students encounter as they progress through this curriculum. It is again important to emphasize that the learning difficulties students encounter cannot be predicted by a nonpsychological mathematical analysis of the mathematical content of the curriculum itself—at least no one has proposed such a theory, and there are good reasons for thinking that no such theory shall be proposed.

It is not a part of arithmetic proper or of geometry proper to make psychological predictions about the difficulties students will have with the different concepts in these disciplines. It is the task of a psychological theory of mathematics-learning to predict and to offer an analysis of the kinds of difficulties that are encountered. The success of mathematics teaching depends upon understanding and providing successful practical remedies for the difficulties that students do encounter. In our increasingly technological age it is of greater importance than ever before that we, as educators, recognize the need for clear analysis of students' learning difficulties and the pressing need to develop theories that adequately deal with these difficulties. I have tried to emphasize in this brief discussion that neither intuition nor sheer empiricism is able to provide adequate answers to our problems. I have rested the case for basic research on the overwhelming practical importance of the solutions one hopes to find. I would like to conclude with some remarks in a somewhat different direction.

PSYCHOLOGY OF LEARNING AND THE NATURE OF MATHEMATICS

It is my own conjecture that as we are able to dig deeper into the development of an adequate psychological theory of mathematics-learning, the results will have an impact on our conception of the nature of mathematics itself.

It is not possible here to defend this conjecture in a detailed way, but there is reason to think that concentration on mathematical thinking and the difficulties students have in learning to think mathematically will lead to a new conception of *invariance*, a conception that goes beyond that now encountered in the various parts of mathematics. Historically, the standard philosophies of mathematics have emphasized differing attitudes toward the nature of mathematical objects, but it is perfectly obvious that in most domains of mathematics the exact nature of the mathematical objects studied is not essential. What is of more central concern are the patterns of thought applied by mathematicians in reaching new results, or by students in finding for themselves solutions of problems or proofs of known theorems.

As yet, theories of learning have little to offer in providing insight into how one learns to think mathematically. The nature of abstraction, or the processes of imagery and association that are surely essential to thinking in any domain of mathematics, have as yet scarcely been studied from a scientific standpoint.

Like mathematics itself, research in mathematics education will necessarily have both basic and applied components. Research that is concerned with particular pieces of curriculum and particular learning difficulties of students will continue to occupy a major portion of research efforts, but it is also to be hoped that the kind of problems I have just been mentioning, problems that represent fundamental puzzles about the nature of human thinking, will come to occupy a larger place in research about mathematics learning.

What's New in Teaching Slow Learners in Junior High School?

SARAH GREENHOLZ

INTRODUCTION

What is new in teaching slow learners in junior high school? They have received little attention and almost no funds in the evolution which is occurring

Reprinted from *The Mathematics Teacher*, LVII, No. 8 (December, 1964), 522–28, by permission of the author and the National Council of Teachers of Mathematics. Copyright © 1964 by the National Council of Teachers of Mathematics. Sarah Greenholz is Supervisor of Mathematics, grades 7 through 12, Cincinnati Public Schools.

in mathematics. Now, however, there is a dramatic turn in attention to the pupils at the other end of the academic achievement scale. There are several reasons for this:

1. Ability grouping causes these pupils to stand out in sharp profile in our schools.
2. Automation has absorbed many of the unskilled jobs which formerly were available to drop-outs. Youngsters who were drop-outs are staying in school.
3. These pupils are asking for opportunities in mathematics beyond the ninth grade.

4. Programs for retraining our adults to enable them to enter employment again involve teaching arithmetic. Some of these adults learn slowly, too.

5. Just as *Sputnik* gave great impetus to training for the capable, so President Johnson gave publicity to teaching the nonachiever when he declared his war on poverty. Much of the money voted for the fight against poverty will be focused on the education of these people.

Mathematics educators had really started in this direction before President Johnson announced his goal. The National Council of Teachers of Mathematics had budgeted $40,000 for a writing project for ninth-grade general mathematics two years ago. During the summer of 1963 a text called *Experiences in Mathematical Discovery* was written by a writing team under the direction of Oscar Schaaf. It is a book designed for pupils with mathematical achievement of 25th to 50th percentile. . . . [1]

Another indication that the slower pupils are receiving attention is that NCTM has formed a committee on mathematics for the noncollege-bound. A conference was held by the U.S. Office of Education and NCTM in March, 1964 on the Low Achiever in Mathematics. The preliminary report on this conference is available from the U.S. Office of Education. SMSG also held a planning conference in April to consider writing for the low achiever.

More textbooks are available now than in the past for slower classes, because the market for these is becoming a more profitable one.

DEFINITION

To what kinds of children are we referring? The NCTM writing group

defines the low achiever as the child ranking below the 30th percentile of the student population in achievement in mathematics. This is the kind of pupil who will be discussed here.

PROBLEMS

There are a number of problems about nonachievers over which teachers have little control. We will mention some of them briefly, but it would seem more profitable to spend time on the learning which takes place in the classroom and the attitudes built there. We would all like to see smaller classes. We all wish that the chronic absentees, the discipline problems, the poor readers, the transients, and the indifferent weren't dumped on us. We all wish that pupils would come to us with a series of experiences which would make them ready for the mathematics we have to offer them. We wish the classes were more homogeneous; instead, they usually contain a wide range of achievement. We wish that the ratio of boys to girls were one to one, but usually the boys predominate in such classes possibly because their maturity rate is slower than that of girls, and the boys do not adapt themselves to sitting in classrooms as easily as girls.

Most of these pupils have failed, and failure hasn't made good students of them. How do we mark these pupils? One of our teachers in the modified program states his philosophy of marking this way:

Give the child the mark that is best for him. If he tries, pass him. How do you motivate him and justify his passing in the eyes of the rest of the class? Since we are not born with equal talents, it is not fair to set a cutoff point on a test and let this determine who passes. Give him credit for daily work turned in, on recitation in class, on a notebook, or on problems assigned for extra credit. If he can't do fractions, grade him on whole numbers.

[1] Oscar Schaaf and Emil Berger, *Experiences in Mathematical Discovery* (Washington, D.C.: National Council of Teachers of Mathematics, 1967).

This teacher is successful in motivating his low achievers without giving many low marks.

Most schools mark the level of mathematics on the report card. Parents accept this now more than they did in the past, but it is never easy for them to face the fact that their child is achieving less well than other children.

GENERAL TECHNIQUES

In spite of the heavy load, there are many teachers who teach less able learners with great skill and derive true satisfaction from seeing these pupils develop number literacy. What are their techniques?

Let us consider some general classroom techniques which have proved successful:

1. Pupils find it difficult to remember directions or materials from one day to the next. To keep the learning process in motion have scratch paper and pencil stubs handy. You may wish to keep your texts in your room and not permit them to be taken home.

2. Provide opportunity for the class to learn through several senses at a time, such as seeing, hearing, manipulating, dramatizing, and doing. An excellent classroom lesson was one where the teacher asked a shorter student to come and stand beside him. He asked the class to compare their sizes. From these answers he led into a lesson on ratio. He was dramatizing the lesson.

3. Frequent changes of activity are necessary because slow learners have a short span of interest. Provide variety within a period: warmup or oral practice, readiness, discussion or laboratory experience to discover the new concept, board work or group practice, games, and supervised study.

4. Have daily routine, with surprises. These children are not so bored with the same routine as we are, and routine gives them a feeling of security. What do we mean by surprises? A surprise could be a puzzle, a student

invited from another class to give a report, a film or film strip, a field trip on the school campus, a bulletin-board display of pupils' work, or a sharing of work via an opaque projector.

5. Never put a child on the spot for an answer if he is dull. Mental arithmetic is hard for him, so avoid this. Board work sometimes embarrasses certain individuals, so let it be optional.

6. Give these pupils immediate satisfaction by checking their work as they do it. Do not return a test several days later. Have short tests over a concept just learned. Circle an error but do not mark the whole problem wrong.

7. Make each daily lesson complete in itself. There will be relationship of ideas from day to day, but do not carry work over from one day to the next. This makes it possible for absentees or new pupils to participate in the learning, even though they have been out the day before. Few of these pupils can work on their own, so provide supervised study within your class period. Assign homework sparingly or for extra credit, but do not require it. Remember that the sense of values of such a pupil is entirely different from yours. He lives from day to day and seldom sees the importance of education or of long-term goals.

8. Never penalize a slow child by forcing him to work longer at mathematics than his brighter peers. Never punish a child for a misdemeanor by giving him computation to do.

9. Always prepare pupils for verbal problems. One or two thought problems each day are more effective than a long list at one time, and the result is better classroom control and less frustration on the part of the pupil. Have the pupils read the problem silently before it is read orally.

10. Always make your directions simple. Instead of saying them, try writing them on the board in the same place every day.

11. Remember that these pupils frequently have low energy levels due to improper eating habits. If it is possible, try to get an early lunch schedule for

them or permit them to eat in the middle of the morning.

12. If a child says, "I don't want to," try to avoid making an issue of it. Usually he will participate in what the group is doing if the lesson is an interesting one.

13. Try to think of new ways to review concepts. For example: Multiplication tables can be taught through a study of prime numbers and factoring. Try using a multiplication grid and let him discover that because of the commutative property he has fewer combinations to learn. When he learns one combination, ask him for others which are related to this one combination.

$$5 \times 9 = \underline{\quad} \quad 45 \div 9 = \underline{\quad}$$
$$45 \div 5 = \underline{\quad} \quad 9 \times \underline{\quad} = 45$$
$$\underline{\quad} \times 5 = 45$$

14. Break content into small repetitive steps and give easy exercises for reinforcement soon after the presentation. Use the techniques employed by programmed texts. Don't give problems requiring sustained computation like long-division problems with large numbers.

15. When a child asks you a question, break his question into a number of simpler ones. For example:

Find the cost of a dozen chocolate bars if they are 3 for 10¢.
How many bars are in a dozen?
Can you draw the 12 bars for me?
Circle each group of 3. How much does each group of 3 cost? [dime] How many groups do we have? How many dimes do we need? How much money is this?

When the child finally arrives at the answer, say, "See, you really answered the question yourself."

16. Do not insist on verbalization if you think a child understands the idea. Accept descriptions and examples if definitions are too demanding. For example, one child said a reciprocal was "bottoms up." In algebra if he can add signed numbers by displacement on the number line, do not insist that he verbalize a rule for this. If a

child can demonstrate the commutative property in addition, do not insist that he give you its name if the child has trouble remembering this word.

17. Always introduce a new relationship with the simplest arithmetic or algebra possible so that the pupil can concentrate on the concept itself and not get bogged down in computation.

$$\frac{1}{5}+\frac{2}{5}=\frac{3}{5} \quad \frac{1}{7}+\frac{2}{7}=\frac{3}{7} \quad \frac{1}{x}+\frac{2}{x}=\frac{3}{x}$$

18. If there are several approaches to a new concept, one per lesson is less confusing to slow pupils than a multiple approach.

There are several new techniques in teaching today: team teaching, television teaching, and programmed instruction. Let us see how each of these works with slow learners.

In team teaching, if each member of the team is conscientious, slower pupils can receive more individual attention and profit from this kind of instruction.

In television teaching, the slower pupil gives up at the point where he does not understand. He stops participating for the rest of the telecast. If the pupil is confronted with a live teacher, the teacher can go back and reteach at the place where he finds that the pupil is confused.

In programmed instruction, the pupil must be able to read. Slow pupils are usually deficient in reading skills. Moreover, the printed page is usually not enough to motivate the slow learner. A teacher can usually do this better than a printed page.

TECHNIQUES IN MATHEMATICS

Let us turn to samples of techniques which have proved successful with slower pupils. Perhaps you will find something that will work in your classroom tomorrow.

1. Use of number line for teaching equivalent fractions, comparing decimals,

rounding numbers (round 287 to the nearest hundred,

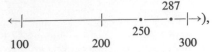

understanding signed numbers, graphing solution sets and inequalities.

2. Vocabulary words on cards with the root of the word emphasized: *Rat*io, Pe*rim*eter.

3. Greenwood method of division:

```
35)1330
   350  10
   ────
   980
   350  10
   ────
   630
   350  10
   ────
   280
   280   8
   ────
      │ 38
```

4. Circling factors equivalent to one in simplifying fractions:

$$\frac{15}{25} = \frac{3 \times ⑤}{5 \times ⑤} = \frac{3}{5}$$

5. In regrouping, use crutches. Rewrite the number completely:

```
             7 16
  286      2 8̸ 6̸
 −49      − 4 9
 ────     ─────
```

6. Making a ruler calibrated in inches by folding a 12″ strip of paper:

$\frac{1}{2}$ of 12 = 6 $\frac{1}{4}$ of 12 = 3
$\frac{1}{3}$ of 12 = 4 $\frac{1}{6}$ of 12 = 2

7. Discovery lesson on positions in which

2 sticks can fall: ═ ╲ ＋

3 sticks: ≡ ⚹ ≠ ⟟

8. Folding a strip of newspaper to represent 50%, 25%, 12½%, 33⅓%, 16⅔%, of the whole. Show placement of common fractions and per cent equivalents on a number line. Adolescents are so afraid that making a concrete model will make them appear childish that sometimes a project like this will not work. Much depends upon how the teacher introduces the concrete aid.

9. Avoid shortcuts with pupils if they cannot remember them:

Not this	*This*
68	68
×20	×20
────	────
1360	00
	136
	────
	1360

Not this   *This*

$$6.7 \div 10 = .67$$

```
            .67
        10)6.70
            6 0
            ───
             70
             70
             ──
```

10. List multiples to find the least common denominator:

$\frac{2}{5}$ 5 10 ⑮
$\frac{1}{3}$ 3 6 9 12 ⑮

CONTENT

Let us turn now to another question. What content should be included for these pupils?

Around the nation, generally, slower pupils do better in computing than in problem solving. This tells you what is going on in classrooms. A teacher who leans too heavily on computation is denying these youngsters part of a general cultural background which should be part of everyone's heritage. Each child should be exposed to some of the structure of mathematics and be taught to apply mathematics by practicing on some of the models he finds around him, in addition to learning how to compute.

These pupils should be taught the relationships in number which dictate why they compute as they do. The Gestalt theory is as valid now as it ever was, and a bag of tricks is an ineffective way to teach competence in number.

In Cincinnati we are experimenting with a tenth-grade course in mathematics for less-able children. Of the four texts being tried, the ones enjoyed most by these pupils are based on structure. Many of these classes have studied so many applications that, to them, a look into the structure is refreshing.

Another observation is that these pupils enjoy thinking at their level more than imitating a model. Let us illustrate.

Find the simple interest for one year on $500 invested at 4%.

$$\begin{array}{r} \$\,500 \\ .04 \\ \hline \$20.00 \end{array}$$

What is the interest on $600 at 5% for one year?

This is learning by imitation.

Now two examples of thinking at their level:

1. Ask the class to consider 9 objects. Separate the set into
   A. 2 sets of objects, one larger than the other
   B. 2 sets, both with an odd number of objects
   C. 2 sets, both with an even number of objects
   D. 3 sets alike
   E. 3 sets different
   (B and C cannot be done)
2. Put on the board these patterns. Let the pupil complete and generalize the patterns.

$$
\begin{array}{lll}
3, 7 \longrightarrow 10 & 7 \longrightarrow 9 & 1 \longrightarrow 3 \\
4, 2 \longrightarrow 6 & 0 \longrightarrow 2 & 3 \longrightarrow 9 \\
1, 8 \longrightarrow 9 & 8 \longrightarrow \underline{} & 10 \longrightarrow 30 \\
15, 5 \longrightarrow \underline{} & \underline{} \longrightarrow 6 & 2 \longrightarrow \underline{} \\
20, \underline{} \longrightarrow 22 & x \longrightarrow x + 2 & \underline{} \longrightarrow 12 \\
\underline{}, 4 \longrightarrow 9 & & n \longrightarrow 3n \\
n, m \longrightarrow n + m & &
\end{array}
$$

Make up some patterns of your own.

Is the material modified or is the same material taught at a slower pace? We must do both. First the material must be modified so that it is less abstract. This is not watering it down. It is providing a simple approach which makes mathematics more reasonable. We also go more slowly and reinforce what we learn with more drill and examples.

What mathematical content seems essential for each pupil to comprehend?

Certainly every pupil should learn the operations with whole numbers and rational numbers, including per cent. He should be numerically literate when he reads newspapers and common magazines and be able to interpret graphs.

He should be taught to keep neat and accurate records and to write checks. He should be taught home and job mathematics and business applications. He can learn simple algebra with emphasis on the use of the formula. He can discover relationships in informal geometry and can do simple geometric constructions.

Every teacher of slow learners must be prepared to help them with their reading. All of these pupils should be encouraged to develop certain attitudes in the class room such as: (1) industry, (2) courtesy, (3) self-discipline, and (4) respect for the other person.

INCREASING YOUR COMPETENCE

What can you do on your own to increase competence at this level?

1. Have a swap session in what has worked in your classrooms.
2. Develop a note book of your own. The teachers in Cincinnati could not find material interesting to adolescents and written for pupils having a low achievement level, so they duplicated lessons which they used successfully with their less-able pupils. They traded these lessons. They tried them, refined them, and bound them together in a curriculum bulletin. This curriculum bulletin is unique because it contains material for direct use in the classroom. Teachers are supplied with classroom sets of these lessons from our central office. If you wish to purchase this curriculum bulletin, it is listed along with other books which we have found work better with slower pupils than with faster ones.

What kind of person is best suited to teach these children? The teacher must possess certain personality traits. He must be a secure person himself. Insecure teachers sometimes demand only bright children to bolster their own ego. The secure one knows in his heart that teaching slow learners is the most difficult teaching assignment of all. This teacher must also have genuine respect for the dignity of every human being. Acceptance of the importance of the assignment to teach less able pupils is all important. He must be challenged by growth in children and by finding ways to modify the content for them. Training to teach in the elementary school provides an excellent background for a teacher of slow pupils.

Our teachers of these pupils prefer the departmentalized curriculum rather than a core program. They find that holding a class for several class periods is exhausting to them and to the children, too. They also find it hard to be a specialist in several areas such as science and mathematics, with content growing as rapidly as it is.

Some critics of public schools suggest that our energies should not be directed toward educating these boys and girls. My answer to such critics would be this: In a few years these young people will pay taxes, vote, serve in the military forces, operate automobiles, buy and sell, marry, and have more children than an average cross section of our population. We will be supporting some because they cannot find employment. How can we, a nation, afford not to educate every child to be the best citizen his talents and ability permit?

What is new in teaching slower pupils? Most of the techniques enumerated here have been in use for a long time, but perhaps now you have more confidence in your own program.

REFERENCES

Materials for slower pupils

1. Grossnickle, Reckzeh, and Bernhardt, *Discovering Structure in Algebra*. New York: Holt, Rinehart & Winston, Inc., 1962 (Grade 9).
2. Hart, Schult, and Irvin, *Mathematics in Daily Use*. Boston: D. C. Heath, 1958 (Grade 9).
3. Hartung, Van Engen, and Knowles, *Seeing Through Arithmetic, Special Book B*. Chicago: Scott, Foresman & Company, 1963 (Grade 7).
4. Mayor, John R., and Marie S. Wilcox, *Algebra, First Course* (2nd Ed.). Englewood Cliffs, N.J.: Prentice-Hall, Inc., 1961.
5. Smith, Lankford, and Payne, *Contemporary Algebra*. New York: Harcourt, Brace & World, 1962.
6. Wiebe, *Foundations of Mathematics*. New York: Holt, Rinehart & Winston, 1962 (Grades 8–9).
7. Wilcox and Yarnelle, *Mathematics, a Modern Approach*. Reading, Mass.: Addison-Wesley Publishing Co., 1963 (Grades 8–9).

Teacher references

1. Cutts, Norma, and Nicholas Moseley, *Teaching the Disorderly Pupil in the Elementary and Secondary School*. New York: Longmans, Green, and Company, 1957.
2. *Mathematics, Modified General Program, Grades 7, 8, and 9, Curriculum Bulletin 113* (1962). Order with remittance to Clerk-Treasurer, Cincinnati Public Schools, 608 E. McMillan Street, Cincinnati, Ohio 45206. $4.50, including postage.

Mathematics Education in the Secondary Schools of the Soviet Union

JAMES M. MOSER

Twenty mathematics educators from the United States and one from England[1] toured mathematics education facilities in the Soviet Union from August 27 to September 9, 1966. The tour was sponsored by the NCTM under the supervision of the Committee on International Mathematics Education, with some financial support from the National Science Foundation. The tour began after the conclusion of the International Congress of Mathematicians which was held in Moscow during the latter part of August 1966. The group visited educational facil-

Reprinted from *The Mathematics Teacher*, LX, No. 8 (January, 1967), 885–92, by permission of the author and the National Council of Teachers of Mathematics. Copyright © 1967 by the National Council of Teachers of Mathematics. James M. Moser is Associate Professor of Mathematics and Associate Professor of Mathematics Education, University of Colorado, Boulder.

Author's Note: The writer wishes to disclaim any credit for the authorship of this article. As secretary of the Committee on International Mathematics Education of the NCTM, he has simply served in an editorial capacity and edited the reports submitted to him by several of the members of the tour described in the following report. The real credit belongs to them.—*James M. Moser.*

[1]Tour participants were Kerry P. Becker, Emil J. Berger, L. Virginia Carlton, Joe Elich, Wade Ellis, Clarence E. Hardgrove, Emanual H. C. Hildebrandt, Shirley Hill, Julius H. Illavaty, Burton W. Jones, Phillip S. Jones, Max Kramer, Clarence B. Lindquist, Robert H. McDowell, James M. Moser, Richard S. Pieters, Henry O. Pollak, Veryl Schult, Dina Gladys S. Thomas, Bryan Thwaites (English), and Bruce R. Vogeli.

ities in Moscow, Kiev, and Leningrad; its primary objective was to visit key persons and institutions involved in the education of the mathematically talented student. Among these were teacher-training institutes, secondary schools, elementary schools, and educational ministries. This particular report, however, is restricted to the secondary school.

A summation of the tour is given below:

August 29—*Kiev Pedagogical Institute* and the *Kiev Engineering Institute.* (Some experimental work in teaching machines is being done at the engineering institute.)

August 30—Conference with Academician A. Markushevich at the *Academy of Pedagogical Sciences.*

August 31—Conference with members of the Mathematics Section of the *Academy of Pedagogical Sciences.* This is headed by Mme G. Maslova.

September 1—The *Lenin Pedagogical Institute.* Visited with faculty members and observed mathematics lectures. Dean of this institute is R.S. Cherkasov. I. Yaglom, noted geometer, is a faculty member.

September 2—The mathematics faculty at *Moscow State University.* Among them were Professors Dynkin and Yaglom (brother of I. Yaglom).

September 3—*Peduchilishche No. 2* (Normal School). Discussion with director and class visitation.

September 5—*Gertsen Pedagogical Institute* in Leningrad. A discussion with faculty members.

September 6—*Experimental School No. 157* in Leningrad. This is attached to the *Academy of Pedagogical Sciences.* It is one of the "computer" schools in the Soviet Union.

September 7—*Isaac Newton Boarding School*,which is attached to the *Moscow State University*. Observed world-famous mathematician Kolmogorov teaching a class of mathematically talented ninth-graders.

September 8—*Special School No. 444* in Moscow. This is an experimental school where new curriculum materials in mathematics are field-tested. It is also a "computer" school.

September 9—*Central Institute for Improving Teachers*. This is essentially an in-service institute for teachers in the field.

GENERALIZATIONS DIFFICULT

Although the tour was stimulating and provided a great deal of insight into certain aspects of the Soviet educational system, it certainly did not create a complete picture of the system. The brief nature of the tour, as well as the loss of precise communication through inadequate translations, makes generalizations difficult. By design and by request, the group visited only the superior institutions and saw representatives of the top 5 to 10 per cent of the student population. One must wonder whether the tour would have been any different if the request had not been made to see the best! Therefore, what follows is mostly the impressions gained by several of the tour members.

This report does not present long lists of statistical data since these can be obtained elsewhere.[2] For a report which gives information on the programs of study in Soviet schools, the reader is referred to Cherkasov's article in the "International Mathematics

Education" section in an earlier issue.[3] In order that the reader may have a frame of reference, several facts relating to the organization of Soviet schools are given.

Soviet children go to school for six days a week during a school year of approximately 233 days. Ten years of schooling are given, beginning at age seven—four years of elementary school, taught by a "generalist," four years of middle school, taught by subject-matter specialists, and two years of secondary, also taught by specialists. For a period of time the secondary school covered three years of instruction, but shortly after the demise of Krushchev it was reduced to two years, its state before his rise to power. Only the first eight years are compulsory, although the great majority pursue the ten years of education. Education is held in very high regard in the Soviet Union and is the major tool by which a citizen may improve his state in life.

SPECIAL PROGRAMS FOR THE MATHEMATICALLY TALENTED

Perhaps one of the strongest impressions gained from the trip was the attention paid to mathematics and science by the Soviet educational system. Thus, it is not surprising that great effort is made to identify the mathematically talented as soon as is possible and to provide them with specialized teaching. This training is effected in several ways, and each will be mentioned in turn.

First, special boarding schools for the mathematically and scientifically talented student have been established recently. There are four of these "internats," each affiliated with a large university, situated at Moscow, Leningrad,

---

[2]W. K. Medlin, C. B. Lindquist, and M. L. Schmitt, *Soviet Education Programs*, U. S. Office of Education Bulletin No. OE-14307 (Washington, D. C.: Government Printing Office, 1960), and Bruce R. Vogeli, *Soviet Schools for the Mathematically Talented* (Washington, D. C.: National Council of Teachers of Mathematics, 1968).

[3]R. S. Cherkasov, "The Development of the Teaching of Mathematics in Soviet Schools," *The Mathematics Teacher*, LVIII (December, 1965), 715–19.

Kiev, or Novosibirsk.[4] These schools draw their students from large geographic regions. As expected, the programs of these schools are heavily weighted in the direction of science and mathematics and are often tied in closely with computer-oriented instruction, i.e., instruction in the use of computers from the viewpoint of the computer's ability to solve physical problems.

It was the privilege of the group to visit the boarding school in Moscow. It is named after Isaac Newton, but almost everyone calls it the "Kolmogorov School" since the renowned mathematician A. N. Kolmogorov has been highly influential in the formation of the program of this school. In fact, he teaches a class of ninth-graders there, and our group had the pleasure of meeting this famous man and watching him teach. The presentation was superb. Through the oft-used example of the mappings of the vertices of an equilateral triangle into themselves, he gave the students insights into ideas such as functions, inverses, groups, and isomorphisms and some combinatorial ideas. When he shifted to the same type of example using the vertices of a square, the eager young students were literally jumping out of their seats to answer. It reminded us of the kind of interaction that George Polya is able to elicit from a group of listeners.

In his talks to us afterwards, Kolmogorov explained the program at the school. Although his instruction was definitely "modern" in its approach, his skepticism about some of the "new" ideas in mathematical instruction became apparent. He prefers to play down the theoretical approach in favor of having the students solve problems, many of which deal with the study of

[4] A. N. Kolmogorov, "A Physics-Mathematics School," *Soviet Education*, VI (October, 1964), 22–24. Trans. from *Uchitel, skaia Gazeta*, February 11, 1964.

physics. In his school there are 360 ninth- and tenth-grade students, only 10 per cent of whom are girls. He personally teaches only two days a week (to a large group), and the rest of the time the students are divided into small discussion groups and problem-solving sessions led by graduate students from the university. In all, there are twenty-seven regular teachers and forty part-time teachers. Although this was a special school, it is indicative of the concern of officials in Soviet education for their superior student. Well-known and highly esteemed university mathematicians believe they should personally give sound instruction to the young students; many part-time instructors are used—some of these give special talks and seminars to the students on such topics as complex variables, conformal mappings, geometric constructions, etc. In this school, some students have twenty class hours a week, out of thirty-six, in a combination of mathematics and physics.

Secondly, there exist in the Soviet Union about a hundred specialized schools for mathematically talented students. These are regular day schools located throughout the country and theoretically open to all, although this is probably not the case. As the age of the electronic computer emerged, the Ministry of Education allowed the development of special programs to train students to become computer programmers. As a result, these special mathematical secondary schools were established a few years ago, and in the beginning programmers were trained. However, the educators found that the computer served as a stimulus for learning more mathematics rather than as an end in itself. Thus, the schools evolved from training schools to their present state of special schools. Apparently, most of these are not special schools in the sense of the four boarding schools, but rather are schools which have special programs, or tracks, for the mathematically talented in much the same fashion that many large high schools in this country have "honors" or "special" programs. The present intention, however, is to have the hundred schools *just* for the talented students. Some of the topics included in the program for the ninth and tenth grades are algebra and elementary functions, probability, linear algebra, linear programming, mathematical analysis, geometry, logic, computer programming. The students study mathematics twelve periods a week in the typical European "parallel" approach, i.e., more than one subject is taken during a given year—perhaps algebra for five periods a week, geometry for five, and programming for two.

The tour included visits to two such schools, one in Leningrad and the other in Moscow. Incidentally, each had a computer in the building. These were old, relatively slow, vacuum-tube machines called the Ural I. Several classes were visited in each of these schools, and perhaps the most significant fact to note was the attempt by the instructors to elicit student participation. This is quite atypical of most European classrooms, which are noted for the lecture-only type of presentation. Both teachers were quite successful, especially Professor Neshkov of the Mathematics Section of the Academy of Pedagogical Sciences, who conducted a lesson that was a pleasure to watch. This was an experimental class of seventh-graders who were investigating the graph of the inequality $|x + 5| + |x - 5| - 12 < 0$. Notions of function and symmetry were brought in to help the students discover the results. The students were obviously selected for this class because of their aptitude for mathematics, but all those who observed the class were impressed by their pleasant appearance, neat-

ness, spontaneity, and enthusiasm for learning.

Finally, there exists a great deal of what could be called extra-class activity. Perhaps the most widespread activity is the mathematics "circles," which might best be described simply as math clubs. They are very similar to clubs which exist in this country in that they are designed for small special-interest groups. Although attendance is voluntary many students did, in fact, come to the meetings for a reason which will be amplified in the next paragraph. These circles usually meet after school or in the evening on a local neighborhood or school basis. The topics for discussion center mainly on subjects which are not formally presented in class. Discussion leaders are university professors or graduate students, many times being former members of the particular circle or a graduate of the school. The tour group did not attend any circle meetings. The Soviet authorities intimated that, with the recent advent of the special schools, circle activity was not as popular or widespread as it once had been.

Part of the popularity of the circles was due to the fact that a large portion of the programs were devoted to a study of and preparation for the Olympiads. The reader is probably familiar with the Olympiad as being a form of mathematical contest.[5] There is a long tradition in the Soviet Union of mathematical Olympiads which are held on the local, municipal, regional, republic,

---

[5] Izaak Wirszup, "The School Mathematics Circle and Olympiads at Moscow State University," *The Mathematics Teacher*, LVI (April, 1963), 194–210; *idem*, "The First Two International Mathematical Olympiads for Students of Communist Countries," *American Mathematical Monthly*, LXIX (1962), 150–55; and D. Shklarsky, N. Chentzov, and I. Yaglom, *U. S. S. R. Olympiad Problem Book*, trans. John Maykovich; rev. and ed. Irving Sussman (San Francisco: Freeman & Co., 1962).

and all-Union level. High importance is attached to performance on these examinations since admission to the special schools as well as the universities and high-ranking institutes depends on that performance. As suggested earlier, advancement to a higher status and better living conditions depends very strongly on the successful completion of formal academic training. Therefore, it is not surprising that many students see fit to join the circle in order to prepare themselves for these Olympiads. In all fairness, there are many students who have a genuine interest in mathematics and find the challenge of competition and the thrill of creativity a real stimulation to them.

It is interesting to note a remark made to the group by one of the educators with whom we spoke in regard to the Olympiads. In referring to the contest as one which explores the depth of understanding as shown by the contestants, he told us of one first-prize winner who did not get one single answer correct! Yet his methods of attacking the problem were such that his paper was considered to be outstanding.

Some of the activity which used to be the domain of the circle now occurs in what is called "faculty activity." This represents a time period after the regular school day when a teacher lectures or discusses in a seminar-type situation a subject of interest *to him*. Pupils are informed of the meeting and the subject and are free to attend or not as they see fit. Again, these are topics which are not part of the regular school program. These meetings occur in the special schools as well as the four boarding schools. As one can infer from this, special attention is given not only to the *quantity* of mathematics taught but also to its *quality*.

Finally, under this category, mention must be made of the small publications which have been prepared by leading mathematicians in the Soviet Union for use by students in the secondary schools. Many of these are familiar to the American reader through translations.

TEACHER EDUCATION IN MATHEMATICS

Although the primary concern of this report is the teaching of mathematics in the classrooms of the special schools of the Soviet Union, some mention should be made of the teacher preparation. This section is not intended to be a technical one, full of details, since much of this is already documented.[6] The education of teachers in mathematics is a primary concern in the Soviet Union. This training is accomplished by special institutions—the pedagogical institutes—designed for that purpose. The tour group visited two such institutes, the Lenin Institute in Moscow and the Gertsen Institute in Leningrad. It is something of a rule of thumb that anything in the Soviet Union which bears the name of Lenin is of high quality. The pedagogical institute which bears his name proved to be no exception to that rule.

Since the secondary mathematics teacher is a mathematics specialist, the guiding philosophy in his or her training appears to be that a strong background in mathematics is a necessary condition for effective teaching. This is not to say that the teaching process in mathematics receives little attention, for pedagogy, too, receives a good deal of emphasis. Yet, in the two institutes

[6]Bruce R. Vogeli and C. B. Lindquist, "Professional Content in Soviet Teacher-Training Curricula in Mathematics," *American Mathematical Monthly*, LXIX (1962), 156–62, and Bruce R. Vogeli, "Mathematical Content in Soviet Training Programs for Elementary School Teachers," *American Mathematical Monthly*, LXXII (1965), 1120–27.

which train mathematics teachers that we visited, over 50 per cent of the curriculum was devoted to mathematics.

In these institutes, we found that there were three basic programs being offered: (*a*) a four-year program which was designed for the teacher in a regular school; (*b*) a five-year program for teachers who were to go to the special schools—this included some work in computer techniques; and (*c*) a five-year program for teachers who will teach mathematics in a foreign language (French, German, or English).

A fact worth mentioning is the large number of females who were students of these institutes. To mention the role of girls and women in Soviet education, it is sufficient to add that there is no distinction between girls and boys in enrollment in the standard elementary and secondary schools. However, in the special mathematical schools, only 13 per cent of the students are girls, and in Kolmogorov's boarding school the per cent was down to 10. On the other hand, about 50 per cent of the university students in the mathematics program at Moscow State University are women. There seems to be some decrease in the per cent of women in more advanced and continued mathematical study. The Lenin Pedagogical Institute had a student body in which almost 80 per cent were girls, while the one normal school that we visited had a graduating class of about three hundred, all but four of whom were girls!

CURRICULUM DEVELOPMENT AND EVALUATION

In a country like the Soviet Union with its particular political system, it is not surprising that all matters of education are closely controlled by a centrally located agency, the Ministry of Education. Yet there seems to be a long-standing tradition of participation of topflight mathematicians in instruction and planning in the schools. Some of the effectiveness of Soviet mathematicians in promoting change and experimentation in schools can be attributed to the fact that A. I. Markushevich, one of Russia's best-known mathematicians and a member of the prestigious Academy of Science, is also vice-president of the Academy of Pedagogical Sciences and Deputy Minister of Education. This man, whose advanced texts in complex analysis are broadly used both in the Soviet Union and in translation in this country, is concerned about, and quite closely involved in, an ongoing program for modernization in the curriculum in the elementary school. Before passing to the secondary curriculum which is part of the main focus of this report, it should be noted that many of the tour members felt that, while the elementary curriculum revision efforts are interesting, they are at least five years behind similar efforts in this country.

Curriculum experimentation and revision—the Soviets use the word "modernization"—seem to be primarily the concern of the pedagogical institutes and the Ministry of Education, the latter of which works through one of its arms, the Mathematics Division of the Academy of Pedagogical Sciences. It is the ministry which finally decides when a revised program is to be introduced into schools in general. It does this on the basis of an evaluation of new materials and their teaching effectiveness after they have been tried out in several schools. The writing and trial teaching of these materials is sometimes initiated by pedagogical institute staffs and even carried out in schools associated with the institutes. This means that when the ministry issues a call for new textbooks embodying new approaches the institute staff members have a certain advantage, but anyone may prepare and submit a manuscript for a text which embodies newly defined changes. We were unable to ascertain the extent of the role of the classroom teacher in the preparation of new materials.

With regard to the evaluation of the new materials, much of the evaluation procedure begins before the actual materials are written. That is, early in the production process objectives are laid out, and discussions take place with respect to the topics to be treated, the way they will be treated, and the characteristics of the pupils for whom the material is intended. Once curriculum materials are written and tried out in classrooms—we found that the trials were very limited in terms of numbers of pupils involved—the formal evaluation procedure takes the following general form:

1. Oral achievement tests are constructed and administered. Pupil performance on these tests is taken as a measure of mastery of the topics. Test items include those easily accessible to pupils as well as some which are different from those in the learning materials. The latter, of course, would provide a measure of transfer of training to different but related problems. It should be noted that Soviet educators are not measurement-oriented in the strict sense, as are their American counterparts. They do little in the way of validating examinations and establishing norms.

2. Teachers who use the materials in the classroom make critical evaluations of their teachability and learnability. Pupil reactions are also noted.

3. Authors and other interested experts observe classes using the materials.

4. Pupil performance on daily exercises is evaluated to assess appropriateness of problems, difficulty level, and pupil understanding in general.

5. Systematic discussions are conducted in which the critical reactions of all those involved are examined.

Pupil characteristics (e.g., ability level) are discussed in relation to the reaction of teachers, writers, and observers and in relation to pupil performance on achievement tests.

6. Systematic modification of materials takes place as a function of the recommendations.

Materials are then tried out once again before adoption for classroom use is recommended. Conversations and discussions with members of the Mathematics Division of the Academy of Pedagogical Sciences indicated that the revisions of the experimental materials at times were quite extensive, almost to the point of starting anew.

At the secondary level, there seems to be some difference of opinion as to the extent to which modern, abstract, and general concepts together with rigorous proofs should be the dominating theme, as opposed to a considerable stress on concrete approaches to abstract ideas and on the relationship of mathematics to the other sciences, physics and mechanics in particular. This latter frame of reference may be a harkening back to the older programs of education in the Soviet Union where everything was of a polytechnic nature —that is, possessing socially useful applications. As noted earlier, Kolmogorov tends to favor this latter stress and to feel that a stress on modern symbolic logic and on abstraction can lead to confusion if introduced too early. Yet, there is considerable interest in "modern mathematics," together with some uncertainty as to the precise definition of it. (You see, we and the Soviets do have things we agree upon!) Such topics as some set theory, linear algebra, and transformation ideas in geometry are all considered modern, but considerable attention is paid to analysis and its physical applications.

Before leaving this section, further mention should be made of the topic of geometric transformations. Not as in the programs of this country (as of this writing), geometric transformations are an integral part of instruction in geometry from the earliest levels. They are used merely as techniques and not as subjects or ends in themselves. That is, the algebraization of this study, looking, perhaps toward groups of transformations, is not the objective—as it is, for example, in certain experiments in the English schools. In view of the joint meeting of the NCTM with the MAA (Houston, January 1967), this information is considered to be of interest.[7]

CONCLUSION

As suggested in the introductory remarks, it is unwise to attempt to draw too many conclusions on the basis of our limited observations. Many times the writer, and I am sure it has happened also to all the other members of the tour group, has been asked: "What was it like in the Soviet Union? What is the condition of their schools and their mathematics programs?" The temptation to sound like an expert giving definitive answers has been

---

[7]W. K. McNabb, ed., *Geometry in the Secondary School* (Washington, D. C.: National Council of Teachers of Mathematics, 1967).

extreme. While giving my impressions, I would often evade the question by saying that the Soviet Union is somewhat like swallowing a raw goldfish—it's just sort of "different," and unless you have tried it or been there yourself it is almost impossible to explain what it is like.

Yet the final impression gained by most of the tour group was that despite certain obvious differences existing between us, we were perhaps more alike than different. Anyone who has taught in different locales or in different countries knows that children are the same the world over. The Russian children we saw were no different from our own. During one of the discussion sessions the group had with our counterparts, one of the American group made the remark that the Russian children were much more earnest and serious of purpose than ours were. The reply was, "Oh, we thought *yours* were more serious." Upon which, general laughter filled the room.

With the exception of one incident with the Intourist Officials, the group was treated with utmost kindness, courtesy, and respect.

We came away with the impression that they still have many problems to solve with regard to their mathematics programs. But, then, so do we!

A Pattern for Research
in the Mathematics Classroom

DONOVAN A. JOHNSON

We have reached a crucial time in mathematics education. Questions are being asked and criticisms made of school mathematics programs. Some of these are difficult to answer. Although several important studies have been made, we have not established criteria; we have not devised measuring instruments; and we have not completed research that would give us valid information about the effectiveness of a mathematics program. However, lack of evidence doesn't mean that a given program or given procedure is not effective. It merely means that we withhold judgment until we have adequate information.

Suppose that you were asked the question: What research basis is there for the principles which you accept in your classroom? Most of us would find this question disturbing and troublesome to answer. Of course, we do not expect to reach the stage where we can discard all ideas that cannot be experimentally validated. But it would seem reasonable that we should be able to differentiate between those ideas supported by research and those that for

Reprinted from *The Mathematics Teacher*, LIX, No. 5 (May, 1966), 418–25, by permission of the author and the National Council of Teachers of Mathematics. Copyright © 1966 by the National Council of Teachers of Mathematics. Donovan A. Johnson is Professor of Education, University High School, University of Minnesota, Minneapolis.

The writer wishes to acknowledge the many contributions of Professor Donald G. Mac-Eachern, University of Minnesota, in the preparation of this article.

the present, at least, rest on philosophical foundations.

In mathematics we emphasize logic and proof, deductive as well as inductive reasoning. We teach probability and statistics, game theory and problem solving, the tools of the research worker. Isn't it strange that at the same time we have not made intensive and organized use of these tools to put our own house in order? We have not used induction or deduction in a consistent, planned fashion in building our new curricula.

NEW EMPHASIS ON RESEARCH

New school mathematics programs are being advocated today for a variety of reasons: New mathematics has been discovered; the computer and automation are changing society; new materials of instruction are available; and so on. In a similar manner, research attains new relevance and importance for these reasons:

1. New research techniques and new measuring instruments make important studies possible to a greater extent than ever before.
2. The computer summarizes data by exhaustive computations at a rate that is practically instantaneous.
3. Research in the behavioral sciences suggests new approaches to the study of human learning.
4. Adequate financial support is available from the federal government and from private foundations. This fact makes

long-range, well-designed studies possible.

In order to emphasize further the need for research in mathematics education, let's look at some of the assumptions we make in school mathematics for which meager support can be found in the literature:

1. The best way to learn mathematics is through discovery activities.
2. Computational skill can best be attained through solving problems.
3. Emphasizing the structure of mathematics is the best means of attaining understanding, application, and retention.
4. The best approach to probelm solving is a flexible, unstructured, independent approach.
5. Homework is essential for attaining maximum competence in mathematics.
6. Given enough time, children can learn complex mathematical ideas at any age.
7. The mathematical competence of our students can be measured by tests and examinations.
8. Geometry is the most appropriate subject for teaching deductive logic.
9. A multiple-track curriculum is an appropriate means of providing for individual differences.
10. The new school mathematics is a better means of attaining competence in mathematics than traditional mathematics.

How then are we to verify such important assumptions as those listed above? It would seem necessary and possible to design research studies that will collect valid information for determining cause-and-effect relationships.

TYPES OF RESEARCH

In considering research in mathematics education we should recognize that there are different types of research designs from which to choose. The type that is considered the most suitable depends on the problem, the setting, and the material involved. Then the confidence we can have in the results of a given study is related to the type chosen.

The least sophisticated type of research is called *action research*. This type usually involves a subjective evaluation of experience without extensive measurements and without control of variables. Usually this type of research is carried out by an individual teacher in his own classroom. This is also the type of research commonly used by experimental programs in developing and trying out new text materials. The reactions of teachers, results on unit tests, or the response of the students to the experimental situation are used to make value judgments about the text material or the method of instruction. Since teachers and students tend to react positively to participation in an experiment, to new content, or to a new method, it is difficult to get unbiased, objective responses in this situation. An advantage of this type of research is that it usually results in the development of usable instructional materials.

Another type of research is called *philosophical research*. In this situation the researcher applies careful thought and reasoning to the situation at hand. This is typically the kind of investigation that extends the frontiers of mathematical knowledge. The research mathematican uses his storehouse of knowledge to think up new theorems, to find solutions to problems, to create new fields of mathematics. He uses his imagination, intuition, and insight as he searches for new relationships and new ideas. Then he builds a new mathematical structure by a series of deductive proofs. This kind of research is typically the method of the inventor as he creates a new product. It is also the type of research used by the mathematician, the educator, and the psychologist to establish the scope, sequence, materials, and methods of a mathematics curriculum based on their knowledge of mathematics, curriculum, and learning theory. Again, it is a type of research that usually results in a product.

A third type of research is called *historical research*. In this case the scholar investigates information or data already in existence to bring out new facts or new insights. It is typically the research of the historian, who searches original documents to complete or correct the information about a specific period. It may also be the type of research done by the scholar who searches the literature of other fields to find information relevant to a specific problem. For example, an educator may wish to relate the research in learning theory to concept formation in mathematics. At present this type of research is needed to evaluate the implications of educational research for mathematics education.

Several other types of research collect original data or information. One such type is the *survey*. In a survey, usually information is collected to determine the status of a certain variable. For example, an investigator may wish to know what per cent of high school students in a given region are registered in mathematics courses. He collects facts and summarizes data in terms of means, percentages, or variances. Typically the analysis of the data involves merely descriptive statistics, although inferential statistics may be appropriate under certain conditions. Hence, this type of research serves the purpose of giving a descriptive picture of a situation without attempting to relate cause and effect. For example, it is the type of research that establishes norms for standardized tests or reports the current status and supply of mathematics teachers.

Another type of research is the *case study*, sometimes called clinical research. It involves the intensive study of individuals or situations. It may involve interrogation and observation of an individual to assess his characteristics and then relate these characteristics to certain performance patterns. In view of the complexity of human learning, it might be fruitful to investigate concept formation, problem solving, motivation, sources of difficulty or errors by this method. However, it is dangerous to state generalizations as if the findings applied to much wider groups, since the samples are usually limited.

The type of research accepted by many researchers as having the greatest promise for finding definitive answers is *scientific experimentation*. This is essentially the method of laboratory experimentation in basic research. It is the method that controls variables in an experimental situation so that we obtain an objective evaluation of the variable being studied. This is the method used to find out whether one treatment is superior to another. It is the method which tests the hypothesis that one curriculum is better than another or that one type of material produces superior learning, as compared to a second type. As an experimental method it makes a variety of measurements and uses the tools of inferential statistics for the data analysis. Thus, this method of experimentation tests hypotheses and establishes probable causality.

This method of scientific research can best be described by an example. Suppose that a scientist wishes to investigate the effectiveness of a certain treatment for the prevention of the common cold. He wishes to determine whether the use of a certain pill is more effective in preventing a cold than a sugar pill. He assumes that, since the sugar pill has no medication, it will have no effect in preventing colds. However, merely taking a pill may have some psychological effect that prevents colds. Consequently, he needs a third treatment for comparison, namely, the complete abstinence from taking pills. For comparison purposes he will then need to consider three groups of people, each group getting a different treatment. He selects these three groups as samples from a certain population. However, he will need to be sure that each of his samples is representative of the population involved and that his samples consist of comparable groups. The samples will probably be considered representative of the population if they are selected in a random manner. The experimenter may also wish to select groups that are comparable in terms of age, sex, occupation, health, home environment, and so on. If one group is significantly younger or healthier than another, the results may be due to these differences rather than to the treatment.

The scientist is now ready to give each of the three selected groups a different treatment for a specified period of time. During the period of the experiment he keeps a record of the incidence of colds in each group. Finally, he analyzes his data to see whether there is a significant difference in the number of colds reported by each group. If the group taking the experimental pill has significantly fewer colds than the other two groups he will conclude that he has found an effective preventative for colds. To gain confidence in his treatment he will probably repeat the experiment with different groups in different localities at different times of the year. Even so, he will need to be careful in examining the limitations of his study.

The example above illustrates how a well-conceived scientific experiment is self-contained. To be self-contained, the investigation must involve at least two comparable groups, usually called experimental and control groups. Only when you have comparable comparison

groups can you make inferences regarding the effectiveness of the experimental factor. One way to determine whether the comparison groups are similar is to compare them in terms of important factors at the beginning of the experiment.

Certain assumptions are made regarding what variables may affect the subjects during the experiment. Then during the experiment the groups involved should have common experiences except for the variables of the experimental treatment involved. Under these conditions, significant differences at the end of the experiment can be ascribed to the treatment involved. It is this control of variables which adds precision to the experiment. However, there will be limitations to the conclusions in terms of the samples used, the time involved, and the measurements made.

The usual way of obtaining comparable groups is to select them at random from the population under study. This randomization tends to reduce the introduction of bias into the experiment. Since statistical inference is based on the notion of randomization, the confidence we may have in our conclusions also depends on it.

Another characteristic of the self-contained study is that it includes the possibility of making a valid estimate of experimental errors. These experimental errors are generally due to variations in the subjects or conditions of the experimental situation that are impossible to control. For example, the physical and emotional well-being of human beings varies from day to day and even from hour to hour. Furthermore, the interactions between individuals and the responses to an experimental situation vary with the individual and the group. To obtain an estimate of these errors, it is necessary that the experiments be replicated under as uniform conditions as possible for experimental and control groups.

A TYPICAL SCIENTIFIC STUDY

Although there are many variations in the designs of scientific studies in mathematics education, let us use an ideal illustration of a well-designed experiment. Suppose that we wish to test the effectiveness of a programmed algebra text in the ninth grade. Since one contradiction is all that is needed to reject a hypothesis, the hypothesis is stated in negative terminology, called the *null* hypothesis, as follows: "There is no significant difference in the attainment of algebraic skills as measured by an achievement test between students who use a programmed text and students who use a conventional text." To control the content to be studied, the investigator will use a programmed text and a conventional text that present the same mathematical concepts with similar vocabulary, symbolism, and problems. We assume that the achievement of the students can be measured by a test of accepted validity and reliability. We also assume that if the experiment is conducted over an eight-month period, the variables are in operation over an adequate period of time.

One of the first problems faced is the selection of treatment groups. Ideally the selection of the schools, the teacher, and the students should be a random choice. In practice, however, we usually must make selections under certain limitations. The schools will probably be confined to a certain geographic location. Only schools and teachers willing to participate may be included. In many cases the teacher effect is controlled by including many teachers and assigning them at random to the different treatments involved. Then teachers of varied ability will probably be equally represented in each treatment group. If the teachers included teach at least two sections of ninth-grade algebra, it would seem reasonable that each teacher teach an experimental and control class. However, it should be noted that teacher bias can never be completely controlled. The assignment of students to the algebra classes should be at random to prevent a selective ability factor from operating. The assignment of treatment to the classes involved should also be random. We now have a set of classes, half of which will use a programmed text, the other half a conventional text.

As a check on the effectiveness of the randomization in providing groups comparable in ability and previous achievement at the beginning of the experiment, a series of pretests are administered. These tests should include a mental-ability test, a mathematics-achievement test, and an algebra-achievement test. The data from these tests can be summarized to determine whether there are differences in the specific measures between the experimental and control classes of each teacher involved. When significant differences exist between groups at the beginning of the experiment, these must be taken into account in the analysis of the data at the end of the experiment.

If one is interested in making a comparison according to different ability levels, it is appropriate to use pretest scores for selecting stratified samples. However, within each stratum of ability students should be assigned in a random manner to the classes involved in the experiment. The advantage of this procedure is that it insures a certain proportion of each ability level in each class and permits comparisons to be made according to ability.

So that other variables may be controlled, the experimental and the control class in each school should be of approximately the same size and should have an equal number of class periods of a given length.

Before the experiment, each teacher involved should be given instruction on the procedure to follow. Factors under his control, such as motivation, assignments, tests, enrichment, discipline, and provisions for individual differences, should be uniform in all experimental and control classes.

The achievement of all students in the experiment should be measured by several types of tests administered during and at the end of the experimental period. To allow the investigator to make a comparison in terms of retention, the classes should be retested after some established period—perhaps six weeks, three months, or one year. It would seem appropriate to use equivalent forms of the pretests of mathematical achievement and algebra achievement to make comparisons in terms of growth.

A careful record of student attendance will need to be kept. Students who are absent for a considerable part of the experiment should be excluded from the analysis. Likewise students who are emotionally disturbed, physically ill, or extremely deviant should also be excluded, or grouped and analyzed separately.

The significance of the differences in the mean achievement of the students in the different classes is determined by a comparison of the post-test scores. The pretest scores may be used to correct the post-test scores for initial differences in achievement and ability. Comparisons may be made within schools, between schools, between teachers, within ability levels, and between ability levels on each post-test. When the probability of obtained differences, given that the null hypothesis is true, is smaller than some prescribed level (such as .05), the dif-

ferences are considered to be statistically significant. Conclusions are then stated on this basis, with the recognition that chance differences will be considered significant 5 per cent of the time. Thus, under these conditions we accept the risk of being wrong 5 times in 100 when we ascribe significant differences to the experimental variable rather than to chance. When the report gives the actual probability (p-value) of the obtained difference, the reader then is free to make his own judgment about the significance of differences.

Stating that the obtained differences are statistically significant means that the null hypothesis is rejected. This is similar to rejecting statements in mathematics as soon as we find one contradiction. When test results are not significantly different, the hypothesis remains in doubt. A statement cannot be accepted as true, no matter how many verifications are found. However, the probability level indicates the likelihood of real differences.

CHARACTERISTICS OF GOOD RESEARCH

The experiment described above has characteristics which are illustrative of the following requirements for scientific research:

1. *Importance.* The problem should involve an important question in mathematics education. The experiment should operate over an adequate period of time, be related to an acceptable goal of instruction, and take into account permanent changes due to treatment.

2. *Randomization.* Since statistical inferences are based on randomness, it is essential that as many assignments as possible be made in a random manner.

This random selection applies to the school, the teachers, the students, and the assignment of the treatments. Although some random choices may be determined by tossing a coin, a more satisfactory method is the use of a table of random numbers.

3. *Control.* A number of variables maybe influencing the results. As many of those as it is feasible to consider should be isolated and controlled so that differences can be ascribed to the operating variable. The major factors influencing achievement in the mathematics classroom appear to be motivation, method of instruction, teaching aids, length of class period, time of day, size of class, assignments, content taught, tests and marking procedures, disciplinary activities, provision for individual differences, and the teacher. One way the researcher in mathematics education attempts to control some of these factors is to have several participating teachers teaching at least one experimental class and one control class. Since we can't control all variables, there will be errors; but randomization insures that the errors are unbiased.

4. *Replication.* To reduce the danger of acceptance of a false conclusion arising from chance errors, the experiment should be repeated several times under similar conditions and in varied locations. When several schools are involved, with both experimental and control classes in each school, then each school may be considered a replication. It is replication that makes it possible to estimate the variability that is due to a given treatment. It is this replication which gives an estimate of experimental errors. Replication adds precision to our tests of significance by assuring that variability due to experimental errors does not mask the real effects of the treatments. Sometimes it is possible to compute the number of replications needed to attain a particular level of precision. Replication thus serves a dual purpose. It adds precision to our experimental results by reducing the experimental errors to which they are

subject, and it provides a means of estimating these errors. However, it is randomization which makes the test of significance valid. Randomization does this by removing bias and making it proper to assume the errors independent.

5. *Measurement.* The data in scientific research are usually a set of measures. In education these measures are usually scores on tests, examinations, rating sheets, or questionnaires. As for all measurements, it should be recognized that the scores obtained are only approximations.

It is the measurement aspect which makes a scientific investigation of the effectiveness of new mathematics curricula extremely difficult. Since the content, the language, the symbolism, and the emphasis of the new school mathematics is very different from that of the traditional courses, tests have not been constructed to measure common achievement. Valid tests for measuring objectives that are independent of content, such as problem solving, logical reasoning, creativity, or attitude, are not now available Thus, the first step in studying an experimental curriculum consists in establishing clearly defined goals for mathematics instruction. These goals must then be stated in behavioral terms so that test items can be written that enable the student to demonstrate his attainment of these goals.

6. *Mathematical Treatment of the Data.* After measurements have been made and properly recorded, the data should be analyzed by appropriate statistical techniques. The principal tests of significance now in use for assessing differences in mean test scores of groups can be performed under the general analysis-of-variance model. This method provides a convenient way of computing estimates of error and of identifying sources of variation. Tests are usually

carried out using an *F*-statistic, which is the ratio of two mean squares (variances), one representing some source of variation and the other the appropriate estimate of error variance. Often, other sources of variation can be purposefully eliminated from the comparison. This method subsumes the older *t*-statistic for the comparison of two means. An extension of this general method is the analysis of covariance, a technique for adjusting the criterion measures for inequalities among groups on various initial measures.

Tests of significance for determining whether the variances of two groups are different can also be carried out using an *F*-statistic. These tests of variances are of considerable importance in education because we expect that effective educational practice will increase variance rather than narrow differences between individuals or groups.

7. *Conclusions:* The results of the analysis must be interpreted impartially and completely. Wherever possible, the probability level (*p*-value) connected with the conclusion should be given. Limitations on the extent to which the conclusion can be generalized should be stated. The investigator should be able to point out the educational implications of the data. In every case the results should be stated in clear, readable language so that the results can be implemented by classroom teachers.

PROBLEMS FOR INVESTIGATION

If the pattern for research described above is followed, it is likely that we shall find answers to many questions that plague us now. We need to use these methods to investigate problems such as the following:

1. What is the relative effectiveness of different methods of instruction?

2. What are significant factors in the formation of mathematical concepts?
3. What are effective ways of providing for individual differences?
4. What are the most effective ways to motivate learning?
5. What is the role of instructional materials in teaching mathematical ideas?
6. Can computational skill be developed through problem solving?
7. What is the relative effectiveness of different methods of solving problems?
8. What topics are most effective in attaining certain goals of instruction?
9. What goals of mathematics instruction are attained as the result of learning the structure of mathematics?
10. What is the role of the computer in learning algorithms and problem solving?

Since research is a complex, expensive venture, it should be a team effort extended over a long period of time and relating many pieces of individual research studies. Research in mathematics education needs the joint efforts of mathematicians, educators, psychologists, test experts, and research specialists. The research design used should be such that the analysis can be done by a computer. Financial support should be solicited so that significant projects can be instituted. Hopefully the National Council of Teachers of Mathematics, the Conference Board of the Mathematical Sciences, the National Science Foundation, or the U.S. Office of Education can offer facilities and services that coordinate efforts for soliciting support.

As mathematics teachers we should be informed of the research that has been done in mathematics education. We should participate in a research project whenever the opportunity arises. Then we should incorporate the conclusions of research into our daily teaching tasks.

REFERENCES

1. Brown, Kenneth, *Analysis of Research in the Teaching of Mathematics.* U.S. Department of Health, Education, and Welfare, Office of Education. Washington, D.C.: Government Printing Office, 1952, 1954, 1956, 1958, 1960, 1962.
2. Collier, R. O., and S. M. Elam, *Research Design and Analysis.* Phi Delta Kappa, 1961.
3. Cooperative Research. *Research Problems in Mathematics Education.* U.S. Department of Health, Education, and Welfare, Office of Education. Washington, D.C.: Government Printing Office, 1960.
4. Gagne, R. M., "Studies of the Learning of Mathematics," *Science Education News*, April, 1963.
5. Henderson, Kenneth B., "Research on Teaching Secondary School Mathematics," *Handbook of Research on Teaching.* American Educational Research Association. Chicago: Rand McNally & Co., 1963.
6. School Mathematics Study Group, *Newsletter No. 15.* April, 1963.

17-202